# OLD ENGLISH LITERATURE

# Old English Literature

Twenty-two Analytical Essays

*Edited by*

MARTIN STEVENS

JEROME MANDEL

UNIVERSITY OF NEBRASKA PRESS · LINCOLN

Acknowledgments for permission to reprint
copyrighted material appear on page 333.

Publishers on the Plains

UNP

Library of Congress Catalog Card Number 68–11565

International  Standard Book Number 0–8032–0181–8

First Landmark Edition Printing: 1976

Manufactured in the United States of America

# *Preface*

THIS BOOK of twenty-two essays is designed for the student of Old English literature. Its aim is to enlarge his background and to suggest various approaches to his reading of the earliest vernacular literature in our culture. Since the beginning student is likely to devote a very large share of his time to mastering the fundamentals of the Old English language, he often is forced to neglect literary considerations. This book, in presenting interpretations of prose selections and poems which are frequently reprinted in standard readers and which therefore serve as an introduction to most learners, hopes to compensate for the necessary linguistic concentration by calling attention to some of the more important textual and literary problems confronting the serious student of Old English. In addition, it is designed to reflect the new and wide-ranging interest in a literature which until recently was studied primarily for what it revealed about its language. The essays in this anthology have all been published within the last twenty years, and many of them have been written by the most noted scholars of Old English on both sides of the Atlantic.

The selections fall into three general divisions. The first of these can be labelled broadly as "Language, Versification, and Critical Approaches." Belonging under this heading are the first seven essays, which include: G. L. Brook's description and illustrations of Old English dialects, Lehmann's discussion of Old English metrics and poetic form, Sisam's observations on the textual accuracy of the Old English poetical manuscripts, Creed's and Stevick's discussions of oral formulae in the composition of Old English poetry, and Leslie's and Greenfield's examinations of Old English syntax as related to literary style. The second major group, "Interpretations of Prose Works," includes the next three essays. The discussions in

this section concentrate on the narrative structure of the famous
"Cynewulf and Cyneheard" episode in the *Anglo-Saxon Chronicle*; the
literary, historical, and geographical background of the accounts of
Ohthere and Wulfstan in Alfred's *Orosius*; and the literary styles of
the two most eminent prose writers in the classical Old English
period, Ælfric and Wulfstan. The last major group is also the
largest: "Interpretations of Poems." Included in this category are
analyses of Caedmon's *Hymn*, *The Wanderer*, *The Seafarer*, *Deor*, *The
Wife's Lament*, *The Battle of Maldon*, *The Dream of the Rood*, *The
Phoenix*, and *Beowulf*. We have selected three essays with different
concentrations on the latter poem: Dorothy Whitelock's chapter on
the audience of *Beowulf*, making the point that the poem is thoroughly Christian in its allusions, diction, and attitudes; Storms'
analysis of the emotive element in the *Beowulf* poet's word choice,
with special emphasis on Hrothgar's celebrated journey to Grendel's
Mere (11. 1399–1417); and Bonjour's demonstration that the so-
called digressions in the poem are really part of a unified larger
structure. This list of contents, as may be evident from the foregoing
enumeration, advances from general considerations to particulars;
it further reflects the progress of the typical beginning course or
textbook in Old English by moving from fundamental explanations
concerning the language, to examinations of prose works and poems,
leaving until last a consideration of *Beowulf*, the longest, most
important, and most complex poem surviving from the period.

   We have made every effort to reflect varieties of approaches to
Old English literature in this book. But, at the same time, we have
deliberately avoided presenting standard interpretations as a matter
of rule. Some of the essays in this collection are, quite frankly, out of
favor with many critics. Few scholars, for example, are likely to
agree with Rudolph Bambas' view that *The Wife's Lament* is really
a man's narrative rather than a woman's. And yet Bambas skillfully
resolves several problems that have vexed critics repeatedly in their
attempts to interpret the poem. While the student may ultimately
be led to reject Bambas' interpretation—and that is, of course, his
right—he cannot do so intelligently without submitting the poem to
close textual analysis and thorough critical examination. A similar
point might be made of Morton Bloomfield's provocative reading
of the poem *Deor* as a charm. Other critics have not thus read the

poem, but Bloomfield makes a strong and instructive, if exceptional, case for his reading. We believe that any criticism which leads to valid new perceptions about a work of literature, even if that criticism is unorthodox, is worthy of recognition and circulation. There is nothing more stultifying than orthodoxy. This point can be illustrated vividly in nearly every published commentary on *The Battle of Maldon*, a poem that has been noted repeatedly for its geographical and historical details. J. B. Bessinger's article, included in this collection, serves to liberate this fine heroic poem from the orthodox "historio-geographic" commentary.

## NOTE ON THE TEXT

The essays appearing in this collection have been reprinted exactly as they appeared in their original published form except when the authors have asked us to incorporate corrections or additions. For the sake of economy and continuity, we have eliminated a few footnotes and cross references. All footnotes are the authors', but, where necessary for the sake of consistency, we have silently added bibliographical information (e.g., publisher or date). We have also silently corrected all obvious misprints, and we have made spelling consistent throughout. In some of the essays footnotes have been renumbered. All abbreviations have been made consistent in line with standard lists of abbreviations, and a table has been supplied in the front of the book for ready reference. Our editorial insertions, most of which are translations from foreign languages, appear within diamond brackets. Three asterisks denote deletions from the original text.

MARTIN STEVENS
*The Ohio State University*

JEROME MANDEL
*Rutgers—The State University*

# Contents

# List of Abbreviations

| | |
|---|---|
| *And* | *Andreas* |
| Ang | Anglian |
| *Brb* | *Battle of Brunanburh* |
| *Bwf* | *Beowulf* |
| *CH* | *Catholic Homilies* |
| *Chr* | *Christ* |
| *Dan* | *Daniel* |
| *DHl* | *Descent into Hell* |
| *EA* | *Études Anglaises* |
| EETS | Early English Text Society |
| *EHR* | *English Historical Review* |
| *Ele* | *Elene* |
| *ELH* | *Journal of English Literary History* |
| *ES* | *English Studies* |
| *Gen* | *Genesis* |
| Gmc | Germanic |
| *Háv* | *Hávamál* |
| *HE* | *Historia Ecclesiastica* |
| *Hel* | *Heliand* |
| *HL* | *Hildebrandslied* |
| *JEGP* | *Journal of English and Germanic Philology* |
| *JGP* | *Journal of Germanic Philology* |
| *Lan M* | *Les Langues Modernes* |
| *MÆ* | *Medium Ævum* |
| *MBo* | *Meters of Boethius* |
| ME | Middle English |
| *MGH* | *Monumenta Germaniae Historica* |
| MHG | Middle High German |
| *MLN* | *Modern Language Notes* |

| | |
|---|---|
| *MLQ* | *Modern Language Quarterly* |
| *MLR* | *Modern Language Review* |
| MnE | Modern English |
| *MP* | *Modern Philology* |
| *N&Q* | *Notes and Queries* |
| *Neophil* | *Neophilologus* |
| Nhb | Northumbrian |
| *NM* | *Neuphilologische Mitteilungen* |
| OE | Old English |
| OHG | Old High German |
| ON | Old Norse |
| OS | Old Saxon |
| *PBA* | *Proceedings of the British Academy* |
| *PL* | *Patrologica Latina* |
| *PMLA* | *Publications of the Modern Language Association of America* |
| *PQ* | *Philological Quarterly* |
| *Rdl* | *Riddle* |
| *RES* | *Review of English Studies* |
| RS | "Rolls Series" (*Chronicles and Memorials of Great Britain and Ireland*) |
| *SN* | *Studia Neophilologica* |
| *SP* | *Studies in Philology* |
| *TLS* | [London] *Times Literary Supplement* |
| *VP* | *Vespasian Psalter* |
| *Vkv* | *Song of Weland, Volundarkviða* |
| WGmc | West Germanic |
| WS | West Saxon |
| *YWES* | *Year's Work in English Studies* |
| *ZDA* | *Zeitschrift für deutsches Altertum und deutsche Literatur* |
| *ZDP* | *Zeitschrift für deutsche Philologie* |

# LANGUAGE, VERSIFICATION, AND
# CRITICAL APPROACHES

G. L. BROOK

# Old English

THE STUDY of the dialects spoken in England during the Old English period, that is before the end of the eleventh century, is rendered difficult by the scarcity of surviving texts. Enough manuscripts have survived to enable us to say what were the chief dialects and what were the characteristic features of each dialect, but the boundaries of the various dialects cannot be precisely indicated. Four main Old English dialects can be distinguished: Northumbrian, Mercian, West Saxon, and Kentish. Very approximately we may say that Northumbrian included the dialects spoken North of the River Humber; Mercian was spoken in the Midlands between the Humber and the Thames; West Saxon was spoken South of the Thames in the ancient kingdom of Wessex; and Kentish was spoken in the South-East over an area rather larger than that covered by the modern county of Kent. Northumbrian and Mercian had some features in common, and the term Anglian is sometimes used to describe the dialect of which they can be regarded as subdivisions. We cannot tell whether the boundaries between these dialects remained the same throughout the Old English period; in view of the unsettled political conditions of Anglo-Saxon England it is probable that they did not. One thing that we can say with confidence is that it is most unlikely that any of the four areas mentioned had a completely homogeneous dialect at any time during the Old English period. Even the scanty texts that are available enable us to distinguish two subdivisions within the dialect of Northumbria, and it is probable that in Anglo-Saxon England there were many dialects of which we have no knowledge because of the accident that no manuscripts have been preserved containing texts written in those dialects. At the end of the Old English period Wessex enjoyed political supremacy, and that is no doubt the reason why most of the surviving texts are written

## OLD ENGLISH DIALECTS

in the West Saxon dialect. The non-West-Saxon texts are so few that in speaking of non-West-Saxon dialects it is safer to speak of the dialect of a particular text rather than that of a particular geographical region. A further advantage of this practice is that it serves as a reminder that the Old English period extended in time over several centuries, and the linguistic differences between two texts may be the result of a difference of date as well as one of dialect.

Since most of the extant Old English manuscripts are written in the West Saxon dialect, West Saxon forms are those with which students of Old English are most familiar. It is, however, important to remember that the Standard English of today is derived not from the West Saxon dialect but from a variety of Mercian, although a few isolated words have been borrowed from other dialects. For example, MnE *hear* cannot be derived from WS *hīeran*; it is from the Anglian *hēran*. *Cheese* is not from WS *cȳse* but from an Anglian form in which the *ā* of Latin *cāseum*, from which the word was borrowed, was fronted to *ǣ* and later raised to *ē*. *Old* and *cold* are from Anglian *ald* and *cald*; the West Saxon forms *eald* and *ceald* would have given MnE *eald* [iːld] and *cheald* [tʃiːld]. Similarly the preterite *sold* is from Anglian *salde*; WS *sealde* would have given *seald* [siːld]. Exceptionally, *chalk* is derived from the West Saxon form *cealc*, as is shown by the initial consonant *ch* [tʃ]; the Anglian form would have given *c* [k], just as Ang *calf* has given MnE *calf*.

Old English dialectal variations are preserved more thoroughly in place-names than in ordinary words, because in place-names the levelling influence of Standard English is less active. Corresponding to the difference between *chalk* and *calf*, we have place-names like *Chalford* (Oxfordshire) and *Chawton* (Hampshire), side by side with *Calverley* (West Riding, Yorkshire), *Caldecote* (Norfolk), and *Coldwell* (Northumberland). The distinction between Ang *ald* and WS *eald* is reflected in place-names. OE Ang *wald*, WS *weald* originally meant "forest, especially on high ground." When forests were cleared, the name often came to mean "open uplands, waste ground." The West Saxon form has survived in *The Weald* of Kent, while the Anglian form is preserved in *The Cotswolds* and in the Yorkshire and Lincolnshire *Wolds*. Another group of place-names shows the developments of three different dialectal forms of the noun meaning "well" or "spring." The usual West Saxon form was *wiella*; Mercian had *wælla*; most other Anglian dialects and Kentish had *wella*. WS *wiella* became ME *wille* or *wulle*, and these forms survive in *Wilton* (Somerset) and *Woolcombe* (Dorset); Mercian *wælla* became ME *walle*, which is hard to distinguish from *wall*, but it is probably found in *Aspinwall* (Lancashire) and *Heswall* (Cheshire); the form *wella* is found in *Well* (North Riding, Yorkshire) and *Wells* (Norfolk). As a result of the influence of Standard English, forms with *e* are liable to occur in any part of the country. Sometimes a sound-change that seems to be dialectal is abundantly illustrated by place-name evidence although literary forms are not very common. Of such a kind is the shift of stress from the first to the second element of the initial diphthong *ĕa*, which had the result that the first element of the new rising diphthong became the semi-vowel [j], spelt *y*. This sound-change is especially common in Devonshire, although occasional examples are found elsewhere. Examples are *Yalland*, the first syllable of which is derived from OE *eald* "old," and *Yeo* (OE *ēa* "river"), a name which is used to describe more than twenty different places in Devonshire.

### Characteristics of the Old English Dialects

There were very few linguistic features of Old English that were to be found exclusively in any one dialect, since dialectal forms were freely borrowed from one dialect into another. The differences between one Old English dialect and another depended for the most part upon the relative frequency of occurrence of a particular group of forms. When we speak of a sound-change being characteristic of a particular dialect, we mean that forms reflecting the change are common or normal in that dialect, whereas in other dialects they are found only occasionally. Sometimes the distribution of variant forms is so complicated that no clear picture emerges, but fortunately there are some forms whose distribution does enable us to make general statements about Old English dialects. Brief mention may be made of the chief texts on which our knowledge of Old English dialects is based and of the chief characteristics of the dialects in order to show what is the justification for the generally accepted classification.

### Anglian

The chief characteristics of Anglian, which includes both Northumbrian and Mercian, are:

(1)   The use of *a* as the development of WGmc *a* before *l* + consonant, whereas West Saxon and Kentish have *ea*. Hence we have Ang *all* "all," *haldan* "to hold" beside WS *eall*, *healdan*. The Anglian forms often spread to West Saxon and Kentish, even in early texts, but the spread of *ea*-forms to Anglian is not common.

(2)   The monophthongization or "smoothing" of the diphthongs *ĕa*, *ĕo* and *ĭo* to *ǣ* (later often *ĕ*), *ĕ* and *ĭ* respectively when they were followed by *c*, *g* or *h*, whether standing alone or preceded by a liquid consonant (*l* or *r*). Thus we have Ang *ǣge*, *ēge* "eye," beside WS *ēage*, Ang *werc* "work" beside WS *weorc*.

(3)   A tendency to keep the front rounded vowel *ǣ*, which in West Saxon was unrounded to *ĕ*. Hence the digraph *œ* does not normally occur in West Saxon texts at all whereas in Anglian texts both *ǣ* and *ĕ* are found. Examples are Ang *œle* "oil," *œpel* "home" beside WS *ele*, *ēpel*.

(4)   The retention of *-u* or *-o* as the ending of the 1st person singular present indicative of verbs. In West Saxon and Kentish this ending is replaced by *-e* from the optative. Examples are Ang *bindu* "I bind," *dǣmu* "I judge" beside WS *binde*, *dēme*.

### Northumbrian

The great period of Northumbrian history extended from the later part of the seventh to the early part of the ninth century. The best-known writer of this period was Bede, who was born near Wearmouth in Durham in 672 and lived for most of his life at Jarrow, where he died in 735. His *Historia Ecclesiastica Gentis Anglorum* is one of the most important sources of our knowledge of Anglo-Saxon history; several manuscripts of the Latin text have been preserved, and there is also a translation into the West Saxon dialect of Old English. A fragment of five lines of verse, generally called *Bede's Death Song*, is preserved in the St Gall MS. No. 254, a manuscript of the ninth century, and this is one of the earliest records that we have of English vernacular writing. Another early Northumbrian text that has been preserved is Caedmon's *Hymn*, a poem of nine lines. In Book IV of the *Historia Ecclesiastica* Bede tells the story of Caedmon, a herdsman and lay brother in the abbey of Whitby in the seventh century, who was endowed with the gift of composing religious verse. Caedmon's *Hymn*, which Bede quotes as a specimen of Caedmon's work, is preserved in its Northumbrian version in some of the manuscripts containing the Latin text of Bede's *Historia*, and a West Saxon version of the *Hymn* is incorporated in the West Saxon translation of that work. A third early Northumbrian poem, consisting of fourteen lines, is known as *The Leiden Riddle* because it is preserved in a manuscript which is now at Leiden, in the Netherlands. There is a later West Saxon version of the same riddle. Another specimen of the early Northumbrian dialect is to be found on the Ruthwell Cross in Dumfriesshire. On this cross are inscribed in runic characters a few lines of an Old English religious poem, *The Dream of the Rood*, which is preserved in a later West Saxon version in the Vercelli manuscript. We thus have four short texts to illustrate the Old Northumbrian dialect, and we are fortunate in having West Saxon versions of three of them available for comparison. The task of comparison is, however, made complicated by the fact that the West Saxon versions are a good deal later than the Northumbrian.

Three longer texts are available for the study of Northumbrian of the tenth century: *The Durham Ritual*, *The Lindisfarne Gospels*, and part of *The Rushworth Gospels*. All three manuscripts are in Latin, but they all contain interlinear glosses in Old English.

The manuscript of *The Durham Ritual* is in the Cathedral Library at Durham and consists of a tenth-century service-book with a Northumbrian gloss.

*The Lindisfarne Gospels* are preserved in a beautiful manuscript, which is now MS. Cotton Nero D. iv in the British Museum. The Latin text was written on the island of Lindisfarne towards the end of the seventh century. The Northumbrian interlinear gloss is two and a half centuries later and was made about 950 by a priest called Aldred at a time when the manuscript had been taken to Chester-le-Street, near Durham, for greater safety. The manuscript was later removed to Durham, where it remained for several centuries.

*The Rushworth Gospels* are so called because they are preserved in a manuscript which was presented to the Bodleian Library by John Rushworth, who was deputy clerk to the House of Commons during the Long Parliament. The Latin text was written in the eighth century, and the Old English glosses were added about two centuries later. They were the work of two scribes: the glosses to the whole of St Matthew's Gospel and a small part of St Mark were the work of

Farmon, a priest "æt harawuda," which may be Harewood, near Ross-on-Wye; the remaining glosses were the work of a scribe called Owun. The two scribes wrote in different dialects. Farmon's work may be regarded as North Mercian; the remaining glosses seem to be copied, with slight variations, from those in *The Lindisfarne Gospels*, and are therefore in a Northumbrian dialect.

The chief characteristics of Northumbrian dialects are:

(1) The development of *a* from WGmc *a* before *r* + consonant, especially when a labial consonant (*p*, *b*, *f*, *m* or *w*) precedes the vowel or follows the *r*. This Northern development spreads to a few Mercian texts, but for the most part the Old English dialects other than Northumbrian have *ea* before *r* + consonant as a result of the sound-change known as fracture. Examples are Nhb *barn* "child," *ward* "protector," beside *bearn*, *weard* in the other dialects.

(2) The tendency of initial *w* to cause rounding of a following vowel or diphthong. Northumbrian often has *o* after *w* in words which, in other dialects, have *eo* as the result of fracture or back mutation, two sound-changes which bring about the diphthongization of front vowels. Thus Northumbrian has *worða* "to become," *cuoða* "to say" beside WS *weorðan* and *cweðan*.

(3) The loss of final *-n*. This loss is especially marked in late Northumbrian, although some categories of words, such as the past participles of strong verbs, are not as a rule affected. Examples are Nhb *bigeonda* "beyond," *wosa* "to be," beside WS *bigeondan* and *wesan*.

*Mercian*

The Mercian dialects have a special interest since it is from one of these dialects that the Standard English of today is derived. Unfortunately we cannot feel so confident about the provenance of the Old English texts that are generally regarded as Mercian as we can about the Northumbrian texts. The earliest texts that have been assigned to a Mercian dialect are the Corpus and Epinal Glossaries of the eighth century. The names of the Glossaries indicate the present location of the manuscripts: Corpus Christi College Cambridge and Epinal in the department of Vosges in France respectively. These glossaries differ from the Northumbrian glosses that have been mentioned in that they are alphabetically arranged and therefore represent a further stage in the development of the dictionary. They consist of lists of Latin words whose meanings are explained sometimes in Latin and sometimes in English.

*The Vespasian Psalter* derives its name from the press-mark of the manuscript in the British Museum: Cotton Vespasian A.i. The manuscript contains the Latin text of *Psalms* and a dozen hymns, generally known as the *Vespasian Hymns*, to which has been added an interlinear gloss of the early ninth century. Professor R. M. Wilson has recently pointed out[1] how slight is the evidence for assigning the glosses to a Mercian dialect. The evidence of Middle English dialects which have some features in common with that of *The Vespasian Psalter* shows that there is no absurdity in assigning the glosses to the Mercian area, but there is much to be said for the cautious approach which avoids localization and refers to the dialect of the glosses as "the dialect of *The Vespasian Psalter*."

The chief Mercian characteristics are:

(1)   The "second fronting" by which *æ* was raised to *e* and *a* was fronted to *æ*. These changes are especially characteristic of the dialect of *The Vespasian Psalter*. Examples are *VP deg* "day," pl. *dægas, feder* "father" beside *dæg, dagas, fæder* in the other dialects.

(2)   The back mutation of *æ* to *ea*, caused by a back vowel in the following syllable. The change did not take place when the intervening consonant was *c* or *g*. As a result of back mutation we find *VP featu* "vessels" beside *fatu* in the other dialects.

## Kentish

The Kentish dialect had a number of distinctive features, though the Old English texts written in this dialect are short and not very well-known. There are several Kentish charters: those belonging to the seventh and eighth centuries are short and in Latin, only the proper names being in Old English, but there are ninth-century

1. *The Anglo-Saxons: Studies . . . presented to Bruce Dickins* (London: Bowes and Bowes, 1959), pp. 292–310.

charters written in Old English. There are also glosses and a Kentish version of the fiftieth Psalm.[2]

The chief characteristics of Kentish are:

(1) The lowering and unrounding of $\breve{y}$ to $\breve{e}$. Thus we find Kentish *senn* "sin" beside *synn* in the other dialects.

(2) The raising to $\bar{e}$ of the $\bar{æ}$ which results from the *i*-mutation of $\bar{a}$, from Gmc *ai*. Thus we find Kentish *ēnig* "any," *mēst* "most," beside *ǣnig* and *mǣst* in the other dialects.

## West Saxon

There are more extant texts written in the West Saxon dialect than in all the other Old English dialects put together. This preponderance is a result of the political supremacy of Wessex during the tenth century, which is the period when most of the extant manuscripts were written. The two great names in West Saxon literature are those of King Alfred and Abbot Ælfric, and they both left works which have been preserved in several manuscripts. Alfred's works, representing the West Saxon dialect of the ninth century, include translations of the *Cura Pastoralis* and the world history of Orosius. Ælfric's works, which belong to the end of the tenth century, include many homilies and a Grammar which shows great ingenuity in the devising of English terms to describe grammatical concepts. Another important late West Saxon text is a translation of the Gospels into West Saxon. The *Anglo-Saxon Chronicle* is in the main in West Saxon, but it is not suitable for the illustration of dialect because it has survived in a number of versions which are not dialectally homogeneous.

The chief characteristics of West Saxon are:

(1) The use of $\bar{æ}$ as a development of WGmc $\bar{a}$ from Gmc $\bar{æ}$, whereas in most other dialects the $\bar{æ}$ was raised to $\bar{e}$. This dialectal feature may date back to a time before the Germanic invasion of Britain, since the raising to $\bar{e}$ is found also in Old Frisian. Examples are WS *dǣd* "deed," *hǣr* "hair" beside *dēd*, *hēr* in the other dialects. One poetical word, *mēce* "sword," has the raised vowel even in the

2. Psalm 50 in the Vulgate, 51 in A.V. ⟨i.e., the King James Version⟩.

predominantly West Saxon poetical manuscripts. This irregularity is thought to be due to the fact that *mēce* was an Anglian literary word not normally used by West Saxon speakers.

(2) The diphthongization of vowels by the influence of preceding palatal consonants. Rather surprisingly, in view of the geographical separation, this is a feature which West Saxon shares to some extent with late Northumbrian, although there are differences of detail between the diphthongizations in the two dialects. Characteristic West Saxon forms are *gielp* "boast" and *forgieldan* "to pay," beside *gelp* and *forgeldan* in the other dialects. In these words *g* had a palatal pronunciation [j], like that of the *y* in MnE *young*.

(3) The change of *ĕa* and *ĭo* to *ĭe* by *i*-mutation. In the other dialects *ĕa* became *ē* and *ĭo* remained unchanged. Examples are WS *hīeran* "to hear," *þīestru* "darkness," *hliehhan* "to laugh," beside *hēran*, *þīostru*, *hlehhan* in the other dialects.

(4) The absence of back mutation in many words which show the change in the other dialects. In West Saxon back mutation took place only when the consonant intervening between the stem-vowel and the back vowel causing the change was a liquid or a labial and the effects of the change were often removed by analogy; in the other dialects it took place before any consonants except *c* and *g* in Anglian. Examples are WS *gebedu* "prayers," *wita* "scholar," beside *gebeodu* and *wiota* in the other dialects.

(5) The use of syncopated forms of the 3rd person singular of the present indicative of verbs; in the other dialects we generally find forms with the ending -*eð* and with the effects of *i*-mutation on the stem-vowel removed by analogy. Thus we find WS *cīest* "chooses," *hielt* "holds" beside *cēoseð*, *haldeð* in the other dialects.

*Specimens of Old English Dialects*

Since Caedmon's *Hymn* has been preserved in a Northumbrian as well as a West Saxon version, it is interesting to compare the two. The Northumbrian version is:

> Nu scylun hergan    hefænricæs uard,
> Metudæs mæcti    end his modgidanc,
> uerc uuldurfadur;    sue he uundra gihuæs,
> eci Dryctin,    or astelidæ.
> He ærist scop    ælda barnum

heben til hrofe,    haleg Scepen;
tha middungeard,    monncynnæs uard,
eci Dryctin,    æfter tiadæ
firum foldu,    Frea allmectig.[3]

The West Saxon version is:

Nu we sculan herian    heofonrices weard,
Metodes mihte    and his modgeþonc,
weorc wuldorfæder;    swa he wundra gehwæs,
ece Dryhten,    ord onstealde.
He ærest gesceop    eorðan bearnum
heofon to hrofe,    halig Scyppend;
ða middangeard,    monncynnes weard,
ece Dryhten,    æfter teode
firum foldan,    Frea ælmihtig.

It is important to remember that the two versions differ in date as well as in dialect. The West Saxon version is more than two centuries later than the Northumbrian, and several of the differences between the two versions are due to this difference of date. Archaisms in the Northumbrian version include the *-æs* of *hefænricæs* and *monncynnæs* and the *-i* of *mæcti* and *eci*. There are other differences which are not due to either date or dialect, such as that between the *-ll-* of *allmectig* and the *-l-* of *ælmihtig*, and some of the distinctive features of the Northumbrian version are merely differences of spelling, such as the use of *c* for *h* before *t* in *mæcti*, *Dryctin*, and *allmectig*, of *u* for *w* in *uard*, *uerc*, *uuldurfadur*, *uundra*, and *gihuæs*, and *th* and *d* for *þ* or *ð* in *tha* and *modgidanc*. There remain, however, several differences that are due to dialect. The *a* in *uard* and *barnum* in the Northumbrian version beside *ea* in the West Saxon, shows the lack of fracture in the neighborhood of labial consonants. The form *ælda* is also Anglian: it is the genitive of a plural word meaning "men," which appears in West Saxon as *ielde*. There was earlier an *i* in the ending which caused *i*-mutation of the stem-vowel. The WS *ie* is from

3. "Now we ought to praise the Protector of the Kingdom of Heaven, the might of the Lord and the thought of his heart, the work of the Glorious Father, as He, the Eternal Lord, made a beginning of every wonderful thing. He, the Holy Creator, first made Heaven as a roof for the children of men. Then the Protector of Mankind, Eternal Lord, the All-powerful God, afterwards created the world, the earth for men."

earlier *ea*, whereas the Anglian *æ* is from *a*, the difference between
the two forms being due to the fact that there was no fronting and
fracture of *a* before *l* + consonant in Anglian. Another Anglian
form is *uerc*, with smoothing of the diphthong found in the corresponding WS *weorc*. In vocabulary the preposition *til* is a rare
Northern form in Old English, although later, reinforced by ON
*til*, it became the everyday non-dialectal English word *till*.

### Northumbrian

An example of later Northumbrian is provided by the Lord's
Prayer as it is preserved in the interlinear gloss in *The Lindisfarne
Gospels*. Since the purpose of the gloss was to translate each Latin
word separately, the following extract does not provide a specimen of
Old English syntax, but it provides a good illustration of Northum-
brian phonology.

> Fæder ure,[4] ðu arð in heofnum. Sie gehalgad noma ðin.
> Tocymeð ric ðin. Sie willo ðin suæ is in heofne and in eorðo.
> Hlaf usenne oferwistlic sel us to dæg and forgef us scylda usra,
> suæ uoe forgefon scyldgum usum, and ne inlæd usih in costunge
> ah gefrig usich from yfle.

The dialectal forms in this passage include some which might occur
in any non-West-Saxon text as well as others which are more
specifically Northumbrian. The non-West-Saxon forms include the
pronouns *ūsih*, *ūsich* (cf. WS *ūs*), the past participle *gehālgad* (cf. WS
*gehālgod*), and the forms *forgef* and *forgēfon* without front diphthongization (cf. WS *forgief*, *forgēafon*). The form *forgēfon* shows also the
non-West-Saxon raising of *ǣ*[1] (from fronting of WGmc *ā*, from
Gmc *ǣ*) to *ē*, since the WS *ēa* is from earlier *ǣ*[1]. Northumbrian forms
include *arð*, (with lack of fracture before *r* + consonant and with
final *ð* corresponding to WS *t*), and *uoe* (where *u* is a spelling for *w*
which has caused rounding of the following *ē*).

### Mercian

The following is an extract from the *Vespasian Hymns*:

> Ic ondettu ðe Dryhten: forðon eorre ðu earð me, gecerred is
> hatheortnis ðin ond frofrende earð mec. Sehðe, God hælend

4. MS. *urer*.

min; getreowlice ic dom ond ne ondredu, forðon strengu min
ond herenis min Dryhten ond geworden is me in haelu.
Gehleadað weter in gefian of wellu[m] haelendes ond cweoðað
in ðæm dege, "Ondettað Dryhtne ond gecegað noman his;
cyðe doð in folcum gemœtinge his; gemunað forðon heh is
noma his. Singað Dryhtne forðon micellice dyde: seggað ðis in
alre eorðan. Gefeh ond here eardung Sione forðon micel in
midum ðin halig Israel." [5]

Some of the dialectal characteristics of this extract are shared by all
the non-West-Saxon dialects, some are Anglian, while others are
characteristic of the dialect of *The Vespasian Psalter*. Non-West-
Saxon forms include *eorre* (corresponding to WS *ierre*, where the
*eo/io* has undergone *i*-mutation), *gecerred*, *gecēgað* (with non-West-
Saxon mutation of *ĕa* to *ĕ*; cf. WS *gecierred*, *gecīegað*), *hēlend* (with *ǣ²*
[which arises by *i*-mutation of *ā*, from Gmc *ai*] raised to *ē* by the
influence of the following alveolar consonant in Anglian; in Kentish,
*ǣ²* was raised to *ē* by an independent change), and *cweoðað* (with
back mutation taking place even through a dental consonant; cf.
WS *cweðað*). Anglian forms include *ondettu* and *ondrēdu* (with the old
ending *-u* in the 1st person singular present indicative; West Saxon
had *-e* from the optative), *dōm* "do" (with the Anglian addition of
*-m* in monosyllabic forms on the analogy of *eam* "am"), *hēh* and *gefeh*
(with Anglian smoothing; cf. WS *hēah* and *gefeoh*), and *gemœtinge*
(with retention of a front rounded vowel as the *i*-mutation of *ō* [WS
*gemēting*]). The two changes that are most characteristic of the dialect
of *The Vespasian Psalter* are reflected in *weter* and *dege* (with raising of
*æ* to *e*), and *gehleadað* (with back mutation of *æ* which in other dialects was retracted to *a*).

### Kentish

The following is an extract from the Kentish Psalm:

> Aðweah me of sennum, saule fram wammum,
> gasta Sceppend, geltas geclansa,
> þa ðe ic on aldre æfre gefremede
> ðurh lichaman leðre geðohtas.
> For ðan ic unriht min eall oncnawe

5. For a translation of this hymn see Isaiah, chap. 12.

and eac synna gehwær selfum æt eagan
firendeda geðrec beforan standeð,
scelda scinað; forgef me, Sceppen min,
lifes liohtfruma ðinre lufan blisse.
Nu ic anum ðe oft syngode
and yfela feola eac gefræmede
gelta gramhegdig, ic ðe, gasta breogo,
helende Crist helpe bidde,
ðæt me forgefene gastes wunde
an forðgesceaft feran mote,
þy ðine wordcwidas weorðan gefelde,
ðæt ðu ne wilnast weora æniges deað.

The clearest indication of the Kentish dialect here is to be seen in the forms with *ĕ* where other dialects would have *ў*. Thus we have *sennum* (WS *synnum*), *geltas, gelta* (WS *gyltas, gylta*), *lēðre* (WS *lÿðre*), *gramhegdig* (WS *gramhygdig*), but it is to be noticed that side by side with these forms there are forms with *y*: *synna, syngode, yfela*. Another Kentish form is *breogo*, with back mutation before a back consonant, whereas *weora*, with back mutation caused by *a*, could occur in any non-West-Saxon dialect. A characteristically Kentish form is *līohtfruma*, with *īo* corresponding to *ēo* in most other dialects. Non-West-Saxon forms are *scelda* and *forgef* (where West Saxon would normally have front diphthongization of *e* to *ie*), *Sceppend* (where West Saxon would have *ie* by *i*-mutation of *ea*), and *firendēda* (where West Saxon would have *ǣ*).

Reprinted from G. L. Brook, *English Dialects*, 2nd ed., The Language Library, ed. Eric Partridge (London: Oxford University Press, 1965), pp. 40–54.

W. P. LEHMANN

# The Old Germanic
# Verse Form

ALLITERATIVE POETRY was maintained to various points of time in the several Germanic languages. The date of its abandonment correlates with the geographical location of the language areas. In Old High German, the southernmost of the Germanic dialects from which literary material has survived, it was abandoned in the middle of the ninth century; in Old Icelandic, the northernmost, it was abandoned only in the thirteenth century, and then not entirely, for here the new form has retained elements of the old. The other Germanic languages in which poetry has been transmitted to us, Old Saxon and Old English, adopted the new form between these dates. Whatever documents have come down to us in other Germanic dialects, Gothic, Old Frisian, and Old Franconian, owe their importance to linguistic, rather than literary, criteria. For Old Saxon, the language spoken in northern Germany, the date of abandonment is uncertain because no poetry has come down to us from later than the ninth century. Yet here the alliterative tradition was stronger than farther south, for a long alliterative epic, the *Heliand*, was composed in Old Saxon shortly before the Old High German monk Otfrid wrote the first Germanic epic in rimed verse.

In England, the alliterative form was in general use until the Norman Conquest; when English verse was resumed again after the interruption from the continent, the new form had replaced the old, except in the north and west. Here there was a curious "revival" of the alliterative form in the thirteenth and fourteenth centuries, continuing into the sixteenth, which is difficult to explain unless we assume a continuous tradition. Even though the southern English poets do not make use of the alliterative form, it seems to have been widely known, for Chaucer was able to let the gentle parson plead inability to handle the verse form of the north with its "rum, ram,

17

ruf" as well as the southern rime.[1] Much as the Middle English alliterative poems differ from the Old English, they contain some of the same characteristics, such as the use of nominal compounds, e.g., *faederhus* "ancestral home." Since these are not found in the Middle English literature written in the new form, the simplest explanation for their use is the assumption of a continuous tradition of alliterative verse.[2] The alliterative form may have survived in these very areas of England because of the powerful Scandinavian influence. Whatever the complex causes contributing to its survival, it was the north—the Scandinavian areas and northern Britain—that maintained alliterative poetry longest, the south that abandoned it earliest.

Although the structure of the alliterative line is parallel in all Germanic poetry, forms longer than the line differ characteristically in the north and south. The northern poetry is stanzaic, the southern stichic. The two forms may be compared with linguistic divisions and length of survival. The three southern languages—Old English, Old Saxon, and Old High German—belong to the West Germanic linguistic group, the northern to the North Germanic group. And though alliterative verse survived in northern England later than the time of Chaucer, it apparently did not escape Scandinavian influence, being in part stanzaic, as in *Sir Gawain and the Green Knight*. We shall, therefore, speak of a northern and a southern type of Germanic alliterative poetry, characteristics of which will be discussed at greater length below.

In both areas the kinds of poetry are severely circumscribed. If we utilize the Aristotelian classification of literature—dramatic, lyric, and epic—we find native poetry resembling only the last. Even the use of this term in Aristotle's sense is difficult to justify by reason of both form and treatment. A favorite feature of the Germanic short epic was dramatic dialogue; for example, all of the *Hildebrandslied*, apart from the introduction and conclusion, consists of dialogue between father and son. Nor does the substance of the *Hildebrandslied* differ appreciably from that of a Greek drama.

1. See "The Parson's Prologue," *The Complete Works of Geoffrey Chaucer*, ed. Fred N. Robinson (Boston: Houghton Mifflin Co., 1933), p. 272.

2. For a fuller discussion see J. P. Oakden, *Alliterative Poetry in Middle English* (Manchester: Manchester University Press, 1935), especially pp. 113–168.

Hildebrand is involved in a tragic situation as inextricably as is Oedipus, though he has yet to perform his tragic act while Oedipus has performed his long before the opening of the drama. Despite this difference the interest in both works lies in the growing awareness of the protagonist that he is involved in a tragic situation and in his form of meeting it.

Nor is the lyric element absent in the Germanic epics as in Niðuð's lament for his sons:[3]

> Vaki ek ávalt,   vilia lauss,
> sofna ek minnzt   síz mína sono dauða!
> Kell mik í haufuð   kǫld ero mér ráð þin, . . .

> [Ever wake I   woe bound
> Sleep flees from me   since my sons' death.
> Cold is my heart   cold was thy rede; . . .]

This and similar short lyric passages depict the feelings of the characters, however, not those of the poet; accordingly the term *lyric* is only partially applicable.

Though we continue to use the term *epic*, in neither the northern nor the southern verse was there emphasis on narration until the long epic was introduced in the south on the pattern of Latin epic poetry. The Germanic audience already knew the stories. It was the task of the poet to depict the most dramatic incident in them, and its effect on the fate of the protagonists. Only in a modified sense may we, therefore, use the term *epic* to describe Germanic verse.

The types of poetry in the north and south are further limited by the choice of medium. In the north, prose became the vehicle for what might have become the longer epic, so that only the short ballad remained for poetry, apart from such genres as ritualistic, magical, and proverb poetry that Heusler calls the "lesser genres."[4] In the south, Latin was generally preferred over the native languages for personal expression, as in the hymns; only from England do we

3. The lines are taken from the Old Norse version of the *Song of Weland*, *Volundarkviða*, stanza 31; \* \* \* see *Edda*, ed. Gustav Neckel (Heidelberg, 1936), p. 118.

4. Andreas Heusler, *Die altgermanische Dichtung*, 2nd ed. (Potsdam, 1941), pp. 26–28, *passim*.

have more than one sporadic poem, such as *Deor's Lament*, which depicts the mood of the writer.

In the north, the surviving poetry consisted of ballads, some of which dealt with the story of a god or ancient hero, others with praise of some living personage. The former are anonymous; the latter were written for specific occasions by well-known poets. The anonymous ballads, known as "Eddic poetry" after a manuscript heading, present incidents from the stories of Germanic (not specifically North Germanic) gods and heroes. The occasional poetry, known as "Skaldic verse" after its writers, the skalds, deals with specific incidents in the life of the acquaintances of the author, usually with his chieftain, assuming for its poetic figures an intricate knowledge of Germanic mythology, but never providing such information. Apart from the Eddic and Skaldic verse, and the "lesser genres," the northern literature was written in prose.

The south, on the other hand, maintained only enough of these genres to assure us that they were employed in common Germanic times. The Old High German *Hildebrandslied* and the Old English *Fight at Finnsburg* may be compared with the northern Eddic poems dealing with Germanic heroes; the Old High German *Ludwigslied* and the Old English *Maldon* with the Skaldic occasional poems. The preponderant genre in the south is the long epic. Most of these deal with Christian story—*Beowulf* is a notable exception—with the life of Christ, with Moses or other Biblical heroes, and with saints. Besides these, and a few short epics, some non-narrative poems survive—especially in England—magical charms, the closely related riddles, and songs of grief. Many of these genres are preeminent too after the change in form; the Middle High German period is eminent on the one hand for long epics, on the other for short lyric poems dealing either with specific occasions (the *sprüche*) or personal emotions (the *minnesang* proper).

Though one characteristic line is used throughout the northern and southern alliterative poetry, we can detect definite patterns of development. The following lines from the various dialects all fulfill the "demand" of two stresses per half-line.

ON *Vkv* 3.1   Sáto síðan   siau vetr at þat,
                 [Sat since   seven years thereafter]

OE *Bwf* 2209  fîftig wintra   —wæs ðā frōd cyning,
[fifty winters   was then the wise king]

OS *Hel* 465  the 'habda at them uuîha sô filu   uuintro endi
sumaro
[who had at that temple so many   of winters
and summers]

OHG *HL* 50  Ih wallōta sumaro enti wintro   sehstic ur lante
[I wandered summers and winters   sixty as
exile]

ME *Destruction of Sodom* 948  To wakan wederez so wylde þe
wyndez he callez
[To wake weathers so wild the
winds he calls]

In other respects, however, these lines show characteristic differences. It is the purpose of this chapter to point out the main lines of development in the various areas from the time when poets who could write competent, or even excellent, verse in the common Germanic form to that when poets could handle as capably the new form with its poetic structure based on end rime and even rhythm. Before undertaking such a sketch we must determine what was the common Germanic form of alliterative poetry. How far back can we trace the Germanic alliterative line? If certain genres, such as the short epic, were already in use in Germanic times, did they follow the stanzaic form of the north or the stichic form of the south? Similarly we must note the stylistic and syntactic innovations in the various areas. After these problems have been discussed we will be able to sketch the changes in poetic form.

All of the oldest Germanic verse that has come down to us is alliterative. While none of this is older than the eighth century, we have runic inscriptions of the third and fourth centuries in the same form. Some of these were apparently intended as verse, and like the inscription on the famous horn of Gallehus:

Ek HlewagastiR HoltijaR   horna tawidō
[I Hlewagastir, the Holtijan,   the horn contrived]

follow the formal "demands" of an alliterative line: (1) The line is bound together by the alliterative *h*'s. (2) These occur at the beginning of accented syllables. (3) The most important word from a

metrical point of view occupies the first stress of the second half-line.
We also find in this inscription the "freedoms" of the alliterative
line: (1) The number of unaccented syllables is not restricted, varying from three with *Hle-* through two with *Holt-* to one with *horn-*.
(2) Anacrusis is permitted before the first accented syllable. (3) The
last accented syllable does not share the alliteration. Lines similar
in pattern can be found in the later Germanic verse, for example
(*HL* 3 and *Vkv* 37.2):

> Hiltibrant enti Haðubrant,   untar heriun tuēm;
> [Hiltibrant and Haðubrant,   their two hosts between;]

> né ek þik vilia, Vǫlundr,   verr um níta
> [nor I, Weland, might wish   worse to harm you.]

We can therefore assume that the form of the alliterative line had
been standardized five centuries before the surviving Germanic
verse was first written down.

The earlier history of Germanic verse remains obscure. Unfortunately, Tacitus and Caesar neglected to preserve any specimens
of the Germanic poetry they allude to. Tacitus' mention, in his
*Germania*, Chapter 2, of the traditional grouping of the Germanic
tribes into *Ingaevones*, *(H)erminones*, and *Istaevones* may preserve for us
the accented sections of a verse with vocalic alliteration. If so, we
may push our date backward several centuries to around the beginning of our era. But beyond this we can only make inferences,
primarily on linguistic evidence.

From the structure of Germanic alliterative verse we can conclude that it did not exist before the Germanic accent shift. In the
earlier stages of Germanic the accent was variable; this we know
from Verner's demonstration that the interchange of consonants,
maintained today in the English past-tense forms *was* : *were*, corre-
lated with the variation of the Indo-European accent, which also
survived in Vedic Sanskrit.[5] At some unknown time before our era
the accent in Germanic became fixed on the first syllable, and was
characterized by strong stress. Alliterative verse on the Germanic

---

5. Formerly this was an interchange of voiceless spirants after accented
syllables with voiced spirants before accented syllables; compare Old English
*wearð: wurdon* "became" with the Sanskrit forms *vavárta: vavrtimá*, in which the
position of the accent is indicated.

pattern was impossible before this shift. Whether it was built on a type of verse that was inherited from the earlier period of Indo-European unity is mere speculation. The *gāyātri* rhythm of the Vedas, if also inherited in Germanic, could readily have been modified to the rhythms of the alliterative line after the change of stress; and alliteration is not unknown in the Vedas. Nor is there any inherent improbability in the theory that such a form could have been maintained to the time of the Germanic accent shift, a period as long as that during which alliterative verse and European rimed verse flourished. However fascinating such speculations may be, in the absence of any literary remains until the eighth century A.D., they remain highly fanciful.

For descriptions of general Germanic verse we have available no materials which permit us to describe segments longer than the alliterative line. For describing the alliterative line we have evidence like the Gallehus horn inscription. Though this was found in North Germanic territory it is so early—dating from before the completion of the Germanic migrations—that few linguistic changes had taken place which would separate its language from Proto-Germanic. And since the literary remains in the various Germanic dialects contain numerous lines like it, we can assume a continuous tradition for the single line.

But very little of the earliest Germanic verse is constructed as a series of lines. Two less simple forms were developed, one in the north, another in the south. In the north we find ballads composed of longer units, stanzas varying from two long lines to four, sometimes more. The southern poetry lacks such ballads, containing instead, besides alliterative epics patterned on Latin epic poetry, shorter poems of fifty to a hundred lines in which there are no regular metrical units longer than the alliterative line; such units as are found in these poems are determined by syntactic and stylistic rather than metrical grouping. Whether the general Germanic verse was composed in stanzas like the northern verse, or in irregular units like the southern, is again unclear.

At first approach it seems more attractive to consider the northern stanzaic ballads the Germanic form. Roman authors speak of Germanic song, a name apparently more applicable to the Old Norse ballads than to the West Germanic short heroic odes. And literary scholars, especially those of the nineteenth century, considered ballads the forerunners of epic verse. But this theory has more arguments against it than in its favor. In speaking of the Germanic song Tacitus singles out its irregularity (*clamor inconditus* ⟨confused noise⟩). Throughout the Germanic territory we find a progression from irregularity towards regularity in form, in the Middle High German *Nibelungenlied* with its four-line stanzas but no less so in the Old Norse Eddic and Skaldic poetry. Moreover, those genres which, apart from the very short charms and similar folk poetry, are agreed to be oldest—the song of praise and the heroic ode—are the ones preserved in the West Germanic irregular form. Furthermore, when the bard in Heorot sings his ballads, in a "southern" poem to be sure, but one dealing with the northern area, the poet does not shift to the Old Norse stanza form. The evidence against considering the stanzaic form the more original is therefore stronger than that in favor of the form maintained in the south.

If we compare two of the oldest poems in both languages, the Old Norse *Song of Weland* and the Old English *Fight at Finnsburg*, we find in both an irregular grouping of lines, from which either the northern ballad or the southern epic forms could have developed. Neither of these poems has escaped the characteristic features of its area, possibly through later modification: the *Song of Weland* contains some stanzas of similar structure, the *Fight at Finnsburg* some lines with syntactic breaks at the caesura rather than at the end. Yet these features are not maintained consistently in either poem, and we may assume that if the homes of these poems had been interchanged so might also such features. With few modifications, such as those suggested below, the *Fight at Finnsburg* might have been written down as a stanzaic ballad, the *Song of Weland* as a short epic. We may conclude, then, that the form of Germanic verse is better preserved in a few of the oldest pieces in our West Germanic literature than in the northern ballads.

The *Fight at Finnsburg* may therefore illustrate for us the characteristic Germanic verse form. The poem begins as follows (2–12):

> Hnæf hlēoþrode ðā    heaþogeong cyning:
> "Nē ðis ne dagað ēastan,    nē hēr draca ne flēogeð,
> nē hēr ðisse healle    hornas ne byrnað;
> ac hēr forþ berað,    fugelas singað,

gylleð grǣghama,    gūðwudu hlynneð,
scyld scefte oncwyð.    Nū scȳneð þes mōna
waðol under wolcnum;    nū ārīsað wēadǣda,
ðē ðisne folces nīð    fremman willað.
Ac onwacnigeað nū,    wīgend mīne,
habbað ēowre linda,    hicgeaþ on ellen,
winnað on orde,    wesað on mōde!"

> [Hnaef counselled then    king untried in war:
> "This is not dawn from the east,    no dragon flying,
> nor here in this hall    are the horns burning;
> but forth they are battling,    birds are singing,
> resound the grey-coats,    zoom the spears,
> shield to shaft answers.    Now shines the moon
> wandering under clouds;    now arise woe-deeds,
> that the wrath of this troop    will arouse.
> But awake now    warriors mine,
> sieze your shields    show courage,
> be first in the ranks,    faithful in mind."]

An examination of these lines shows how little they are removed from the Germanic form. Almost every line might be independent, as are the individual lines of the oldest charms and the Old Norse ballads; line 9 alone is connected syntactically to the preceding line. Only lines 7 and 8 show the characteristic West Germanic form of the alliterative line with their enjambment, that is, syntactic breaks in the middle of the line rather than at the end. And here only do we find the stylistic device of variation—the repetition of a concept in different words—which with the syntactic device of enjambment was the innovation that distinguishes the southern poetry from the northern. Stylistically, then, these lines are out of keeping with the rest of the poem. The first half-line of 8 is a poetic description of the moon, adding no new material; and 7*a* too is little more than a varied form of 6*b*. If these half-lines were omitted the passage would approximate an Old Norse heroic ballad, with no loss in essential material. Half-line 7*b* would then stand as the first half-line to 8*b*, and to bring about alliteration the *wēa-* of 8*b* might be replaced by an element beginning with *m*, such as *mān-*. Omission of 8*a* would harm the passage little; Klaeber comments on it:[6] "A stereotyped expression is here put to a fine, picturesque use." Old Norse poetry

6. Fr. Klaeber (ed.), *Beowulf and the Fight at Finnsburg*, 3rd ed. (Boston: D. C. Heath and Co., 1936), p. 251.

and early West Germanic poetry rarely engage in such picturesque expressions. Half-line 7a, "shield to shaft answers," is a bit premature in the passage; wēadǣda "dire deeds" is hardly more pertinent than māndǣda "evil deeds."

By these modifications this is not suggested as an "earlier form" of the introduction of the *Fight at Finnsburg*, but is merely used to illustrate how little was the difference between the northern ballad form and the early southern heroic ode. The recomposed forms of ancient verse that one sometimes finds in handbooks, such as the Old Norse version of the alliterative lines on the Tune stone, may have some pedagogical value in linguistic studies, but for study of literary form they are as absurd as similar passages of Chaucer would be if one kept Chaucer's words but strained them through the sound laws.

With these changes this part of the *Fight at Finnsburg* would consist of two stanzas: the first dealing with the portents, visual and aural; the second, after a transition through a sensual image, with the actual situation. Unequal stanzas of eight and ten half-lines would be quite normal in such an early ballad, but if the poem had been transmitted in the northern tradition the second stanza might also have been reduced to eight half-lines through omission of the last two half-lines. That these omissions and changes are not wholly arbitrary, that they are based on the contrasts in style between such lines as 6 and 8, may be noted by comparison with the early West Germanic charms. There too we find symmetry of structure like that of lines 5b, 6a, 6b, and 11b, 12a, 12b, but no enjambment or variation; emotion is heightened by repetition of similar patterns as in the first Merseburg charm:

> suma hapt heptidun,   suma heri lezidun,
> suma clubodun . . .
>
> [Some binding bonds,   some banning hosts,
> some chopping away . . .]

The *Fight at Finnsburg*, as it stands, is a stylistic confusion between the older and newer forms.

Through such stylistic analysis we may detect in the *Fight at Finnsburg* and the early heroic odes, such as the Old High German *Hildebrandslied*, the germs of two opposing tendencies, one of which was to take root in each of the Germanic areas: enjambment in the south, in the West Germanic area; strophic form in the north, in the North Germanic area. These contributed to making West Germanic alliterative poetry of the ninth and subsequent centuries so different from its contemporary North Germanic poetry. In the *Fight at Finnsburg* neither of these tendencies is carried through, or is even characteristic. Nor could one expect both to develop fully side by side. For enjambment is rare in any poetry with stanzas and lines as short as those in Old Norse. And only in highly sophisticated verse, such as Goethe's *Mailied* or Chaucer's *Troilus and Criseyde*, do we find a rigid stanza structure broken effectively by the emotion. In Germanic verse, too, there arose no balance between them. West Germanic poetry developed enjambment and variation, North Germanic poetry the stanza form and the *kenning*, a poetic compound consisting of two or more elements suggested by poetic fancy rather than by the context. In their extreme form, as in the Old Saxon *Heliand* and in some of the Skaldic poems, both literatures developed these tendencies to their utmost conclusion, and the conclusion of poetry.

But neither the northern nor the southern poetry ever broke through the stichic character of alliterative verse. Even in the most regular stanzas of the skalds and in the late Old English poetry, where syntactic pauses rarely coincide with rhythmic pauses, the characteristic unit remained the alliterative line. None of the gifted craftsmen who wrote in alliterative verse ever found a way of welding together successfully two successive lines.

An appreciation of Germanic rhythms requires only that the rhythms of the single line be understood. Though the Germanic poetic rhythms are based on those of prose and though the rhythm of each individual line is therefore ascertainable, in the over-all scheme of the Germanic alliterative line there has been considerable dispute among scholars; for the lines vary greatly in precisely those characteristics that modern verse has standardized: the relative position of the stresses and the number of unstressed syllables per line. Some lines of the southern and northern poetry are quite similar in structure, for example (*Bwf* 195 and *Vkv* 25.1):

> gōd mid Gēatum,  Grendles dǽda;
> [good mongst the Geats,  Grendel's deeds;]

> en ór augom     iarknasteina
> [but from the eyes    ornate stones]

others quite dissimilar (*Hel* 1096 and *Háv* 76.1):

> gibrengan uppan ênan berg then hôhon:    thar ina the balouuîso
> [bring upon a mountain high:    where him the baleful one]

> Deyr fé,    deyia frændr,
> [kine dies,    kinfolk die]

But all have the same basic structure. This is built around two characteristics: the alliterations and the stressed syllables.

The principles governing choice of alliteration in Germanic poetry are clear, not only from the poetry itself but also from a contemporary treatment, a treatise on it by a master-poet, Snorri Sturluson. Every long line was divided by a caesura into two parts, usually referred to as half-lines, but these were bound together by the alliterations of at least one of the two stressed syllables in each part. The important alliteration fell on the first beat of the second half-line; it determined the alliteration of the entire line, and only rarely, virtually only in the Eddic verse, yielded this function to the second beat of the second half-line. Apart from such rare lines the second beat of the second half-line almost never shared the alliteration. Both beats of the first half-line usually alliterated, as in the lines cited above; when not, the first more commonly than the second (*Fight at Finnsburg* 5, 9, 10, 11, 12). The single consonants alliterated with each other—likewise the groups *sp, st, sk*—but any of the vowels could be associated. Throughout the whole area and time of Germanic verse these principles are observed with absolute consistency. Confronted by such regularity, scholars have been able to find problems only in extremely minor points, chiefly whether cross alliteration, that is, alliteration of either the first or second stressed syllable in addition to the regular alliteration, as in the *Hávamál* line cited above, is deliberate or accidental.

The problems in the rhythm of the alliterative line, however, more than make up for the lack of them in alliteration. Here scholars have not attained even the uneasy agreement that is sometimes termed unanimity among them. For the characteristic rhythm is made up of two predominant elements—quantity and stress—which do not admit a simple relationship. There is no problem about the predominant elements of the line: these are four syllables, two in each half-line, which are elevated by stress, quantity, and two or three of them by alliteration. In these four syllables stress and quantity correlate, as does alliteration with the qualification stated above. Because of the interplay of stress and quantity, the term *lift* is used for the elevated syllables of Germanic verse, the term *drop* for the others. When, however, one attempts to set up a pattern for the nonpredominant syllables as well, the correlations end. Scholars have accordingly selected either stress or quantity as the predominant characteristic and on this have built their metrical systems. Two systems stand pre-eminent among the many proposed: that of Sievers, and that of Heusler and Leonard. Each of these reflects the approach of its proponents toward poetry.

Sievers, whose approach to literary works was analytic, found five recurrent patterns of stress in the alliterative line and succeeded in classing all alliterative lines in one of these patterns or a slight variant. The patterns are as follows: / symbolizes chief stress, \ medial stress, x lack of stress, — a long syllable, ‿ a short syllable.

```
A   ´x´x
B   x´x´
C   x´ ´x
D   ´ ´ `x
E   ´ `x´
```

All of them occur in *Beowulf* 7*b* to 10:

|  |  |  |
|---|---|---|
| hē þæs frōfre gebād, |  | B |
| wēox under wolcnum    weorðmyndum þāh, | A | E |
| oð þæt him æghwylc    ymbsittendra | A | D |
| ofer hronrāde    hȳran scolde, | C | A |

> [solace for this he found;
> he prospered on earth,    with honors he throve,
> until everyone    of the areas round
> beyond the whale-road    should worship him.]

The validity of these patterns was easily established in all areas of alliterative poetry, for they occurred with somewhat the same frequency in Old Norse as in Old English, some of them diminishing in frequency as the languages changed (D and E are less frequent in both Old Saxon and Middle English alliterative verse than in Old English). Furthermore, they were very useful in textual studies;

many emendations of corruptions introduced in transmission were effected with their help. But the over-all irregularity in pattern displeased those students of Germanic poetry whose approach was literary rather than linguistic; the variety of unit patterns struck them as a metrical contradiction.

The attempts to find a consistent unit pattern in Germanic poetry are now associated with the work of two such scholars, although they had numerous predecessors: Heusler, a German literary historian, and Leonard, an American poet and scholar. They turned to the other predominant element of the Germanic alliterative line, quantity, and developed rhythmic systems based on time rather than on accent periods. If we let – represent a half note, x a quarter note, # a quarter rest, we would indicate Heusler's scansion of *Beowulf* 11:

> gomban gyldan;  þæt wæs gōd cyning!
> [tribute to pay;   that was a true king!]

$$\text{—̀x\#  —́x\#   xx—́\#\#  x́x\#\#}$$

By Sievers' system it would be scanned:

$$\text{—́x —́x   xx—́  ⌣x}$$

The systems based on quantity admit no variety in the unit patterns: all normal half-lines are made up of two feet or measures, and all feet were alike in time. Where Sievers had assumed a variation extending from one stressed syllable ⌐, to a stressed plus a medially stressed plus an unstressed ⌐ ⌐x, Heusler assumed equal measures, comparable to musical measures in 4/4 time. In Sievers' pattern ⌐ ⌐x, linguistic material would fill up Heusler's measure; in Sievers' pattern ⌐, however, the linguistic material, depending on its weight, might correspond to a whole note, or a half note, and to fill out the measure a half rest would be assumed. With the aid of a complex series of rules Heusler was able to fit all alliterative lines into his system.

Systems so diverse naturally invited dispute among their adherents. Heusler's condemnation of Sievers stands or falls with his contention that poetry demands à recurrence of equal units. The adherents of Heusler maintained that Sievers' principles ruined Germanic verse as poetry, but upon admitting that Sievers himself read Germanic verse with feeling and understanding, declared that in his reading he failed to follow his system. Sievers himself seems tacitly to have admitted this contention, for he never ceased attempting to find one underlying principle for Germanic verse. Whether such a basis for poetry is essential, is, however, open to question. So far as I know neither Sievers nor Heusler ever investigated the living poetry of non-Indo-European languages. To readers in the European tradition, some such poetry, for example, Eskimo, conveys an impression exactly like that Germanic poetry produced on Tacitus, of an irregular noise. There seems to be no recurrence whatsoever of like units. That modern Europeans look for these in current poetry does not preclude their absence in old Germanic verse; for whichever system of metrical analysis one adheres to, that of Sievers or Heusler, it is clear that an aesthetic revolution has intervened between old Germanic and current Germanic verse, and before this revolution no need may have been felt for recurrent equal units.

But, either with Sievers or with Heusler, we agree on the basic outline of the alliterative line. It contained four lifts, that is strongly stressed syllables whose quantity, either inherently or by resolution, was long. Anacrusis was common and was not limited to one syllable—the American metrist J. C. Pope, however, has attempted to fit even anacrusis into a set pattern, analyzing all lines of the *Beowulf* according to a 4/8 time pattern, in which the first measure may be heavy or light, but the second always is heavy.[7] Nor was the number of unstressed syllables per stress circumscribed. We can disagree only in the assignment of these, and the use of pauses. Unless one has firm aesthetic convictions, either arrangement, that of Sievers or Heusler, permits one to manage the Germanic line. Current favor rests with Heusler; but earlier scholars worked effectively with Sievers' system, and one has the feeling that it too would have been favored by at least one contemporary observer, Tacitus.

While the alliterative line remained basically unmodified in northern poetry, the southern epic introduced expanded lines, as in the passage cited here from *Beowulf* 1166:

æt fōtum sæt frēan Scyldinga;   gehwylc hiora his ferhþe trēowde,
   [sat at the feet of the master of the Scyldings;   each of them
                                             his mind trusted,]

7. J. C. Pope, *The Rhythm of Beowulf* (New Haven: Yale University Press, 1942).

Some scholars read expanded lines with two chief stresses per half-line, others with three. Expanded lines were employed chiefly in passages of strong emotion, and did not lead to a departure from the basic rigidity of Germanic verse form. The characteristics which determined the development of the alliterative line were linguistic and stylistic rather than metrical: a tendency to terseness in the north, to a free-flowing form in the south.

* * *

While the northern poets were exploiting the terseness inherent in the alliterative line, the southern poets were breaking through its stichic rigidity. In contrast to the northern poets, they extended the narrative possibilities of Germanic verse at the sacrifice of its form. For the chief device used in the south was enjambment, opposition between syntactic and metrical units. Metrical devices to link two or more alliterating lines are but sporadic, such as the use of the initial sound of the fourth stress for the alliterations of the next line, as in *Beowulf* 36–37:

> mærne be mæste.    Þǣr wæs mādma fela
> of foerwegum    frætwa gelǣded;

> [The mighty one at the mast.    There was many a fortune
> from far countries    furnished, as treasure;]

or the repetition of alliterating sounds in two or more lines, as in *Beowulf* 1520–21:

> hildebille,    hond sweng ne oftēah,
> þæt hire on hafelan    hringmǣl āgōl

> [(a mighty blow he gave)
> hewing with the battle-sword,    his hand did not slight the
>                                                                    stroke,
> so that hewing on her head    the hissing sword sang
> (a fierce war-song).]

Even though these devices may not be accidental they never succeeded in becoming a feature of Germanic poetry. Syntactic stops came to be characteristically located in the middle of the line. The early Old English poets used this device with moderation and effect; in *Beowulf* such breaks are found about once in every five lines. But later it was carried to an extreme: by the North German *Heliand* poet of the ninth century who even ended eighteen of his seventy-one fits in the middle of a line; and in England by the tenth-century *Judith* poet. The northern poets choked their alliterative poetry by packing too much material in the line; the southern poets, on the other hand, permitted it to dissolve in a torrent of words.

In the south, just as in the north, the poets developed a stylistic feature which enabled them to fulfill the requirements of their form; this probably contributed in turn to its trend of development. In the north, metaphors within metaphors enabled poets to convey to those initiates who could unravel the figure a wealth of material in the few syllables that their line granted them. The southern poets had no need to seek terse expressions, and such metaphors are almost entirely absent in much of their verse, especially that from the continent. Here, as in England too, the characteristic figure is the variation, an appositional construction restating previous material while introducing few or no new concepts but contributing to expansion. While the kenning is often obscure through terseness, the variation often contributes little besides words; through it the poet pulls his syntactic breaks to the middle of a line, as in lines 2413–14 of the *Heliand*:

> Thô sâtun endi suîgodun    gesîðos Cristes,
> uuordspâha uueros:

> [There sat and were silent    the Savior's companions,
> those eloquent men:]

Here "eloquent" is hardly more than inept. Like the northern kennings, the variations developed in complexity. Other arrangements are found besides the appositional, such as the chiastic, as in lines 1580–82 of the *Heliand*:

> Heliðos stôdun,
> gumon umbi thana godes sunu    gerno suuîðo,
> uueros an uuilleon:    uuas im thero uuordo niut,

> [The great men stood,
> the disciples about that Son of God    with no slight joy,
> the heroes all happy:    they wished to hear those words,]

Accordingly, syntactic and stylistic devices accompanied prosodic innovations in the south, as well as in the north, as the alliterative line was adapted to epic poetry. But in carrying these innovations to excess, the southern poets destroyed the external form of the alliterative line. To the same number of stressed syllables as are found in the northern verse, they added many unstressed syllables, both in anacrusis and between the stresses. The resultant lines are so padded that often the two alliterating stressed syllables fail to hold them up. That such expansion was due rather to attempts at development than inability to handle the form is clear from the "expanded lines." Such lines, containing half again as much speech material as the normal lines, are introduced in scenes of special dignity, as in some lines of the Sermon of the Mount in the *Heliand*, e.g., 1687:

> Gerot gi simbla êrist thes godes rîkeas,   endi than duat aftar
> them is gôdun uuercun,

> [Keep ever your minds set on God's kingdom above all,
> and then do good works accordingly.]

Under such a weight the Germanic alliterative line collapsed. The rhythm was built around two stresses per half-line in the south as in the north; yet one could scarcely imagine a greater difference than that between the southern (*Hel* 1931*b*)

> simbla sôkiad gi iu thene bezton sân
> [always seek for yourselves the best straightway]

and the northern (*Háv* 77)

> deyr fé
> [kine dies.]

The southern "expanded verses" may be the result of an attempt to extend the structure of the Germanic line—to proceed beyond the two central stresses, but if they were, the attempt was unsuccessful; even an additional stress could not support the extra material. Alliterative poetry in the south foundered under the weight of unstressed syllables.

Revivals of the alliterative form were attempted in England, especially in areas under Scandinavian influence. Some of the Middle English poems, for example, *The Destruction of Troy*, have a more rigid form than the late Old English epics; of 14,044 lines, 13,999 have, according to Oakden, an alliterative pattern like that of the first line:[8]

> Maistur in Magesté,   Maker of alle,

8. Oakden, *op. cit.*, p. 188.

But even when the older Germanic patterns are kept, often the structure is merely external. Words that were unstressed in Old English, such as prepositions and even unimportant verbs like *is* and *are* may alliterate in Middle English; in other words the alliteration may vary from syllable to syllable, as in *Morte D'Arthur* 3966 *al*las, but 1153 al*las*. The alliterative form was apparently unable to support both the unaccented inflectional endings and the mass of function words, especially the articles and verbal auxiliaries, which had come into use in the Germanic languages after the eighth century.

Alliterative poetry was abandoned earliest on the continent. Despite the small amount of poetry that has survived from this area we have within fifty years an epic characterized by the extreme development of the alliterative form, the *Heliand* of about 830, and one in the new rimed form, Otfrid's *Krist* of about 860. The last alliterative Old High German poem that has survived, the *Muspilli*, was a contemporary of the *Krist*; whatever verse was produced in Germany after it is in the new form.

\* \* \*

By the thirteenth century the various Germanic languages had turned from the original Germanic verse form to the Latin-Romance form. Though the rate and course of change vary, in none of the three important literary areas of the Germanic world was verse form still governed by the Germanic principles. In Iceland, the most conservative area, alliteration was still retained as a structural feature, but in combination with rime and regular rhythm; in the main stream of poetry of the English area, and in the German area, alliteration had merely become a stylistic feature. Apart from Icelandic verse—which never again reached its early dominant position in Germanic literature—and the alliterative poetry of north England, the Germanic world had turned completely from irregular rhythm and alliteration to even rhythm and rime.

Reprinted from W. P. Lehmann, *The Development of Germanic Verse Form* (Austin, Texas: The University of Texas Press, 1956), pp. 23–63. Several pages, dealing primarily with Skaldic and Middle High German poetry, have been omitted.

# The Authority
# of Old English
# Poetical Manuscripts

I

*Genesis B* 313–17 (MS. Junius xi):

> þær hæbbað heo on æfyn   ungemet lange
> ealra feonda gehwilc   fyr edneowe;
> þonne cymð on uhtan   easterne wind,
> forst fyrnum cald;   symble fyr oððe gar,
> sum heard gewrinc   habban sceoldon;

For manuscript *gewrinc*, modern editors accept Grein's *geswinc*, which renders *tribulatio* in some Biblical texts. But, whatever the explanation of *gar* in *fyr oððe gar*, these words indicate violent tortures, so that *geswinc* gives a weak effect. Read *geþwinc* = *geþwing*, Old Saxon *gethuing* "torment" as in *Heliand* 2144 f.:

> Thar ist gristgrimmo   endi gradag fiur,
> hard helleo gethuing,   het endi thiustri.

In the only other English example, *Genesis B* 696 *hellgeþwin*, the erasure of final *g* in the manuscript indicates that the word was unfamiliar; and at line 802, for which the Old Saxon source is available, the verb *thuingan* is translated by OE *slitan*.

*Genesis B* 327–329:

>            hie hyra gal beswac,
> engles oferhygd,   noldon Alwaldan
> word weorþian;   hæfdon wite micel: etc.

The use of *engel* after their Fall deserves notice, though it is easier to explain than the singular *engles* in a plural context. Certainly Lucifer's arrogance has been referred to earlier in the poem (262, 272); but that does not justify the interpretation *engles* = "Lucifer's" in this passage, where it is emphasized that arrogance is the

36

fault of all the fallen angels (332, 337), and where *engles oferhygd* is naturally taken as a variant of *hyra gal*. Nor does Old English usage allow us to take the singular as generic, translating "angelic arrogance."

Must we be content with the manuscript reading even though it involves such difficulties? Recent practice favors that choice: an editor's reputation for soundness would gain rather than lose by his tenacious defense of the manuscript, unless its reading were as patently wrong as *gewrinc* in the previous passage. If this attitude has a basis in reason, it implies that the extant manuscripts of Old English poetry represent the original compositions with a high degree of accuracy. Yet there seems to be no modern work which attempts to establish a thesis so fundamental. To say that "an accurate scribe did not as a rule depart from the *wording* of his original except as a result of oversight"[1] is begging the question, unless the editor goes on to inquire whether the scribes with whom he is concerned were accurate in this sense, and whether, since the assumed date of composition, the transmission of the text has been entirely in the hands of scribes who aimed at copying what was before them. A following section deals mainly with the first of these questions; and in anticipation of the argument, I propose to read

1. R. W. Chambers' Preface to *Beowulf with the Finnsburg Fragment*, ed. A. J. Wyatt, rev. R. W. Chambers (Cambridge: Cambridge University Press, 1914), p. xxvi. There is much that should be common ground in this persuasive manifesto of the school which makes the defense or conservation of the MS readings its ruling principle, and is therefore called "conservative." The term does not imply a generally conservative attitude in criticism.

The history of opinion has its interest. The headship of this school in Old English poetry belongs to R. P. Wülker, who succeeded Grein as editor of the *Bibliothek der angelsächsischen Poesie*. In the Preface to his first volume (1883) he announced: "In bezug auf die textherstellung habe ich mich . . . bemüht möglichst die lesungen der handschrift zu wahren" ⟨In regard to the reproduction of the text . . . I have endeavored wherever possible to preserve the scribal readings⟩. The best textual critics of that brilliant time were grateful for the materials he provided, which were then not so accessible as they are now; but they joked at his obtuseness: Cosijn pencilled *unsinnigen* ⟨senseless⟩ before *lesungen* ⟨scribal [readings]⟩ in his copy of the volume. In 1894, when Wyatt declared in his Preface to *Beowulf* that anyone who himself proposed emendations suffered from "the greatest disqualification for discharging duly the functions of an editor," he drew a protest from Zupitza, who excelled in editorial judgment. In 1914 Chambers could fairly say that the battle for conservatism was won.

here *egle oferhygd* "(their) pernicious arrogance." *Oferhyd egle* occurs in *Daniel* 679. In *Guthlac* 935 (= 962) the manuscript has *engle* for *egle*, in *Christ* 762 *englum* for *eglum*.

## II

*Was the poetry accurately transmitted?*

This subject could well occupy a monograph, and even a selective treatment requires many illustrative examples. One might start from the considerable number of gross errors that appear in the principal manuscripts; but single lapses are not necessarily inconsistent with a high general level of accuracy, and that is the quality to be discussed.

Nearly all the poetical texts depend on a single manuscript; but the contents of three out of the four great codices show a very small overlap. Thus both the Exeter Book and the Vercelli Book contain a poem on the Soul and the Body. The following specimen is set out in short or half lines for convenience of comparison, and substantial differences are italicized in both texts:

| **A** | Exeter Book | Vercelli Book |
|---|---|---|
| | Sceal se gæst cuman | Sceal se gast cuman |
| | gehþum hremig | geohðum hremig |
| 10 | symle ymb seofon niht | symble ymbe seofon niht |
| | sawle findan | sawle findan |
| | þone lichoman | þone lichoman |
| | þe heo ær longe wæg | þe hie ær lange wæg |
| | þreo hund wintra | þreo hund wintra |
| | butan ær *wyrce* | butan ær *þeodcyning* |
| | *ece dryhten* | |
| | ælmihtig god | ælmihtig god |
| | ende worlde | ende worulde |
| | | *wyrcan wille* |
| | | *weoruda dryhten* |
| 15 | Cleopað þonne swa cearful | Cleopað þonne swa cearful |
| | caldan reorde | cealdan reorde |
| | spriceð grimlice | spreceð grimlice |
| | gæst to þam duste | *se* gast to þam duste |
| | hwæt dru*gu* þu dreorga | hwæt dru*h* ðu dreorega |

| | |
|---|---|
| to hwon dreahtest þu me | to hwan drehtest ðu me |
| eorþan fylnes | eorðan fulnes |
| eal forweornast | eal forwisnad |
| lames gelicnes | lames gelicnes |
| lyt þu gepohtes | lyt ðu gemundest |
| 20 to won þinre sawle sið | to hwan þinre sawle þing |
| siþþan wurde | siðþan wurde |
| siþþan heo of lichoman | syððan of lichoman |
| læded wære. · | læded wære. |

The next specimen from the *Daniel-Azarias* verses allows a comparison of the Exeter Book with MS. Junius XI. It does not show the widest divergencies of content, but evidently contains a deep-seated corruption:

| **B** | Exeter Book (*Azarius*) | MS. Junius XI (*Daniel*) | |
|---|---|---|---|
| | þu him gehete | þu him *þæt* gehete · | |
| | þurh hleoþorcwid*as* | þurh hleoðorcwyd*e* · | |
| | þæt þu hyra fr*o*mcynn | þæt þu hyra fr*u*mcyn · | |
| | *on* fyrndagum | *in* fyrndagum · | |
| | ycan wolde | ican wolde · | |
| | *þæt hit* after him | *þætte* æfter him · | |
| 35 | on *cyneryce* | on *cneorissum* · | |
| | cenned wurde | cenned wurde · | |
| | *yced on eorþan* | *and seo mænigeo* | 320 |
| | *þæt swa unrime* | *mære wære* · | |
| | *had* to hebban | *hat* to hebban*ne* · | |
| | swa heofonsteorran | swa heofonsteorran · | |
| | buga*ð* bradne hw*e*arft | *be*bugað bradne hw*y*rft · | |
| | oð brimflodas | oð *þæt* brim*faro* · *þæs* | |
| | *swa wa*roþa sond | *sæ*faroða sand · | |
| | ymb sealt w*æter* | geond sealt*ne wæg* · | |
| 40 | *yþe geond eargrund* | *me are gryndeð* · | |
| | þæt *swa* unrime | þæt *his* unrim *a* · | |
| | ymb wintra *hwearft* | *in* wintra *worn* · | 325 |
| | weorðan sceolde. | wurðan sceolde. | |

Two manuscripts are available for lines 30–94 of *Solomon and Saturn*, MS. CCCC ⟨Corpus Christi College, Cambridge⟩ 422 of the second half of the tenth century and a fragment in the margin of

CCCC 41 which may be a century later.[2] Lines 75–84 will serve as a sample:

| **C**   *MS. CCCC* 422 | *MS. CCCC* 41 |
|---|---|
| 75 He is modigra | He is modigra |
|  middangearde |  middangeardes |
|  staðole strengra |  staðole *he is* strengra |
|  ðonne eal*ra* stana gripe |  þone eall*e* stana gripe |
|  lamena he is læce |  lamana he is læce |
|  leoht wincendra |  leoht winciendra |
|  swilce he is deafra duru |  swilce he is deafra duru |
|  *dumbra* tunge |  *deadra* tunge |
|  scyldigra scyld |  scilidgra scild |
|  scyppendes seld |  scippendes seld |
| 80 flodes ferigend |  flodes feriend |
|  folces nerigend |  folces neriend |
|  yða yrfeweard |  yða yrfeweard |
|  earm*ra* fisca |  earm*a* fixa |
|  *and* wyrma *welm* |  wyrma *wlenco* |
|  wildeora holt |  wildeora holt |
|  *on* westenne weard |  westen*es* weard |
|  weorðmynda geard. |  weorðmynta geard. |

I am concerned only with the amount of variation and the nature of the variants, not with their merits. There are differences of inflection, e.g., **B** *hleoporcwidas: hleoporcwyde*, sometimes with other modifications, as **C** *on westenne weard: westenes weard*, or **A** *forweornast: forwisnad*. Minor words are added or omitted, e.g., **C** *staðole* [*he is*] *strengra*, or **A** [*se*] *gast*. Prepositions are varied, e.g., **B** *ymb wintra hwearft: in wintra worn*. Substitution of one word for another is

---

2. I have not seen this MS, but have noted (*MÆ*, XIII [1944], p. 35) that it was nearer to the original than the earlier MS in omitting the runes for PATER-NOSTER. The latest editor, Robert Menner, whose readings I follow, dates the hand "at the end of the eleventh or beginning of the twelfth century." Mr. Neil Ker tells me he would place it considerably earlier. It is disadvantageous to use such a late copy, because the great bulk of the poetry is contained in MSS of the second half of the tenth century—Exeter Book, Vercelli Book, Junius "Caedmon" (original part), Beowulf MS, MS. CCCC ⟨Corpus Christi College, Cambridge⟩ 422 of *Solomon and Saturn*; and new factors affecting transmission may arise in MSS written much after that time. I have excluded the poems contained in the *Chronicle* partly for this reason, partly because they are all late compositions transmitted in an unusual way. Similarly *Be Domes Dæge* is left out of account.

common: sometimes the forms are similar, e.g., **C** *welm: wlenco*; and, with inferior alliteration in the first reading, **B** *swa waroþa: sæfaroða*. Sometimes the words have the same alliteration and rough sense, as **B** *ymb sealt wæter: geond sealtne wæg*; sometimes only the alliteration is the same, as **B** *cyneryce: cneorissum*; sometimes only the meaning and syllabic weight, as **A** *geþohtes: gemundest*. Omissions or additions with considerable rearrangement occur at **A** 13 f. There is a new composition at **B** 320, and *þæt swa unrime* in the *Azarias* text recurs below. **B** *yþe geond eargrund: me are gryndeð* shows the making of a crux. At **B** 322 the *Daniel* scribe fails to recognize *brimfaroþes*, and points the verse before the last syllable, which he takes to be the word *þæs*. At **A** 17 both copies bungle the formula *Hwæt druge þu?* (*Genesis* 888 *Juliana* 247), so creating, even for Bosworth-Toller's Supplement and the latest editors,[3] a noun variously identified as *druh, drug, druhþu, druguþu*, and supposed to mean "dust."

In sum, the number of variants is very large. Though they are of a pedestrian kind,[4] many of them cannot be accounted for by simple errors of a scribe's eye or ear. More often than not they make meter and some sense: even **C** *deadra tunge* might be defended if there were no second manuscript to support *dumbra*. But as compared with the variants in classical texts, they show a laxity in reproduction and an aimlessness in variation which are more in keeping with the oral transmission of verse. An editor who has these passages in mind will not regard the integrity of a late manuscript as axiomatic.

All the major manuscripts already sampled were written within one half-century, and all come from the South or South Midlands, an area which was fairly homogeneous in literary language and culture at that time. It is possible to reach back into earlier times and different conditions because three short pieces, recorded in the eighth or ninth centuries, are also found in late-tenth-century copies:

3. George P. Krapp (ed.), *The Vercelli Book* (New York: Columbia University Press, 1932), p. 126; Krapp and E. van K. Dobbie (eds.), *The Exeter Book* (New York: Columbia University Press, 1936), pp. 175, 317; W. S. Mackie (ed.), *Exeter Book* (EETS, 1934), p. 74 f.

4. A variant is exceptionally preserved in the MS at *Christ* 1653: "ðær is leofra lufu, lif butan ende deaðe," where *ende* makes an almost inevitable phrase and the alternative *deaðe* matches the group of opposites that follows.

they are Caedmon's *Hymn*, the *Leiden Riddle*, and the Ruthwell Cross runic inscriptions.

The Ruthwell Cross runes, which are not necessarily as old as the Cross itself, give four groups of verses that can be identified in the Vercelli Book between lines 38 and 64 of *The Dream of the Rood*. The latter poem is so different in bulk and so uneven in quality that a comparison could not favor the hypothesis of accurate transmission; and the first inscription differs remarkably from the corresponding lines in the Vercelli Book:[5]

> (on)geredæ hinæ god almegttig   þa he walde on galgu gistiga
> modig f(ore allæ) men   bug . . .
> Ongyrede hine þa geong hæleð,   þæt wæs God ælmihtig,
> strang and stiðmod.   Gestah he on gealgan heanne,
> modig on manigra gesyhðe,   þa he wolde mancyn lysan.
> Bifode is þa me se beorn ymbclypte;   ne dorste ic hwæðre bugan
>    to eorðan . . .

The absence of any probable alliteration in the second runic line is evidence of adaptation to the special purpose, and it would be unsafe to make much of the detailed variants where the conditions of recording are so abnormal.

The exceptional character of Caedmon's *Hymn* is marked by the many copies in which it appears.[6] If manuscripts later than the tenth century are excluded, the reproduction of the original words is good, with five variants, four minor and one major, of which only the last, *eorðan (bearnum)* for *aelda*, can be traced back to the ninth century. But it is a very short piece of miraculous origin, and it has been preserved as a quotation in historical prose texts, either the Latin of Bede's *History* or the late-ninth-century English translation from it. Here the conditions of transmission are abnormal, and again it is unsafe to rely on the evidence.

There remains the *Leiden Riddle*, found in a ninth-century Continental manuscript and in the Exeter Book. A specimen is un-

5. See *The Dream of the Rood*, ed. Bruce Dickins and A. S. C. Ross (London: Methuen and Co., 1945).

6. See *The Manuscripts of Cædmon's Hymn and Bede's Death Song* by E. van K. Dobbie (New York: Columbia University Press, 1937). I omit *Bede's Death Song*: the Northumbrian text is preserved in Continental MSS from the ninth century onwards; but, for comparison, there is only a very late West Saxon text, equally uniform, preserved in MSS from the twelfth century onwards. Its four variants from the Northumbrian text have no claim to authority.

necessary because the two manuscripts have often been printed side by side.[7] Apart from details of inflection and uncertainties of reading in the Leiden manuscript, there are half a dozen variants of some importance in sixteen corresponding lines, and the last two lines of the Leiden version, which are supported by the Latin original, have been replaced by a conventional riddle-ending in the Exeter Book. The degree of variation is not very different from that exhibited in the much shorter Riddle 31, of which two copies survive by an exceptional chance in the Exeter Book.

In these three pieces the tenth-century texts show no attempt to reproduce the archaic or dialectal forms and spellings of the earlier copies: Bodleian MS. Tanner 10 of Caedmon's *Hymn* and the early-eighth-century Moore MS. are identical only in a few invariable words. Ample evidence from other sources confirms that copyists of Old English texts were not expected to reproduce their originals letter for letter, as they were when copying Latin and especially Biblical texts. Modernization of forms in the course of transmission was allowed and even required by the use for which Old English works were intended,[8] and the practice was obviously dangerous for the wording.

7. See especially *Three Northumbrian Poems*, ed. A. H. Smith (London: Methuen and Co., 1933).

8. This has a bearing on attempts to defend the MS reading *wundini golde* in *Bwf* 1382, where the slight emendation *wundnū = wundnum* had become established. It is not quite certain that *wundini* is the reading of the MS, and it is very doubtful whether a form *wundini* ever existed: in the recorded *-numini*, all the examples of which may go back to a single late-seventh-century gloss, the stem is short. But if there were no such doubts, it is most unlikely that this extraordinary ending would survive for three centuries, in a common word and phrase, to appear in the Beowulf MS. It would require, in this one place only, a suspension of the normalizing practice of scribes, and minutely accurate unintelligent copying throughout the whole long chain of transmission. That the acceptance of this reading leads to startling conclusions about the written tradition of *Beowulf* is another reason for preferring the simpler solution *wundnum*.

The habit of normalizing helps to explain some corrupt readings. In the Paris Psalter LXII. 11 *sine causa* (*justificavi cor meum*) ⟨without cause (I have justified my heart)⟩ is rendered, according to modern editors: "þeah þe ic on [me] ingcan ænigne [ne] wiste," etc. It is more likely that *ic intingcan* was the original reading, that *t* dropped out leaving *ic in ingcan*, and a scribe changed *in* to *on*, as he would the preposition. The only other place where *causa* has to be translated is Paris Psalter LXIII. 21 *iudica causam tuam* ⟨justify your own cause⟩: "dem þine nu ealde intingan."

A defender of the manuscript readings might well say that the evidence so far adduced is not ample or varied enough, and might argue that the scribes were well trained, and that they knew more about Old English usage, thought, and tradition than a modern critic can. I doubt if this holds good for the earlier poetry. In *Beowulf*, recent editors agree that the first scribe writes *gara* (*cyn*) 461 clearly and boldly for *Wedera* (*cyn*), without sense or alliteration, with no likeness in script or sound, or anything in the surrounding verses to mislead him; and the aberration is passed over in their commentaries. For *Cain* 1261 (misread as *cam*) he writes *camp* "battle," just as in *Genesis* 1938, 2400, *Loth* becomes *leoht* with no glimmering of sense. At a critical point in the Finn episode (1127 ff.), he leaves us the meaningless "Hengest . . . wunode mid finnel unhlitme." Rather different is 1960 f.: "þonon geomor woc hæleðum to helpe," where, misled by a possible spelling or pronunciation of the initial diphthong, he has taken the proper name *Eomær* for the common adjective *geomor* "sad."[9] I have previously noted[10] a similar instance in the Exeter Book, where *onsyne beorg* appears in *Christ* 876, 900 for *on Sione beorg*, because the scribe mistook *onsione* for the common noun meaning "face"; and MS. Junius XI shows the same misunderstanding in *Exodus* 386 *onseone* (*beorh*) for *on Sione*. All these are proper names, which I have preferred because there can be little doubt about the true reading when a name is miswritten. To show

9. The MS reading *geomor* has been defended, e.g., ⟨by Edith Rickert, "The Old English Offa Saga,"⟩ *MP*, II (1904), 54 ff. Faith in the accuracy of this scribe, or his kind, underlies the doctrine that, in one poem or tradition, the same person sometimes has two authentic names, metrically equivalent and similar in script, but etymologically different in the significant first element: e.g., *Bwf* 467 *Heregar* beside *Heorogar* 61 and *Hiorogar* (second scribe) 2158; or *Oslaf* 1148 beside *Ordlaf* in the Finnsburg fragment. That two names, having such practical inconveniences and no technical purpose, should be maintained for centuries within a single poem or tradition seems to me to be a major improbability, which is not much lessened by evidence (e.g., in Fr. Klaeber's *Beowulf* [Boston: D. C. Heath and Co., 1936], p. xxxii, n. 5) that some persons who can be identified in both literatures have Old English names differing in formation from their Scandinavian names. It is more likely that a scribe has slipped again, where he should have written *Heorogar*, *Or(d)laf*.

10. *RES*, X (1934), 340. [The confusion occurs in psalter glosses: XIII. 7 *ex Sion* = Vitellius E XVIII (G) *on seone*; Tiberius C VI (H) *ansyne*; Arundel 60 (J) *ansine*.]

that the scribe misunderstood the meaning of common words we must use conjectural emendations, and, though I shall indulge in conjecture from this point, there is a risk of arguing in a circle. But in *Juliana* 482 the bad form *hyradreorge* (for *heoru-*) arose because the first element was mistaken for the pronoun *heora*, which usually has the form *hyra* in the Exeter Book.[11] In *Genesis* 2174 f.

> Hwæt gifest þu me, gasta waldend,
> freomanna to frofre, nu ic þus feasceaft eom?

it can hardly be doubted that a scribe has lost the sense by substituting *freomanna*, a legal not a poetical word, for *fremena* gen. pl. "benefits" depending on *hwæt*. And because one can seldom prove that the scribe was alert when he wrote something wrong, it is worth noting a scrap of evidence at *Beowulf* 1981: "hwearf | geond þæt (side) reced Hæreðes dohtor." Here the copyist has added *side* as a correction above the line, which shows that his attention was directed to an error; and, for the sake of the alliteration, the editors must either reject his correction, or assume a lacuna after *reced* which escaped him. But there is no need to multiply indications that the scribes were often ignorant, or inattentive to the meaning.

As a last resort, it might be argued in defense of the poetical manuscripts that their authority is confirmed because they have passed the scrutiny of Anglo-Saxon readers, who knew things unknown to us. In fact there is hardly a trace of intelligent scrutiny. It is a curious feature of the great poetical codices that no early reader seems to have noticed the most glaring errors left by the scribe.

My argument has been directed against the assumption that Anglo-Saxon poetical manuscripts are generally good, in the sense

11. *RES*, *X* (1934), 340. Should not *Exodus* 218 *habban heora hlencan* be read *habban heorahlencan* (Sievers' expanded D-type, with extra alliteration which is not objectionable in the context)? In MS. Junius xi the elements of a compound are often separated, and the MS arrangement here is the same as in *Exodus* 181 *heorawulfas*. *Hioroserce* occurs in *Bwf* 2539; *wælhlence* in *Exodus* 176; but *hlence* by itself nowhere means "coat of chain-mail," and such a meaning for the simplex is not likely. The passage has been used to emend *Finnsburg* 11 *habbað eowre landa*, which has a modern ring. Here we have to do with what Hickes and his printer made of the lost MS, and perhaps *habbað (h)eorelinda* is worth considering, though that compound is not recorded.

that, except for an inevitable sprinkling of errors, they faithfully reproduce the words of much older originals. It does not attempt to establish that all the poems have survived in bad texts: three such pieces as *Widsith*, *Juliana*, and the *Gnomic Verses*, all preserved in the Exeter Book, may well have been subjected to different chances in their earlier transmission, and there may be reasons for believing that some poems were lucky.

Nor should acceptance of this argument discourage the habit of constant recourse to the manuscripts. Long after all the letters that can be read in them are settled in cold print (and not many finds like Mr. J. C. Pope's *Geatisc meowle*[12] at *Bwf* 3150 can now be expected) they will repay close study, because they are the primary witnesses. If there were enough of them, all the facts about the written transmission would be in evidence.

But when, as is usual for Old English poetry, only one late witness is available, there is no safety in following its testimony. The difference between a better reading and a worse is, after all, a matter of judgment; and however fallible that faculty may be, the judge must not surrender it to the witness. To support a bad manuscript reading is in no way more meritorious than to support a bad conjecture, and so far from being safer, it is more insidious as a source of error. For, in good practice, a conjecture is printed with some distinguishing mark which attracts doubt; but a bad manuscript reading, if it is defended, looks like solid ground for the defense of other readings. So intensive study with a strong bias towards the manuscript reading blunts the sense of style, and works in a vicious circle of debasement.[13]

12. *The Rhythm of Beowulf* (New Haven: Yale University Press, 1942), p. 233.
13. The process extends to grammar. It is enough to quote the most distinguished English commentator of the conservative school, R. W. Chambers, defending the MS reading *licað leng swa wel* at *Bwf* 1854 against Grein's conjecture *sel*: "If one finds gross anomalies in accidence in the *Beowulf*, why should one look for a flawless syntax?" ⟨*op. cit.*, p. 90⟩. (Here, it should be noticed, there is confusion between the late MS of *Beowulf*, to which the *if* clause must refer, and the text to be derived from it by critical methods, to which the apodosis refers.) The principles of phonology must also yield: in Boethius *Metra* XXXI. 11 the editors and modern dictionaries accept *fierfete* "four-footed" on the evidence of Junius' transcript of a leaf since destroyed, though *fier-* is against all rules, and the regular word is *fiðerfete*.

As a simple example, the Vercelli MS. reading *Hwæt, druh ðu
dreorega* in *Soul and Body* 17, already mentioned, provides not only a
ghost-word *druh*, but a form of apostrophe new to Old English verse
in its word order. A more complex example comes from the narrative
passage in *Genesis A* which describes the flight of the raven and the
dove from the Ark, lines 1443 ff.:[14]

> Noe tealde,   þæt he on neod hine,
> gif he on þære lade   land ne funde,
> ofer sid wæter   secan wolde
> on wægþele;   eft him seo wen geleah;
> ac se feond[e] gespearn   fleotende hreaw:
> salwigfeðera   secan nolde.
> He (*sc.* Noe) þa ymb seofon niht, etc.

The last two complete lines are interpreted "but he (the raven),
rejoicing, alighted on a floating corpse: the dark-feathered (bird)
would not seek." I find them ungrammatical, for *secan* is never left
in the air like this in a sound text, and it is the more intolerable with
*secan wolde* just above, and *sohte, secan* in the following lines, all with
the regular object. The abruptness of the expression is equally dis-
turbing, because the narrative in the whole passage is full and easy,
and the poet has gone to a commentary for more about the raven
than the Bible tells. The indications are that at least a line is missing,
probably after *hreaw*, which contained the object of *secan*. But if such
a manuscript text is regarded as sound, the chances are small that
any lacuna of a line or more will be admitted on internal evidence.
In fact, few are admitted by modern editors.[15]

14. The text is that of F. Holthausen *Die ältere Genesis* (Heidelberg: C. Winter,
1914) and Krapp *The Junius Manuscript* (New York: Columbia University Press,
1931).

15. When there is only one MS, gaps other than those due to its physical condition may sometimes be established from our knowledge of the subject-matter.
But generally lacunae are conjectural. The weakness of such conjectures is that
they are vaguer than specified readings, and therefore easy. Still, they should be
considered on the balance of probability. Note:

(i) The mechanical dropping of one or more verse lines, which is common in
MSS of Latin poetry, is not so likely in Old English MSS, because in them the
written line rarely corresponds with the verse. If the copyist dropped a line or
more of his pattern MS, the ragged parts of two verses would usually be brought
together, and meter as well as sense would show up the fault. If the omission
escaped the copyist, subsequent patching up is likely.

There is, then, no escape from the task of questioning our single witness, beginning with tests of general credibility like those I have suggested already. If the results are not satisfying, we must examine and cross-examine on every sign of weakness in particular places. Thus in line 1446 of the passage just quoted, how is *eft* to be accounted for in the second half-verse? Noah has not been disappointed before, and the formula *him seo wen geleah* is elsewhere a complete half-verse (*Gen* 49, *Bwf* 2323, *And* 1074). Here the manuscript pointing of the verse is at fault. In the next line *feonde* "rejoicing" for manuscript *feond* was suggested by Grein and confirmed by Cosijn; but there is no good evidence for a simple verb *feon* beside regular *gefeon*, and it is especially awkward in the present participle. Then again, a demonstrative pronoun *se* "he" so clumsily separated from

---

(ii) But one would expect a kind of omission to which Latin verse is not subject: the feeling for alliteration was strong, and when the scribe had written part of a verse, his eye might drop to a verse below with the same alliteration. So a lacuna could occur with no break in the alliteration. This possibility should be taken into account in such places as *Bwf* 1931, where Old English usage gives the clear indication that *modþryðo* is a compound abstract noun, object of *wæg* (*Gen* 2238 *higeþryðe wæg*; *Guthlac* 982 *hygesorge wæg*, 1309 *gnornsorge wæg*; *Elene* 61 *modsorge wæg*, 655 *gnornsorge wæg*; *Bwf* 152 *heteniðas wæg*, 2780 *ligegesan wæg*: all second half-lines). See also W. A. Craigie, "Interpolations and Omissions in Anglo-Saxon Poetic Texts," *Philologica*, II (1923–1924). [There is another reason for suspecting a lacuna here: the name of a new and important character, especially where it is suddenly introduced, should be emphasized by the alliteration; cf. *Sigemund* 875, *Heremod* 901, 1709.]

In *Azarias* 109 ff.,

þu þæs geornlice
wyrcest wuldorcyning wæstmum herge
bletsien bledum, etc.,

pretty clearly a subject has been lost before *wæstmum* or after *herge*, and the Latin *benedicat* terra *Dominum* ⟨let the earth *praise the Lord*⟩ confirms it. But rather than admit a lacuna, modern editors (Grein-Wülker ⟨*Bibliothek der angelsächsischen Poesie* (Kassel: Georg H. Wigand, 1883), vol. 2, p. 517⟩ and Krapp-Dobbie ⟨*op. cit.*, p. 271⟩) assume an unknown fem. pl. *herge*, a meaning "groves" otherwise unrecorded in Old English, and the free choice in this context of a word with peculiarly heathen associations—although *hergen* "let them praise" occurs six times elsewhere in this paraphrase of the *Canticum Trium Puerorum*, thrice in association with *bletsien*. It is an example of the speculation which is induced by too much faith in the MS.

its noun *hrefn* is hardly possible: it is better to take *se* as a consequence of the misreading *feond*, and to substitute *he* as a necessary part of Grein's proposed emendation.

The cluster of difficulties in these few lines shows how complicated corruption may be. If the average text offered by the manuscripts were open to so many doubts, a critic's work would be hopeless. But long stretches have no such obvious faults: whether or not they represent the exact words of the original composer, they make good sense, grammar, and meter by the standards at present available. So a proper respect for the manuscripts is consistent with a critical and independent attitude towards their evidence. Nothing is to be gained by judging them with a hostile bias, and occasionally they still offer readings which modern editors have rejected and which deserve to be restored.[16]

16. In *Elene* 925 "Gen ic findan can ... wiðercyr wiððan," the editors since Grein read *siððan* with feeble sense. In *Guthlac* 465 "Ic eow soð wiððon secgan wille," they again alter to *siððon*. In *Menology* 146 "hæfð nu lif wið þan," the alteration is not possible. The meaning in *Elene* and *Guthlac* is "Still I can devise a counter-stroke *against that*," etc., and the MS readings are sound. *Wið þan* fills a similar place in the verse in Paris Psalter CXVIII. 158: "and ic þand wið þan þe hi teala noldan  þinre spræce  sped gehealdan," where *þriste* should be read for MS *teala*.

Again, in his edition of *Genesis A*, Holthausen has the courage to say that he does not understand line 1400 in the account of the Flood:

> Fiftena stod
> deop ofer dunum    se drenceflod
> monnes elna.    Þæt is mæro wyrd:
> 1400 þam æt niehstan wæs    nan to gedale,
> nymþe heo[f] wæs ahafen    on þa hean lyft, etc.

Bouterwek, who established this punctuation in 1849, described the passage as "sehr dunkel," and it troubled P. J. Cosijn and E. Sievers (Paul and Braune's *Beiträge* ⟨*zur Geschichte der deutschen Sprache und Literatur*⟩, XIX (1894) 448 f.). If MS *heo* is restored instead of Sievers' suggestion *heof* "lamentation," and if *þæt is mæro wyrd* is bracketed as a parenthesis, for which there is an exact parallel at *Gen* 2566, the MS reading makes grammar and sense: "Fifteen of our (*monnes*) ells above the mountains stood the whelming flood (that was a great marvel!); and at last there was none to divide the flood (*þam ... to gedale*) unless it (sc. *seo dun*) rose up to the high firmament." This is not far from the Latin: "opertique sunt omnes montes excelsi sub universo caelo. Quindecim cubitis altior fuit aqua super montes quos operuerat" ⟨All the lofty mountains under the universal sky were covered. The water rose fifteen cubits above the mountains which were covered⟩.

Because our means of criticizing the manuscripts are still so small, and some of them are weak from disuse, the change of approach which I suggest would not produce texts very different from those that are now reckoned good. Editors would less often write as if they were presenting a distant original exactly, except for its archaic and dialectal forms. They would also be less ready to cumber the text with palaeographical features or linguistic oddities from the late manuscript: the first are useless in an age of cheap and good photography, for palaeography cannot be learnt from type; the second raise more delicate problems, but the retention, for example, of the normal nominative plural form *yrfeweardas* at *Bwf* 2453, where it stands for the normal genitive singular *yrfeweardes*, is a nuisance to the reader.[17]

One might expect a considerable increase in the number of places marked as cruces, i.e., places where the manuscript reading is

17. The historical grammar of Late West Saxon is a neglected subject, but poetical MSS and commentaries on poetry are not the places in which it can best be studied, and the editors are far from consistent. Thus the Beowulf MS has *Ecgþeow* fourteen times, but *Ecþeow* 263 with *g* added later by the scribe, and *Ecþeow* unaltered 957; *Ecglaf* four times, but *Eclaf* 980; and *sec* 2863. Chambers follows the MS at 957, 980; "corrects" *sec* to *secg*; and fails to note that *Ecþeow* was originally written at 263. Klaeber, who assembles the facts, regularizes throughout. But instead of normalizing MS *siexbennum* 2904 to *seax-*, Klaeber reads *sex-*, which is a conjectural form based on an assumed confusion with the numeral. In the Beowulf MS *siex-* would be an exceptional form of "six," and an alternative explanation is possible. There is a late *ie* for *ea* which has escaped Sievers' grammar. It is common in the mid-eleventh-century Cambridge Psalter (ed. Wildhagen, 1910), which has *ie* not only in *wiex* = *weax* n., *gepieht*, *iec* = *eac*, and in *ciestyr* = *ceaster*, but also in *iert* = *eart*, *sielm* = *sealm*, *lies* = *leas*, etc. This MS has Canterbury connections, and the second hand of the Beowulf MS shows South-Eastern forms; but as some other examples of late *ie* = *ea* are not clearly South-Eastern, I merely note the alternative explanation. An inclination toward standard spellings in the printed text has a further advantage, because in these details too scribes make mistakes, not all of which can be accounted for. Beside *missere*, editors and dictionaries accept a form *missare*, which is a possible alternative in Old Norse but not in Old English. It is inferred from the dat. pl. *missarum* in *Gen* 2345, where I have little doubt that the scribe thought of *missarum*, gen. pl. of the familiar Church Latin *missa* ⟨mass⟩. In Old English there are such errors due to the religious preoccupations of the copyists. Thus *heofon* for *geofon* "ocean" occurs in the MS of *Andreas* 393, 1508, and 1585, where the corrections were made by Kemble (1843). And *amen* for *agmen*, *angelo* for *angulo* in classical MSS (see L. Havet *Manuel de critique verbale* [Paris, 1911], p. 263 f.) are in the same kind as *engle* for *egle*, which was our starting point.

judged to be unsound and there is no convincing conjecture to replace it. Klaeber in his standard edition of *Beowulf* (1936) marks only one crux (*mwatide* 2226) and one lacuna of a few words at line 62; Chambers marks the lacuna but not the crux; Sedgefield admits neither. For a text of the form and content of *Beowulf*, subject, according to these editors, to the vicissitudes of three centuries, this residue of faults detected and not made good is incredibly small. It indicates that comfortable conventions have become established, so that healthy doubts have been stilled.

An increase in the number of recognized cruces would cause some conjectural readings to disappear from the text. But, in compensation, some others would replace manuscript readings which are now retained on the assumption that a single late manuscript has extraordinary authority; and there would be a real gain if conjecture, instead of being reserved for the useful but disheartening task of dealing with obvious or desperate faults, were restored to its true functions, which include probing as well as healing.

Reprinted from Kenneth Sisam, *Studies in the History of Old English Literature* (Oxford: The Clarendon Press, 1953), pp. 29–44.

ROBERT P. CREED

# The Making of an Anglo-Saxon Poem

I

THE DICTION of *Beowulf* is schematized to an extraordinary degree.[1] Roughly every fifth verse is repeated intact at least once elsewhere in the poem. An essential part of about every second verse—such a part as a whole measure, or a phrase which straddles both measures, or one which encloses the two measures of the verse—is repeated elsewhere in the poem. Many of these verses or essential parts of verses bear such a resemblance to certain others as to suggest that the singer "knew them"—in the late Milman Parry's words—"not only as single formulas, but also as formulas of a certain type."[2] In composing a line containing any one of these verses, therefore, he was guided by the rhythm, sound, and sense of other verses belonging to this type or "system."[3]

The degree of the schematization of his diction suggests that the singer of *Beowulf* did not need to pause in his reciting or writing to consider what word to put next. His diction was one which, in Goethe's words, did his thinking and his poetizing for him, at least when he had completely mastered that diction and its ways. Precisely *how* that diction might have done his poetizing for the Anglo-Saxon singer is the subject of the present paper.

1. The evidence for this statement is contained in Appendix A, "Supporting Evidence," of my "Studies in the Techniques of Composition of the *Beowulf* Poetry . . ." (unpublished dissertation, Harvard, 1955), pp. 200–385.

2. Milman Parry, "Studies in the Epic Technique of Oral Verse-Making. I. Homer and Homeric Style," *Harvard Studies in Classical Philology*, XLI (1930), 85.

3. Parry uses the term *system* to designate a group of formulas of similar construction (pp. 85–89). For a discussion of certain systems of formulas in Anglo-Saxon poetry, see Francis P. Magoun, Jr., "Oral-Formulaic Character of Anglo-Saxon Narrative Poetry," *Speculum*, XXVIII (July, 1953), especially 450–453, and also my "The *andswarode*-System in Old English Poetry," *Speculum*, XXXII (July, 1957), 523–528.

I cannot attempt to deal in so brief a study with the way in which the singer puts together the larger elements of his poem. I shall therefore take only a very small portion of *Beowulf*, eight verses (four lines), and attempt, by means of references to similar verses and lines in the rest of the poem and in other surviving Anglo-Saxon poems, to illustrate the thesis that the making of any Anglo-Saxon poem was a process of choosing rapidly and largely on the basis of alliterative needs *not* between individual words but between *formulas*.

A formula may be as large as those whole verses repeated intact to which I referred earlier, or even larger. There are whole lines and even lines-and-a-half repeated within *Beowulf*. At the other extreme a formula may be as small as those trisyllabic prepositional phrases which end certain A-verses, or even as small as a single mono-syllabic adverb, *if* the adverb makes the whole spoken portion[4] of the measures and thus makes it possible for the singer to compose rapidly.

This last fact is important. The essential quality of the formula is not its memorable sound—although some formulas are, even for us, memorable—but its *usefulness* to the singer. To be useful to a singer as he composes rapidly a phrase or word must suggest to him that it belongs at only *one* point, or possibly only two points, in his verse or line; that is, it must be a significant segment of his rhythm. To be useful to the singer every phrase or word which is metrically significant should also be a syntactic entity, that is, if it is not a poly-syllable which by itself makes a whole verse or whole "crowded" measure, it should at least be a phrasal group or a clause. It should be, for example, an article and its noun, or a noun or pronoun and its verb, or a verb and its object, or a preposition and its noun, *not* such syntactically meaningless groups as, for example, an adverb and a preposition.

The formula in Anglo-Saxon poetry is, then, to paraphrase and somewhat emend Milman Parry's definition of the formula in Homer, a word or group of words regularly employed under certain strictly determined metrical conditions to express a given essential idea.[5]

---

4. As opposed to that portion of the measure accounted for by a rest or harp-substitution. See John Collins Pope, *The Rhythm of Beowulf* (New Haven: Yale University Press, 1942).

5. See Parry, *op. cit.*, p. 80.

In a formulaic or traditional poem we are frequently able, because of this schematization of the diction, not only to examine the formula which the singer chose, but also to guess at with some measure of assurance, and to examine, the system or entire group of formulas from *among* which he chose at a given point in his poem. When we have studied his tradition with care we are able to appreciate his poetry in a unique way, because we can perform in slow motion the very process which he of necessity performed rapidly: we can unmake, and make in new fashion, each line according to the rules of the game, and thus approximate what the singer himself might have done in a different performance of the same tale.

## II

At line 356 of his poem the singer has got Beowulf safely across the sea from Geatland to Denmark, and has placed him outside the hall Heorot. Wulfgar, Hrothgar's herald, has just learned from Beowulf who he is and what his mission is at Hrothgar's court.

> Hwearf þá hrædlíce    þǽr Hróþ-gár sæt,
> eald and unhár,    mid his eorla ʒedryht;
> éode ellen-róf    þæt hé for eaxlum ʒestód
> Deniʒa fréan;    cúðe hé duguðe þéaw.[6]

[Then he (that is, Wulfgar) turned quickly to where Hrothgar sat, old and very hoary, with his troop of men; famous for his courage (he, Wulfgar) went until he stood before the shoulders of the lord of the Danes; he knew the custom of the comitatus.]

There are several different ways by which the singer could, in good formulas, have got Wulfgar or anyone else from one place to another. Not many lines before this passage the singer has got Beowulf out of Geatland with the following verse: *ʒewát þá ofer*

---

6. Quotations from *Beowulf* and other Old English poems are cited in the normalized spelling proposed by Francis P. Magoun, Jr., in "A Brief Plea for a Normalization of Old-English Poetical Texts," *Lan M*, XLV (1951), 63–69, and adopted in Magoun's own classroom edition of the poem, *Béowulf and Judith, Done in a Normalized Orthography* ... (Cambridge, Mass.: Harvard University Press, 1959). [This edition is based primarily upon Charles Leslie Wrenn, *Beowulf with the Finnesburg Fragment* (London-Boston: George G. Harrap and Co., 1953).]

*wǽʒ-holm.* At line 720 the singer will get Grendel to Heorot with the following verse: *cóm þá to rećede.* At line 1232 he will get Wealhtheow to her seat with *éode þá to setle.*

We can be sure that each one of the verb-adverb groups (*ʒewát þá, cóm þá, éode þá*) which begin these lines is a formula not only because it fits the conditions of usefulness and significance, but also because the singer has used each of these phrases in this same position more than once.

But at our point in the story the singer chose to say *hwearf þá,* like these other verb-adverb groups a demonstrable formula since it appears at the beginning of line 1188, 1210 and 1573. We can find good reasons for his choice of *hwearf þá* in this passage. *Ʒewát þá* suggests a journey longer than the length of a hall, *cóm þá* suggests a new arrival rather than a return. The singer might then have said *éode þá* as he will do at 1232 and 1626 (*éodon . . . þá*), or simply *éode* as he does at eight other places in his poem. That he said *hwearf þá* here suggests that he had already thought ahead not only to the adverb with which *hwearf* incidentally alliterates, but to *Hróþ-gár* in the second verse of the line, which is the excuse for the adverb itself. The singer had no particular need to get Wulfgar from Beowulf to Hrothgar with haste; he *did* need to get him to Hrothgar with alliteration.[7]

---

7. Quite by accident the study of this passage (which, by the way, I chose at random) led me to what seems to be a rather dramatic demonstration of this principle. In my reflections on what the singer *might* have said here it seemed to me that, had he chosen not to mention but rather to allude to Hrothgar in his second verse, he might have substituted for *Hróþ-gár* a vowel-alliterating noun or phrase such as *se ealdor.* In consequence he would probably have substituted for *hrædlíće* the adverb *ofostlíće* in the second measure of the first verse. The point is that the singer is likely to have regarded such synonymous and metrically equivalent poly-syllables as interchangeable. As a matter of fact, the singer of *Beowulf* uses at line 3130 *ofostlíć(e)* exactly as he uses *hrædlíće* here, that is, as the second measure of a C-verse which begins the line: *þæt híe ofostlíć[e] / ut ʒeferedon / díere máðmas . . . .* But another singer, the singer of *Genesis,* at one point in his poem appears to have supplied one of these two adverbs where he intended the other. In "*Genesis* 1316," *MLN,* LXXIII (May, 1958), 321–325, I discuss this fascinating slip of the singer more fully. Had I not been, in effect, performing the part of the apprentice singer by seeking here for a different polysyllabic adverb than *hrædlíće* I should not have stumbled so soon across this slip, nor so quickly have grasped what I found in *Genesis* 1316.

In *Beowulf* 356, then, the singer has correctly established his alliterative bridge-head with *hrædlíce* for an assault on the second verse of the line. That verse, *þǽr Hróþ-gár sǽt*, does not divide neatly into two formulas each of which makes a single measure as does 356a. Verse 356b belongs to a type the pattern of which can be expressed by *þǽr* x *sǽt*, where x equals the subject of *sǽt*. Eight hundred lines after this passage, at line 1190, the singer has composed another verse of this type, *þǽr se góda sǽt*, in which the substitution for the sake of alliteration is perfectly straightforward. Just seventy lines before our passage, however, the singer has apparently used the same container, *þǽr ... sǽt*, with a different kind of alliterating content: *þǽr on wicge sǽt*. Apparently the singer does not restrict himself to employing the same kind of substituting element within the framework of this simple substitution system. Or perhaps it would be more correct to say that he shows signs at such points as these of thinking in terms of two complementary types of formula which he can readily combine to make a single verse.

This verse, *þǽr Hróþ-gár sǽt*, completes a line, and might, had the singer so chosen, have completed a thought. He does not so choose; he amplifies in the following line this brief mention of Hrothgar seated into a noble picture of the aged king surrounded by his retainers. But before we turn our attention to this picture in the next line of this passage, let us first observe how this line as a whole has helped to prepare the singer to make another whole line later in his poem.

Some eight hundred lines after this passage the singer moved Wealhtheow not into but across the hall with the following line: *hwearf þá be bence | þǽr hire byre wǽron ...* (1188). The design of this line is very similar to that of the one we have just studied. Both lines begin with the same formula; the second verse of both lines is enclosed by a similar phrase (*þǽr ... sǽt, þǽr ... wǽron*). The singer requires, however, a different alliteration in each line: he wishes to name Hrothgar in the first and to refer to Wealhtheow's sons in the second, consequently he uses a different second measure (*hrædlíce, be bence*). We shall return to this later passage in a moment to indicate how the earlier passage has influenced even further the construction of the later.

To sum up my rather extensive remarks on this single line: the singer appears to have composed his line of at least three separate formulas, *hwearf þá, hrædlíce,* and *þǽr* x *sæt.* He seems to have chosen the second formula, which carries the important alliteration of the first verse, in order that he might name Hrothgar in the second verse. He was, finally, guided in the shaping of the line as a whole by the *association* in his mind of these three formulas, as his later line 1188 seems to prove.

Line 357 presents fewer problems. The first verse, *eald and unhár,* belongs to a type long recognized as a formula, the so-called *reim-formel* ⟨rhyme formula⟩. Formulas of this kind have sometimes been regarded as a particularly characteristic kind of formula in Anglo-Saxon poetry or elsewhere.[8] Such formulas are indeed distinctive and decidedly ornamental; in fact, so far as getting any real work done is concerned, they are more ornamental than useful. For this very reason they can hardly claim to be the type of formula *par excellence.*

In making this verse the singer was guided by its simple and rather pleasing A-rhythm. At three other places in his poem the singer was guided by the same play of sound and rhythm to link *eald* with another alliterating word (*eald and infród,* 2449, for example).

The vowel-alliteration of *eald* gets him easily to the second verse of this line. Had he wished to name Hrothgar in the first verse of this line, or, for any other reason to employ *h*-alliteration or even *s*-alliteration he would have been faced with no problem in making the second half of the line. *Mid his eorla ȝedryht* is an even better example than verse 356b of the simple substitution system. For *h*-alliteration the singer replaces *eorla* with *hæleða,* as he does at line 662; for *s*-alliteration he replaces *eorla* with *secga* as he does in line 633 and 1672.

8. Klaeber [Fr. Klaeber (ed.), *Beowulf . . . ,* 3rd ed. (Boston: D. C. Heath and Co., 1950)] gives a prominent place to *reim*-formulas (which he more accurately but also more ponderously calls "copulative alliterative phrases") in his list of "formulas, set combinations of words, phrases of transition, and similar stereotyped elements" (p. lxvi). John S. P. Tatlock, in "Laȝamon's Poetic Style and Its Relations," in *The Manly Anniversary Studies in Language and Literature* (Chicago: University of Chicago Press, 1923), p. 7, calls attention to these formulas in Lawman: "One *chief function* of his *shorter epic formulas* was as expletives to fill in a half-line [a whole verse in Old English poetry] for which he had no matter, that he might not be obliged to introduce a new theme." (My italics.)

The noble picture is complete with this fourth verse; the singer pauses momentarily, and editors punctuate accordingly. If, during that pause, we turn again to that later picture of Wealhtheow at which we have already glanced, we shall see even further similarities between these two passages. Line 1188, like 356, is followed by a *reim*-formula, *Hrép-ríc and Hróp-mund*, in this case a *reim*-formula which, like 357a, amplifies the alliterating core of the previous verse. Again like 357a, and probably to some degree because of 357a, 1189a is followed by the mention of the troop of warriors, "sons of heroes," seated around the two princes: *and hæleða bearn*. But this later passage does not end with the fourth verse; *hæleða bearn* itself is amplified by the following verse, *ʒeoguþ ætgædere*. Thus the two passages are alike but not identical. We can only with increasing difficulty deny, however, that the rhythms and ideas which governed the making of the first passage played some part in the making of the second when we note that *ʒeoguþ ætgædere* is followed by the paradigm of 356b: *þǽr se góda sæt. Se góda* in verse 1190b refers not to Hrothgar but to Beowulf, whose name and whose location *be þǽm ʒebróðrum twǽm* completes in eight verses a reflection of the noble picture we have seen condensed into four.

But perhaps it is not quite correct to say that the earlier picture is yet complete, since, in verse 358a, the singer returns to the idea contained in the first measure of 356a. The singer has made the second measure of the later verse not out of a single adverb but a single substantive, *ellen-róf*. Eighteen lines before this he has made the entire second measure of a B-verse out of this word; twenty-eight hundred lines later in his poem he will again make *ellen-róf* the second measure of a D-verse.

But to stop with these observations of the other appearances of this compound as a compound is to ignore an important and interesting point of the singer's technique. That point may be expressed as a kind of rule-of-thumb which runs something like this: the first element of any compound noun or adjective will more often than not exist for the sake of alliteration rather than for the sake of a more precise denotation. We can demonstrate the operation of this rule in the present case by noting that the singer has elsewhere combined *hiʒe-* with *róf* to mean something synonymous with *ellen-róf* but having a different alliteration and a different metrical value.

He has also combined *beadu-*, *brego-*, *gúþ*, *heaðu-* and *siʒe-* with this same adjective *róf* to obtain slightly different meanings and three more different alliterations.

Verse 358b, *þæt hé for eaxlum ʒestód*, appears to be made of two such complementary formulas as appear in 356b. The container, *þæt hé . . . ʒestód*, is made in the same fashion as the container of 356b. Again, the container does the real work of the verse, that is, it functions syntactically as a complete clause with its subject pronoun and verb. The easily replaceable contained element, *for eaxlum*, both carries the alliteration and delimits the action of the verb.

This verse might indeed be spoken of as a delimiting formula, or as a formula for indicating distance. Once the singer has learned to isolate the container from the alliterating content of the verse, as we have just done, he has learned a most useful technique. That the singer of *Beowulf had* so isolated the container is evident from the following verses in which he indicates, at various points in his poem, different distances travelled by inserting a different prepositional phrase into this same container:

| | |
|---|---|
| þæt hé on héorðe ʒestód | (404) |
| þæt hit on wealle ætstód | (891) |
| þæt hit on hafolan stód | (2679) |

Compare also

| | |
|---|---|
| þæt him on ealdre stód | (1434) |

The problem of indicating before whose shoulders it was that Wulfgar came to a stop caused the singer little difficulty. He knew several kinds of whole verse formulas for referring to Hrothgar. The most numerous group of these formulas, or, to express it properly, the most useful group, is the x *Scieldinga* group, to which belong *wine Scieldinga*, which he employs in the poem seven times, *fréa Scieldinga*, which he employs four times, *helm* (three times), *eodor*, *léod*, *þéoden* (each twice). This group alone provides him with six different alliterative possibilities.

But before speaking 359a, the singer must have thought ahead to the *duguðe* with its *d*-alliteration in 359b. Hence he provided himself here with a *d*-alliterating epithet, *Deniga fréan*, as he had done at line 271 and was to do at 1680.

359b, *cúðe hé duguðe þéaw*, has no very close analogues in *Beowulf*. If, however, we compare it with verse 1940b, *ne biþ swelć cwǽnlić þéaw*, we can observe some similarity between the second measures of these two verses.

If the two second measures are derived from the same play of sounds and ideas, the two first measures which accompany them are not. *Cúðe hé*, which appears nowhere else in *Beowulf*, is quite unlike *ne biþ swelć* in 1940b, which appears again in line 2541. It has been suggested that, in such lightly stressed first measures as these, the singer has a kind of escape valve, or a measure into which he can cram, without worrying about alliteration, needed but metrically annoying words and phrases. Perhaps this is so, but it is also true that the singer composed many of these lightly stressed measures out of formulas.[9]

### III

At the beginning of this paper I noted that we can both unmake and make again each of the singer's lines if we are careful to follow the same rules which seem to have guided the singer. It might be amusing, and perhaps even instructive then, for such a novice singer as I—who have, however ridiculous this idea seems, been training myself and the careful reader to be a singer, and in a way not unlike that by which the singer trained himself—to attempt to do just that: to remake this passage from *Beowulf* which we have just unmade, attempting to say as closely as possible but with other formulas what the singer has said:

Éode þá ofostlíće     þǽr se ealdor sæt
hár and hiʒe-fród     mid his hæleða ʒedryht;
éode hilde-déor     þæt hé on héorðe ʒestód
freân Scieldinga;     cúðe hé þæs folces þéaw.

There is my poem. If you analyze it properly you will find every single formula elsewhere in *Beowulf* or in other poems in the Anglo-Saxon corpus, and used exactly as I have used it here. I must however claim credit for combining *hár* with *hiʒe-fród* and, I had

---

9. See my "Studies in ... *Beowulf* Poetry" (n. 1, above), Chapter VI, especially pp. 90–94, and the chart which accompanies this chapter on pp. 118–120.

thought, even for the manufacture of *hiȝe-fród*. I needed a *reim*-formula with *h*-alliteration and hit upon *hiȝe-fród* by following that rule-of-thumb I spoke of earlier. Only afterwards I discovered *Genesis* 1953, *háliȝ and hiȝe-fród*, along with marginal notes indicating that I had been reading this portion of that poem not very long ago.

I don't like my poem nearly so much as I like the singer's.[10] Yet my poem is composed of the same formulas out of which this singer and other Anglo-Saxon singers of ability created their poems. The diction of my poem is schematized to no greater degree than the diction of most other surviving Old English poems. What my experiment helps to prove, then, is that the simple use of formulaic diction is no guarantee of aesthetic success. Conversely, the use of a formulaic diction does not make such success impossible. *Beowulf*, with its highly schematized diction yet continually marvelous subtlety, is sufficient proof to the contrary.

If my feeble attempt to compose formulaic poetry only serves to demonstrate once again the subtle art of the singer of *Beowulf* I shall be satisfied. I should be more than satisfied if the experiment should serve also to remind the reader that this subtle art is a traditional and formulaic art, and that it is possible to praise the four lines of *Beowulf* I have chosen to examine as, for their purposes, the best of all possible *combinations of formulas*.

Reprinted from *ELH*, XXVI (1959), 445–454.

10. A close comparison of my poem with the *Beowulf* singer's seems to me to show a sharp contrast between the ceremonial slowness with which the Anglo-Saxon gets Wulfgar in the D-verse *éode ellen-róf* before his lord and the rather discourteous bump with which in the B-verse *éode hilde-déor* I get him into the royal presence. Nor do I like, for describing Hrothgar, the jigging rhythm of my *hár and hiȝe-fród* so well as the singer's *eald and unhár*. My *éode þa* is also a vaguer introduction to the passage than the singer's more precise suggestion of Wulfgar's turning *away* from Beowulf in order to move *toward* Hrothgar in *hwearf þá*. But then this is where I've got by *trying* to be different from a great singer.

# ROBERT D. STEVICK

# *The Oral-Formulaic Analyses of Old English Verse*

THE SCANT REMAINS of Old English verse provide only a thin and uneven fossil record for the palaeontologist of literature. Interpretations of that record, of course, have never been lacking. In the earliest stages of Old English study they seemed to require only the taxonomist's inspection and classification or the trained judge's identification of the hybrid characteristics of, say, the Germanic *burh* and the Christian monastery. For the most part, however, the nature and development of poetry of the Anglo-Saxons neither appear in the certitude of self evidence nor sustain a simplicity of analysis. If our present understanding of the nature and history of this body of verse is more complex, more tentative, but presumably more accurate, it has become so through the ingenuity of scholars in erecting upon that meager record some remarkably cogent accounts of literary evolution. Without an appreciable increase in the fossil record, this scholarly achievement has been primarily the result of resourcefulness in seeking new methodology for dealing with historical data.

The methodological breakthrough identified with Francis P. Magoun, Jr., is a prominent current example of scholarly resourcefulness. Applying the methodology developed by Milman Parry and Albert B. Lord in the study of a living oral poetry, he was able to discern the pervasiveness of the oral-formulaic character of Old English verse. In the few years since he published "The Oral-Formulaic Character of Anglo-Saxon Poetry"[1] and "Bede's Story of Caedmon: The Case History of an Anglo-Saxon Oral Singer"[2] several things have happened to his discovery. None of them should surprise us if we recall the history of almost any major breakthrough

1. *Speculum*, XXVIII (1953), 446–467.
2. *Speculum*, XXX (1955), 49–63.

in knowledge; nor should their diverse and random character necessarily be distressing.

One of the most engaging applications of oral-formulaic analysis of Old English verse is Robert P. Creed's attempt to reconstruct the process of composition of a passage from *Beowulf*.[3] Enacting the process in slow motion, he unmakes and then makes anew the verses according to the inferred rules of the game. To test the process, furthermore, he remakes the same passage using different formulas, producing his own version of that portion of the poem. In so doing he purports to offer an illustration of how the formulaic diction does the poetizing for the Anglo-Saxon singer, how, in fact, the rapid and extempore composition before an audience was accomplished.

A deliberate narrowing of the field of investigation is undertaken in Robert Diamond's analysis of the diction in the four signed poems of Cynewulf.[4] His procedure, he says, is to apply Magoun's ideas to Cynewulf's poems "just as he [Magoun] takes the ideas of Parry and Lord on formulaic poetry in general and applies them to Anglo-Saxon poetry." The results of this analysis show us several aspects of the scope, the grammatical structure, and the metrical forms of formulaic phrases and formula systems; the conclusions to be drawn are that Cynewulf composed in the traditional formulaic style— since the poems are, by Diamond's analysis, about 63% demonstrably formulaic—though it is not easy to make precise distinctions between oral poems set down, poems composed "in the ordinary modern way," and poems composed by learned poets using traditional (i.e., oral) formulas.

Inevitably there have been reservations expressed with respect to Magoun's theory or parts of it, for the most part in the form of suggestions for modification and refinement. The tendency of these reservations is generally consistent. Claes Schaar, for example, points out the error of equating the two propositions "all oral poetry is formulaic" and "all formulaic poetry is oral."[5] It may well be, he argues, that the surviving texts may be the products of a transitional

3. "The Making of an Anglo-Saxon Poem," *ELH*, XXVI (1959), 445–454.

4. "The Diction of the Signed Poems of Cynewulf," *PQ*, XXXVIII (1959), 228–241.

5. "On a New Theory of Old English Poetic Diction," *Neophil*, XL (1956), 301–305.

period, when there were written texts, and lettered poets were using and modifying the oral-formulaic materials; there may indeed be influence, in the common literary sense, of one poet drawing on the text of another rather than drawing solely from the common formula stock. Jackson J. Campbell, applying the "touchstone" for oral verse, finds that *The Seafarer* is neither plainly oral nor plainly lettered.[6] Rather, he infers from oral-formulaic tests together with tests for poetic diction that an older poem full of the older (oral) conventions has been remembered and reworked by a lettered homilist-poet—a man with full knowledge of the style of oral poetry and even a certain reduced command of its formulas. Once again, the existence of a transitional period is insisted upon; the records we have are, thus, more likely to be the works of English monks and churchmen rather than scops; they were educated in Christian Latin literature, and were in practice carrying over oral traditions into lettered poetry, not merely transcribing performances of oral singers.

Further reservation is expressed by A. G. Brodeur in context of his discussion of the diction of *Beowulf*.[7] By questioning Magoun's assumption that a lettered poet would be incapable of composing in the formulaic manner, he attempts to establish the *Beowulf* poet as a trained scop, who at the same time is literate and cultivated. The richness of his diction, the prominence of unique compounds and kennings, the style and structure of the poem, he asserts, point to a man we must again place in a transitional poetic milieu, when the ability to read, to invent new diction, and to compose with delibera-tion were not inconsistent with a man's training as a professional scop.[8]

6. "Oral Poetry in *The Seafarer*," *Speculum*, XXXV (1960), 87–96; still further, Wayne A. O'Neil, "Another Look at Oral Poetry in *The Seafarer*," *Speculum*, XXXV (1960), 596–600.

7. *The Art of Beowulf* (Berkeley and Los Angeles: University of California Press, 1959), Chap. I.

8. It may strengthen Brodeur's case for the poet's training and method of composition to consider the factor of length of the poem. So long a poem—even if conceived of as recited in three sittings (or singings)—if composed in a purely oral way from the common formula stock, would in all probability have more frequent repetitions or "favorite" formulas, fewer unique compounds, and more frequent lapses or other flaws in structure and style.

These several examples define, I believe, the direction of the applications and modifications offered for Magoun's oral-formulaic theory of Old English verse. In the meantime, application and extension of the theory have produced important re-interpretation of several poems. Stanley Greenfield's exploration of "The Formulaic Expression of the Theme of 'Exile' in Anglo-Saxon Poetry"[9] is one of the best, particularly for its inclusion of aesthetic considerations of the advantages and disadvantages of formulaic composition and of the nature of originality within this tradition.

In this cursory review of publications dealing with a new phase of Old English literary study two things are prominent. First, the amount and ingenuity of the scholarly activity are impressive: the new methodology applied to several segments of the extant Old English verse is rapidly producing results whose security and significance are noteworthy. Second, however, the total character of these investigations is disappointing. We may begin obliquely by saying that, if we consider the contributors *as a group* working on a single problem, their metaphysics are muddled. It is unfair, of course, to the individuals to impute to them the faults of the group. Yet, without clearly formulated and mutually shared postulates, without regular comparison and scrutiny of methodologies, without sufficient scope or clarity of purpose, the laborers in this literary museum may be thought of as assembling some quite startling palaeontological exhibits, possibly as unhistorical as they are ingenious.

On the one hand, for instance, there is strict adherence by some to the postulate of the "singer" and avoidance of the concept "poet." The text, if it is heavily formulaic, is then a "performance" (perhaps modified a little in the process of being captured in writing) rather than a poem composed by a poet. On the other hand, others talk of the "poet" and his "poem," of writers working within a tradition, with traditional materials, as they compose poems and, at times, put the traditional materials to uses quite foreign to the source of their formulas.

As a specific case we may consider Magoun's inferences from his analysis of Caedmon's *Hymn* about the history of Old English

9. *Speculum*, XXX (1955), 200–206.

Christian verse and its distinctive formulas. His argument, replete with charts and lists of evidence, is that the poem is formulaic, its language quite traditional, inasmuch as 83% of its diction is demonstrably formulaic—i.e., the dictional elements appear elsewhere in the corpus of Old English verse. Now, he says, the eight references to the Deity compose 44% of this formulaic poem; and since, *if Caedmon was a "singer"* it is unlikely that he would compose *new* such a proportion of his poem, we may conclude that there was a Christian formulaic vocabulary for verse developing before Caedmon. (And, we should add, developing for some considerable time, if we consistently maintain that singers learned and preserved traditional formulas to a far greater extent than they invented new ones.)

To call Caedmon's *Hymn* "formulaic" may mean either of two things: (a) that it is made up of formulas, that it uses ready-made poetic components—"formulaic" in a substantive sense; or (b) that it is made in the manner of formulaic verse, that it somehow resembles it (perhaps even using some traditional formulas)—"formulaic" in an attributive sense. In the first case, however, he needs either to adduce instances of formulas from earlier texts or to present an independent body of evidence confirming the hypothesis that there were earlier instances of these formulas. The first alternative we may write off for absence of records; the second, besides straining the earlier limit of Anglo-Saxon Christianity, requires convincing reason to reject the opposite assumption that other occurrences of these formulas are borrowings, directly or indirectly, from Caedmon or his imitators and successors. Unless this reason appears, we have no substantial warrant to accept the inference of a body of Christian formulas available to Caedmon. And this reason has not yet appeared. Moreover, to call the *Hymn* formulaic in the attributive sense permits no inference at all about prior development of a Christian poetic vocabulary.

We may feel it in our hearts that Magoun's assertions concerning Caedmon's *Hymn* in particular and the history of Christian poetic formulas generally may be substantially accurate; but empathy has always been an untrustworthy historical prop, however valuable it may be heuristically. The networks of inferences and their postulates still must appear in sound historical array.

Let us consider one more instance. Creed's slow-motion enactment of the process of composition of the *Beowulf* passage is performed on the postulate of a singer (not a poet) putting together verses rapidly in accordance with rules of measure, verse, and alliteration, under the requirements of his narrative, and with respect to aesthetic effect. It implicitly discounts any possible differences between the "text" of a live performance and a written text (in an age neither skilled nor motivated to capture pure examples of traditional art) and any possible differences between the neat extant text and earlier manuscripts by which the *poem* was transmitted. The process described is essentially that of commencing with a common formula, then adding a measure or verse at a time, hardly looking farther ahead than the next alliterative stave. Now, while the psychology of poetic improvisation still lies in the limbo of guesswork, we may take some clues from an analogous process—musical improvisation. Perhaps the nearest parallel among familiar forms is jazz. We may affirm immediately the position that, in the process of improvisation, each successive phrase of formula is to some extent determined by its immediately preceding context, as well as by the cumulative effect of all that goes before it. This is about as far as Creed's analysis goes, and it is certainly the process most susceptible to simple explanation. But if there are similarities between poetic and musical improvisation beyond this—and I am convinced there are[10]—then much more needs to be said if we are to understand the methods, stages, and accomplishments of formulaic composition. For example, the performer of jazz will employ anticipations, larger as well as smaller structural patterns, overlapping patterns, contrapuntal movements—will, in short (if he is a good musician), deliver a highly complex performance, an adequate description of which would be exceedingly long and, in the present state of musical terminology, surpassingly difficult. Moreover, in a traditional oral (or musical) art form—as opposed to a tradition perpetuated in writing or notation—memory of past performances will have a very large

10. There is hardly a flaw in the parallel between Albert B. Lord's description of oral-epic improvisation, in *The Singer of Tales* (Cambridge, Massachusetts: Harvard University Press, 1960), and the nature and history of improvisational (traditional) jazz.

effect on any further performance; any familiarity at all with successive jazz performances suggests strongly that performers (and particularly professional ones) repeat earlier performances as entities,
subject only to such changes as faulty memory, momentary experiments, or effects of audience reaction may produce. They do not
build each performance merely a phrase at a time. Composition, in
this respect, represents relatively slight modifications within an
entire "piece" or a substantial stretch of the selection being presented. But composition in improvisational art, for traditional
themes handled repeatedly by professional performers, can hardly
be conceived of entirely as fresh creation measure-by-measure,
phrase-by-phrase, line-by-line, as Creed has represented it. In fact,
Creed's reconstruction equally suits the procedure of a lettered poet
composing pen-in-hand in a formulaic manner.

The problem inherent in Creed's reconstruction of the making
of a formulaic poem can be restated as follows. There is an ambiguity in the concepts of "composition," "singer," "poem," and
"performance." What Creed has apparently given us is a rational,
analytic reconstruction of the cumulative effects on some verses of a
large number of performances and the tradition in which they
participate—effects, moreover, possessing a more complex and
fortuitous history than his analysis allows us to conceive. Reconstruction of the process of composing—of putting together—a perfor-
mance-text is not identical to reconstruction of the history of
modifications of a traditional, repeated "piece" when that history
is terminated in a stipulated text; yet the two in traditional art are
inseparable. Composition, in other words, is a process of both singer
and tradition. This is the ambiguity of "composition." It is inseparable from the ambiguity of "singer" as one who "sings," as those
singers who have contributed to the surviving shape of a piece of
verse, and as that one who produced a given text (or performance).
It is the ambiguity of the "poem" as an evolving archetype ever
represented anew and as a designated member in a series of successive modifications of a whole piece within a body of tradition. It is
the ambiguity of "performance" as act and as object.

Now if we inquire into causes of these difficulties in oral-
formulaic analyses of Old English verse, we may be able to discover
some obstructions to refinement of the oral-theory for Old English;

we may be able to recognize and remove some limitations to its utility. Inquiry is facilitated by recent publication of Albert B. Lord's *The Singer of Tales*, embodying the acknowledged base for the oral-theory in Old English studies; a systematic inquiry may be preferable to an historical one.

The cogency of the Parry-Lord theory is maintained for the *oral epic song*—a narrative in verse, developed and perpetuated within an unlettered tradition, manifested in traditional formulas and themes, and distinct from "ballads and comparatively short epics." The definitions and restrictions for "oral song" are explicit, and the theory limited to that specific art form. Nevertheless, oral-formulaic analyses for Old English verse take their evidence from all poetic forms—from Caedmon's *Hymn* to *Beowulf*. It is possible, of course, that in Old English verse the distinction between *The Seafarer*, say, and *Beowulf* is unimportant in this respect. Yet Lord's book would not lead us to expect this.[11] Moreover, these analyses for Old English regularly recapitulate the Parry-Lord postulates about rapid, extempore composition (performance) of extended narrative songs, thereby putting the hymns, lyric-elegies, and moral and homiletic pieces in the appearance of anomalies as sources of data or topics of generalization for the oral-theory.[12] It may be that these non-narrative poems in Old English are of a different order from the epic oral narratives, and may prove intractable—even disruptive—to the narrative-based theory.

Over-extension of the oral-theory may be in itself sufficient cause for some difficulties we have described. It may also be a contributing cause to difficulties over the question of transitional aspects of Old English verse. In Lord's analysis the most careful distinctions between oral and literary texts of epic songs precede the assertion that the relationship between the two types, or styles, is not only one of *either-or*, but also one of *not both*. While a period, a career, or a repertory may be termed "transitional" in combining oral and

11. This is the tenor of the exposition of the oral-theory and the analysis of *Beowulf, including its supporting evidence.*

12. Looking back at my analysis of "Formal Aspects of *The Wife's Lament*," *JEGP*, LIX (1960), convinces me that, whatever the proportion of formula-content of *The Wife's Lament*, its close, intricate, symmetrical patterns together with its brevity are incompatible with extempore oral composition. This is one poem, for a start, that I believe should be excluded from oral-formulaic analyses.

literary techniques, the categories are held to be exclusive for individual texts or for individual singers at a particular time. In reaching the decision that in all his data there is no such thing as a transitional text, Lord insistently confines his argument to the traditional epic song form and to the technical requirements of a performer within the tradition of oral epic song.

Faced with the contradiction between denial of the possibility of transitional texts and the conviction that, in Old English verse at least, some texts *must* be transitional, we may seek the resolving distinction in the nature of the evidence on both sides. Whether there is a relevant distinction between epic song and other, especially non-narrative, verse becomes a crucial question. If the distinction is significant, then transitional texts (for non-epic songs) can perhaps be described more directly than as products of a transitional period. If it is not significant, then the Parry-Lord theory has only analogical, suggestive value for Old English studies, requiring thorough re-examination and reconstruction of concepts and inferences regarding oral-formulaic aspects of Old English poetry.

That the contributions to study of the oral-formulaic character of Old English verse have been random and diverse, I shall re-affirm, should not necessarily be distressing. That the total product of contributors to this study has been fragmentary, piecemeal, and not entirely consistent is less than we might have hoped for. But that, as a result of these conditions, even some of the contributions[13] turn out upon inspection to lack historical rigor or conceptual clarity is a clear sign (*tacen sweotol*) that all is not well.

A remedy is more easily urged than prescribed. Perhaps the over-all requirement is that of unified and systematic procedures, together with stipulation of specific purposes; these purposes, I assume, are primarily (not exclusively) those of accurate literary history. Instead of random methods, there is need for a self-correc-tive methodology. Instead of merely techniques of investigation, techniques oriented to comprehensive theories. In ultimate terms: instead of loosely related experiments, a science. Or, from the scholar-teacher's point of view, rather than ask "Who is the best judge?" ask "How is the best judgment to be made?"

13. I have deliberately selected, for extended analysis, essays by Magoun, as the originator of this special area of study, and by Creed, as a highly productive contributor to its development.

The practical problem of how to achieve more unified and systematic procedures can be solved only in practice itself, of course. Some areas of endeavor may be more promising than others for the inevitable trial and error attempts at progress. Some have already been implied. Distinctions need to be made in order to remove ambiguities and bring the terminology under control: whether "formulaic" is used in a substantive or attributive sense, whether "performance" denotes an act or an object, whether "singer" is particular or generic, whether "composition" is process or product, of an individual or a tradition or both, whether a "poem" is a text or an abstraction—these are some immediate problems of definition. Further, since we have established a time in which poetry was oral and formulaic and a somewhat later time in which poetry was composed in writing, and the evidence indicates a material continuity between those times, we infer, with Schaar, Campbell, Brodeur, and others, that there was a gradual transition. The need now is to establish the stages of that transition—at least in schematic form— so that a particular poem, or section of one, can be placed in the historical continuum and interpreted according to its context. We need, in other words, a denser historical record. But this in turn requires careful delimitation of oral texts and styles together with distinctions, probably, between the styles and techniques of oral epic narrative and shorter, non-narrative verse.

Beyond these "internal" areas, there are others that may provide useful resources for continued progress. Historiography, for instance, seems to have advanced rapidly (for some time now without the help of literary historians) and may well save the historian of literature much of the effort of discovery or the frustration of fruitless speculations. The history of physical anthropology may yield a lesson that endless fact listing and classification, without orientation to a comprehensive theory, produces only facts and groups of facts whose significance is open only to speculation—that the gathering of facts produces problems but does not solve them. Magoun's "supporting evidence" for his analysis of Caedmon's *Hymn*, in relation to his assertions about Old English Christian poetic vocabulary, is a case in point. Other art forms, like jazz, may provide suggestive analogies for investigation of the nature of a popular form of art, of its performers, of its history, and of its methods. From such a variety of fields of knowledge may come models or patterns—at least experience—on the basis of which to develop investigative patterns and integrate them into a comprehensive schema.

Investigations of Old English literary history, obviously, could also profit by taking a larger scope: indeed, this may be the most likely method for achieving through practice those unified, systematic procedures which, at a certain stage of development, begin to operate in a self-corrective manner. In the continuing effort to expand and correct the accounts of literary evolution in the Anglo-Saxon period, we may recall the history of the theory of organic evolution and conclude with the kind of praise known where knowledge has progressed conspicuously: the major trouble with the methodological breakthrough embodied in the oral-formulaic analyses of Old English verse is that it needs to be succeeded by refinements and still further breakthroughs and ultimately assimilated into a comprehensive literary history.

Reprinted from *Speculum*, XXXVII (1962), 382–389.

R. F. LESLIE

# Analysis of Stylistic Devices
# and Effects in
# Anglo-Saxon Literature

IN THIS PAPER I shall attempt to illustrate how style and structure
are intimately related in Anglo-Saxon poetry. Although it is true
that the relationship is often a highly formal one, a concern with
form has often obscured the profound effect of the poetic theme upon
the style of individual passages or complete poems. The result of
concentration on the primarily formal features of Old English
poetry has been the widespread belief that it contains ornate and
rigid stylistic elements, into which have been fitted—sometimes
felicitously, sometimes incongruously—all sorts of poetic material.
I hope to give some indication that the stylistic devices of the
Anglo-Saxons were far from being mechanically applied.

As recently as 1935 it was possible for Miss Bartlett, in *The
Larger Rhetorical Patterns in Anglo-Saxon Poetry*, to write that many of
the studies of style had been confined either to one text or to one
figure, usually the kenning, that little had been written on Anglo-
Saxon poetry as a relatively homogeneous and independent body of
verse, and even less that was concerned primarily with its style. But
in her work also, there remained the belief that the poet was, as she
said, "more interested in the elaborate detail than the composition
of the whole."[1]

The view that many of the stylistic features of Old English were
superimposed on, or arbitrarily inserted into, the flow of the verse,
was one which could remain dominant largely because the study of
syntax had fallen far behind the study of figures such as the "kenning." It is perhaps significant that, two years after Marquardt's
definitive work on kennings, it was necessary in 1940 for S. O.
Andrew in *Syntax and Style in Old English* to explain in his preface that

1. A. C. Bartlett, *The Larger Rhetorical Patterns in Anglo-Saxon Poetry* (New York:
Columbia University Press, 1935), p. 7.

his study was "an attempt to drive a few main lines through the almost unexplored tract of Old English syntax."[2] Both in this work and in its successor, *Postscript on Beowulf,* Andrew has—by and large—shown that sense units in Old English are more thoroughly integrated than the traditional punctuation of texts leads us to suppose, that there is in fact more hypotaxis and less parataxis in the literature than has previously been admitted.[3] Perhaps he has gone too far in some of his claims, and laid himself open to the criticism that he has "in all probability unconsciously been a slave to his modern linguistic instincts," which Alarik Rynell made in 1952 in his Lund monograph entitled *Parataxis and Hypotaxis as a Criterion of Syntax and Style, especially in Old English Poetry.*[4] Nevertheless, I believe that enough cases can be made out on the objective grounds of textual harmony to justify us in assuming a much closer texture to Old English verse than has usually been allowed; e.g., in *The Wife's Lament* 36–38, the woman must walk alone

> under actreo geond þas eorðscrafu,
> þær ic sittan mot sumorlangne dæg,
> þær ic wepan mæg mine wræcsiþas.

Editors generally begin a new sentence with the first *þær,* whereas the demonstrative adjective "these" before *eorðscrafu* indicates that *þær* is to be taken as a conjunction, not an adverb.

Linked with this syntactical approach to the question of style and structure has been a reappraisal of many passages that had been held, because of their digressionary or repetitive or didactic nature, to be stylistically inept. M. Adrien Bonjour's work on *The Digressions in Beowulf* in 1949 shows, as he says, that "each digression brings its distinctive contribution to the organic structure and the artistic value of the poem"[5]; and in an article on the technique of parallel

2. S. O. Andrew, *Syntax and Style in Old English* (Cambridge: Cambridge University Press, 1940).

3. S. O. Andrew, *Postscript on Beowulf* (Cambridge: Cambridge University Press, 1948).

4. Alarik Rynell, *Parataxis and Hypotaxis as a Criterion of Syntax and Style, especially in Old English Poetry,* Lunds Universitets årsskrift. N.f. avd. 1. bd. 48. No. 3 (Lund, 1952), p. 22.

5. Adrien Bonjour, *The Digressions in Beowulf,* Medium Ævum Monographs, No. V (Oxford: Basil Blackwell and Mott, Ltd., 1950).

descriptions in *Beowulf*,[6] he compares the return of the Danes from the lake where Beowulf fights Grendel's mother with the return of the Geats from the same spot, pointing out how the poet made use of parallel parts of the same plot to effect a simple and telling contrast. In his comment on this article in *The Year's Work in English Studies* (published in 1954), R. M. Wilson concludes: "when considering the art of the poet we must take into account the parallelism of parts and other structural features to a greater extent than has previously been the custom."

I turn to examine how these larger structural features echo, use, or grow from the various stylistic devices frequently used in minor contexts, devices which in *their* turn are related to the antithetical interlacing patterns of the alliterative verse medium itself, on which so much has been written. From a structural point of view, probably the most widespread stylistic feature is "variation," a term not always unambiguously used, but by which I mean simply the repetition of an idea in a different word or words. Basically the device adds emphasis to a word or group of words, and can be used in a number of different ways. Claes Schaar in *Critical Studies in the Cynewulf Group*[7] devotes a long chapter to listing and analyzing examples from the Cynewulfian and related poems. You may recall that he makes a division between "close" and "loose" variation. In the first, the variant word or group of words corresponds syntactically to its correlative; e.g., in *Elene* 460–461, where Christ is described as:

> cyning on roderum,
> soð sunu meotudes, sawla nergend.

and with chiasmus in *The Wanderer* 13–14:

> þæt he his ferðlocan fæste binde,
> healde his hordcofan, hycge swa he wille.

In "loose" variation the variant expression corresponds semantically, but not formally, to its correlative, as in *The Wanderer* 99–100:

> Eorlas fornoman asca þryþe,
> wæpen wælgifru, wyrd seo mære.

6. "The Technique of Parallel Descriptions in *Beowulf*," *RES*, N.S. II (1951), 1–10.

7. Claes Schaar, *Critical Studies in the Cynewulf Group*, Lund Studies in English, XVII (Lund: C. W. K. Gleerup, 1949).

The arrangement is frequently chiastic, as in Christ 677–678:

> ofer sealtne sæ sundwudu drifan,
> hreran holmþræce.

Schaar would confine his definition of "loose" variation to variants where nothing is added to the sense. Although such a definition often holds good for the Cynewulfian poems, with their ornate and rather leisurely style, it does not apply so well to *Beowulf*, and rarely to the elegiac lyrical poems, where something is almost always added in the variant expressions. While I concur with Schaar in having two categories of variation, I would extend the scope of his "loose" variation, calling it for comparative stylistic purposes, *conceptual variation*, in contrast to "close," or *formal variation*, where the variants are syntactically equivalent, and—in their simplest form—include most kennings.

There is a distinct similarity between the stylistic employment of *formal* variation in minor contexts, encompassing only a few phrases, and the use of *conceptual* variations which encompass whole passages, and sometimes whole poems. Sometimes the variant passages are interlaced with other matter in a distinct pattern, often in the form ABA which has been called an envelope pattern. Sometimes the effect of this interlacing is heightened by conscious antithesis with the passage or passages between the conceptual variants. These larger patterns appear to have grown out of an expansion of the chiastic arrangement of formal variants, of the kind that I have already quoted. We can see this expansion with the chiastic arrangement of relatively simple conceptual variants in the following passage from *The Phoenix* 34–41:

> Wæstmas ne dreosað,
> beorhte blede, ac þa beamas a
> grene stondað, swa him god bibead.
> Wintres ond sumeres wudu bið gelice
> bledum gehongen; næfre brosniað
> leaf under lyfte, ne him lig sceþeð
> æfre to ealdre, ærþon edwenden
> worulde geweorðe.

A negative statement is followed by a positive one; then follows another positive variant, followed by a negative one. It is notable that we find nothing of this configuration in the Latin source, the poem by Lactantius, which simply has: "Here is the grove of the Sun, a holy wood thickly planted with trees, green with the glory of never-failing foliage."

Chiasmus as a stylistic device in Old English poetry would not have been possible without the development of what Kemp Malone calls "plurilinear" units.[8] Within the bounds of the presumably early end-stopped lines a certain amount of straightforward variation was possible, but the development of chiastic phrases and patterns would require a syntactical pause in the middle of a line and would stimulate, or be stimulated by, the development of multilinear sentences as in the *Phoenix* passage just quoted. The increasing importance of the medial pause led to many sentences beginning in the middle of the line, and in later poetry *most* of the sentences begin and end in the middle of the line. Malone says of *Judith* that "the verses give the effect of a never ending flow, but this continuous effect is gained at a heavy structural cost." In this swift narrative poem perhaps we should not expect *major* structural patterns, but there are ample effective local uses of chiasmus and variation which give form to the narrative and provide contrast and vivid description, without holding up the flow of the verse, e.g., in lines 253–256:

> Mynton ealle
> þæt se beorna brego and seo beorhte mægð
> in ðam wlitegan træfe wæron ætsomne,
> Iudith seo æðele ond se galmoda.

—a neat use of variation and inversion, the variants being separated by a line of other matter.

I should like to turn now to two other stylistic devices which are used effectively, not only in minor contexts, but in large-scale patterns, where—like variation—they may have a pronounced bearing on the structure of a passage or poem. The first of these is "antithesis," which can be either implicit or explicit. In implicit antitheses contrast is obtained by the mere juxtaposition of phrases, without conjunctions, by adversative asyndeton. Schaar regards it as

8. "Plurilinear Units in Old English Poetry," *RES*, XIX (1943), 201–204.

stylistically primitive and accuses the *Andreas* poet of using the device indiscriminately. A simple example occurs in *Andreas* 505–506:

> Ðu eart seolfa geong,
> wigendra hleo, nalas wintrum frod.

It is true that this appears rather artless beside the polished balanced phrasing in *The Wanderer* 32–33, where the poet says of the exile:

> wara∂ hine wræclast nales wunden gold,
> fer∂loca freorig nalæs foldan blæd.

Explicit antitheses, with adversative conjunctions, appear to be most common with *ac*, as in *Christ* 1049:

> Ne sindon him dæda dyrne, ac þær bi∂ dryhtne cu∂.

A sustained use of antithesis effectively culminates Wiglaf's long speech in *Beowulf* 3007–3027. Here is the final vivid contrast of life and death for the warrior:

> For∂on sceall gar wesan
> monig, morgenceald, mundum bewunden,
> hæfen on handa, nalles hearpan sweg
> wigend weccean, ac se wonna hrefn
> fus ofer fægum fela reordian,
> earne secgan, hu him æt æte speow,
> þenden he wi∂ wulf wæl reafode.

This sentence repeats a figure which occurs several times in the preceding nineteen lines, the sandwiching of the negative element in the antithesis between two positive ones, forming an envelope pattern.

Interlacing of this kind is carried still further in *The Seafarer*, where it comprises a major structural element in the poem. The early part falls into two distinct sections—the speaker's past experiences of coastal voyages, and his projected experience of an ocean voyage. The predominant tone of each is different, the first being concretely descriptive, the second reflective and imaginative. Yet they are linked by a contrast which runs through both.

In the first section the speaker describes the hardships of sailing in wintry weather, then in line 12 comes the contrast:

> þæt se mon ne wat
> þe him on foldan fægrost limpeð,
> hu ic earmcearig iscealdne sæ
> winter wunade, wræccan lastum,

His distress is reinforced by the terse glimpse of the storm, *hægl scurum fleag*. The next passage indicates not physical but mental suffering, and in line 27 comes the contrast:

> Forþon him gelyfeð lyt, se þe ah lifes wyn
> gebiden in burgum bealosiþa hwon,
> wlonc ond wingal, hu ic werig oft
> in brimlade bidan sceolde.

Again the poet reinforces his sufferings by a graphic description of the elements, in terse asyndetic clauses, contrasting in verse texture, as well as in content, with the complex sentence just quoted:

> Nap nihtscua, norþan sniwde,
> hrim hrusan bond, hagl feol on eorþan,
> corna caldast.

In both passages we have the ABA sandwich pattern which we found in the *Beowulf* passage discussed above.

In the second voyage section the speaker describes his longing for the high seas, and the signs that urge him on to the ocean. The tone of the passage is exalted, and builds up towards a climax through two anaphoric series, with repetition of the negative particle *ne*, the second culminating in an antithesis with the conjunction *ac* (lines 39–43, and 44–47). There follows the lovely lyrical passage on the signs of spring—and how poignant are the Anglo-Saxons on this theme—then the constrasting motif of the fortunate landdweller is repeated, this time formally parallel to its first introduction in line 12:

> þæt se beorn ne wat,
> sefteadig secg, hwæt þa sume dreogað
> þe þa wræclastas widost lecgað.

The antitheses themselves, we see, are subject to variation, forming

an ABA pattern, and to anaphora or repetition of words or phrases—
a device to which I now turn.

Like variation, anaphora can be either formal and compact, or
intimately woven into the structure of a poem. The formal expression may be relatively simple, as in *The Wife's Lament,*

under actreo in þam eorðscræfe               (28)

and

under actreo geond þas eorðscrafu            (36)

where the repetition links a descriptive and reflective passage with
a preceding narrative one, emphasizing at the same time the
potency of the woman's environment.

The device of repetition can be built up into a powerful rhetorical pattern, a purpose for which the negative particle *ne* is frequently
employed. The structure of *The Phoenix* 14–21 is a good illustration,
and—with its culminating *ac* clause—it is very similar in structure to
*The Seafarer* 44–47, referred to above.

Ne mæg þær ren ne snaw,
ne forstes fnæst, ne fyres blæst,
ne hægles hryre, ne hrimes dryre,
ne sunnan hætu, ne sincaldu,
ne wearm weder, ne winterscur
wihte gewyrdan, ac se wong seomað
eadig ond onsund.

Other adverbs and the pronoun *sum* are used in the same way.

Repetition is more closely woven into the texture of the poem in
*Beowulf* 702–731, in the tense and vivid description of the approach
of Grendel to Heorot. The echoed words and phrases, each some
seven or eight lines apart, mark decisive stages in Grendel's advance,
while the intervening lines flash back and forward to events before
and after. The technique is almost that of the film camera. The
relevant phrases are:

Com on wanre niht scriðan sceaduganga . . .
Ða com of more under misthleoþum Grendel gongan . . .
Com þa to recede rinc siðian . . .
Geseah he in recede rinca manige . . . .

Atmosphere is built up in calculated phases.

I should like in conclusion to refer to the lines which follow this passage in *Beowulf*. They contain several antitheses with hints of the outcome of Grendel's expedition; then follows an accumulation of short sharp paratactical clauses, with no links, indicative of swift action:

> slat unwearnum,
> bat banlocan, blod edrum dranc,
> synsnædum swealh.

These bring a considerable change to the texture of the verse, and constitute what Schaar calls a "compound series," which is reserved for incidents and actions important to the plot, and for vivid description. Passages with a predominance of subordinate clauses he calls "complex series," and claims that they serve primarily a reflective and explanatory function, giving the result or consequence of what precedes.

It will be seen, then, that the stylistic features of Old English poetry are not merely decorative, but have an important functional part in the total structure, and that the syntactical constructions in their turn are diversified to suit the requirements of the style.

Reprinted from Paul Böckmann (ed.), *Stil- und Formprobleme in der Literatur* (Heidelberg: Carl Winter Universitätsverlag, 1959), pp. 129–136. The original article has no footnotes. The present footnotes have been provided to supply more detailed bibliographical information than appeared in the text of the original article.

STANLEY B. GREENFIELD

# Syntactic Analysis
# and Old English Poetry

DESPITE THE FACT that Old English poetry is highly conventional, stylized, and formulaic, it was possible, as many studies have shown, for the poets writing in that tradition to be individual in their stylistic talent. Professor Bonjour has demonstrated, for example, that the theme of the beasts of battle is handled uniquely and with great effect by the *Beowulf*-poet,[1] and I, for example, have elsewhere suggested that exilic formulas, even in thematically similar poems like *The Wanderer* and *The Seafarer*, are capable of multiple exploitations.[2] But in no study that I am aware of has much been done with the contributions of syntax and word order to the individual poetic effect. Those studies in syntax and style that have appeared have mainly been concerned with such arrangements as parataxis and hypotaxis as norms, as indicators of a particular poet's syntactic signature, though some attention, it is true, has been given to the appropriateness of coordinating or subordinating elements to the subject matter of poems. But even in such a study as Claes Schaar's on the poems of Cynewulf,[3] there is no comment on what seems to me a predominant and highly effective word-order pattern in the speech of the Cross in *The Dream of the Rood*—I refer to the many a- and b-verses beginning with verbs, the reiterated pounding of which moves the descriptive narrative along at a steady pace unlike any I know of in other Old English poems.

    I have become interested in exploring syntactic arrangements in poetry through exposure to Winifred Nowottny's *The Language Poets*

1. "*Beowulf* and the Beasts of Battle," *PMLA*, LXXII (1957), 563–573.

2. "The Formulaic Expression of the Theme of 'Exile' in Anglo-Saxon Poetry," *Speculum*, XXX (1955), 200–206; "Attitudes and Values in *The Seafarer*," *SP*, LI (1954), 15–20.

3. *Critical Studies in the Cynewulf Group*, Lund Studies in English, XVII (Lund: C. W. K. Gleerup, 1949).

*Use*, wherein the author most articulately reveals the contribution of syntax and word order to the meaning and poetic effect of four lines of Pope.[4] I am heartened in my endeavors by Morton Bloomfield's recent comment: "I see here a new and important field for literary critics and scholars."[5] I should like to suggest that such a study can be a valuable entry into the specific poetic quality of Old English poems, in a way that the study of themes and formulas is incapable of. To this end, I wish to analyze briefly, but I hope cogently, but one sentence in *The Wanderer*. That sentence is the one beginning at line 19, in which the exiled speaker declares that he has had to lock his thoughts in fetters since his lord died and he had to seek a new dispenser of treasure, fruitlessly, it would seem:

> 19 swa ic modsefan    minne sceolde,
> oft earmcearig,    eðle bidæled,
> freomægum feor    feterum sælan,
> siþþan geara iu    goldwine minne
> hrusan heolster biwrah,    ond ic hean þonan
> wod wintercearig    ofer waþema gebind,
> 25 sohte sele dreorig    sinces bryttan,
> hwær ic feor oþþe neah    findan meahte
> þone þe in meoduhealle    min mine wisse,
> oþþe mec freondleasne    frefran wolde,
> weman mid wynnum.[6]

The sentence has an undeniable majesty and sweep, bearing the listener with the speaker from an earlier action in the past to a later action in the past, from a mood of despair to one of hope, however frustrated. What are its specific syntactic features, we may ask, that carry its narrative and emotive burden?

4. (London: Oxford University Press, 1962), especially pp. 11–13.

5. "A Grammatical Approach to Personification Allegory," *MP*, LX (Feb., 1963), 162. Mr. Bloomfield's *here* refers to "the application of grammatical (and rhetorical) analysis to literature"; he wisely adds the caveat that such analysis must "be done by linguists and philologists with some literary sensitivity." Mr. Bloomfield has himself the requisite sensitivity; may this article suggest that I have!

6. From the edition of *The Exeter Book* by George P. Krapp and E. van K. Dobbie (New York: Columbia University Press, 1936), with one change: *heolster* for their *heolstre* in line 23; see below ⟨p. 84⟩.

The sentence consists of a main clause (lines 19–21) and a subordinate clause, *sippan geara iu* . . . . The subordinate clause contains within it coordination, *ond ic hean ponan* . . . , and within that coordinating element there is further subordination with *hwær ic feor oppe neah* . . . , relative subordination within that adverbial clause in *pone pe in meoduhealle* . . . , and finally coordination within that relative subordination in *oppe mec freondleasne* . . . . Surely it is not too much to suggest that this complex of clauses is in itself, apart from emotive words, a vital element in conveying the sense of movement and frustration that the more referential linguistic features specify? We may notice, too, how the subject of the main clause is *ic*, and the speaker continues to make himself subject of the action in the *ond ic hean* . . . clause and in the *hwær ic feor* . . . clause; but in the last two clauses the speaker becomes the object of the action: *min mine wisse* and *mec freondleasne frefran wolde*. This syntactic inversion mirrors the change in the speaker's viewpoint of his actions: from his past dependence on his own behavior, his relying on himself alone for his existence, to that devoutly-to-be-wished-for state wherein he can depend on another, have another care for him.

There is only one clause, as I interpret the sentence, where the speaker is not subject or object of the action, and this occurs, fittingly, at the pivotal point in the action, the break between the former life of joy within the comitatus and the beginning of the frustrated searching for the establishment of a new lord-thane relationship (I emend, with many, the MS *heolstre* to *heolster*): *sippan geara iu goldwine minne / hrusan heolster biwrah*. The death of the speaker's lord is presented objectively as the "darkness of earth covered my gold-friend"—and this pivotal accident of nature or of war is emphasized syntactically by the placing of the verb *biwrah* at the end of the a-verse.[7] This is the first of but nine such placements in the poem, and only four of the nine, moreover, are not auxiliaries. (Contrast this rarity of end-placed verbs in the a-verse in *The Wanderer* with the frequency of such placement in *The Seafarer*, for example, where

7. Although final position was normal for the verb in a subordinate clause, such word order was not mandatory in Old English syntax; see Randolph Quirk and C. L. Wrenn, *An Old English Grammar*, 2nd ed. (London: Methuen and Co., 1958), p. 94. The *Wanderer*-poet himself uses SVO ⟨subject-verb-object⟩ order in the *peah pe* clause in lines 2b–5a.

there are twenty-two occurrences, only one of which may even be considered an auxiliary!)

Clustered with the verb *biwrah* at the center of the sentence's action are two other finite verb forms, *wod* and *sohte*, both appearing as the first word and the first stress in the succeeding a-verses (again, such word order is rare in *The Wanderer*). Such verbal emphasis, by finite form and position as well as by stress and alliteration, contributes to the sense of motion, to what I have called the sweep of the sentence. As something of a contrast to this "actional" mode the verb in the main clause consists of an auxiliary and an infinitive; in addition, two whole lines separate *sceolde* from *sælan*, and while separations of this kind are common in Old English poetry, such lengthy ones are not. The ideational referent here, of course, is a mental or spiritual one, and the difficulty of keeping to the heroic code which demands one keep one's mouth shut in such circumstances is, I think, suggested by the suspended verbal phrase. Finally, in connection with verbs, we may remark that the only variation in the sentence which is dependent on a prior word is the infinitive *weman* in the last clause, varying *frefran* and dependent on *wolde*—a variational lingering, as it were, highly appropriate to the thoughts of consolation it calls up in the mind of the speaker.

A moment ago I mentioned that the sentence's sweep is partially conveyed by the finite verb forms; also, I would add, by the very succession of clauses that contribute to its linguistic complexity. What about the sentence's majesty? Old English poetry, with its repetitions, its variations, its envelope patterns, is notoriously balanced and stately; but the sentence under consideration goes further in this direction than most. Consider, for example, its adjectives and adjective phrases.

First, there is the triple modification of the subject *ic* in lines 20–21a: *oft earmcearig, eðle bidæled, | freomægum feor*. The wretched state of mind (adjective) is ideationally the *effect* of the deprivation of native land (participle with dat. complement) and of kinsmen (adjective with dat. complement), though it is positionally parallel to them. This triple modification is reinforced in the subordinate clause's second coordinating element, describing the speaker's actions to find a new lord; but this time there are three adjectives: *hean, wintercearig, dreorig* (all referring to the state of mind), and they occupy only parts of half-lines. In the last clause of the sentence there is but one modifying adjective: *freondleasne* (referring to deprivation of companions), a modification that reinforces the threefold repetitions of the earlier segments of the sentence but which by its very singularity allows the hope that the last clause implies to filter through. The triple modification in *earmcearig, eðle bidæled, | freomægum feor*, representing the state of mind, the deprivation of land, and the alienation from kinsmen, is also reflected in the larger structure of the sentence: lines 19–21 emphasize state of mind, lines 23b–25 stress movement into a new land, and lines 26 ff. reinforce the absence from kinsmen by concentrating on the search for comfort in the understanding and benevolence of a hypothetical liege-lord.

For a final commentary on syntax, we may consider another of the balancing elements in the sentence. Both the ideas of the old lord buried and the wished-for new one unfound are given expression in b-verses: *goldwine minne* as the object of *biwrah*, and *sinces bryttan*, not as direct object but variationally as a dependent genitive on *sele*, the direct object of the verb, in the a-verse. Would it be too far-fetched to observe that within the b-verse counterparting of old and new lords, the dependent genitive suggests syntactically the inevitably less personalized new and unfound treasure-dispenser, while the direct object is a syntactic "objective correlative" for the old and known departed gold-friend?

Perhaps in this last statement, and in some of the others I have made here, there is much unprovable, much subjectivity in inference; and perhaps, too, many of the syntactic features and word-order arrangements I have called attention to are but the concomitants of the demands of meter, alliteration, and formula. Nevertheless, I am convinced that the Old English poet, orally or in writing, had some flexibility in these matters; and that he could use and did use, consciously or unconsciously, these linguistic counters, as he did diction, formulas, and themes, to contribute uniquely, in many cases, to his poetic effect.

Reprinted from *Neuphilologische Mitteilungen*, LXIV (1963), 373–378.

# CRITICAL INTERPRETATIONS

# OF PROSE WORKS

TOM H. TOWERS

# Thematic Unity in the Story of Cynewulf and Cyneheard

THE STORY of Cynewulf and Cyneheard, the *Anglo-Saxon Chronicle* entry for 755, is unique among the pre-Alfredian entries both for its artfulness and for its complexity. As Charles Plummer noted in the nineteenth century, most of the early entries give no connected account of either single or multiple events; they do not "chronicle" a year or period so much as they "characterize" it.[1] Typically the pre-Alfredian entries make only the barest allusions to discrete events, and the style of those entries is suitably sparse and unadorned. By comparison, the entry for 755 seems almost poetic. Under a single annual heading the author compresses history properly belonging to a thirty-year span, and he clearly implies that his narrative has some kind of causal and contextual unity. Further, he writes a vigorous and living language that suggests considerable literary skill and consciousness. Finally, the author of this entry is obviously aware of the dramatic possibilities of his material, and he selects and arranges it to emphasize what he apparently thinks of as the dramatic climaxes.

Paradoxically, the very literary qualities which distinguish this entry from the rest of the early *Chronicle* also result in a good deal of narrative and thematic confusion.[2] The brevity and compression of the piece lead to certain obvious difficulties, and in the usual

1. Quoted by G. N. Garmonsway (ed.), *The Anglo-Saxon Chronicle* (New York: E. P. Dutton, 1953), p. xviii. See also Kemp Malone, "The Old English Period," *A Literary History of England*, ed. Albert C. Baugh (New York: Appleton-Century-Crofts, 1948), p. 100.

2. For discussions of this entry see the following: George K. Anderson, *The Literature of the Anglo-Saxons* (Princeton: Princeton University Press, 1949), p. 294; R. H. Hodgkin, *A History of the Anglo-Saxons* (Oxford: Oxford University Press, 1935), II, 393–395; Francis P. Magoun, "Cynewulf, Cyneheard, and Osric," *Anglia*, LVII (1933), 361–376; Charles Moorman, "The 'Anglo-Saxon Chronicle' for 755," *N&Q*, CIC (Mar. 1954), 94–98; C. L. Wrenn, "A Saga of the Anglo-Saxons," *History*, XXV (1940), 208–215.

Anglo-Saxon manner the author is irritatingly careless about such basic narrative matters as the identification of actors and speakers. Most important of all, the very compression of a story historically so prolonged suggests a unity which seems obscured by the selection of detail and the apparent looseness of construction.

As the following translation shows, the narrative itself is fairly direct, except of course for the typically vague pronoun references:

775. In this year Cynewulf and the West-Saxon council because of unlawful deeds, deprived Sigebryht of his kingdom except for Hampshire; and he retained that until he slew the aldorman that had remained with him longest. And then Cynewulf exiled him into the Weald and he dwelled there until a swain stabbed him to death at Pryfetes stream—and he [the swain] avenged the aldorman Cumbra. And Cynewulf often fought great battles against the Welsh; and about thirty-one winters after he came to power, he wished to exile a noble that was called Cyneheard— and that Cyneheard was Sigebryht's brother. And then he [Cyneheard] learned that the king [with] a small band [was] in the company of a woman at Merton, and then he [Cyneheard] overtook him [the king] there and surrounded the chamber from without before the men who were with the king discovered them [Cyneheard and his men].

And then the king became aware of that [attack] and he went to the door and defended it in no mean fashion until he discovered the aetheling [Cyneheard], and then he [the king] rushed out upon him [Cyneheard] and severely wounded him; and they all [Cyneheard's men] fought against the king until they had slain him. And then, by the woman's screams, the king's thanes discovered the disturbance; and then whichever of them were ready and first prepared ran thither [to the woman's chamber]. And the aetheling [Cyneheard] offered to each of them money and immunity, and not one of them would accept it; but they fought constantly until they all [the king's party] lay dead except one Welsh hostage, and he was severely wounded.[3]

3. Though Moorman suggests that this survivor is a Welsh retainer of Cynewulf here captured and taken hostage by Cyneheard, it seems more likely that he is a Welshman held hostage by Cynewulf. It was common Anglo-Saxon practice for potential enemies such as the West Saxons and the Welsh to exchange hostages; in the event of war, especially such an internecine quarrel as this, the hostages fought on the side of their present lord.

Then in the morning the king's thanes who were behind him [i.e., those left behind when the king proceeded to Merton] heard that the king was slain. Then they rode thither, and his [the king's] aldorman Osric and Wiferth his thane and the men he had left behind him earlier; and they met the aetheling [Cyneheard] at the stockade where the king lay dead (and they [Cyneheard's men] had locked the gates against them [Osric's party]) and then they [Osric's force] went thereto. And then he [Cyneheard] offered them their own choice of money or lands if they would grant him the kingdom; and he told them that their [Osric's and Wiferth's] kinsmen were with him and would not desert him. And then they [Osric and Wiferth] told him that no kinsmen were dearer to them than their lord [the king] and they would never follow his murderer. And then they proposed to their kinsmen that they come away safe and unharmed, and they [the kinsmen] said that that same offer had been made to their [Osric's and Wiferth's] companions who were formerly with the king. Then they [the kinsmen] said that they did not consider it worthy [of] them [selves] "any more than of your[4] companions who were slain with the king." And they then fought about the gate until they [Osric's party] got inside, and they slew the aetheling [Cyneheard] and all the men that were with him except one who was the aldorman's [Osric's][5] godson; and he [Osric] saved his [the godson's] life, though he [the godson] was often wounded.[6]

Clearly the narrative breaks into two more or less distinct major sections. First there is the deposition and eventual murder of Sigebryht; later there are the two connected battles at Merton. Joining the two major segments is a single sentence describing the reign of Cynewulf. But that transition is abrupt, and the narrative relationship

4. Two manuscripts of the entry read "their," and Moorman, attributing the quotation to Osric, chooses that reading. "Their" can be readily explained, though, as a scribal error; but for the momentary and most unusual direct discourse, the third person would undoubtedly have been used.

5. Moorman holds that the author is speaking of Cumbra's godson, not Osric's, because the latter would not have followed the disloyal Cyneheard. The taking of godsons, however, like the arrangement of marriages, was a common means of reconciling discordant factions. The *Chronicle* entry for 894, for example, records such an attempted reconciliation that failed.

6. The above is a translation of the entry for 755 from the Parker MS of the *Chronicle* as it appears in James W. Bright, *Anglo-Saxon Reader*, rev. James R. Hulbert (New York: Holt, Rinehart, Winston, 1957), pp. 14–15.

between the deposition and the battles seems to break down. Neither do the three great scenes, the deposition and the two battles, lead to any apparent dramatic climax or resolution. There is not even the link of a single dominant character uniting the parts of the story. Still, though the entry seems to lack unity in all these areas, it achieves, I think, a clear thematic harmony that provides the necessary artistic structure.

The identification of a uniting theme is the major concern of the two principal critical studies of the entry. Francis P. Magoun suggests that the story demonstrates chiefly the traditional values of the comitatus. In Magoun's reading, the narrative leads up to the testing of comitatus solidarity in the two battles at Merton. In both, the comitatus holds firm. Though defeated in the first fight, the comitatus, under Osric, triumphs ultimately, and its spirit and values are vindicated.

On the other hand, Charles Moorman argues that the narrower theme of personal loyalty unites the story. Moorman suggests that the principal vehicle for the theme of personal loyalty is a "protagonist," a single character who appears in all three major scenes, first as the avenging swain, then as the Welsh hostage, and finally as the preserved godson. (Moorman thinks the character is the godson of Cumbra, not of Osric. Hence, according to Moorman, he is a fit avenger for the aldorman; and Cumbra's name suggests a Welsh background.) The loyal protagonist is contrasted in the deposition passage with the unlawful and perfidious Sigebryht and in the two battles with the treasonous and deceitful Cyneheard. Though he suffers throughout the story, the loyal protagonist, in Moorman's opinion, at last survives the villainy of his enemies. Moorman also maintains that the contrast between loyalty and treachery is further supported by a "false parley" before the second battle at Merton. According to Moorman, Cyneheard lies when he suggests that in the stockade are kinsmen of Osric loyal to the murderer of Cynewulf. Moorman reasons that any such kinsmen would have to be hostages taken at the first battle, and that the account of that fight precludes such a possibility. Magoun, in contrast, suggests that the kinsmen are quite simply kinsmen of Osric who have chosen the cause and the company of Cyneheard. Moorman rejects that thesis because he contends that the comitatus is primarily a tribal structure that never crosses blood lines.[7]

Moorman's explanation of the story is ingenious, and it has the advantage of comprehending all three scenes of the narrative. It seems to me, however, both implausible and illogical. Moorman suggests that in a single two-page narrative the same character appears in such various guises as an avenging swain, a Welsh hostage, and the godson of a great noble. Similarly he suggests that the author of the entry neglects to name or even to describe consistently his "protagonist," while at the same time he is careful to identify such relatively minor figures as Cumbra and Wiferth. Again Moorman argues that Cyneheard is disloyal when he sacrifices comitatus to blood ties; but at the same time he maintains that it is unthinkable that Osric's kinsmen could betray blood ties out of loyalty to Cyneheard's cause. Similar objections might be raised to Moorman's theory that the godson of the second battle is not Osric's, but Cumbra's. In short, Moorman's reading of the selection seems to depend ultimately on doubtful aesthetic premises and on serious oversimplification of Anglo-Saxon social customs. His theory of a "protagonist" who remains always in the background is aesthetically unconvincing, and the idea of a false parley rests on doubtful historical assumptions and seems introduced chiefly to provide an opposition of loyalty and deceit in the third scene. At best the theme of "personal loyalty" seems only a simplified refinement of the comitatus theme.

But if the "unity" discovered by Professor Moorman is more ingenious than satisfying, Magoun's location of unifying theme in the comitatus spirit also seems inadequate because it fails to comprehend the deposition of Sigebryht. Certainly the idea of the comitatus is very important to the narrative; dramatically, the displays of the comitatus spirit in the two battles at Merton are the

7. Wrenn, however, claims that "this sacred *comitatus*-loyalty was supreme over any blood-relationship" (*op. cit.*, p. 215). Certainly the political exploitation of marriage and other family connections was common in the period. Especially in such a situation as this entry describes—royal deposition and "counter-revolution" —it should be neither surprising nor illogical to find apparently large, powerful families divided in their loyalties. Magoun's interpretation here seems to me both more reasonable and more realistic than Professor Moorman's.

most striking aspects of the story. Still, the comitatus loyalty is, I think, no more the theme of the entry than is chivalry the theme of Shakespeare's *I Henry IV*. I propose that the first section of the narrative, the deposition of Sigebryht, provides the key to interpretation.

Though the chronicler devotes only two long sentences, about one-sixth of the entire story, to the fall of Sigebryht, the deposition is the background against which all the subsequent action is played. Sigebryht, although apparently the legitimate ruler, had committed unlawful deeds serious enough to lead to his dethronement. It is not necessary here to consider the possibility of a degree of constitutional government among the West Saxons of the eighth century;[8] but it is clear that Cynewulf came to power with the consent and possibly with the help of the royal council or *witan*. Thus, Cynewulf's rise results from a *coup d'état* in the name of proper and orderly government. The chronicler does not explain why Cynewulf allowed Sigebryht to continue to rule in Hampshire, but it seems fair to speculate that the new king did not yet have the power to banish the old king completely.[9] Sigebryht's murder of Cumbra seems to have provided the occasion for the further and ultimate harassment of the deposed ruler. The eventual killing of Sigebryht must have been inevitable in any event; it is an axiom as old as kingship that the new ruler, especially the usurper, is never secure until the old king is finally and safely out of the way.

The whole narrative is sympathetic to Cynewulf and his party. The chronicler is careful, I think, to provide evidence that Cynewulf was a good king. Such, I believe, is the thematic purpose and significance of the statement that Cynewulf fought many great battles against the Welsh. The very title of the West-Saxon and Kentish kings of this period—the Bretwalda—suggests that the chief kingly function was defending the realm against the always troublesome Welsh neighbors. The tone of the whole entry further implies that

8. For discussions of the role of the *witan* in the selection of kings, see H. M. Chadwick, *Studies on Anglo-Saxon Institutions* (Cambridge: Cambridge University Press, 1905), pp. 361–363; Anderson, *op. cit.*, pp. 13–17; and Magoun, *op. cit.*, p. 368.

9. Magoun (pp. 368–369) suggests that Hampshire under Cumbra defied the *witan* and remained loyal to Sigebryht.

Cynewulf was a good king, and the proposed exile of Cyneheard is then justified in terms of national good. Although there is again no explicit evidence, it seems reasonable that Cyneheard, Sigebryht's brother, must have fallen heir to the leadership of whatever disaffected elements remained in the land. Cynewulf's decision to banish Cyneheard suggests that whatever threat Cyneheard posed had grown too great to be tolerated longer. Certainly Cynewulf's decision might logically be supposed to have forced Cyneheard's hand—direct and immediate action becomes Cyneheard's only alternative to banishment and the effective renunciation of all ambition. Faced with exile, Cyneheard, already a logical pretender since his brother's death, acts to usurp the throne. All doubt of his intention evaporates in the parley with Osric where Cyneheard offers the loyalists money or land on their own terms if they will "grant him the kingdom," that is, if they will support his claim to the throne.

Thus, the background of the story and, I think, its theme are boldly political. The concern of the narrative is not personal loyalty or disloyalty, though such considerations enter the story; neither is the concern only the comitatus-tribal spirit. The political concept in this chronicle is much more sophisticated than the comitatus, and it comprehends the comitatus. The basic interest here is the personal ambition of Cyneheard seeking to disrupt a sound and orderly national system represented by Cynewulf. The issue, as in Shakespeare's history plays, becomes ultimately the disposition of the realm.

Nor does the chronicler pose himself a simple, black-or-white problem. Cyneheard, though he lacks the support of the *witan*, has an hereditary claim to the throne at least as strong as Cynewulf's. Confronted with the threat of banishment, Cyneheard rebels for the sake of political, and perhaps physical, self-preservation. Families are divided in the dispute that erupts at last into open rebellion. The claims of kin, comitatus, and state are at odds. Before the issue is finally resolved in favor of political order, the comitatus twice has its faith put to the extreme test, and Osric has to subordinate the loyalties of kinship to the loyalties to king and country. Though only a sketch, the chronicle contains material enough for a major political drama. And by recognizing and emphasizing the moral and social complexity of his subject the author derives from that subject a high degree of drama and of art.

Though Anglo-Saxon heroic poetry is apt to be wholly concerned with the comitatus, it is not surprising that such a relatively sophisticated political narrative should appear in the *Anglo-Saxon Chronicle*. From at least as early as the seventh century the direction of Anglo-Saxon political development was toward a kind of national state.[10] Similarly, the very title of Bede's eighth-century history speaks for the existence of a well-developed national consciousness at about the time of the events narrated in this selection. The great climax of national feeling in the Anglo-Saxon period came in the ninth century of Alfred; and, therefore, it is hardly peculiar to find one of Alfred's scribes recounting an old tale of princely ambition, rebellion, and royal reform. Indeed, the unusual compression and connection of events in this chronicle demonstrate the chronicler's awareness of the political interest latent in the narrative. Matters such as that recounted here have interested English writers of all ages, and it should not be surprising to find the anonymous ninth-century scribe working at the same kind of problem that attracted Shakespeare.

Reprinted from *JEGP*, LXII (1963), 310–316.

10. Malone, *op. cit.*, p. 4.

# ELEANOR DUCKETT

# The Accounts of
# Ohthere and Wulfstan

ALTHOUGH * * * WE CANNOT be certain of the order and time of translating these various works ⟨St. Gregory's *Dialogues* and *Pastoral Care* and Bede's *Ecclesiastical History*⟩, it is once more reasonable to think that Alfred turned from instructing his people of Wessex in the Church history of their own England to teaching them something of the past history of their world as a whole. This time, indeed, and from this time onward, we may safely hold him himself as the translator.

His original he found in the work of a Catholic priest, possibly born in Spain, but far more probably in Portugal. This priest's name was Paulus Orosius. He lived and wrote in the early years of the fifth century after Christ; and he was a devoted follower of the great St. Augustine of Hippo in North Africa.

In these 400's of our era the Roman Empire throughout its vast extent, from the Tiber to the Rhine and the Danube, and among the peoples of the Mediterranean, was suffering from those barbarian invasions which preceded and prophesied its fall in the West, from massacres and plunderings and plagues unnumbered. Naturally its citizens, of whom so many still stoutly adhered to the pagan faith of their ancestors, were declaring that these manifold and terrible visitations were being brought on them through the wrathful vengeance of the gods of ancient Rome, who would not brook their supplanting by the new worship of one named Christ. Augustine, therefore, who himself was preparing an answer to this pagan fallacy in his *City of God*, requested Orosius to write by way of supplement a narrative, as Orosius describes it, "based on all the histories and annals available, of all the grievous wars, foul epidemics, baneful times of famine, ghastly earthquakes, unheard-of floods, fearful conflagrations, savage blasts of lightning, storms of hail, wretched

97

murders and crimes" which had descended on men in past heathen ages. This persuasive story, at Augustine's bidding, was to be "brief and well-ordered."

Orosius was delighted at the task. Here was an honor given him by his beloved master; here was a work for the Church and for the heathen whom he longed to convert; here was business of much research. He set to with all his might and by the year 418 had produced *Seven Books of History against the Pagans*, books crammed with details, bristling with names of peoples, persons, and places in almost every paragraph, and punctuated by exhortations: "See now, you heathen, and believe, you who jeer at our present Christian age, so far happier than the past!"

The narrative ran from the earliest times of which Orosius could find knowledge to his own century. It became a classic in the earlier Middle Ages, a text book for Christian readers of history. To Alfred it was an obvious, even an ideal choice; but it also offered to him an undertaking of almost insuperable difficulty. After the comparatively clear and simple Latin of St. Bede, after the ordered, if "unclassical," periods of St. Gregory the Great, he now faced the diffuse Latin flood poured out by Orosius, bearing, as it swept along, its swirling burden of facts, or at least what Orosius regarded as facts.

The king of Wessex, however, true to his nature, was undaunted. From this seething mass he made in his Anglo-Saxon a story written in as simple and popular, as clear and direct, a style as he could devise, hoping thereby to descend to the level of his uninstructed readers. Many names he recast in an English form. Roman terms he explained, as, for instance, when the Roman vestal virgin becomes "a nun" and Roman cohorts are described as "what we now call *truman*," or troops. The errors of Orosius did not concern Alfred; indeed, he makes hair-raising mistakes of his own. Names are continually misspelled by him; persons and places are confused; words are entirely misunderstood, causing complete mistranslation; the caution which Orosius now and again expressed in making a statement is here neglected; and matters noted as doubtful or possible by him are stated simply by Alfred as true. Much, moreover, of the Latin work is here omitted, especially material relating to the times of the Caesars; and the seven books of the original are represented in the Anglo-Saxon by six. Alfred was fortunate, of course, in having a Christian authority in Orosius for all this pagan matter. Even so, he adds here and there a purely Christian touch on his own. He makes the pagan Leonidas place his trust "in God" and declares that Hannibal "said within himself that he was longing and hoping for dominion over Rome, but that God would not allow it."

In spite, however, of all the king's strenuous endeavor, many men of Wessex in this ninth century must have found their minds sinking and slipping as in a bog of clay when they strove to read this Anglo-Saxon version of Orosius. One hopes that their eyes lighted up when they fell on a few pages near the beginning of the book, amid Alfred's translation of a discourse on world geography which Orosius had placed before his long treatment of history. For here the king, most happily for all his readers, medieval and modern, decided to insert a substantial addition of his own in regard to the Germany and the Scandinavia of this ninth century, those countries so well known by name in his England and among his own people.

His description of Germany's geography is of deep interest to scholars, since it shows the knowledge of that country current in Alfred's time. But the famous picture of the northern lands of Europe is even more fascinating. And here the king had first-hand evidence. He was drawing his words from two explorers who had travelled far in the north and had themselves, he said, told him of what they had seen.

The name, in Anglo-Saxon form, of one of these sailors was Ohthere, and he is here described as acknowledging Alfred, king of Wessex, as "his lord." Ohthere, however, was a Norwegian, and many have wondered what this statement means. As one observer has remarked, it can hardly have been due to gratitude for hospitality received by him in Wessex. Nor is there any evidence that Ohthere had met Alfred before he made his explorations in the north. He told the king that he lived farther north in Norway than any of his fellow-countrymen, on the coast of the "West Sea," by which he meant the Norwegian Sea, and that his "shire" of Norway was Helgeland.

In this region one enters the Arctic Circle. It is known to many for the islands which cluster about its shore, broken by long, narrow fjords, for its valleys and the great waterfalls that roar down their cliffs in its southerly part, and for that far-stretching glacier, the

Svartisen, the field of "Black Ice." This land, Ohthere said, extended very far in length, but was very narrow in width. He could use for pasture or for ploughing only that part of it which lay near the sea, and even that was very rocky here and there. Farther inland rose wild mountains, inhabited by Lapps (he called them "Finns"). North of him the land stretched on, holding only a few Lapps who lived by hunting in the winter and by fishing off the coast in summer-time. In Helgeland, Ohthere told Alfred, there was such excellent whale-hunting that he and five other men had killed sixty whales in two days. Across the mountains from its more southerly part lay Sweden, and facing the more northerly part was a region which Alfred wrote down from Ohthere's report as "Cwenaland." This may have lain at the north end of the Gulf of Bothnia. Its people, the "Cwenas," now and then made raids across the mountains upon the men of Norway, carrying with them their boats, very small and very light, which they used in ferrying across the large fresh-water lakes among the mountains. These "Cwenas," it seems, were of Finnish race. Ohthere said that they in their turn were raided by the men of Helgeland, the "Northmen," as he called them.

He himself, he said, was one of the leading men of Helgeland and very wealthy in one of its sources of revenue, the wild reindeer, which he hunted and sold. At the time he came to Alfred he had six hundred of these deer in stock, tame and awaiting sale, as well as six most precious "decoy reindeer," which he used for capturing others of their kind. For all his standing, however, and his wealth of deer, he had no more than twenty head of horned cattle, twenty sheep, twenty pigs, and some horses with which he ploughed a small tract of soil.

Another source of his income, as he reported it, is of interest. It consisted of tribute paid in kind, to him and to his neighbors in that northerly region, by the Lapps: furs and skins of reindeer, bear, marten, and otter; feathers of birds; ship's ropes made from hides of whale and seal. Tribute was exacted from these Lapps, he said, more or less in amount, according to the rank and importance of each one of them among his fellow-tribesmen.

This detail of Ohthere's story has brought forth an interesting suggestion which might explain his coming to Alfred. Historians of Norway are now inclined to date the great battle of Hafrsfjord, in which Harold Fairhair finally won dominion over its land, about the

year 885. Even before this time Harold had been winning lordship
and control; and there is evidence which at least points towards his
seizing of the *finnskattr*, these taxes paid by the Lapps, as his own
royal prerogative. It is known that many brave men sailed away
from Norway in their anger against what they held as the usurpation
of Harold Fairhair. Perhaps Ohthere was one of these; perhaps he
sailed to Wessex to enter the service of another king, one by this time
renowned for the defense of his own people against invasion.

Ohthere went on to tell of his voyages. He had been curious, he
told Alfred, to find out how far land extended north of his own most
northerly point and whether any people, except those few Lapps,
lived in its solitudes. He had, therefore, started out in his boat from
his home in Helgeland on a journey due north to explore. As Alfred's
geography here is difficult to understand, and as the political geography of Europe has changed within recent years in regard to
borderlands and the names of towns, it will be better perhaps to
describe the explorations of these two sailors, Ohthere and Wulfstan,
in modern terms.

Ohthere, then, took his boat northward past islands innumerable,
past Hammerfest, past the North Cape, as far as the entrance to the
Barents Sea. Then he voyaged south-east, waiting at times for a
favorable wind, and quite uncertain of what he would find as he
went on. Past Varangerfjord and onward he continued for four days.
By their end he had reached the bend of the Kola Peninsula, and
now he turned towards its southern border and the entrance to the
White Sea. He sailed into the sea and continued in its waters for five
days, along the southern coast of the peninsula, until he reached the
mouth of a great river. During the whole of his course hitherto he
had seen only Lapp hunters. But now he, and the man or two whom
he had taken with him for his aid, saw that the land beyond this
river's mouth was inhabited, and they were afraid of encountering
some enemy tribe if they continued on their course as before.

This river was probably the Varzuga, which flows down through
the southern part of the Kola Peninsula into the White Sea. Ohthere,
wisely cautious, turned his boat up the river and there found more
cultivated land. Again fearing attack, he did not dare to put his boat
into shore. But soon he came upon men who dwelt along the
Kandalaksha Gulf, probably in what is now Karelo-Finnish territory; in Alfred's narrative these men are called "Beormas." They

must have been friendly, for, Ohthere said, they told him "many tales." He had already heard of their people in his own country; for the Norwegians, who thought of them as dwellers in "Bjarmaland," believed this to be a faraway region of magic, of a people who confounded their enemies by mysterious incantations which caused the heavens suddenly to burst open at time of battle and hurl down fearful deluges of rain and hail. The "Beormas" told Ohthere about Lapp neighbors of theirs who, it would seem, spoke almost the same language as themselves. Alfred wrote of these neighbors as the "Terfinnas"; and we may think of them as living along the south shore of the White Sea. Ohthere's chief interest in visiting this region was its walrus-hunting, and he brought some walrus tusks as a gift to the king.

There were other voyages, too, of which Ohthere told Alfred. He had sailed not only north from Helgeland but also south, past Iceland in the distance, although, as several scholars have noted, he did not mention it; along the Norwegian Sea into the North Sea and round into the Skagerrak, until he reached the coast of Vestfold in southern Norway. And then again he had sailed on from there, skirting the west coast of Sweden for three days, along the Kattegat into the Store, or the Great Belt, past the Danish islands of Fyn and Sjælland, of Langeland and Lolland, to the port of Hedeby, near Slesvig.

The other voyager, Wulfstan, the second source of Alfred's additions to Orosius, was apparently an Englishman. He had taken his boat from Hedeby, then a Danish port, past Lolland and Bornholm into the Baltic Sea, to reach the country about the mouth of the Wista and the Gulf of Danzig. Here, he told Alfred, he had met the people who lived near the Zalew Wislany, the salt-water inlet which lies between Gdansk in Poland and Kaliningrad in the Soviet Union. Wulfstan went on to describe their manner of living. They possessed many towns, he said, each one ruled by a king. They lived largely on fish and honey; mares' milk was the drink of the dominant minority who were steppe folk, and mead was left for the poor and the slaves. No ale was brewed among them.

But, especially, the customs attending death among this people seem to have impressed Wulfstan. He reported to Alfred that the body of the dead lay in state among his kinsmen and friends for a month, or two months, sometimes even for six. The higher the rank of the dead, the longer it lay. All this time, around the bier in the house, there was carousal of drinking and celebration of funeral games. At last came the day decided upon for the burning of the body. Then the dead man's treasures, those which could be carried, were divided into five or six or even more shares, according to their number and value. The richest portion was laid on the ground about a mile from the dead man's home, and all the other portions at points between the first one and the home, each one nearer than the last, the portion of least value being placed nearest the house. After this had been carefully done, all the men who owned the swiftest horses rode from a point five or six miles distant in a race to pick up these treasures, and the prizes fell to those who reached them first. Finally, the cremation of the dead man, clothed in his best and girded with his weapons, was solemnly fulfilled.

Swift horses, as we may imagine, sold for a high price in that country. If anyone asks how its dead could remain so long within their homes, the answer of Wulfstan is that certain men dwelling there possessed the secret of refrigeration; even in summertime, he said, they could keep water frozen into ice.

To all these tales of Ohthere and Wulfstan, Alfred had surely listened with rapt mind. Books, we know, were worth the world to him; yet in reality his world was the people of his land. To pass on to them, not only books, but the narratives of those who themselves had heard and seen strange things, and heard and seen, too, things that concerned the Europe of Alfred's own day, narratives that told of the Northmen from whom had descended so much tribulation upon England and who were even now settled on wide regions of English land—this to the king of Wessex was welcome and happy work, good both for himself and for those whom he longed to teach.

Reprinted from Eleanor Duckett, *Alfred the Great, The King and His England* (Chicago: University of Chicago Press, 1956), pp. 141–148.

STANLEY B. GREENFIELD

# Ælfric and Wulfstan

* * * ÆLFRIC'S ACCOMPLISHMENTS may be viewed in three stages: the first concludes with the publication of his *Lives of the Saints* in 1002; it begins with the two series of *Catholic Homilies* (989, 992) and includes a translation of Bede's *De Temporibus Anni* and of the *Heptateuch*, the Latin works mentioned above ⟨the *Grammar, Glossary,* and *Colloquy*⟩, and the *Letter to Wulfsige* (in which Ælfric attempted to clarify, for the Benedictines whom Wulfsige had invited to Sherborne, essential doctrine and incumbent duties). The second stage, 1002–1005, consists of more homilies and "occasional" pieces, the result of his reputation by this time; these pieces he used to expand his instructions to parish priests, to state the fundamentals of monastic life, to offer moral guidance, and to synthesize his earlier themes. The last stage, after his establishment as Abbot of Eynsham, contains still more homilies, the Latin *Vita Sancti Æthelwoldi,*[1] two pastoral letters to Archbishop Wulfstan (in Latin and in English), and the *Letter to Sigeweard* ("On the Old and New Testament").[2] Those works which have most engaged the attention of students and critics of Old English literature have been the *Catholic Homilies,* the *Lives of the Saints,* the *Heptateuch,* and the *Colloquy,* and it is to these that we now turn.[3]

1. There are two versions of this Life, the longer attributed to Wulfstan, the precentor of Winchester. Critical disagreement exists as to which has precedence in point of time; see the Introduction to the translation of the shorter Life (Ælfric's) in *English Historical Documents,* I, ed. Dorothy Whitelock (London: Eyre and Spottiswoode, 1955), pp. 831–839.

2. I have followed the dating indicated by P. Clemoes, "The Chronology of Ælfric's Work," in *The Anglo-Saxons: Studies Presented to Bruce Dickins* (London: Bowes and Bowes, 1959). For a somewhat different chronology, see Kenneth Sisam, *Studies in the History of Old English Literature* (Oxford: The Clarendon Press, 1953).

3. C. L. White's *Ælfric: A New Study of his Life and Writings,* Yale Studies in English #2 (Boston: Yale University Press, 1898) is still the most comprehensive study. For more recent bibliographical material and considerations, see G. K. Anderson, *The Literature of the Anglo-Saxons* (Princeton: Princeton University Press, 1949), pp. 308–339, and Clemoes, *op. cit.*

The two series of *Catholic Homilies* and the *Lives of the Saints*[4] may be commented on together for at least two reasons. First, they were viewed by Ælfric as something of a continuum, whereby he first made accessible in English an account of and commentary on the facts and doctrines of Christianity, including the Scriptures, the origins and spread of Christianity, and the lives of its saints. Many of the "Homilies" are really saints' lives and many of the latter incorporate homilies; and Ælfric's Preface to the latter work explains that he is now devoting himself to saints celebrated among the monks themselves, whereas formerly he had been concerned with those honored on festival days. Second, they reveal a development in Ælfric's methodology and style; and it is Ælfric's mature style for which he is celebrated as a literary figure, a style which * * * is taken by many scholars as the standard not only of late West Saxon, or classical Old English, but as the norm for the teaching of the language.

These three series of homilies and saints' lives consist of approximately forty sermons each. Their sources are named by Ælfric himself: mainly Gregory the Great, St. Augustine, St. Jerome, and Bede—though Ælfric may have found the homilies of these fore-runners conveniently collected in some version of the popular homiliary of Paul the Deacon.[5] But Ælfric, though no innovator or speculative philosopher or theologian, was also no mere translator: he expanded, condensed, embroidered in the light of his specific purpose to expound to Englishmen the truths of Christianity. Sometimes these truths were controversial: Ælfric preached the Eucharistic belief of Ratramnus, for example, that the bread and wine were mystically symbolic of the body and blood of Christ, a view that was

4. For the best edition of the former, see B. Thorpe (ed.), *The Homilies of the Anglo-Saxon Church*, I (London, 1844); of the latter, see W. W. Skeat (ed.), *Ælfric's Lives of the Saints*, EETS, 76, 82, 94, 114 (1881–1900).

5. See C. J. Smetana, "Ælfric and the Early Medieval Homiliary," *Traditio*, XV (1959), 163–204, and J. E. Cross, "Ælfric and the Mediæval Homiliary—Objection and Contribution," *Studier utg. av KHVL: Scripta Minora* (1961–1962:4). Father Smetana observes that Ælfric does not maintain a strict distinction between *sermon* (a discourse on a dogmatic or moral issue for instructional purposes) and *homily* (a commentary and exegesis on Scriptural text). Of the eighty-five actual homilies in the *Catholic Homilies*, he further points out, fifty-six may properly be termed exegetical; twelve are topical sermons and expanded Gospel texts; seventeen are saints' lives. See also his "Ælfric and the Homiliary of Haymo of Halberstadt," *Traditio*, XVII (1961), 457–469.

to be condemned, ultimately, at the Synod of Vercelli in 1050 in favor of the doctrine of transubstantiation. Yet Ælfric was extremely conservative and careful in his teachings, never asserting dogma (such as the Assumption of the Virgin) that he had doubts about. In handling his Biblical material, Ælfric condensed his sources to make effective narrative and to heighten dramatic potentialities as well as to remove unfamiliar elements which might cause confusion in the faithful.[6] To this end, too, he, like the Old English poets before him, used Old English social, political, and legal nomenclature to translate Biblical relationships and even the smallest features of daily life of Scriptural times. He used similes from these areas, too, as had Alfred, though the sources of his similes were more likely Patristic rather than "life," as when he compares the joys in heaven over the conversion of a sinner to "the greater love which a chieftain feels in battle for the soldier who after flight boldly overcomes his adversary, than for him who never took to flight, nor yet in any conflict performed any deed of valor" (*CH*, I, p. 343).[7] Still, Ælfric followed in his methodology the typological-allegorical-symbolic tradition of exegesis that he found in his originals. In *CH*, II, page 282, for example, he explains the crossing of the Red Sea on a fourfold level of meaning: literally, the crossing of the Israelites from servitude to the promised land; allegorically, the passage of Christ from the "middle-earth" to the heavenly Father; tropologically, the moving in this present life from sin to virtue; and anagogically, the crossing in the next life after our resurrection to eternal life in Christ.[8]

The first series of *Catholic Homilies* is largely Scriptural and exegetical in content, while the second is more legendary, less didactic, and more concerned with the appearance of Christianity in England. In the latter and in the *Lives of the Saints*, the narrative assumes greater prominence than the moralizing, the saints' lives in particular resembling later medieval tales of wonder. Stylistically in

6. See Charles R. Davis, "Biblical Translations in Ælfric's *Catholic Homilies*" (unpublished dissertation, New York University, 1949).

7. Ælfric's source for this simile was Gregory, *Hom. XXXIV in Evang.* §4. I gratefully acknowledge Dr. J. E. Cross's identification of this source and his many helpful comments on other portions of this text.

8. See H. Schelp, "Die Deutungstradition in Ælfrics Homilæ Catholicæ," *Archiv*, CXCVI (1960), 273–295. On the fourfold method of interpretation, see B. Smalley, *The Study of the Bible in the Middle Ages* (London: Oxford University Press, 1941).

these three series, Ælfric moves from a prose heightened occasionally by alliteration and other rhetorical effects to an almost regularly metrical style: balanced, antithetical, synonymic, and richly alliterative—so much so that earlier critics disputed as to whether the *Lives* was not meant to be poetry (Skeat printed many of the *Lives*, or portions of them, as such, and Jost has reverted to this practice in his edition of Wulfstan's *Institutes of Polity*—see below). Whether Ælfric derived this style which, though found in other Old English prose, even to some extent in Alfredian prose, has come to be his hallmark, from the rhymed Latin prose of the time (his familiarity with it is evidenced by his Latin *Vita Sancti Æthelwoldi*), with a substitution of alliteration for the rhyme and even an attempt to capture Latin rhythm, particularly the *cursus* ⟨rapid movement⟩; or whether he drew mainly upon his native English poetic and prose heritage, however inspired he was by Latin literature, is still a matter of debate among literary historians.[9]

The *Heptateuch* (so named by Thwaites, its first editor, in 1698) is a translation of and commentary on the Pentateuch, Joshua, and Judges. Ælfric's actual share in the Pentateuch translation is still not conclusively established.[10] But we know he was not as happy translating the Old Testament Vulgate as he had been in his work on the New. He was afraid, for one thing, that *sum dysig man* "some foolish man" might think he could live under the New Law as the patriarchs had lived under the Old. Still, he acceded to the request of his powerful patron Æthelweard that he do the job, and he performed in his typical fashion, interchanging epitomes of the history in the Old Testament with more extensive translation, and omitting "catalogs" and abstruse passages. At the end of his paraphrase of

9. The former view is enunciated by G. H. Gerould, "Abbot Ælfric's Rhythmic Prose," *MP*, XXII (1925), 353–366; the latter by D. Bethurum, "The Form of Ælfric's *Lives of the Saints*," *SP*, XXIX (1932), 515–533. A more recent commentator, R. Vleeskruyer, *The Life of St. Chad* (Amsterdam: North-Holland Publishing Co., 1953), stresses the use of Old English poetic formulas and alliteration as the basis of Old English prose style, and sees Ælfric (and Wulfstan) as continuing and developing a Mercian (rather than Alfredian) vernacular prose tradition of the ninth century. For differences of opinion among literary historians, see K. Malone, "The Old English Period," in *A Literary History of England*, ed. A. C. Baugh (New York: Appleton-Century-Crofts, 1948), p. 101, and G. K. Anderson, *op. cit.*, pp. 311–312.

10. See J. Raith, "Ælfric's Share in the Old English *Pentateuch*," *RES*, N. S. III (1952), 305–314.

Judges, which treats in detail only of Samson, Ælfric updates his material by expounding the typology-allegory of Samson, commenting on the consuls and Caesars of Rome, especially on Constantine and the elder and younger Theodosius, and concluding with a paean of praise for Alfred, Æthelstan, and Edgar, the three "victorious" kings of Wessex and England.

Finally we must look at the *Colloquy*, with which most students of Old English become acquainted early in their study of the language, despite the fact that the Old English gloss they read is not Ælfric's but presumably the work of a cleric of a generation or two later. Written as a supplement to his Latin *Grammar* and *Glossary*, the *Colloquy* is the first use of the "direct method" of language instruction. It is the most engaging and literarily effective example of a type of medieval dialogue that "became the drudge of monastic pedagogues, and in the role of a literary Cinderella laboured in obscurity in monastic classrooms to help boys learn their lessons."[11] The realism of this work has often been noted, as has its sociological picture of the occupational strata of Old English society. Less noted has been its fine organization and structure, dramatic in effect, with its pairing and contrasting, for example, of the king's bold hunter and the independent, timid fisherman who would rather catch fish he can kill than hunt those (whales) which can destroy him and his companions; and with its lively disputation toward the end about which occupation is the most essential. Ælfric's work is a good illustration of how even the most unpromising material, from a modern point of view, can become "literature" in the hands of a master craftsman.

Ælfric has until recently received much more attention than his colleague and contemporary Wulfstan. But the great administrator and adviser to kings (Æthelred and Cnut), the legalist and homilist, has fully received his due in the researches of the last fifteen years.[12]

11. G. N. Garmonsway, "The Development of the Colloquy," in *The Anglo-Saxons: Studies Presented to Bruce Dickins*, p. 249. The best edition is Mr. Garmonsway's (London: Methuen and Co., 1939).

12. The most significant works: D. Bethurum, *The Homilies of Wulfstan* (Oxford: Oxford University Press, 1957); K. Jost, *Wulfstanstudien*, Swiss Studies in English, No. 23 (Bern: A. Francke, 1950), and his *Die "Institutes of Polity, Civil and Ecclesiastical,"* Swiss Studies in English, No. 47 (Bern: A. Francke, 1959); D. Whitelock (ed.), *Sermo Lupi ad Anglos*, 3rd ed. (London: Methuen and Co., 1964); A. McIntosh, "Wulfstan's Prose," *PBA*, 1949, XXXV (1950), 109–142. For earlier editions and further bibliography, see these works and the following notes.

His first appearance on the religious scene is as Bishop of London from 996 to 1002; from 1002 to his death in 1023 he was Archbishop of York and Bishop of Worcester, though he relinquished the latter see in 1016, or at least had it ruled by a suffragan. Though there is no record of his belonging to any of the well-known eleventh-century monastic houses, Wulfstan was a Benedictine and was buried at Ely, as the one medieval account of his life, in the twelfth-century *Historia Eliensis*, informs us.[13] During his tenure as Bishop of London he established his reputation as a preacher, probably with his eschatological homilies—the approach of the millennium and the incursions of the Danes gave rise to a rash of such homilies; in this period his nom de plume *Lupus* appears on documents for the first time. As Archbishop of York, he instituted reforms in the northern Church, which had suffered severely from Danish depredations, and probably helped rebuild the York library by encouraging manuscript collection. As adviser to and lawmaker for Æthelred from 1008 to 1012, he concerned himself with the problem of moral regeneration; Codes V–X *Æthelred*, for example, attempt to provide legal sanctions for the infringement of Christian ethics. The presence of heathen Danes in England made Wulfstan conscious that the amalgamation of civil and ecclesiastical laws, such as existed in the Continental Carolingian laws, would not suffice for England; and in his legal writings—the *Canons of Edgar*, the *Peace of Edward and Guthrum*, the *Institutes of Polity*, and *I* and *II Cnut*—the concept of the division yet interrelation between divine and civil obedience and jurisdiction becomes more and more explicit.[14]

The *Institutes of Polity* is Wulfstan's greatest accomplishment in the fields of law and politics. Three main manuscripts survive, indicating a first (*I Polity*) form and a greatly expanded revision (*II Polity*).[15] This work defines the duties of all classes of men, though it

13. Wulfstan, Archbishop of York and Bishop of Worcester and homiletic writer (Wulfstan II of York), should not be confused with St. Wulfstan, Bishop of Worcester (d. 1095) (Wulfstan II of Worcester), the last of the Anglo-Saxon bishops in Norman England.

14. The *Canons* was Wulfstan's first major work, a learned and comprehensive set of instructions to his secular clergy to combat the abuses he had earlier preached against. See R. G. Fowler, "'Archbishop Wulfstan's Commonplace-Book' and the *Canons of Edgar*," *MÆ*, XXXII (1963), 1–10.

15. Jost, *Die "Institutes of Polity* . . ."; a valuable critical summary and review by D. Whitelock appears in *RES*, N.S. XII (1961), 61–66.

does not include the specific lay obligations of thegns, *ceorlas*, and slaves except as they impinge upon their religious duties. Beginning with the responsibilities of the king, Wulfstan moves to the doctrine (taken from Ælfric's *Letter to Sigeweard*) of the three supports of the throne: preachers, workers, and warriors—then to the duties of those in authority, starting with the highest ecclesiasts, and moving to secular government in the persons of such as earls, reeves, judges, and lawyers. By defining the limits of power, Wulfstan tries to clarify the interrelationship of the Church and the secular state. Probably also by Wulfstan, at least as a rewriting—an attribution made by a study of style—is the *Rectitudines Singularum Personarum* and its second part *Gerefa*.[16] If this attribution is correct, it would nicely complement the *Institutes*, treating as it does of the lay duties of tenants of a great fief to their temporal lord and in more detail of the manorial duties of the reeve.

Students of English literature, however, have rightly been most interested in Wulfstan as a homilist. Unlike Ælfric's, Wulfstan's sermons (they are really more sermon than homily—see n. 5) were not written around the calendar of saints' days; Miss Bethurum (n. 12) groups them around subjects: eschatology, the Christian faith, archiepiscopal functions, and evil days. It is one of the last group (Miss Bethurum's xx) that has made the greatest impression upon readers, the famous *Sermo Lupi ad Anglos*.[17] This "Sermon of Wolf to the English," extant in five manuscripts, was preached in the troublesome times between Æthelred's expulsion in 1013 and his death in 1016, most likely in 1014. The pulpit orator is nowhere more thunderous than in this denunciation of the English for their sins, sins which had occasioned their destructive persecution by the Danes. Toward the end of his sermon, Wulfstan makes specific mention of Gildas' earlier excoriation of the Britons for their sinful responsibility for the Anglo-Saxon persecutions; actually, he took

16. See D. Bethurum, "Episcopal Magnificence in the Eleventh Century," in *Studies in Old English Literature in Honor of Arthur G. Brodeur*, ed. Stanley B. Greenfield (Eugene, Oregon: University of Oregon Books, 1963), pp. 162–170. The text is edited by F. Liebermann, *Die Gesetze der Angelsachsen*, I, (Halle a. S., 1903–1916), 444–455.

17. In addition to her separate edition (see above, n. 12), Miss Whitelock furnishes a translation in *English Historical Documents*, item 240, from which I cite below.

this Gildas reference from Alcuin, who had used it to point the same
moral to the monks at Lindisfarne after the Viking raids of 793!
Wulfstan begins:

> Beloved men, realize what is true: this world is in haste and
> the end approaches; and therefore in the world things go from
> bad to worse, and so it must of necessity deteriorate greatly on
> account of the people's sins before the coming of Antichrist, and
> indeed it will then be dreadful and terrible far and wide
> throughout the world.

Over and over again he calls attention to treachery and disloyalty
as the cardinal sin: "There has been little loyalty among men,
though they spoke fair enough"; "For now for many years, as it
may seem, there have been in this country many injustices and
wavering loyalties among men everywhere"; "Nor had anyone had
loyal intentions toward another as justly he should, but almost
everyone has deceived and injured another by word or deed"; "For
here in the country, there are great disloyalties both in matter of
Church and State . . . [he proceeds to some detail, including mention of the death of Edward the Martyr and the expulsion of
Æthelred]"; "Many are forsworn and greatly perjured, and pledges
are broken again and again." And, in somewhat atypical fashion for
Wulfstan, he resorts to realistic detail to characterize the evil days
that have befallen the English; for example, "And often ten or a
dozen, one after another, insult disgracefully the thegn's wife, and
sometimes his daughter or near kinswoman, whilst he looks on, who
considered himself brave and mighty and stout enough before that
happened."

In this sermon as in others, Wulfstan's method of composition
was careful and painstaking: he collected Latin selections on the
topic from the most authoritative sources and then translated and
expanded them into a sermon, pausing in the development to
reflect on religious or ethical truths suggested by his sources.
Rhetorical questions or exclamations frequently introduce such
reflections.

Realistic detail, or specificity, which Wulfstan generally felt
unsuitable for his sermons (perhaps he had a "Puritan" fear that the
audience would enjoy the details for their own sake?), is more

characteristic of Ælfric. In other ways, too, the archbishop's subject matter and style differ from the abbot's. In line with his avoidance of realism and his practical morality, he does not use metaphors, similes, or analogical interpretation of Scripture. He eschews the lives of saints, and except where his sources make it requisite, he avoids straight narrative technique. Though he uses a rhythmic prose which superficially resembles that developed by Ælfric from his *Lives of the Saints* onward, Wulfstan intensifies his rhythms into a strong two-stress system based on independent syntactic units, or at least on breath groups, that somewhat resembles that of classical Old English verse.[18] He heightens the emotional pitch of his sermons still further by a profusion of intensifying adjectives and adverbs; and he uses more alliteration and rhyme and a greater parallelism of word and clause than Ælfric. Rhetorically, he depends heavily on the repetitive devices prescribed in medieval manuals of rhetoric, such as Alcuin's, which were mainly based on Cicero. And he has certain pet phrases and tricks of expression, as well as favorite vocabulary items, that distinguish him from Ælfric (for example, the "beloved men" salutation at the beginning of the *Sermo Lupi ad Anglos*, and the use of *dryhten* "Lord" where Ælfric has *haelend* "Savior").[19] A short passage from Ælfric's *De Falsis Deis* ("On Heathen Gods"), and Wulfstan's rewriting of it for *his* sermon, will illustrate various of these differences:

> Ælf.:  *A*n man waes *ea*rdigende / on þam *e*glande Creta, // *S*aturnus gehaten, / *s*wiðlice and wælreow, // swa þæt he a*b*at his sunan, / þaþa hi ge*b*orene wæron, // and un-*f*æderlice *m*acode / heora *f*læsc him to *m*ete; // he *l*æfde swaþeah / ænne him to *l*ife, // þeahþe he a*b*ite / his ge*b*roðra onær.
>
> [There was a man dwelling on the Island Crete, called Saturn, cruel and bloodthirsty, so that he ate his sons as

18. This style has been carefully analyzed by A. McIntosh (see above, n.12). For expansion and modification, see O. Funke, "Some Remarks on Wulfstan's Prose Rhythms," *ES*, XLIII (1962), 311–318. Jost edits major portions of the *Institutes of Polity* in two-stress lines to give reality to McIntosh's findings. See reservations in n. 20 below.

19. For a thorough study of Wulfstan's stylistic traits, see the sections on "The Canon" and on "Style" in Bethurum, *Homilies*. On pp. 93–94 Miss Bethurum gives a fine detailed analysis of a Wulfstanian sentence.

soon as they were born, and in an unpaternal way made
their flesh his meat; he left, nevertheless, one alive, though
he had eaten his brothers formerly.]

Wulf: *A*n man wæs on geardagum // *ea*rdiende on þam *i*glande /
þe Creata hatte // *s*e wæs *S*aturnus gehaten; // ond se
wæs swa wælhreow // þæt he fordyde // his agene bearn //
*ea*lle butan *a*num // ond unfæderlice macode // heora *l*ife
to *l*yre // sona on geogoðe. // He *l*æfde swaþeah *u*neaðe //
*æ*nne to *l*ife, // þeah ðe he fordyde // þa broþra elles.

[There was a man in days of yore, dwelling on the island
which is called Crete, who was called Saturn; and he was
so bloodthirsty that he destroyed his own children all
except one, and in an unpaternal way brought their life
to loss straightway in youth. He left, however, unwillingly
one alive, though he had destroyed the brothers otherwise.]

I have attempted in the markings of the above passages to indicate
the difference in breath groups, phrasing, and alliterative patterns
in the two men: Ælfric's phrasing is longer, and its two halves are
often bound by alliteration, whereas Wulfstan's are shorter (two-
stress) with alliteration predominantly within the two-stress phras-
ings. Wulfstan's characteristic softening of realistic detail appears,
moreover, in his handling of Saturn's eating of his children. His use
of intensifying adjectives and adverbs is not revealed, however, in
these sentences.

The difference between Ælfric's and Wulfstan's rhythms and
Alfred's may be seen by viewing the above lines side by side with the
following from the voyage of Ohthere that Alfred inserted into his
translation of Orosius' *History*:

Ohthere sæde his hlaforde, Ælfrede cyninge, ðæt he ealra
Norðmonna norðmest bude. He cwæð ðæt he bude on ðæm lande
norðweardum wið ða Westsæ.

[Othere told his lord, King Alfred, that he dwelt furthest
north of all the Norsemen. He said that he dwelt in that land
(which is) northwards along the West {i.e., North} Sea.]

Alliteration and phrasing in the Alfredian sentence have not been
marked; the sentence can be read in several ways. But the style

exhibits a simplicity, limpidity, and periodicity that is very attractive.[20]

Of Wulfstan's other works, the prose portions of *The Benedictine Office* are of some significance. The *Office* is the English liturgy adapted from the Benedictine Rule, with introductory material from Hrabanus Maurus, the Carolingian expositor, and metrical paraphrases in the native Cædmonian tradition. The latest editor[21] believes that Wulfstan rewrote an existing vernacular text, which he postulates was Ælfric's translation; but the attribution of such a hypothetical text to Ælfric is dubious, and much still remains to be clarified about the literary relationship of the two most eminent prose stylists of early eleventh-century England.[22] * * *

Reprinted from Stanley B. Greenfield, *A Critical History of Old English Literature* (New York: New York University Press, 1965), pp. 47–58.

20. I cannot agree with O. Funke (see above, n. 18), that "neither speaker nor hearer would feel any rhythmical movement in these periods [he pauses after *hlaforde, cyninge,* and the first *bude* only]; it is ordinary non-metrical prose." By pausing additionally and naturally after *Norðmonna,* the second *bude,* and *norð-weardum,* I can even obtain satisfying two-stress groups! The point so far as Wulfstan's rhythms is concerned is that we should not inflexibly try to fit his prose into the Procrustean two-stress phrasing, nor call that which does not fit "bad" prose. MS pointing may be a good guide, but when we are left "unpointed" we should proceed with extreme caution.

21. J. M. Ure, *The Benedictine Office* (Edinburgh: University Press, 1957).

22. See P. Clemoes, "The Old English Benedictine Office, CCCC MS 190, and the Relations between Ælfric and Wulfstan: a Reconsideration," *Anglia,* LXXVIII (1960), 265–283.

CRITICAL INTERPRETATIONS OF POEMS

BERNARD F. HUPPÉ

# *Caedmon's* Hymn

CAEDMON's *Hymn* survives because Bede included a Latin translation of it in his *Ecclesiastical History* (and because an early scribe saw the value of including the English original in his copy). The manner in which the first Christian poem in English is preserved is fortunate because the poem can be studied from an established frame of reference, Bede's concept of the purpose and function of poetry. Bede's reaction to the poem provides a test of the applicability of Augustinian poetics to the study of Christian poetry in English. He tells the story of Caedmon's *Hymn* thus:[1]

> In the monastery of Abbess Hild was a brother [named Caedmon] specially marked and honored through divine grace for he did create songs of piety and faith. Whatever he learned of divine Scripture through scholars, in a brief space of time he adorned and brought forth in the poetic form of the English tongue, well wrought and of the greatest sweetness and inspiration. And through his songs made for the people, the hearts of many men were enkindled to turn from the world toward the companionship of eternal life. Likewise many another in the English nation followed his lead in making songs firmly fixed in the faith, but none might equal him in this because not by means of men nor through any man had he learned the art of song, rather had he been divinely inspired and had received the art of verse through the grace of God. And for this reason he could never make idle or lying songs but only such as were appropriate to true faith and fitting for his faithful tongue to sing.
>
> Now this man had remained in the secular state until he was advanced in age and had never learned any song. Thus often at

1. The translation follows the OE version of the *History*, ed. T. Miller (London: K. Paul, Trench, Trübner, 1890–1891). For the *Hymn* see *Three Northumbrian Poems*, ed. A. H. Smith (London: Methuen and Co., 1933).

the feast when there was adjudged an occasion for rejoicing and each in turn was to sing to the accompaniment of the harp, then as he saw the harp near his place, he arose for shame from the feast and went home to his house.

At a certain time when he had done this and had left the house of feasting, he went out to the cattle-barn, for that night was his to watch. When he had, at the proper time, laid his limbs to rest and slept, then in his sleep a man stood before him, hailed and greeted him and called him by name, "Caedmon, sing me something."

Then he replied and said, "I can sing nothing, and that is why I left the feast and came hither, because I knew nothing to sing."

Again he who was speaking with him spoke: "Nevertheless you must sing for me."

Then he said, "What shall I sing?"

Said he, "Sing to me of the Creation."

When he had received this answer, then forthwith he proceeded to sing in praise of God the Creator, verses and words which he had never heard, the order of which is this:

> Nu we sculan herian   heofonrices weard
> metudes myhte   ond his modgeþanc
> wurc wuldorfæder.   Swa he wundra gehwilc
> ece drihten   ord onstealde.
> He ærest gesceop   ylda bearnum
> heofon to hrofe   halig scyppend.
> Middangearde   mancynnes weard
> ece drihten   æfter tida
> firum on foldum   frea ælmihtig.

[Now we should praise the Ward of heaven's kingdom: / the Might of God and His Wisdom, / the Work of the Glory-Father. So he of each wonder, / the Eternal Lord, established the beginning. / He first created for the sons of men / heaven as a roof, the Holy Creator. / The middle-earth the Ward of Mankind, / the Eternal Lord, thereafter adorned / for men on earth, the Almighty Joy. / ]

Then he arose from his sleep, and all that he had sung sleeping he retained in his mind, and to these words he soon joined in the same meter many another song worthy through God.

Subsequently, according to Bede, Caedmon was brought to the abbess, and his miraculous gift of song was tested. Convinced by these tests, Hild had scholars teach him. What he learned he turned into songs, which, in turn, the scholars transcribed. He wrote poems based on Genesis, Exodus, and other books of the Old Testament and on Christ's ministry, Passion, and so forth. His purpose was "in all these writings," as Bede says, "to draw men away from the love of sin and evil deeds and to arouse them to an eagerness and love for good deeds."

What was important for Bede in this story, we may be sure, was the miracle that solemnized the birth of Christian poetry in English. Yet in telling the story Bede shows no overwhelming surprise at the strangeness of the event; he simply treats the story seriously, with reverence. He had ample precedent, of course, for the connection of poetry with religious inspiration. The word itself had been connected even by pagans with religious ceremonial in praise of their gods. More important for Bede, the Bible, the word of God, contained poetry that was by definition divinely inspired and was considered to be the first poetry written by men.[2] That God should specially mark with the honor of divine grace the first Christian poem in English must have seemed to Bede miraculous but, paradoxically, not surprising. Consequently he felt none of the doubts that today we feel and had no need to explain what in his account we now find difficult to understand. Nevertheless, for the students of literature the miraculous poem presents a special problem in critical judgment: Does the poem itself represent a worthy beginning to English poetry, or does its only worth rest in its historical position?[3]

2. Isidore of Seville, "De Poetis," *Etymologiae*, ed. W. Lindsay (Oxford: Oxford University Press, 1911), VIII, vii. See Smith, *op. cit.*, p. 14. The primacy of biblical poetry is enunciated by Jerome. (See the Preface to Eusebius' *Chronicle*, *PL*, 27, 36; Preface to Job, *PL*, 28, 1081.) See Isidore's "De Metris," *Etymologiae*, I xxxix, 11. Christian writings contain many examples of the achievement of knowledge through divine inspiration. See Augustine's preface to his *De doctrina*; his *De civitate Dei*, XVIII, xlii; and *De doctrina*, IV, vii, 15–21; also Cassian, *De institutis cenoborium*, V, xxxiii.

3. It is most instructive to read C. L. Wrenn, *The Poetry of Caedmon* (London: Geoffrey Cumberlege, 1947), p. 9: "At first the Hymn may seem to have little intrinsic worth as poetry. Yet the more one reads it and allows it to become assimilated in one's mind, the more one feels it has qualities of balanced and rhythmic grandeur which still have some poetic appeal"; and then to read the review by George Kane in *MLR*, XLIII (1948), 250–252: "The Hymn has hardly enough literary merit to allow of discussing it at any length as a piece of poetry. . . . Finally, not everyone will be as certain of the high literary quality of Caedmon's poem as either Bede or Professor Wrenn appears to be."

First of all, Bede was probably not much concerned about anything but the miracle itself and its revelation of God's meaning. "His business was religion; even his interest in the actual poetry produced by the miracle is a religious one."[4] Another way of saying this is that his attitude toward poetry is Augustinian. Thus, without compromise of religious seriousness he responded to the beauty he perceived in the poem and testified to his inability to translate it since translation involves "loss of beauty and loftiness."[5] For Bede God, through his angel, was the true author of the *Hymn*. Since God is the source of all beauty, it follows that for Bede the *Hymn* had some relation to the divinely inspired poetry of Scripture. Angelic inspiration implies revelation: The angel brings to a chosen vessel, characteristically humble, the obligation to receive and to be the first to communicate God's word in English poetry. In consequence and within the limitations of its language, Caedmon's *Hymn* must for the believer have seemed as nearly perfect as man's work may be; either the poem was beautiful to the eyes of faith, or there was no miracle. It is impossible that God should have inspired what is inferior or merely workmanlike. Since the demands of faith on the little poem were very large, Bede must have seen in it much more than the best disposed modern is likely to allow. Hence the question: How could Bede have found in the brief and simple hymn an exemplification of true Christian poetry? In short, how would he have found in the *Hymn* that exercise of the mind which promotes understanding?

4. Kane, *op. cit.*, p. 251. Kane is quite rightly protesting against Wrenn's conjecture that the miracle had primarily "artistic" interest (p. 12); but Kane's remark has itself pejorative implications against which it is well to put such a vigorous defense of the purposes of early Christian writers as that by O. Kuhnmuench, *Early Christian Latin Poets* (Chicago: Loyola University Press, 1929), pp. 3–4. See P. C. De Labriolle, *Histoire de la littérature latin chrétienne*, rev., G. Bardy (Paris: Belles-Lettres, 1947), *passim*; also E. K. Rand, *Founders of the Middle Ages*, 2nd ed. (Cambridge, Mass.: Harvard University Press, 1941), Chap. VI.

5. He translates Caedmon's hymn into Latin prose. The remark is found only in the Latin original, of course (*Historia ecclesiastica*, in *Venerabilis Baedae Opera Historica*, ed. C. Plummer [Oxford: Oxford University Press, 1896], I, 259–260): "Hic est sensus, non autem ordo ipse uerborum, quae dormiens ille canebat; neque enim possunt carmina, quamuis optime conposita, ex alia in aliam linguam ad uerbum sine detrimento sui decoris ac dignitatis transferri" ⟨This is the meaning and not the same order of words which he was composing while asleep; for the poems, although very well composed, can not be translated from one language to another without detriment to their beauty and dignity⟩.

Since Caedmon sings of the creation and celebrates the might of God in establishing the beginning of created things, in particular of heaven and earth, his *Hymn* is to be related to the opening verses of the first chapter of Genesis: "In the beginning God created heaven and earth. . . ." But surely, even for Bede, there must have appeared something of an anticlimax if all that was involved in the angelic inspiration was the simple elaboration of the beginning of Genesis in the repetitive parallels of OE verse. An approach toward understanding what Bede saw in the *Hymn* is provided by biblical commentary on the opening verses of Genesis.[6] For the Fathers of the Church, as for the priest delivering a sermon to the people, the opening verses of Genesis had acquired dogmatic connotations. The verses did not stand alone. Their underlying meaning had become a basic and indispensable part of Christian doctrine.[7]

Bede himself wrote synoptic commentaries on Genesis.[8] As he points out, he relies chiefly on the authoritative hexameral commentary of Basil, as translated into Latin by Eustathius, on the commentary of Ambrose, and on that of Augustine. These commentaries, to which may be added that of Isidore, are basic and indispensable, and they, along with Bede's own commentary, should afford us some guide to the meaning that Genesis had for him.[9] We discover immediately that the opening verse of Genesis was considered especially to reveal the divine source of scriptural inspiration. The first verse of Genesis was said to have been written by Moses "in the spiritual excellence of revelation as if he were a witness of divine truth." Caedmon, too, was inspired, for according to Bede his

6. See C. Spicq, *Esquisse d'une histoire de l'exégèse latine* (Paris: 1944), pp. 10–30; B. Smalley, *The Study of the Bible in the Middle Ages* (London: Oxford University Press, 1941), pp. xiv–xv; D. Robertson and B. Huppé, *"Piers Plowman" and Scriptural Tradition* (Princeton: Princeton University Press, 1951), pp. 1–20; De Labriolle, *op. cit.*, pp. 408–409; Kuhnmuench, *op. cit.*, p. 2.

7. The last part of Augustine's *Confessions* (XI–XIII) consists in commentary on the opening of Genesis, verses basic to his faith, thus part of his spiritual autobiography. Compare Ælfric's "On the Old and New Testament" and "Preface to Genesis," in his *The Heptateuch*, ed. S. J. Crawford (London: Oxford University Press, 1922 ⟨EETS 160⟩), pp. 15–29 and 76–80. See also Augustine's *De catechizandis rudibus*; Eucherius, *Instructiones ad Salonium*, *PL*, 50, 773.

8. Spicq, *op. cit.*, pp. 30–31; M. Laistner, "Bede as a Classical and Patristic Scholar," in *Transactions of the Royal Historical Society*, 4th ser., XVI (1933), 79–94.

9. Bede, "Preface" to the *Hexameron*, *PL*, 91, 9–11.

*Hymn* was "a heavenly gift" (*caelestiem gratiam*) granted him by God. Genesis was said to be pure and without the worldly taint inherent in works written "in the conviction of human wisdom or in the pretenses and disputes of philosophy."[10] Caedmon's *Hymn* was written by a man so far from pretension to worldly learning that he even lacked the knowledge of song possessed by his unlettered fellows. To underscore the divine inspiration and purpose of Genesis, St. Basil calls Moses not the writer but "the *editor* of this scripture . . . Who, equal to the angels in having seen God, makes known to us what he heard from God." Thus the words of Moses, read in the light not of "human wisdom" but of spiritual doctrine, aided in "the salvation of those who learn."[11] Similarly, through Caedmon's "songs made for the people, the hearts of many men were enkindled to turn from the world toward the companionship of eternal life." And again, "Caedmon labored to remove men from the love of wickedness and to excite them truly to an eagerness and love of good deeds."

Comparison of the power of Caedmon's poem with the efficacy of the opening of Genesis provided Bede with a pragmatic test of the worth of the poem, although he did not, of course, believe that Moses and Caedmon were really comparable. Moses had seen God face to face and in this was the "equal of the angels"; whereas Caedmon was inspired to write in praise of God's creation in a vision and through the intervention of an angel. Yet a clear line of relationship connects Caedmon, the poet who wrote about Scripture in the vernacular, and Moses, who, in the language of Adam, wrote Scripture itself. Although Bede would have distinguished degrees of veneration to be accorded the word of God as reported by Moses and a divinely inspired poem, he would have expected each, in its degree, to contain some revelation and therefore to be worthy of the closest study.

For Bede the best evidence of the authenticity of Caedmon's vision would have been that the *Hymn* reflects some of the divine truths implanted by God through the agency of Moses in the beginning of Genesis. These truths—or some of them at least—had been

10. Ambrose, *Hexameron*, *PL*, 14, 136.
11. Eustathius, *In hexameron S. Basilii latina metaphrasis*, *PL*, 53, 868–869. Cf. Augustine, *Confessions*, XI, iii, 5.

brought to the knowledge of the faithful through the commentaries of the Fathers. Not only the verse, but also the very form, the order of words, *in principio fecit deus coelum et terram* ⟨in the beginning God made heaven and earth⟩, was considered by the Fathers to be divinely inspired and uniquely beautiful.[12] What literary criticism meant to the Christian of the early Middle Ages is suggested by St. Basil's delighted discovery that the very form of the first verse is itself meaningful: "*In principio fecit Deus,* Lo! the beauty of order in which Moses placed the beginning first," for thus Moses set forth the fundamental truth that God *created* the world, that it was not "engendered or innate." Immediately thereafter he set down the verb, *fecit,* Basil continues, to show "that the miracle of the creation is a little part of the excellence of the Maker." Then to teach man to "seek Who is the Maker, Moses, as if fixing a sign of his care, reverently introduced the name of God," *Deus.*[13] St. Ambrose also exclaims at "the excellent ordering" of placing *in principio* first, "so that Moses asserts that first which heretics were wont to deny." Ambrose finds even further artistic subtlety in the order of words, with *fecit* following *in principio*: "And beautifully Moses added *fecit* lest there be supposed a delay in creation." Furthermore, Moses in adding the subject, *Deus,* immediately after the verb, *fecit,* takes advantage of the natural human desire "to seek the Maker Who gave a beginning to so much work, Who so quickly made it." The result for Ambrose is absolute conviction: "You have heard the Author, you cannot doubt. . . . You can see because man did not discover this, rather God announced it."[14] St. Augustine eloquently agrees with Ambrose concerning the power of the opening verse of Genesis: "Marvelous the profundity of Thy words whose outer show is before us guiding the little ones. Terror there is in looking within, the terror of honor and the trembling of love."[15]

12. It was, of course, understood that the Latin was itself a translation, but a translation felt to possess something of the beauty of the original. The Greek Septuagint was felt to be divinely inspired, but although Augustine in the *De doctrina* gives the Septuagint precedence over the Latin, he used the Latin in his study of biblical eloquence. The weight of his authority was sufficient to sanction the letter of the Latin.

13. Eustathius, *PL,* 53, 870.

14. Ambrose, *PL,* 14, 137.

15. *Confessions,* XII, xiv, 17.

Although these judgments by men whose business was religion are basically religious, they are, nonetheless, aesthetic. As the *De doctrina* suggests, the Fathers were concerned with spiritual meaning, but they were concerned with the beautiful as well, with the placing of the best words in the best possible order. For them harmony and number are beautiful only because they reveal in outward formal symmetry the spiritual harmony and order of the Creator.[16] St. Basil and St. Augustine considered the first verse of Genesis to be beautiful because the form reveals an inner meaning consonant with spiritual truth. In its perfect fusion of form and meaning the verse serves as a model for the beautiful in Christian writing. Caedmon's creation hymn, to seem divinely inspired, must have appeared to reflect the supreme excellence of its source. Bede's "appreciation" of the *Hymn* would in turn have derived from a method of reading it similar to that which led to his appreciation of the biblical verses on the creation, except that in the *Hymn* he would seek not original revelation, but simply reaffirmation of biblical truths. It is against these truths that the arrangements of the parts of the *Hymn* must be balanced. Biblical commentary may provide a method for approaching the poem and a key to its order and meaning.

The *Hymn* falls naturally into three main divisions. The first two and one-half lines state the theme of praise:

> We should praise the Ward of Heaven:
> the Might of God, His Wisdom,
> the Glory-Father's Work.

There follows a general statement about God's creation:

> So He of each wonder
> the Eternal Lord established the beginning.

Finally comes the paraphrase of the first verse of Genesis:

> He first created for the sons of men
> heaven as a roof, the Holy Creator,
> then the middle-earth, the Ward of Mankind,
> the Eternal Lord, thereafter adorned
> for men on earth, the Almighty Joy.

What might Bede have perceived in this arrangement?

16. E. De Bruyne, *Etudes d'esthétique médiévale* (Brussels: Rijksuniverstat te Gent, 1946), I, 36, and *passim*.

The initial theme of praise he would have felt to be especially appropriate to a creation hymn. Ambrose considered that heaven and earth were created in the beginning "in evidence of things unseen," and he cites Psalm 18:1, "The heavens proclaim the glory of God and the firmament announces the works of His hands," to show that the function of the creation is to praise God.[17] Significantly, the theme of praise of the Creator by his creatures formed from the very earliest times the substance of the Preface in the Ordinary of the Mass: "Vere dignum et justum est, aequum et salutare, nos tibi semper et undique gratias agere, domine sancte, Pater omnipotens, aeterne Deus" ⟨Indeed, it is worthy and just, right and commendable, that we give thanks to you always and everywhere, holy Lord, almighty Father, eternal God⟩. This is the portion of the Mass, according to Walafrid Strabo, "in which the will of the people is directed toward thanksgiving."[18] Inspired by the words of the Preface and finding in them an excellent introduction to his poem on Genesis, St. Hilary of Arles begins his *In Genesim*:

> Dignum opus et iustum semper tibi dicere grates
> omnipotens mundi genitor, quo principio cuncta
> natalem sumpsere diem atque exorta repente
> post tenebras stupidi spectarunt lumina caeli.

> [Worthy and right is it always to say thanks to You / Almighty Creator of the world, in which Beginning all things / assumed their natal day and, suddenly born / after the shadows, amazed, looked at the lights of heaven.][19]

Caedmon in English is making the same connection of ideas. The purpose of God's creation is to praise and glorify His name. This purpose is especially revealed in the creation itself. In beginning

17. Ambrose, *PL*, 14, 141.

18. *De rebus ecclisiasticis*, *PL*, 114, 948. The formula of the Preface, *Vere dignum* ⟨Indeed worthy⟩, is found in the earliest liturgies. See, for example, the Gregorian liturgy (*PL*, 78, 24–25); see also the *Catholic Encyclopedia*, *s. v.*, "Preface." The office of the Mass seems a more likely influence on the yet secular Caedmon than the monastic office of the hours suggested by I. Gollancz, *The Caedmon Manuscript* (Oxford: Oxford University Press, 1927), p. lxi. The *nu* is probably a generalized, not a specific, expression.

19. *PL*, 50, 1287.

with the theme of praise, Caedmon seems to give emphasis to what is most important for man to learn: that he should praise God in word and works. Bede would certainly have perceived the connection of ideas and would have appreciated the opening theme of praise for its appropriateness to the subject of the *Hymn,* the creation.

In his admonition to praise God, Caedmon develops the reasons for praise of the Ward of Heaven in three parallel epithets: "the Might of God," "His Wisdom," "the Glory-Father's Work." In these three epithets Bede might well have found a trinitarian significance. The belief in "God the Father Almighty, Creator of heaven and earth," as triune was established by St. Athanasius as the basic article of Christian faith. In this regard the opening verses of Genesis were especially important because they represented for the Fathers the *locus classicus* of scriptural evidence for the Trinity. Ælfric, much later than Caedmon but in his language, gives succinctly the conventional patristic interpretation:

> The Almighty Creator showed Himself through the great work which he created in the beginning, and He wished his creatures to perceive his glory and dwell with Him in glory eternally. . . . Here is the Holy Trinity in these three persons: the Almighty Father, born of no other, and the great Wisdom born of the Wise Father alone without beginning. . . . Now is the Love of Both ever the same with Them, that is the Holy Ghost, Who vivified all things.

Ælfric here summarizes the standard interpretation of the beginning of Genesis, by which the verses are made to reveal not only the Creator, but also the three elements or parts of the act of creation. The three elements distinguished are aspects of the Creator, manifest in His act of creation; and they represent the Three Persons in One Creator. As Ælfric explains in one of his Catholic homilies, the creation was accomplished through the act of the Father, by the agency of Wisdom, the Son, and completed in Love, or Will, the Holy Spirit.

How the fathers arrived at this underlying meaning is illustrated by Ælfric in his Preface to Genesis:

> *In the beginning God created the heaven and earth.* It is literal truth that God Almighty, as He wished, made in the beginning, created things. Nevertheless according to the spiritual under-

standing that beginning is Christ, just as He Himself said to the Jews, "I am the Beginning Who speak to you." Through this beginning God the Father wrought heaven and earth, because He created all creation through the Son Who was eternally born of Him, the Wisdom of the Wise Father. Afterward, in the next verse in the book stands . . . *The Spirit of God brooded over the waters.* God's Spirit is the Holy Spirit through Whom the Father vivified all creation which He shaped through the Son.[20]

Ælfric is quoted not because the ideas he expressed are in any way original with him, but simply because he wrote in English and with masterful clarity. He is, of course, reiterating a patristic common-place.[21] The Fathers ascribe "to the Father the creation of the world, to the Son, the disposition of things, to the Holy Spirit, the vivifying

20. "On the Old and New Testament" and "Preface to Genesis" in Crawford (ed.), *op. cit.*, pp. 16–17 and 78; "Sermon on the Creation," in the *Homilies of the Anglo-Saxon Church*, ed. B. Thorpe (London, 1849), I, 10.

21. Ambrose, *PL*, 14, 150: "*Et spiritus Dei superferebatur super aquas* . . . nos tamen cum sanctorum et fidelium sententia congruentes, Spiritum sanctum accipimus, ut in constitutione mundi operatio Trinitatis eluceat. Praemisso enim quia *in principio fecit Deus coelum et terram*, id est, in Christo fecit Deus, vel Filius Dei Deus fecit, vel per Filium Deus fecit; quia omnia per ipsum facta sunt, et sine ipso factum est nihil, supererat plenitudo operationis in Spiritu" ⟨*And the spirit of God brooded over the waters* . . . we, however, in accord with the opinion of the saints and the faithful, accept the holy Spirit, so that the work of the Trinity may shine forth in the creation of the world. The premise being that *in the beginning God made heaven and earth*, that is, God created it in Christ, or the Son of God, as God, created it, or God made it through the Son; since all things were created through him, and without him nothing was created, the perfection of the work survived in the Spirit⟩. Augustine, *De Genesi ad litteram*, I, vi, 12: "Et quemadmodum in ipso exordio inchoatae creaturae, quae coeli et terrae nomine, propter id quod de illa perficiendum erat, commemorata est, Trinitas insinuatur Creatoris, nam dicente Scriptura, *In principio fecit Deus coelum et terram*; intelligimus Patrem in Dei nomine, et Filium in principii nomine, qui non Patri, sed per seipsum creatae primitus ac potissimum spirituali creaturae, et consequenter etiam universae creaturae principium est: dicente autem Scriptura, *Et spiritus Dei ferebatur super aquam*, completam commemorationem Trinitatis agnoscimus" ⟨It has been mentioned how, in the very beginning of creation, namely heaven and earth, on account of what was necessary for its carrying out, the Trinity of the Creator is involved; for when the Scripture says, *In the beginning God made heaven and earth*; we recognize the Father in the name "God," and the Son in the name "beginning" who, not through the Father but through his own self, was created first and most powerful of spiritual creation, and consequently in even the beginning of all creation: when the Scripture says, *And the spirit of God brooded over the waters*, we recognize the complete commemorization of the Trinity⟩.

or ornamenting of all things." [22] In the representation of the Trinity
through the creation, God the Father is the Power or Might, the Son
is the Shaping Wisdom, the Holy Ghost, the Perfection of the Work.

These commonplaces of patristic interpretation might well have
prepared Bede to perceive the mystery of the Trinity in the three
aspects of God's creation singled out in the *Hymn* as demanding
praise:

> metudes myhte   ond his modgeþanc,
> wurc wuldorfæder

[The Might of God and His Wisdom (the thought of his mind), /
the Work of the Glory-Father.]

The three phrases reflect the traditional division of the three Persons
of the Trinity as they are revealed in Genesis: the Might of God, the
Creator, would represent the Father; the Thought of the Father,
His plan and disposition of creation, the Son; the Work, the Holy
Ghost. Insofar as the opening lines seem to reflect in their ordering
the eternal truth, that is, God, they also reflect the radiance of God,
the only source of beauty. To discover, in the ordering of the words
of the *Hymn*, the revealed truth was for Bede to perceive its formal
beauty.

The first part of the *Hymn* consists in an exhortation to praise the
Creator and possibly in an implicit suggestion of the mystery of the
Trinity as revealed in the creation. In the second part of the poem
Caedmon paraphrases "in the beginning":

> So He, of each wonder
> the Eternal Lord, established the beginning.

This beginning occured, according to St. Basil, outside time, for
"just as the beginning of the way is not the way, and the beginning
of a house is not yet the house, thus also the beginning of time is not
yet the fullness of time, nor even a small part of time." [23] "In the

---

22. Honorius of Autun, *Hexameron*, PL, 172, 254. For the Holy Spirit as the
perfection of the work, see the phrase of Ambrose, n. 21 above, "plenitudo operationis in Spiritu" ⟨the perfection of the work in the Spirit⟩. Bede translates Caedmon's three epithets as *potentiam, consilium, facta* ⟨power, counsel (wisdom),
action⟩. (See above n. 5.)

23. Eustathius, PL, 53, 874.

beginning" teaches us that God created outside of time in His eternity. He established the beginning of all from nothing (*ex nihilo*). Moreover, that act of creation in the beginning "gives the form of the future circles of the years." All that was to be in time was created in idea in the beginning.[24] This mystery of time and eternity, of which Augustine speaks at length in his commentary in the *Confessions*, is suggested in the second section of Caedmon's *Hymn* by the setting off of the adjective "eternal" against the noun, "beginning." The verses thus specifically describe, not the creation of all things, but the creation of their beginning.

Patristic exegesis has more to reveal about the underlying meaning of "in the beginning." The creation in the beginning was not of the heaven and earth "as man now sees them."[25] The earth, we are informed immediately in Genesis, was then *idle* and *empty*. But why should the idle emptiness of the earth be introduced "without mention of the heaven, except that nothing like this is to be understood of that heaven; for this is the very higher heaven which, secret from all condition of this revolving world, remains always quiet in the glory of divine prescience."[26] The world, which exists in time, could not yet exist in the beginning, which, timeless, gives the form of time; therefore the heaven created in the beginning must have been the eternal heaven, the *coelum coeli* ⟨heaven of heavens⟩, of which God is Ward.[27] In contrast the earth is yet formless. The eternal heaven was inhabited in the beginning by spiritual beings, "not coeternal with the Trinity, but participating in that eternity."[28] For simultaneously with the creation of the spiritual heaven, as Bede says, "it was filled with the blessed troops of angels, . . . called

24. Ambrose, *PL*, 14, 139: "Dedit ergo forman futuris annorum curriculis mundi primus exortus, ut ea lege annorum curriculis mundi primus exortus" ⟨Therefore, the initial origin of the world gave form to the future courses of the years as, by that law, the initial origin of the world [gave form] to the courses of the years⟩. Eustathius, *PL*, 53, 875.

25. *Confessions*, XII, viii, 8: "Sed illud coelum coeli tibi, Domine; terra autem quam dedisti filius hominum cernendam atque tangendam, non erat talis qualem nunc cernimus et tangimus" ⟨But that heaven of heaven is yours, Lord; but the earth which you, as the Son, gave to man to look upon and touch was not the same as we now look upon and touch⟩.

26. Bede, *PL*, 91, 13–14.

27. Augustine, *Confessions*, XII, xi, 12.

28. *Ibid.*, XI, ix, 9.

the sons of God to distinguish them, in truth, from the saints, who
were created later."[29] But, as St. Ambrose points out, in another
sense, the heaven created in the beginning was created for man. For
the spiritual heaven was a model for the heaven that man sees as
"the highest of visible things." The temporal heaven, which is "the
ornament of the world," is also "the representation of things in-
visible, the evidence of things unseen, as in the prophecy, *the heavens
declare the glory of God, and the firmament announces the works of His
hands.*"[30] The heaven of the beginning is not the heaven man sees,
but the spiritual meaning of that visible heaven.

In the light of such detailed interpretation of the creation *in
principio* a reader like Bede would not have found it difficult to see a
hidden significance in the order of the *Hymn*, which first states, "The
eternal Lord established the beginning of all wonders," then says:

> He first created for the sons of men
> heaven as a roof, the Holy Creator,
> then the middle-earth, the Ward of Mankind,
> the Eternal Lord, thereafter adorned
> for men on earth, the Almighty Joy.

The second and the last divisions of the poem seem to reflect the
patristic distinction between the creation *in principio* and the creation
of heaven and earth for the sons of men, which exists in time. In
contrast to the adjective "eternal" of the second division, we have
the adverbs, "first," "then," and "thereafter" of the final division.
Furthermore, the one metaphorical description in the poem,
"heaven as a roof," might well have suggested to Bede the spiritual
symbolism that related the heaven seen by man to the heaven of
heavens. Ambrose says that if we wish to discover the true nature of
the heaven above us we must ponder Isaiah 40:22: "God made
heaven like to a room."[31] In the same vein, Bede quotes St. Clem-
ent's summary of the creation, "In the beginning when God made
the heaven and earth, he made it like to one house"; in the course of
creation "the water, which was between heaven and earth as a
frozen solid, thawed"; the resulting firmament between the true

29. Bede, *op. cit.*, 13–14.
30. Ambrose, *PL*, 14, 141.
31. *Ibid.*, 143–144. See Eustathius, *PL*, 53, 876.

heaven and the earth "God called heaven." Thus, what in the
beginning "was one house, He divided into two regions; the reason
for this division was that the upper region was the dwelling of
angels; the lower, in truth, He granted to men."[32] Heaven and
earth were given man as a home, and the heavens, which form the
roof of that house, "declare the glory of God." They teach man to
praise God and to live so that he may see the eternal heaven that
was at the beginning. In short, God "first created for the sons of
man / heaven as a roof," as a reminder that "now we should praise
the Ward of Heaven."

Finally, Caedmon says of the earth that the *eternal* God *adorned it*
after He had made the heavens. Both the sequence of events and the
image of God's adorning the earth are in accord with Scripture as
the Fathers understood it. St. Ambrose says, for example, concerning the order of creation, "Primo fecit Deus, postea venustavit"
(First God created, thereafter he adorned).[33] This order reveals that
God is the only source of the beautiful.[34] Thus, the beauty of the
earth comes from God and proclaims its Creator.[35] The earth in its
beauty, like the heavens, reminds us to praise God and to think of
the uncorrupted beauty of the eternal. The order of phrasing in the
*Hymn*, "the middle-earth ... thereafter He adorned," reflects
Ambrose's understanding of the order of creation, the leading idea
of which is that "we should praise the Ward of Heaven."

The end of the *Hymn* returns us to its beginning. There Caedmon
rightly sings first of man's need to praise God, the Creator. The
Creator is the Trinity, the Might of the Fatherhood, the Wisdom of
the Word, the Perfection of the Holy Spirit. The mystery of the
Trinity demands our wonder and our praise. Caedmon gives now
another reason for praise: that though He was timeless, the eternal
Lord in His Love chose to create a beginning, not only of eternal
things, but also of temporal things. For He created the heavens to
be as a roof for mankind in token of the spiritual heaven above, his
home. The visible heavens not only declare the glory of God, but
also teach man to praise Him. Man's dwelling place in time, the

32. Bede, *PL*, 91, 19–20.
33. Ambrose, *PL*, 14, 148.
34. *Ibid.*, 149, and 153.
35. Cassiodorus, *De anima*, XII, *PL*, 69, 1304.

middle-earth, God afterward adorned so that man might perceive the Origin of beauty, God the Creator, and give thanks. The theme of the poem, explicitly stated at the beginning, is carried out implicitly in the underlying meanings suggested in the poem. Moreover, this thematic development is carried out in the details of word choice. As the three epithets that signify the Trinity are reflected in the tripartite division of the poem as a whole, so the poet's use of the remaining epithets for God seems further to reveal his adaptation of form to substance.

Caedmon first calls God the "Ward of Heaven," that is, of the *coelum coeli*, where He dwells eternally, Protector of His angels and saints. Next he speaks of Him as "the Eternal Lord," in the context of His establishing the beginning of all things; the epithet emphasizes the mystery of the creation of time by the Timeless. Only when Caedmon turns to the actual creation of heaven and earth for man does he call God the "Holy Creator"; it is in the visible works of God that man, inexorably bound in time and space, sees his Maker. With the mention of the earth, in contrast to the first epithet, "Ward of Heaven," Caedmon now calls God the "Ward of Mankind." The earth is man's temporal dwelling place; God is the Protector Who will lead him from the earth to his true home in heaven. To emphasize the greatness of the Protector He is again called the *Eternal Lord*, heedful of His people, but unknowable to a mind bound in time. The final epithet, *Frea Ælmihtig* (Almighty Joy or Almighty Lord), returns us to the thematic statement at the beginning of the poem. For *frea* means both joy and Lord, as God is both man's joy and his Lord. The true pleasure of man is to rejoice in the Creator. To sing of the creation, is, in fact, to rejoice in God, to praise Him as "we now should do."

The possibility of deliberate word selection in the *Hymn* links the English poem to Christian Latin poetry, with its problem of adapting a pagan vocabulary to new uses. And Bede's contrast between Caedmon's songs and the lying songs of others suggests that Bede thought of Caedmon as the first in England to call the poetic diction of his ancestors out of foreign bondage back into the service of the Master. The *Hymn* itself reveals that Caedmon is not content to give a simple, literal translation of biblical terms. A study of the diction of the poem serves to suggest the deliberate employment for Christian purposes of the pagan vocabulary of native heroic poetry. The vocabulary of Caedmon's *Hymn* is, in fact, likely to be the most striking aspect of the poem for the modern reader, who feels a certain clash between the military, even pagan, connotations of the epithets for God and the Christian idea of God the Creator. Thus, God is called "Ward of Heaven, Ward of Mankind." God establishes the *ord* (point or beginning), a word of military connotations. Caedmon refers to the earth as the "middle-earth," a word perhaps related to the cosmogony of Germanic myth.

In discussing Caedmon's choice of his epithets for God no estimate may be made of how much or how little pagan connotation remains as effective counterpoint to the Christian idea expressed. Study of Caedmon's adaptation of a pagan poetic diction is handicapped by the lack of recorded pre-Christian pagan verse. We cannot be sure how much has been changed and modified in the process of Christian transmission.[36] As a result, no absolute standards of comparison exist as they do for Latin Christian poetry. Caedmon's choice of the epithet for God, "Ward of Heaven," may have derived either from a similar biblical term, translated from the Latin in a sermon Caedmon may have heard, or from ancestral poetry.[37] In his use of the term, with its connotations of a ruler protecting his followers from armed assault, he may simply have been thinking of the King of Heaven, the Duke of the Celestial Host, Who protected His throne and His followers from Lucifer. On the other hand, he may have been guided in his choice of words by memory of the heroic king of his native history and fable. It is not certain, but it seems probable, that his choice depended in large part upon the appropriateness of the pagan word to its new Christian context. If, as seems probable, the epithet "ward" retained connotations of the activities of the heroic king, it would have served admirably to represent an important symbolic meaning of God.

The connotative force of the first epithet is enforced by Caedmon's selection of the phrase *ord onstealde* to describe the creation of the beginning. In its most concrete meaning *ord* refers to the point

36. See F. M. Stenton, *Anglo-Saxon England* (Oxford: Oxford University Press, 1947), p. 192: "The English poetry of the heathen age was first written down by Christian clerks, and most of it survives in texts which are affected by Christian ideas and imagery."

37. Scotus Erigena discusses in his *Expositiones*, *PL*, 122, 145–146, the meaning of the military figures used to represent heavenly beings.

of the sword, but this military denotation serves an important figurative purpose. In patristic commentary the fact was stressed that the beginning is not yet in time, "for the beginning of a house is not yet the house." Similarly the point of the sword is not the sword. Moreover, *ord* also refers to the front of battle, the foremost point, which the heroic king first establishes and where he makes his stand to the end. The establishment of this *ord*, or point of battle, does not constitute the battle, but it does represent the beginning of the battle. Derived from this is the compound *ord-fruma*, which is used in OE poetry to refer both to God, the Creator, and to an earthly prince.[38]

The epithet *wuldorfæder* (Glory-Father) may fit, though perhaps more doubtfully, into the pattern of military or heroic connotation, contrasting with and enforcing the underlying Christian meaning. The Glory of God is a Christian commonplace; the heroic king also fought for glory (*wuldor*). The glory of God is nowhere more manifest to men than in His creation; the glory and fame of a king of heroic myth was nowhere more apparent than in his words and deeds when, before battle, he established the battlefront. But beyond the reputation gained in the forefront of battle the glory of the heroic king sprang from his reputation as a protector, a ward, of his people—at least that is the impression one gains from *Beowulf*, although the impression is not decisive, since the heroic motifs in *Beowulf* seem themselves to have been adapted to a Christian purpose. At any rate, Caedmon appears with some degree of artistry to have contrived by his choice of epithets a counterpoint of connotations suggesting the kingliness of God, Who is, in fact, the True King. The idea is, of course, Christian, whatever were the original connotations of the words.[39]

Caedmon's choice of the epithet "middle-earth" to signify the earth on which man dwells may reflect the pagan cosmogony of Germanic myth. Therein the earth was pictured as set between the home of the gods above and the home of their enemies, the giants, below. But Aldhelm in his Riddle 100, *Creatura*, speaks of penetrating

38. For the various meanings of *ord* see C. Grein, *Sprachschatz der angelsächsischen Dichter* (Heidelburg: C. Winter, 1912). The word *hlaford* may also have been in Caedmon's mind.

39. See Augustine's mirror of the true king in *De civitate Dei*, V, xxiv.

the secrets of the Thunderer above, and of seeing below the earth Tartarus.[40] For the earth in the Christian spiritual cosmology stood midway between heaven and hell, considered as the ends of man's activity on earth. Man himself was created, according to Augustine, "in the middle of things, below God and above the bodily." As Olympus, a word of pagan concept, could be used to suggest the Mount of Sion, the word "middle-earth," though it may originally have expressed a notion of pagan myth, was most useful in suggesting that the earth was created for man. On the middle-earth man journeys toward Jerusalem above or loses his way and ends in Babylon below.

Caedmon's inspired effort to adapt pagan poetic diction to the demands of Christian meaning is in accord with the practice of the Latin Christian poets, and particularly with that of his fellow English poet, Aldhelm. What he is doing accords also with Augustine's willingness, in theory, to make practical use of human means in the instruction of men. If a phrase of Caedmon's reflected, as was unavoidable, any phrase of pagan heroic poetry, so much the better, because the Christian meaning would gain in symbolic strength from use of the memorable pagan phrase—that is, if one loved the truth and not the word. The Christian had to accept the fact that his language had been spoken by men who did not know the teachings of the Church. He could, however, by exploiting the residual symbolic force of words, make a providential virtue of pagan necessity. If those who heard Caedmon's *Hymn* perceived in his epithets a reflection of ancestral poetry, their minds were actually being prepared, even though unconsciously, through the memory of the well-known and the poetically admired, to receive the Christian truth embodied in the pagan phrase. In restoring to the Master what is rightfully His, the poet takes from the Egyptians whatever is of worth; for example, the image of the true and good king of pagan poetry. Like Aldhelm's reported singing of the old songs to gain hearers for the Gospel, Caedmon's employment of words rich in the connotations of heroic pagan poetry was justified by a very practical theory.

Everything being considered, there seem to be grounds for Bede's justification of Caedmon's *Hymn* as divinely inspired. The

40. Ehwald, *Aldhelmi Opera*, *MGH* (Berlin, 1919), p. 146.

miracle lies not in the details of the angelic visitation, but in the concrete, empirical truth, as Bede saw it, that a man unlearned in Scripture, with its great intellectual demands, had the insight to proclaim what he never formally learned. Caedmon's dream, unsupported, might well have been dismissed; in accordance with Gregory the Great's principles dreams were in general looked upon with suspicion.[41] But the poem itself was visible evidence of unseen grace. Whatever guess may be made about Caedmon's own understanding of what he wrote and about the sources—sermons and the like—which might have supplied him with his material, the fact remains that the poem demonstrably contains the meaningful beauty that Bede associated with Scripture, the basic model of the beautiful. By employing the techniques established to reveal the truth and beauty of Scripture, it has been possible to show that to the pious mind determined to find hints of thematic truth, the form and diction of the *Hymn* would have given such hints.

On the other hand, the modern reader will wish to find a source —other than angelic—for Caedmon's inspiration. Caedmon was, of course, both illiterate and uninstructed when he composed the *Hymn*, but he was a Christian and he went to church. Simple as this fact may appear to be, it is a sufficient explanation of Caedmon's source of inspiration: his poem was the result of a long gestation of ideas and of unconscious imitation. In church, he would have had explained to him his creed and the meaning of the words, let us say, of the Preface; also he would have heard homilies, many of them translations of the Latin homilies of Augustine, Basil, Ambrose, Gregory. These homilies were, in general, exegetical in method; indeed many of the commentaries, cited above, exist as connected series of homilies. In addition it is likely that Caedmon possessed a powerful memory, more common than uncommon in the days before printing. St. Augustine takes for granted feats of memory staggering to the modern mind; in his *De catechizandis rudibus*, for example, he advises the instructor when he reviews biblical history for the catechumen not to recite the Bible from Genesis through Acts "verbatim

41. *Moralia, PL*, 75, 827: "Somnis non facile credendum. Cur daemon sanctorum corda somniis officere sinatur" ⟨One must not trust readily in dreams. For the devil is allowed to try the hearts of saints in dreams⟩.

as he has committed them to memory."[42] Facility of memory and the opportunity frequently to hear homilies, some presumably on the subject of the creation, would have been sufficient to afford a nonmiraculous genesis for the *Hymn*. The angelic vision would have served as a catalytic agent to precipitate ideas stored in Caedmon's memory, and he himself would have been unaware of the process until it flowered. His later poetry, written under direct monastic influence, was a result of imitation. As Bede explains, Abbess Hild had Caedmon "taught the whole course and succession of biblical history; he, then, remembering what he had learned in listening, and like to an innocent animal chewing the cud turned it all into delightful poetry."

Another problem still remains: What is the likelihood that Caedmon's poetry would have been read "exegetically," for its underlying meaning? To answer this question it is necessary to reconstruct the attitude of mind which looked toward the skies and saw them proclaim the glory of God. This is difficult. The modern man may, with Keats, see in the heavens symbols of high romance; normally he does not see in them the precise and ordered symbols, which, organized through the interpretation of Scripture, appeared to the medieval man. Yet if the modern reader is to judge the works of the Christian poets of the Middle Ages he must make an effort at such historical reconstruction.

A grasp of the principles of Augustine's theory of literature helps at least to remove "surprise" that Caedmon's poetry is "subtle." Caedmon's poem is, in fact, not subtle; rather it is enigmatic and allusive. This style is the natural result of the influence upon Caedmon of a Christian ideal that pervaded the consciousness of Western Christendom. The "subtlety" results from the Augustinian resolution of two apparently opposite attitudes: that of late classical rhetoric, with its interest in elegancies and refinements, and that of Christian rhetoric, with its insistence on discovering single-mindedly, through whatever confusion, an underlying meaning consonant with the Faith. In Bede's view—and in Caedmon's view, because

42. See also the *De doctrina*, 4, 7 (5) and 2, 14 (9); H. Chaytor, *From Script to Print* (Cambridge: Cambridge University Press, 1945), pp. 115–119. See F. Magoun, "Bede's Story of Caedmon," *Speculum*, XXX (1955), 49–63.

he was Christian—poetry that did not force the mind to an intense appreciation of such underlying truth was without function.

Furthermore, to recall the apparent complexity of the English *Be Domes Dæg* is to suggest that Caedmon's unlearned audience may very reasonably be granted such awareness of symbolic meaning as would be necessary even partially to understand the verbal and stylistic potentialities of the *Hymn*. In his reading of the poem Bede would have been guided by Christian theory of literature, which would have led him automatically to look for the underlying meaning of angelically inspired verse. The letter of the *Hymn* for Bede could have meant only a shell to be cracked for the kernel of hidden meaning that alone would have given the poem the Christian beauty demanded by its angelic inspiration. The English poems already considered seem to have been written by poets governed by the same theory as that which governed Bede. Certainly they expected that their audiences would, in varying degrees, be able to grasp the meaning implicit in such a poem as Caedmon's *Hymn*. * * *

Reprinted from Bernard F. Huppé, *Doctrine and Poetry* (Albany: State University of New York Press, 1959), pp. 99–130. The last paragraph, which points forward to the next chapter in Professor Huppé's book, and two footnotes (numbered 41 and 42 in the original text) have been omitted.

R. F. LESLIE

# The Wanderer :
## *Theme and Structure*

*The Wanderer* has been a favorite anthology piece, much admired and much discussed for over a century. It is one of a group of Old English poems similar in elegiac tone and lyrical feeling. Universal in their significance, they illustrate typical human situations to which they give immediacy by portraying them through the eyes of individuals. The identity of the speaker in *The Wanderer* is of little moment, but the depth of feeling he displays preserves his individuality in the midst of the generalizations, gnomic utterances, and formulaic patterns which give a wider validity to his own experiences.

Most nineteenth-century scholars believed that the poem was fundamentally a product of pagan times and were concerned to show that the Christian references in it were interpolations by monastic revisers, whose alleged contributions were deprecated. A strong reaction in support of the integrity of the text as it has been transmitted was led by W. W. Lawrence.[1] Although the interpolation theories lingered on for several decades, scholars in increasing numbers accepted the poem as it stands, and controversy shifted to its theme and structure. There was, however, a valuable legacy from these early discussions: attention was focused on points of apparently abrupt transition of thought or mood, which called for explanation.[2]

1. For Lawrence's account of the various theories see "*The Wanderer* and *The Seafarer*," *JGP*, IV (1902), 460–480.

2. In a recent article, "The Wanderer (and The Seafarer)," *Neophil*, XLVIII (1964), 237–251, published since this book went to press, A. A. Prins has questioned the integrity of the transmitted text. He contends that the present abrupt transition in the center of both poems is the result of a misplacement of folios in an earlier manuscript; restitution of the "correct" order of the folios would bring together the seafaring parts of *The Wanderer* and *Resignation* into one poem.

For some critics the narrative and elegiac parts of the poem are the essence of the poetic inspiration and the Christian references sops to the new religion;[3] for others the poem is a blend of pagan and Christian elements which do not readily coalesce.[4] More recently discussion has been concerned with elucidating the structural as well as the textual unity of the poem,[5] and there is now a considerable measure of agreement that, far from there being any inconsistency between the secular and the religious passages, there is a deliberate juxtaposition whose purpose is to illustrate a contrast in theme between the transience of this world and the changelessness and security of the heavenly kingdom.

The whole poem is not intended to be taken as the utterance of the poet in his own person, as can be seen from lines 6–7, 88–91 and 111, in which reference is made to a speaker or speakers. The determination of the limits of the main monologue and of the number and extent of any other speeches has an important bearing on any interpretation of the structure of the poem.

The wanderer's monologue has frequently been held to begin, not with the opening lines of the poem, but with line 8, because at this point the pronoun in the first person is introduced after the *swā cwæð* construction in lines 6 and 7. But a construction of this type normally has a summary or retrospective function; there is no clear evidence that it can point exclusively forward.[6] A case for the opening of the monologue at line 8 has been put forward on the basis of the similarity of lines 8 ff. to the opening lines of *The Seafarer* and *The Wife's Lament*, both of which begin with a first person formula of elegiac lament.[7] But the hardship depicted in the

3. Cf., especially G. K. Anderson, *The Literature of the Anglo-Saxons* (London, 1949), p. 159, and F. Mossé, *Manuel de l'Anglais du Moyen Age* (Paris: Aubier, 1945), I, 403.

4. Notably N. Kershaw, *Anglo-Saxon and Norse Poems* (Cambridge: Cambridge University Press, 1922), pp. 3–5, and E. E. Wardale, *Chapters on Old English Literature* (London: K. Paul, Trench, Trübner and Co., 1935), pp. 58–59.

5. For a summary of these views see T. C. Rumble, "From *Eardstapa* to *Snottor on mode*: The Structural Principle of *The Wanderer*," *MLQ*, XIX (1958), 225–230.

6. Cf., E. E. Ericson, *The Use of Swā in Old English* (Baltimore: Johns Hopkins Press, 1932). Clear evidence for the use of the construction in the middle of a speech is to be found in *Christ and Satan*, 125–128.

7. S. B. Greenfield, "*The Wanderer*: A Reconsideration of Theme and Structure," *JEGP*, L (1951), 456–457.

first five lines is similar to that in the openings of the poems cited; moreover, since there is alternation between the first and third person throughout much of what is generally accepted as the wanderer's speech, there is no reason why he should not choose to begin in the third person. On balance, therefore, there is good reason to include lines 1–5 in the monologue and to accept lines 6–7, introduced by *swā cwæð*, as parenthetical.

The first five lines consist of generalizations by the wanderer. Lines 1–2a have been held to contrast the mercy of God with the inexorability of fate, exemplified in lines 2b–5.[8] But these are not capable of being contrasted; the wanderer is maintaining that God in His mercy often chooses to override the otherwise inexorable course of events; cf. *Beowulf* 1056–1057, where it is said that Grendel might well have perpetrated further wickedness *nefne him wītig God wyrd forstōde | ond ðæs mannes mōd*, and *Andreas* 459–460:

> þæt næfre forlæteð    lifgende God
> eorl on eorðan,    gif his ellen dēah.

It should be noted that in both passages the display of fortitude is a prerequisite of God's intervention. That a great man should possess both fortitude and wisdom is a common homiletic motif, whose presence in Old English poetry has been amply demonstrated by R. E. Kaske.[9] Throughout the poem the wanderer is concerned to show first how fortitude should be displayed in the face of acute personal suffering, and second how a wise man should comport himself as he contemplates human misery and the complete futility of dependence on the things of this world.

The reference in lines 2b–5 to an exile wanderer neatly summarizes his own situation, which he develops and makes personal in the passage which follows. The earlier reference, to God's mercy, is not explicitly picked up again until the last lines of the poem; but the wanderer is not concerned exclusively with worldly matters in the meantime. His use of the demonstrative "this" with reference to "world" or "life" on no fewer than six occasions, the use of *hēr* (108–

8. Cf., B. Huppé, "*The Wanderer*: Theme and Structure," *JEGP*, XLII (1943), 526.

9. "*Sapientia et Fortitudo* as the Controlling Theme of *Beowulf*," *SP*, LV (1958), 423–456.

109) and of *woruldrīce* (65),[10] all show that throughout he is implying the existence of an eternal world which, as the closing lines show, is contrasted with this earthly one. A similar technique is employed in the celebrated opening description of the Earthly Paradise in *The Phoenix*.

When the poet in his own voice interrupts the monologue at lines 6 and 7, it is with one precise object in view: to emphasize the wanderer's experience, to point out that the latter has suffered the worst that life can visit upon him in the society to which he belongs and is, therefore, well qualified to speak authoritatively on the feelings and philosophy of an outcast.

The wanderer's monologue is resumed on a more personal note, recounting in lines 8–9a his own former friendless state. It is important to note the use of the past tense here; the wanderer no longer "stands in the midst of sorrow" as has been claimed.[11] It is the failure to recognize that the wanderer's troubles are over and done with which weakens Elliott's claim that we have to deal with a particular history rather than a personal but typical fate in the lament of the wanderer.[12] He believes that the wanderer has a guilty secret which he dare not acknowledge to anyone. Although this interpretation seems to find support in the verb *durre* "dare" (10), it overlooks the force of *nū* (9). There is no longer anyone left alive to whom he dare speak openly because he has outlived his friends, the men of his own generation; cf. lines 7, 31. He has become a wise man with a good share of years in the world, and he must follow the code of behavior of such. Elliott's supposition that he dare not speak because of the guilt he hides would be more cogent if he were surrounded by his own friends, which he is not. He makes clear why he dare not speak his mind. In lines 11–14 he alludes to the custom of keeping one's thoughts to oneself, because fortitude is one virtue that will be expected of him now. To do this does not come easily to him, as is indicated by the phrasing of lines 11b–12, which imply that he knows something to his cost: cf. the

10. This compound indicates the kingdom of this world, as opposed to the kingdom of heaven, in its frequent occurrences in OE religious poetry: e.g., eight times in *Genesis*, twice each in *Exodus* and *Elene*, and once in *Christ* and *Juliana*.

11. Cf., Huppé, *loc. cit.*, p. 535.

12. R. W. V. Elliott, "The Wanderer's Conscience," *ES*, XXXIX (1958), 195.

similar phrasing in *Juliana* 546b–549:

> Hwæt, þū mec þrēades
> þurh sārslege; ic tō sōþe wāt
> þæt ic ǣr ne sīð ǣnig ne mētte
> in woruldrīce wīf þē gelīc.

Lines 15 and 16 have the appearance of a piece of gnomic wisdom, but Miss Williams has observed that the thought expressed is to be found nowhere else in passages or poems of gnomic verse in Anglo-Saxon literature.[13] Elliott sees in the fact that they do not constitute a stereotyped expression an indication that they arise out of a real situation[14]; but it has recently been pointed out that, though the idea of defying fate may be foreign to the Germanic peoples, it is to be found in Boethius, and in a particularly apposite form in Book 4, Prose 7[15]; cf. the Old English translation: *Ac ǣlc mon scyle āwinnan ægþer ge wiþ þā rēþan wyrde ge wiþ ðā winsuman.* Because a sad and disturbed spirit is of no avail in resisting fate, the wanderer goes on in lines 17–19 to point out that men desirous of a high reputation generally keep their sorrows to themselves. Commonly regarded as Germanic and heroic, this concept may also owe much to classical and Christian precepts; both St. John Chrysostom and St. Ambrose in consolatory sermons advise that a man should endure his grief in silence and not publish it by outward show.[16]

In lines 19–29a the wanderer makes specific application of this reflection to his own past and gives us more information about his own life, indicating that his troubles began with the burial of his lord (22–23), which precipitated his departure from his native land (20b) and his voyage across the sea to seek another lord in whose service he could find security (25–29a). Here ends the personal history of the wanderer. His time of wandering was turbulent; cf. *oft . . . mīne ceare cwīþan* (8–9) and *oft earmcearig* (20). Insufficient

---

13. *Gnomic Poetry in Anglo-Saxon* (New York: Columbia University Press, 1914), p. 47.

14. Elliott, *loc. cit.*, p. 194.

15. W. Erzgräber, *"Der Wanderer*: Eine Interpretation von Aufbau und Gehalt," *Festschrift zum 75. Geburtstag von Theodor Spira*, ed. H. Viebrock and W. Erzgräber (Heidelberg: C. Winter, 1961), p. 61.

16. J. E. Cross, "On the Genre of *The Wanderer*," *Neophil*, XLV (1961), 66.

attention has been paid to *geāra iū* in line 22. These emphatic adverbs make clear that all these things happened a long time ago, and
underline his present ripeness in years and experience. In the following lines the use of stereotyped exile-wanderer imagery suggests
that his fate is shared by many.[17] We do not know whether his quest
was successful, whether he found a new temporal lord, but he suggests
that he found peace under God's protection. He sought a "giver of
treasure" (25), one who could comfort him (28); Cross points out
that *frēfran* can mean "console" as well as "comfort,"[18] and the
importance he attaches to it in his thesis that the poem belongs to
the genre of *consolatio* would appear to be borne out in the closing
lines of the poem, in which the wanderer echoes this quest for consolation by saying that it is good for a man to seek consolation from
God, *frōfre tō fæder on heofonum* (115a), for with Him alone is there
security (115b).

Since the use of the first person is interrupted at the end of this
passage (29), the wanderer's monologue has sometimes been closed
at this point.[19] But although the poem goes on to describe in the
third person the hardships of a lonely man, the first person is resumed at line 58 for four and a half lines which lament the passing
of kinsmen and are thus connected through identity of content, as
well as identity of grammatical person, with lines 8–29a.[20] Moreover, the tendency to generalize personal experience in an impersonal form is characteristic of Old English poetry, as is the use of the
*þām þe* formula to characterize such generalizations in lines 31 and
56.[21]

Although the case for ending the monologue here is not a strong
one, the middle of line 29 does mark a change of tone. The central
issue of the poem to this point is the personal experience of the
wanderer, cast in elegiac form and referred to in the past tense; but

17. S. B. Greenfield, "The Formulaic Expression of the Theme of 'Exile' in
Anglo-Saxon Poetry," *Speculum*, XXX (1955), 205–206.

18. Cross, *loc. cit.*, p. 66.

19. By Flom, Miss Kershaw, Mossé, and Krapp-Dobbie in the introduction of
their edition of *The Exeter Book* (New York: Columbia University Press, 1936),
p. xxxix, but not marked in their text.

20. Cf., Huppé, *loc. cit.*, p. 520.

21. Cf., the use of this formula in an impersonal passage of the same type in
*The Seafarer*, line 51, and at the intense climax of *The Wife's Lament*, ll. 52–53.

the pattern has been varied by the alternation of individual experience and behavior with general truths, referred to in the present tense. These generalizations are unlike those which follow line 29a in being closely related to the wanderer's own feelings and called forth by his own circumstances.

In the long passage in the third person (29b–57), the appeal is to the experience of all lonely voyagers. The *winelēas guma* (45) represents the type, of which the *eardstapa*, the wanderer himself, is an individual member. Since the passage generalizes the sorrow of the outcast it is in the present tense, as such philosophical passages generally are in Old English poetry; for the same reason it contains the common generalizing phrases with *sē þe* and *þām þe* formulas.[22] There appears to be little justification for beginning a new section with line 37.[23] The generalizing present tense and third person begin at line 29b and continue through to line 57. The *wāt sē þe* formula first introduced in line 29b is repeated in line 37; the *þām þe* formula which first appears in line 31 is repeated in line 56. Moreover, when we examine the subject matter, lines 29b–33 are seen to be a general introduction to a single topic, the evocation of the past by the lonely voyager; there are three sub-sections corresponding to three kinds of evocation, the first of which is introduced at line 34, the second at line 37, and the third at line 50b.

The wanderer opens the passage by describing the state of mind of all solitary travellers (29b–33), emphasizing from personal experience how bitter a companion sorrow can be (29b–30) to one who is entirely alone; the characteristic litotes of line 31 underlines this utter loneliness. He voices their plight in lines 32–33 with a dramatic juxtaposition of the happy past and the doleful present, such as we find as a major theme in *The Riming Poem* and in *The Seafarer* 20–22. He then proceeds to illustrate the psychological phenomena which overtake the solitary one when mind and spirit are taxed by sorrow. His experience is clearly of three kinds, each involving the resurrection of the past in a different form, each more intense and less subject to his control than the one which precedes it: memory, dream, and hallucination.

22. Cf., *Guthlac*, ll. 1348–1356, *The Wife's Lament*, ll. 42–53, *The Seafarer*, ll. 39–57, and *Vainglory*, ll. 67–77.

23. As proposed by Krapp-Dobbie, *op. cit.*, p. 135, and Erzgräber, *loc. cit.*, pp. 63–64.

The realization of what he lacks, *wunden gold*[24] and *foldan blǣd* (32–33), leads naturally to remembrance of former happy days. Memory recalls, not particular occasions, but the habitual pleasures of his environment, the ministrations of servants, the giving of treasure, the patronage of his lord at the feast (34–36); then he recalls that all this joy has vanished—*wyn eal gedrēas*.

When he falls asleep exhausted (39–40), deprivation of his lord's company causes him to dream (41a) that he is enacting the ceremony of paying homage to his lord.[25] In memory he dwelt passively on past pleasures, but in the dream he participates in a key ceremony in all its detail. He awakens to a stark reality (45–48); seabirds preening replace his enthroned lord, falling rime and snow replace the walls of the hall.

The keen disappointment of his return to the lonely, harsh present has made his heartache the heavier with longing for his beloved prince (49–50a); so the scene is set for the third and most powerful evocation of the past, hallucination. The wanderer makes clear that his solitary man is aware that he is dreaming by the phrase *þinceð him on mōde*, and then tells us specifically of his awakening (45). What happens next is beyond the solitary man's control and understanding. A key phrase for the lines that follow is *Sorg bið genīwad* (50); but the force of this observation is obscured by the punctuation of Krapp-Dobbie, who place stops after *geseldan* and *on weg* (53). Since the images which rise up before him in lines 51–53 are those of friends, it cannot be that their appearance causes him sorrow; his distress arises from the fact that they are mirages (54–55). That we have to do with hallucination and not voluntary recollection is made clear by comparison of line 34 with line 51. In the former it is *hē* who *gemon* "remembers"; in the latter it is the remembrance itself, *gemynd*, which invades the man's imagination, as the past, unbidden, forces itself upon the lonely, unhappy man.[26] In explanation of the peculiar power of past joys over the minds of

24. As Cross points out (*loc. cit.*, p. 66) *wunden gold* is a metonymy for the generosity of a lord.

25. See Notes to lines 41b–44 ⟨in R. F. Leslie's edition of *The Wanderer* (New York: Barnes and Noble, 1966), pp. 74–75⟩.

26. For a detailed discussion of the syntax of this passage see Notes to lines 50–55 ⟨in Leslie's edition mentioned in the preceding note⟩.

seafarers in particular, the wanderer inserts the parenthetic remark that the minds of seafarers often swim away.[27] The concept of the detachment of mind from body is repeated more explicitly in the next few lines (55b–57) and is somewhat similar to that in *The Seafarer* 58–60.

The first half of the poem has been devoted to the experience and limitations of the individual in the clutches of adverse fortune. The theme is now broadened in scope to include the whole of man's existence. Because the use of *ic* extends to the sentence ending in line 62, it has generally been assumed that the wanderer's speech goes as far as this line at least, even by Huppé, who believes that the tone of the second part of the poem is sufficiently different to justify its being given to a different speaker.[28] It is difficult, however, to separate the philosophic tone of lines 58–62 from that of the lines which follow. If there is a second major speaker, it is more credible that he should be introduced at line 58 than at line 62, as in Professor Pope's recent thesis.[29] He points out that if there are two speakers, both will naturally use the first person pronoun. Pope's major justifications for the introduction of a second speaker here are the sharp cleavage at line 58, the fact that the change comes not gradually but all at once, and the sweeping generalization of the latter part of the poem, "so much greater in range and abstraction than the wanderer's, and so objective, as having nothing to do with the speaker's personal losses."

The abrupt transition can, nevertheless, be attributed to the deliberate intention of a single speaker, switching from the particular to the general for effect, and the completeness of the change has perhaps been overemphasized. The wanderer remains a serious candidate for the views expressed in the latter half of the poem, especially if he is shown to be mature enough to utter them, and if attributing them to him illuminates their complexities more adequately than placing them in the mouth of a second speaker. The

27. Unnecessary emendation of MS *oft* to *eft* has frequently misdirected criticism of this passage.

28. Huppé, *loc. cit.*, pp. 522–527.

29. J. C. Pope, "Dramatic Voices in *The Wanderer* and *The Seafarer*," *Franciplegius: Medieval and Linguistic Studies in Honor of Francis Peabody Magoun, Jr.* (New York: New York University Press, 1965), pp. 165–167 ⟨or see pp. 163–168 in this volume⟩.

wanderer has not only reached a state of comparative tranquillity, as Pope states, but is a man of mature years, for it is made clear in line 22 that he buried his lord a long time ago, *geāra iū*. If we grant him the percipience in the first five lines[30] to see the grace of God operating to counter the otherwise fixed course of events, then we may grant him the capacity to philosophize in the second half of the poem.

The state of mind of the speaker at line 58 is relevant to the significance of the latter part of the poem. It has been claimed that his mind is saddened by what he sees[31]; but he states no more than that the things of this world are calculated to make him sad. Lines 58–59 are nothing more than a rhetorical comment on what is to follow, namely the wanderer's explanation of how wisdom brings peace of mind despite loss of earthly fortune.[32] He does not, in these lines, identify himself with the "wise man" of lines 73–74 and 88–89, whose view is bounded by the visible world. He has seen beyond it, as indicated in lines 114–115, and is therefore concerned to point out the utter instability of this world, and, at the end of the poem, to draw a moral from it. Throughout there is implied a contrast of this world with the kingdom of heaven, of a type familiar in Old English homiletic literature,[33] and the use of *fæstnung* (115) to describe heaven is but the final explicit emphasis on what has been implicit all through the poem.

The wanderer sets the stage for his broader theme in lines 58–63; all men depart and creation daily decays. Two words, *Forþon* the opening word and *eal* (60), show a connection with the preceding part of the poem. *Forþon* as an adverb generally has a linking function, however vague, and *eal* refers to the whole life of men, that is, not simply the experience of one individual with which the wanderer has just been concerned. Pope, in support of a second speaker here, suggests that the possessive *mīn* in line 59 takes on an extra meaning which explains why it carries the alliteration; the thinker is saying

30. These lines are accepted by Pope as part of the wanderer's speech.

31. Ida L. Gordon, "Traditional Themes in *The Wanderer* and *The Seafarer*," *RES*, V (1954), 6, and Cross, *loc. cit.*, p. 67; see also Notes to lines 58–59 ⟨in Leslie's edition cited above in n. 25⟩.

32. Cf., R. M. Lumiansky, "The Dramatic Structure of the Old English *Wanderer*," *Neophil*, XXXIV (1950), 108.

33. Cf., especially Vercelli Homily XIV.

"*my* mind also, like the wanderer's." But we are not really justified in taking this construction as anything more than a stylistic device for, twice in the earlier part of the poem, in lines 10 and 19, *mĩnne* in the second half-line alliterates with *mōdsefan* in the first; the use of a similar construction in line 59 supplies evidence, therefore, not for a new speaker but for continued reference to an earlier one.

As at the outset of his personal elegy, the wanderer crystalizes his theme in the opening lines of his impersonal elegy. He follows it with a bridge passage, which has troubled many critics, before he goes on to deal with the two parts of his general theme, first the disappearance of man and then the disappearance of man's works and environment. The function of lines 64–72 has generally been underestimated and their presence condemned; but they have a significant part to play in the poem. The clue to their interpretation lies as much in the speaker's stress on the wisdom of the man referred to in lines 73, 88, and 90, as in the preceding lines, in which general gnomic reflections follow naturally from the speaker's observations on the mortality of men. The particular reflection in lines 61–62a prompts the general one in lines 62b–63; the connection of ideas is indicated by *swā*, for as individuals perish, so does the world.[34] One reflection continues to prompt another, and so in line 64 the speaker states the paradox whereby the passage of time, which carries all things to oblivion, including man himself, is yet a paramount requirement for gaining the cardinal asset—wisdom.[35] A somewhat different interpretation of these lines suggests that although earthly things are perishing daily, man cannot recognize the universality of this decay till the experience and reflection of many years have brought it home to him.[36] But recognition of the universality of decay is not yet a point at issue, as it becomes in the passage beginning with line 73. Whether the adverb *Forþon* (64) is taken adversatively to mean "and yet," or as a loose connective "and so," the point emphasized in the *Forþon* clause is the same—namely that wisdom comes with ripeness of experience; this wry reflection is

34. Cf., Blickling Homily V (EETS edition), p. 59: *þes middangeard daga gehwylce fealleþ and tō ende efsteþ.*

35. Cf., *wintrum frōd* in *Beowulf* 1724, 2114; Hroðgar's age as well as his wisdom is emphasized.

36. Greenfield, *JEGP*, L (1951), 458.

prompted by the otherwise entirely destructive function of the passage of time indicated throughout the preceding six lines.

The continuity of thought in this passage militates against closing the wanderer's monologue at either line 62 or 63.[37] Although the use of the first person ends here, there is no sudden change from narrative to didactic verse; that change has already taken place at line 58. Huppé's argument that the contents of lines 62–87 make them incompatible with the previous lines, which are certainly in the monologue, is based on the assumption that the monologue reveals only a pagan attitude to life, and that the didacticism which follows is not consonant with it. But the use of preconceptions about the character of the monologue to determine its boundaries weakens his argument, and there are inconsistencies in his deductions about the use of the pronoun *ic* which have been clearly demonstrated in the article by Greenfield quoted above.

After discussing the prerequisite for gaining wisdom, the wanderer enumerates the elements of which it consists (65b–72), the principal stress being laid on the value of moderation. The succession of formulaic expressions consisting of *ne tō* followed by an adjective indicating a trait of human nature is one which is found in the works of Anglo-Saxon homilists, where the sentiments expressed are often similar,[38] although those admonitions which are as much heroic as Christian, namely *ne tō wāc wiga, ne tō wanhȳdig* (67), and *ne tō forht* (68), appear to have no precise counterparts in the homilies. But there is a comparable passage in the Christian poem *Andreas*, in which there is considerable sympathy with these old heroic sentiments: *Ne bēo ðū on sefan tō forht,/ne on mōde ne murn* (98–99). That

---

37. Huppé alone has followed Klipstein in closing the monologue in the center of line 62. The revised edition (14th) of H. Sweet's *Anglo-Saxon Reader* (Oxford: Oxford University Press, 1959), by C. T. Onions has quotation marks at the end of line 63. Sweet himself in earlier editions had indicated no closing point for the monologue.

38. See Miss Dorothy Bethurum, *The Homilies of Wulfstan* (Oxford: Oxford University Press, 1957), VIIIe, ll. 168–171; and Xe, ll. 97–100; and cf. Miss Kershaw, *op. cit.*, pp. 164–165; Fr. Klaeber, "Notes on Old English Poems," *JEGP*, XII (1913), 259; and Miss Elizabeth Suddaby, "Three Notes on Old English Texts," *MLN*, LXIX (1954), 465–466. Miss Bethurum notes that the idea of the Golden Mean was not found by Wulfstan in his sources, nor was this manner of expression.

a wise man's code of moderation may have a similar expression in both pagan and Christian teaching appears from a comparison of an inscription cited by Plutarch with writings by Ambrose and Jerome, who quote the saying of the Seven Wise Men of Greece, "nothing in excess." [39] From an Irish source, to be dated to the early ninth century in its present form, comes a passage similar in content and form to that in *The Wanderer*. It appears in one of the gnomic collections of instructions to young aristocrats, *The Instructions of King Cormac MacAirt*:

> Be not too wise, be not too foolish,
> be not too conceited, be not too diffident,
> be not too haughty, be not too humble,
> be not too talkative, be not too silent,
> be not too harsh, be not too feeble. [40]

The last three lines of this passage (70–72) have been described as a "feeble expansion of line 69." [41] But the prominent position of the lines at the end of a passage of maxims, as well as the extent of the "expansion," should make us pause. Is it true that "twice the speaker warns men against uttering boasts before they know fully how things are going to turn out"? [42] The injunction in line 69 is part of a list of exhortations to moderation that a wise man should heed; *gielpes tō georn* probably refers to the aspiration to glory, which should be kept within bounds. [43] The absolute use of the verb in the clause *ǣr hē geare cunne* indicates that it is to be taken with all the injunctions. The last three lines are, however, outside this framework. They are distinct in that they do not apply only to the wise man of line 65, but to men in general, as indicated by *beorn*, and in that they refer to a particular *bēot* "vow" or "promise," [44] stressing

39. J. E. Cross, *loc. cit.*, p. 68.

40. Edited and translated by Kuno Meyer, Royal Irish Academy, Todd Lecture Series XV (Dublin, 1909), p. 45.

41. A. J. Wyatt, *An Anglo-Saxon Reader* (Cambridge: Cambridge University Press, 1919), p. 264.

42. R. W. V. Elliott, *loc. cit.*, p. 195.

43. Cf., *gilpgeorn* in the Old English translation of Bede, and the discussion of *gelp* which constitutes section X in *The Meters of Boethius*.

44. Cf., *Beowulf* 80, 523, *The Battle of Maldon* 15, 213, and *gebēot* in *The Husband's Message* 49.

the necessity of being certain of what one intends before giving one's pledged word. There is a repetition of this admonition in a decidedly Christian homiletic form in line 112; but what is striking here is the phrasing of the admonition as a piece of gnomic wisdom, using *bēot* with its predominantly heroic associations. This two-fold approach to the same code of behavior is a variant of a duality which runs through the whole passage of injunctions. None are predominantly to be associated with Christian teaching, although many are to be found in similar homiletic lists, the exceptions being those appropriate to a warrior (67–68b); and yet the form which they take is a familiar homiletic one. This calculated ambiguity is repeated several times in the latter part of *The Wanderer* and embraces both Christian teaching in readily identifiable stereotyped forms and the noblest of the heroic virtues, as if to emphasize that the wise man postulated by the wanderer in his monologue is but a step from Christianity in his code of behavior. Yet his philosophy is one of despair, for he lacks the ultimate salvation of the Christian, permanent security under an all-powerful Lord.

Lines 73–87 contain the first part of an impersonal elegy on the decay of the works of men, similar in style to another Old English elegiac lyric, *The Ruin*. This vivid picture of ruin gives a foretaste of what it will be like when the whole world shares the same fate (73–74). Here is the point of fusion of the themes stated in lines 63 and 65a, namely the daily decay of the world and the wisdom gained only in maturity. The man who has lived long enough to recognize the inevitability of decay is the wise man who can project his experience into the future, and who has the imagination to realize how terrible it will be when all the riches of the world stand desolate (73–74). Ambrose lists this ability as one of the prerequisites of wisdom:

> Sed etiam futurorum interpres sapientia est,
> scit praeterita, et de futuris aestimat. Scit
> versutias sermonum, et solutiones argumentorum.
> Signa et monstra scit antequam fiant, et eventus
> temporum et saeculorum.[45]
>
> ⟨But wisdom is also the fore-seer of the future;
> she knows things past and appraises the future.

45. *PL*, XIV, col. 492.

She knows the cunning of speech and the solutions for debates.
Signs and portents she knows before they occur,
and the outcome of eras and ages.⟩

The wanderer then proceeds to exemplify and give substance to his projection in his poignant description of crumbling walls and mouldering buildings, commenting on the fate of those who had left them behind to decay. Huppé suggests that this description is a Christian reference to Doomsday, but, as has been pointed out, the tone of the passage is not exclusively Christian.[46] Early Christian writers used this theme, which they had taken over from their pagan predecessors,[47] and the reference to God in the last three lines indicates that the Last Judgment was not absent from the mind of the poet; but the emphasis on the effects of storm and rime, and later of snow and hail, are Anglo-Saxon modifications in *The Wanderer*. Even in the one explicit reference to the Christian God, the *ælda Scyppend* (85), there is ambiguity; with fine irony the kenning referring to His creative activity is used in a passage describing His destructive role.

The impression that the ambiguity is deliberate is reinforced by the use the poet has made of the *sum . . . sum* formula (80–84). In an article on the incidence of the figure which includes this formula in Old English prose and poetry, Cross has shown its prevalence in Latin and Greek Christian literature to exemplify ways of bodily destruction.[48] That the poet has drawn upon this well-known Christian theme seems likely, as Cross suggests, both from the contents of the list and from the formula in which it is expressed. But it must not be forgotten that the poet has adapted the theme to his context, and that the limits he sets upon it are those appropriate to that context. The wanderer has just informed us that the buildings have crumbled and all the men have fallen by the wall (79–80). The following lines contain four successive statements introduced by forms of the indefinite pronoun *sum*. The first opens with the plural form *sume*, when the wanderer declares that war carried some off.

46. S. B. Greenfield, *JEGP*, L (1951), 459.

47. J. E. Cross, *loc. cit.*, pp. 68–69.

48. "On *The Wanderer* lines 80–84: A Study of a Figure and a Theme," *Vetenskaps-Societetens i Lund* (Årsbok 1958–1959), pp. 77–110; cf. particularly the short lament of Gregory Nazianzen which combines this figure with the *ubi sunt* motif as in *The Wanderer* (p. 94).

A list of fates of men after battle in *Elene* 131–137 begins in precisely the same way, but goes on to discuss the fates of others in groups, whereas the wanderer takes up in turn the different fates of individuals in the three following phrases, each opening with *sumne*. We cannot be certain whether the use of the singular is distributive, so that each of the fates which follows refers to men struck down by war, as indicated in the *sume* phrase (80)[49] and suggested by lines 79–80a which tell how all fell in the prime of their manhood, or whether they are to be taken as fates in addition to that of men killed in battle. Whichever may be the case, the use of the singular serves to make the fates typical and hence stereotyped, as they are throughout the Old English poem *The Fortunes of Men*.

The fate of one man is to be carried off across the deep sea by a bird. This may be a thematic bird[50] or * * * a sea-eagle, one of the "beasts of battle"; but we do not have to decide between them, for both may well be intended. That one of the "beasts of battle" is intended in the fate of the second man is highly probable. Almost all the Greek and Latin Christian texts, and all the Old English homilies which deal with the ways of bodily destruction, contain a reference to death by the agency of unspecified wild animals. Specific reference to the wolf as an agent of death is made only in the Old English poetic treatments of the theme, in *The Wanderer* and in *The Fortunes of Men* 12–13. It is not enough to explain this fact simply as a desire for realism. When poets choose to depart from their sources to introduce an animal so charged with significance as the wolf, which hovers frequently, along with the carrion birds, near scenes of carnage in Old English poetry,[51] we cannot exclude symbolic intent. Here is one more example of a common theme of Christian writings being first evoked and then given an Anglo-Saxon orientation. The third man is given normal burial by a friend who has survived him; a touch of individuality is given, not to the dead, but to the man who buries him and who is described as

49. This suggestion by Bright is supported by J. C. Pope, *loc. cit.*, p. 172 and footnote 13.

50. Cross, "On *The Wanderer* lines 80–84," p. 92.

51. See F. P. Magoun, "The Theme of the Beasts of Battle in Anglo-Saxon Poetry," *NM*, LVI (1955), particularly p. 88 and footnote, also A. Bonjour, "Beowulf and the Beasts of Battle," *PMLA*, LXXII (1957), p. 568 (footnote), and E. G. Stanley, *Anglia*, LXXIII (1955), 442–443.

*drēorighlēor* "sad-faced." We may assume from this adjective that he is emotionally involved with the deceased, who was his comrade, or perhaps his lord, and the wanderer may be remembering his burial of his own lord, described in lines 22–23; the speaker may also be touching on the elegiac motif of the last survivor, which is so movingly developed in *Beowulf* 2236–2270.

The identity of the man *Sē . . . þās word ācwið* in lines 88–91 has been the subject of considerable discussion. Since a new speaker is introduced here, the end of line 87 has been suggested, though rarely adopted, as a closing point for the wanderer's monologue, and the speaker introduced at line 88 can be held to be another major character.[52] But since *þisne wealsteal* (88) and *þis deorce līf* (89) point back to the previous passage, and since *ācwið* (91) is in the present not the past tense as is *cwæð* in lines 6 and 111, lines 88–91 should be taken to introduce a speech within the wanderer's monologue by the "wise man," who is the wanderer's "man of straw," none other than the *glēaw hæle* of line 73, who has observed the decay portrayed in lines 75–87.[53] The devastation which he has observed gives him the subject matter for his meditations and leads him almost inevitably to generalization and quotation of a version of the well-known *ubi sunt* formula. He is the man who "ponders this dark life deeply," wise by the standards of this world, whose outlook the wanderer has been discussing since line 65. The wanderer agrees with his postulated wise man, who has learned that nothing in this world is stable; but he does not restrict himself to the wise man's this-worldly wisdom. Lines 88–89 echo in part the wanderer's words in lines 58–60 but with a significant difference; whereas life is accepted as dark by the wise man in line 89 and his cry in lines 92 ff. is one of deep pessimism, the wanderer had stated that life would cause him to despair only if his observations were confined to the present world (58–60). Here is the vital distinction to be made between the wanderer and his puppet. While the latter speaks with earthly wisdom at his disposal and the apparent futility of life defeats him, the wanderer can refrain from despair because he sees the other-worldly goal which gives this life its significance. It is not, however, until he has

52. See Miss Kershaw, *op. cit.*, p. 3; and Huppé, *loc. cit.*, pp. 519, 527.

53. Cf., Lawrence, *loc. cit.*, p. 474, whose first "man of straw" is *sē þe cunnað* (29), now generally held to be the wanderer himself, generalizing his own experience.

driven home the hopelessness of a this-worldly philosophy that he lights up, briefly but positively, this desolate landscape with the certain knowledge of the world to come, which has buoyed up his own faith and enabled him so steadfastly to contemplate the suffering and ruin which he has experienced.

In lines 92 ff. we have the substance of the wise man's lament. In the light of Cross's comparative survey of the *ubi sunt* passages in Old English texts, there can be little doubt about the indebtedness of this passage to the *ubi sunt* formulas widely current in medieval Christian homilies.[54] There were two major versions of the basic formula: one asked where had gone either named heroes of antiquity or the various kinds of potentates such as kings, princes, emperors, as in *The Seafarer* 82–85; the other version asked where had gone an often copious variety of past splendors and joys, the objects themselves reflecting the tastes of the period and society in which the writer lived, from the early centuries of our era onward, and from all over the known world from Syria to Ireland.

A close parallel to the phrasing of *The Wanderer* is to be found in the Latin homily which begins

> Ubi ergo abierunt illa omnia?   Ubi pompa,
> ubi schemata?   Ubi exquisita convivia?[55]
>
> ⟨Where have they all gone?   Where the pomp,
> where the fashion?   Where the elaborate feasts?⟩

The question form, the references to past splendors, the use of *abierunt* ⟨they have gone away⟩ in place of the more common *sunt* ⟨are⟩, all constitute precedents for *The Wanderer*. There is an Old English translation of this homily, Blickling Homily VIII, which furnishes parallels for the poet's version of the formula. The Latin verb *abierunt* is translated as *gewiton*, and the questions are asked in the form *hwǣr cwōm* as well as *hwǣr byð*.[56] The diversity of lists of things, qualities, and people whose passing is noted in various versions of the formula provides a basis for the compilation by the

54. "'Ubi Sunt' Passages in Old English—Sources and Relationships," *Vetenskaps-Societetens i Lund* (Årsbok 1956), pp. 25–44; cf. particularly pp. 39–41.

55. *Sermones ad Fratres in Eremo* 58, in Migne's *PL*, XL, col. 1341; this sermon is repeated as No. 75 of the collection, with a different and shorter introduction, a clear attestation of its popularity.

56. Cf., the *ubi sunt* passages in Blickling Homily X and Vercelli Homily X.

*Wanderer* poet of his own list, although individual items may have their counterparts elsewhere. It should be noted that the subjects of the exclamatory part of the passage, introduced by *Ēalā*, are of a similar type to those in the formal questions. As with the *sum sum* formula, the form of the passage owes much to Latin Christian models, but the spirit which informs it has strong heroic overtones. Once again the calculated ambiguity of the poet is apparent.

It has generally been assumed that the wise man's speech continues to the close of line 110, coincident with the end of the wanderer's speech, of which it forms a part.[57] But the *ubi sunt* formula, which he exists to utter, ends with line 96, as can be seen from comparison of lines 95b and 96 with Isidore of Seville's famous *ubi sunt* prototype, which concludes, after the series of questions, with the following words:

> quasi umbra transierunt velut somnium evanuerunt;
> quaeruntur et non sunt.[58]

> ⟨as though shade they have passed away, as though a dream they
> have vanished;
> they are sought and do not exist.⟩

Many versions of the formula have this or a similar "answer" to the questions and, like the line and a half in *The Wanderer*, suggest that the objects or persons might well never have existed. *The Meters of Boethius X* deals, like the latter part of *The Wanderer*, with the conduct and outlook of the wise man; it too has a version of the *ubi sunt* formula, in which the poet asks where are the wise men of antiquity such as Brutus and Cato; like the *Wanderer* poet, he adds a Germanic note to the formula, in his case by asking where are the bones of Weland, who is unknown to the Latin text of Beothius. He ends the *ubi sunt* section:

> Hī wǣron gefyrn forð gewitene:
> nāt nǣnig mon, hwǣr hī nū sindon.

Since the wise man has been chosen by the poet of *The Wanderer* to utter a stereotyped form of lament, it is reasonable to suppose that

---

57. Cf., Greenfield, *JEGP*, L (1951), p. 460; Kennedy alone closes it earlier, at the end of line 96, in *Old English Elegies* (Princeton: Princeton University Press, 1936), p. 50.

58. *PL*, LXXXIII, col. 865.

his utterance closes with the end of that lament. Moreover, line 97 begins a passage in a different vein; we are back with the ruins and the vanished warriors of lines 75–80. We are also back with the present tense, which continues to line 110, broken only by two parenthetic explanatory lines (99–100); lines 92–96 are isolated by being in the past tense.

In lines 97–110 the impersonal elegy of lines 73–87 is resumed by the wanderer in his own person, but from a slightly different point of view. In the foreground now are not the fallen warriors of lines 79–84, but the wall by which they fell. His concern here is to point out how the works of man have outlasted him; but just as man is destroyed by weapons, so his works in their turn are destroyed by the merciless elements. The culmination is reached in line 110 with the statement that all the world grows waste. The line echoes, but also enlarges the scope of line 87; there the buildings stand empty of inhabitants, now they themselves are included in the general destruction.

Many have followed Grein in closing the wanderer's monologue at the end of line 110, seeing in *Swā cwæð snottor on mōde* (111a) an indication that the speech is finished.[59] Huppé has argued that line 110 closes only the speech beginning at line 92 with the *ubi sunt* formula; but the verb *ācwið* which introduces this speech is in the present tense and is to be taken as iterative, as indicated by *feor oft gemon* in line 90. The speech to which it refers cannot, therefore, be closed by *cwæð* in line 111, which must refer to a speech begun prior to line 88, namely the wanderer's monologue.

Line 111 is, like lines 6–7, to be taken as an interpolation by the poet in his own person,[60] at a convenient point in the wanderer's speech, in which he draws attention to the fact that the reflective part of the poem, from line 62, is part of the train of thought of the wanderer, who is wise by experience. The interpolation is necessary because the wanderer has had no occasion to identify himself by the first person pronoun as he did earlier in the poem. Pope acknowledges the plausibility of the argument that "having appeared to us at first as merely an *eardstapa*, he has earned by his discourse the epithet of a wise man, a *snottor on mōde*." Nevertheless he sees in the difference of epithet confirmation, in the poet's own words, of his

59. They include Lawrence, Kennedy, and Greenfield.
60. Cf., Lumiansky, *loc. cit.*, p. 105.

thesis that there are two different major speakers in the poem.[61] The poet's own words may, however, be held to point to a quite different conclusion. He has established the identity of his speaker by the noun *eardstapa* in line 6 and the descriptive adjectival phrase in line 111 emphasizes another facet of the same man. Pope's suggestion, that *swā cwæð snottor on mōde* is a self-contained statement of the same order as *swā cwæð eardstapa*, is difficult to sustain in face of the Old English poetic practice of providing a referent, either noun or pronoun, for an adjectival phrase of this kind.[62] The only possible referent here is *eardstapa*.

Another question of some importance, but difficult to answer decisively, is whether *on mōde* is to be taken with *cwæð*, to stress the inward nature of his meditations,[63] or as part of a stereotyped phrase with *snottor*, similar in kind to *frōd in ferðe* (90) or *wīs on gewitte* (*Andreas* 470). The difficulty is that there are no analogous *snottor* phrases; *mōd* is usually linked to *snottor* in the oblique cases,[64] and poets appear to prefer alliteration in phrases such as *snottor in sefan* (*Exodus* 439). Pope believes that even if we take the phrase "as meaning primarily 'sat apart communing with himself' it suggests that he would normally have been expected to be communing with others." This expectation might be justified if the phrase were *tō rūne* as in the parallels he cites,[65] but here it is *æt rūne*, "in counsel," whereas the contexts of *tō rūne* indicate that a meaning "in consultation" would be the appropriate one. That the counsel the wanderer takes is inward is a possible interpretation of *on mōde*; that he is apart from others is indicated by *sundor*. This interpolated line meets the objection that the wanderer's monologue violates the noble custom that a man should keep his woes to himself (11–14).[66] We are reminded that the wanderer is in fact "thinking as he will" (14b).

61. Pope, *loc. cit.*, pp. 165–167.

62. Cf., *frōd in ferðe* (90) whose referent is *Sē* (88); *rædum snottor, wīs on gewitte* (*Andreas* 469–470), whose referent is *cempa* (461) varied by *ōreta* (463); and, after a speech, *hildedēor* (*Beowulf* 312), whose referent is *weard* (286).

63. Cf., *þinceð him on mōde* (41).

64. Cf., *mōde snottor* (*Riddle* 84. 35), *mōdes snottor* (*Precepts* 87), and *mōde snottre* (*Riddle* 86. 2).

65. *Beowulf* 171–172 and *Andreas* 1161.

66. Cf., Susie I. Tucker, "Return to *The Wanderer*," *Essays in Criticism*, VIII (1958), 233.

The last four lines of the poem contain sentiments which are
similar in kind to those in lines 65–72, but which have a more specifically Christian formulation and application. In lines 112–113 the
wanderer once again warns against overhasty conduct, as Elliott has
pointed out.[67] But whereas, in the earlier passage, reference was to
the consequences of a vow, here any form of extravagant emotion
indulged on impulse is deprecated. The concept is similar to that
expressed many times in the Book of Proverbs,[68] but particularly in
29:11:

> A fool gives full vent to his anger,
> but a wise man quietly holds it back.

It is not only the concept but also the manner of expression which is
subtly different in this closing passage. The speaker uses formulas
closely associated with homiletic writing. Line 112a has no exact
counterpart, but the formula, adjective followed by *biþ sē þe*, is an
established one in didactic passages in Old English poetry.[69] As has
been pointed out, *til* is used in Old English of God's goodness,[70] and
the adjective is associated with fidelity in *Riddle* 26, on the Bible
codex, in line 23, where friends are referred to as *tilra ond getrēowra*.
Beside the virtue of self-control the speaker puts that of fortitude;
that *ellen* can be a specifically Christian virtue is made explicit in
*Andreas*:

> Forþan ic ēow tō sōðe    secgan wille,
> þæt næfre forlǣteð    lifgende God
> eol on eorðan,    gif his ellen dēah.          (458–460)

The key to the wanderer's emphasis on prudent behavior and fortitude is his insistence throughout the poem on the failure of this
world to provide consolation. The early Christian fathers had been
well aware that things of this world offer no real consolation, and
Cicero before them had stated that secular consolation was poor
consolation.[71]

---

67. Elliott, *loc. cit.*, p. 195.

68. E.g., 10:19; 13:3; 15:28; 21:23; 29:20.

69. E.g., *Dol biþ sēþe* . . . in *The Seafarer* 106, *Maxims I* 35, *Solomon and Saturn*
225, *Ēadig bi ð sē* . . . in *The Seafarer* 107, and *Bald bi ð sē* . . . in *Solomon and Saturn* 243.

70. Susie I. Tucker, *loc. cit.*, p. 232.

71. Cross, "On the Genre of *The Wanderer*," p. 70.

The last line and a half provide a solution to the whole problem of the transitoriness of all things, which has been posed throughout the poem. Reliable consolation is at hand if one seeks the grace of God; in *frōfre* is an echo of lines 25–29, where the wanderer as a young man sought a lord who would comfort him in his friendless state, *sōhte . . . þone þe . . . mec frēondlēasne frēfran wolde.* In form these last one and a half lines are typical of Christian exhortations not only in the prose homilies, but in poetry also, as in *The Phoenix* 516–517: *Wel biþ þām þe mōt in þā geōmran tīd Gode līcian,*[72] and *Beowulf* 183–188:

> Wā bið þæm þe sceal
> þurh slīðne nīð    sāwle bescūfan
> in fȳres fæþm,    frōfre ne wēnan,
> wihte gewendan!    Wēl bið þǣm þe mōt
> æfter dēaðdæge    Drihten sēcean
> ond tō Fæder fæþmum    freoðo wilnian!

This formula, adverb followed by *bið þām þe,* is simply a variant of the adjectival one in line 112 already discussed. The use of *fæstnung* in the abstract sense "stability"[73] is unique in Old English, but when one considers the world's wealth which *wēste stondeð* (74), and the buildings which *īdlu stōdon* (87), it is not surprising that stability should be the feature of the eternal world which is stressed.

The view that the introduction and conclusion are closely unified by explicit mention of the contrast between pagan and Christian ideas "in supplementation of each other,"[74] presents too stark an antithesis. Rather is there a contrast between the man who ignores, or is ignorant of, the world to come, and yet experiences God's grace (1b), and the man who actually seeks that mercy (114b). The virtues which are extolled in the gnomic passages are remarkable for being consistent with either a heroic or a Christian society, and those which are urged in the closing lines are the noblest of the not exclusively Christian virtues: fidelity, self-control, courage. These, of course, are not enough; the wanderer himself had

---

72. Cf., the practically identical passage in *Christ* 1079b–1080, also *Christ and Satan* 364, and *Andreas* 885–886.

73. Cf., Susie I. Tucker, *loc. cit.*, p. 237; Erzgräber, *loc. cit.*, p. 76 n. 70; and note to this line ⟨in Leslie's edition cited above in n. 25⟩.

74. Greenfield, *JEGP*, L (1951), p. 465.

demonstrated in the first fifty-seven lines of the poem that they provided neither consolation nor peace of mind. They are not the highest virtues of which man is capable under the inspiration of Christianity, such as loving one's neighbor as oneself, laying down one's life for one's brother, or turning the other cheek. The poet, however, is not concerned here with the specific virtues of Christianity, but rather to point out that the best of the heroic virtues are insufficient for lasting security, and that the gloom and despair which consideration of this world alone may arouse in the breast of even the wisest non-Christian, may be avoided by recognition of the fact that stability is to be found in God alone.

Reprinted from R. F. Leslie (ed.), *The Wanderer* (New York: Barnes & Noble, Inc., 1966), pp. 1–25.

JOHN C. POPE

# Dramatic Voices in
## The Wanderer *and* The Seafarer

IN THIS ARTICLE I propose to reconsider the structure and certain aspects of the meaning of *The Wanderer* and *The Seafarer*. *The Seafarer* even more than *The Wanderer* has been the subject of a great deal of interpretation, and much of it has enduring value; but certain very basic issues are still in doubt—largely, I believe, because we have not reached a full understanding of its structure. My view of the structure is only a little different from some others that have been advanced both long ago and recently; yet I think the difference makes the basic idea more acceptable, and this idea itself needs to be brought into relation with what other critics have had to say about the probable meaning of certain passages. *The Wanderer*, by contrast, has seemed a relatively clear and well-organized poem and the usual view of its structure, though in my opinion incorrect, has had only a few undernourished rivals. Hence my interpretation is novel enough to need careful demonstration. But it is not entirely without antecedents, and is really more obvious than the interpretation of *The Seafarer*. Certain parallel features of the two poems strongly suggest the same basic structure, and certain features peculiar to *The Wanderer* seem to point the way to a fuller understanding of that structure. For the sake of clarity, therefore, I shall begin with *The Wanderer*.

I

The prevailing view of *The Wanderer* in its formal aspect has been that it consists principally of a long dramatic monologue, lines 8–110, spoken by a man who is introduced in line 6 as an *eardstapa* or wanderer. This monologue is enclosed by a seven-line introduction and a five-line epilogue spoken impersonally by the poet, and it contains within itself a subordinate speech by a purely hypothetical person, introduced as *se . . . pisne wealsteal . . . deope geondpenceð*, he

163

who deeply considers this foundation.[1] The hypothetical speech, coming at the end of the monologue, is a lament for all that men care for on earth and for the earth itself. It puts what the principal speaker has to say in a grandly objective way. When it is finished the wanderer himself stops talking and the poet adds the epilogue.

But now, at the head of the epilogue, we read,

> Swa cwæð snottor on mode,     gesæt him sundor æt rune.

That is, "So spoke one wise in spirit, sat by himself at counsel." To whom is the poet referring? Those who take lines 8–110 as the wanderer's speech generally assume, as surely they must, that the poet is referring by this new epithet to the wanderer himself. He can hardly mean the speaker of the closing lament in lines 92–110, for that indefinite person is merely a rhetorical figment, and his speech is introduced by the present-future *acwið* "will say," to which the preterite *cwæð* here does not properly correspond. It is plausibly argued that the wanderer has spoken not only of his personal sufferings (ll. 8–57) but with philosophical breadth of the losses all men must sustain in this unstable world (ll. 58–110). Hence, having appeared to us at first as merely an *eardstapa*, he has earned by his discourse the epithet of a wise man, a *snottor on mode*.

This is roughly the view set forth by Max Rieger in 1869,[2] and very ably reasserted by S. B. Greenfield in 1951.[3] There are some variations of it that are of interest though they do not change the basic conception of the structure. Thus it was assumed by Thorpe in the first modern edition of the poem, and later by Gollancz and others, that the wanderer rather than the poet spoke the first five lines—a very probable inference which will prove to be of some importance.[4] A logical extension, though somewhat less inviting, is

---

1. Quotations are from *The Exeter Book*, ed. G. P. Krapp and E. V. K. Dobbie (New York: Columbia University Press, 1936), pp. 134–137. Once or twice I have altered the punctuation.

2. "Über Cynewulf," *ZDP*, I (1869), 313 ff.; on *The Wanderer*, 324–330.

3. "*The Wanderer*: A Reconsideration of Theme and Structure," *JEGP*, L (1951), 451–465. Greenfield's analysis has recently been elaborated by Willi Erzgräber, "*Der Wanderer*, Eine Interpretation von Aufbau und Gehalt," *Festschrift zum 75. Geburtstag von Theodor Spira*, ed. H. Viebrock and W. Erzgräber (Heidelberg: C. Winter, 1961), pp. 57–85.

4. *Codex Exoniensis*, ed. B. Thorpe (London, 1842), p. 286; *The Exeter Book*, Part I, ed. I. Gollancz (EETS 104 [London, 1895]), p. 287. Their punctuation is briefly supported by W. S. Mackie, *MLN*, XL (1925), 92.

a recent suggestion that the last four lines also are spoken by the wanderer, so that only the lines describing the speaker, 6–7 and 111, are the poet's.[5] Real dissent from the prevailing view has been rare,[6] though it should be remembered that some of the most reputable editors have been unwilling to commit themselves as to where the wanderer's speech ends. They put a quotation mark before line 8 for the beginning (or resumption) of his speech, but one looks in vain for a corresponding mark of conclusion.[7]

If one is to object to the prevailing interpretation it must be rather for what it leaves unexplained than for any demonstrable error. It does not openly conflict with the development of meaning in the poem, and it explains plausibly what the poem itself says, in lines 6 and 111, about who is talking. But this explanation is not inevitable, and there are other points at which we may wonder whether we are on the right track. Most notably, there is a sharp cleavage between the first half of the poem, lines 1–57, and the second, lines 58–115.[8]

5. T. C. Rumble, "From *Eardstapa* to *Snottor on Mode*: The Structural Principle of 'The Wanderer'," *MLQ*, XIX (1958), 225–230.

6. For example, Norah Kershaw (Mrs. Chadwick), in *Anglo-Saxon and Norse Poems* (Cambridge: Cambridge University Press, 1922), pp. 8 ff., limits the wanderer's speech to lines 8–29a, after which the first person gives way to the third; but in her introductory remarks on p. 6 she expresses uncertainty. Emily Doris Grubl, in her *Studien zu den angelsächsischen Elegien* (Marburg: Elwert-Gräfe und Unzer, 1948), pp. 15 ff., limits the wanderer's speech to lines 8–57, attributing all else to the poet himself until the conclusion, 112–115, which she attributes to the *snottor on mode*. Her analysis on p. 31, however, disregards speakers and treats the poem as consisting of prologue (ll. 1–5), Part I (ll. 6–57), Part II (ll. 58–110), and conclusion (ll. 111–115).

7. The list includes Sweet, Gollancz, Bright, Kluge, and (perhaps unintentionally) Krapp and Dobbie. See Huppé's article, cited below in n. 9, pp. 518 f.

8. Fernand Mossé prints the poem with an extra space between lines 57 and 58, and in his notes calls lines 58–115 the "seconde partie de la poème" (*Manuel de l'Anglais du Moyen Âge*, I, *Vieil-Anglais* [Paris: Aubier, 1945], pp. 290 and 404). F. P. Magoun, Jr., setting off the introduction and conclusion, divides the middle section into Part I (ll. 8–57) and Part II (ll. 58–110) of the wanderer's speech *Anglo-Saxon Poems . . . Normalized*, Second Corrected Printing [Cambridge, Mass.: Department of English, Harvard University, 1961], pp. 18–21). Earlier Ernst Sieper had tried to show that lines 58–110, along with the prologue and epilogue, were not part of the original poem. (*Die altenglische Elegie* [Strassburg: Trübner, 1915], pp. 197 ff.). Grubl (above, n. 6) and Erzgräber (above, n. 3) observe the same division into two parts between lines 57 and 58 but treat these parts (with prologue and epilogue) as members of a carefully unified whole.

In the first half the wanderer is dwelling on the sorrows he himself has endured, generalizing them only enough to include others whose lot closely resembles his own. A cold and desolate sea provides the setting for poignant descriptions of the loneliness that attends a friendless and lordless retainer. In the second half he seems to have put aside his personal sorrows, indeed all his past experience with its desolate seascapes, in exchange for thoughts about mankind at large, for images of walls and cities in ruin, for the sweep of history and the awesome prospect of the end of the world. And the change comes, not gradually, but all at once. We may easily begin to wonder whether the speaker is really the same, whether it is advisable to identify the *eardstapa* with the *snottor on mode*.

An unsuccessful but nevertheless significant effort to separate the two characters was made some twenty years ago by Bernard F. Huppé.[9] His basic feeling, that the poet was making a distinction between a man hemmed in by his own bitter experience and a man whose mind could range freely over the universe with philosophic detachment, was grounded in the contrast to which I have already alluded. Unfortunately a slip in reasoning caused him to ignore the natural division between lines 57 and 58 and to assert that the *eardstapa*'s speech extended to line 62a. His reason was that the pronoun *ic*, after giving way to the third person in lines 30–57, had reappeared in the sentence at 58–62a and that therefore the *eardstapa* must still be speaking. This was a fatal deduction, for lines 58–62a are lines that introduce a broad consideration of human life and if they are spoken by the *eardstapa* they mark him as a philosopher, so that there is no reason to deny him any of the ideas that follow. Mr. Greenfield, in the article cited above, accepting as an obvious truth the fallacy in Mr. Huppé's reasoning about the pronoun, had no difficulty in showing that the latter's analysis of the structure was inconsistent in itself and much less satisfactory than the traditional view. Additional trouble was created by Mr. Huppé's effort to identify the wise man's speech with the concluding lament, lines 92–110, so that he was obliged to designate the lines between speeches, 62b–91, as a bridge passage spoken by the poet. The result of this analysis could only be general confusion. The important perception at the root of it was nearly obliterated.

9. "*The Wanderer*: Theme and Structure," *JEGP*, XLII (1943), 516–538.

What did not occur to Mr. Huppé, probably because he had already assigned lines 92–110 to the *snottor on mode*, was that if there are two speakers in a poem they can both use the pronoun of the first person. Suppose we start with the possibility that the *eardstapa* and the *snottor on mode* are different characters, as the different epithets suggest, and ask ourselves how much of the poem, in that event, is appropriate to each. The answer is very clear: Lines 1–5 and 8–57 are appropriate to the *eardstapa*; lines 58–110 (including the imaginary lament, 92–110) are appropriate to the *snottor on mode*. Lines 6–7, identifying the first speaker, line 111, identifying the second, and lines 112–115, bringing down the curtain with a combination of gnomic wisdom and pious reassurance, may best be left to the poet. The hypermetric form of the last five lines helps to set them off as an epilogue.

If now we look more narrowly at the two speeches thus distinguished we shall find that we have replaced one vaguely inclusive character with two firmly defined ones. The wanderer's speech becomes the perfectly rounded utterance of a person whose own bitter experience has made him an authority. Having achieved some measure of resignation to his lot, he is expressing for all who have suffered similar losses just what this kind of sorrow is made of. His concluding generalization,

> Cearo bið geniwad
> þam þe sendan sceal   swiþe geneahhe
> ofer waþema gebind   werigne sefan,

should not be taken primarily as an appeal for sympathy. It is concurrently, and more importantly, a truth gleaned by suffering. From beginning to end he is telling us what he has learned about life. His personal history gives him the right to speak.

And since we have thus limited his speech, it is important to make sure that it has a proper beginning. The first five lines do not say anything that is beyond the range of such a character, and they say much that is appropriate to him:

> Oft him anhaga   are gebideð,
> metudes miltse,   þeah þe he modcearig
> geond lagulade   longe sceolde
> hreran mid hondum   hrimcealde sæ,
> wadan wræclastas.   Wyrd bið ful aræd!

The opening clause keeps the consoling possibility of God's ultimate mercy in view without assuring us that the speaker has already obtained mercy. He does seem to have reached a state of comparative tranquillity, but his past sorrows are still vivid in his mind, and they form the substance of what he has to communicate. As he begins to recall them he thinks of the inexorable power of fate. It is characteristic of him to generalize out of his own experience, so that his hypothetical characters are but projections of himself. Thus the word *anhaga* (repeated in line 40) sums up his own loneliness. (We may remember that it is used of Beowulf in a similar situation, when he swims back to his country alone after having witnessed the death of Hygelac and all the Geatish host.) And the image of one stirring the rime-cold sea anticipates the climactic seascapes of lines 37–57. So long as the wanderer is thought to be responsible for speaking most of the poem one may toy with the idea that the poet speaks the opening lines in such a way as to anticipate the wanderer's own point of view while he adds a bit of piety. But if the bulk of the poem consists of two complementary speeches, this kind of introduction is less appropriate. Besides, the wanderer's speech needs some sort of generalization at the start to hold it together. His words at line 8 are not a beginning but a development proceeding out of what has been said in lines 1–5. Thus, although the pronoun of the first person appears in line 8 for the first time, the sentence is not otherwise comparable to the sentences with which *The Seafarer* and *The Wife's Lament* begin. And the *Swa cwæð eardstapa* at line 6, though there is precedent for such an expression (under somewhat different circumstances) as an introduction to a speech, is much more likely to refer to something already said.[10]

In the second speech we find just as consistent a characterization as in the first. The *snottor on mode* proclaims himself at once as a person who relies, not on direct experience, but on the wide reach of his thought:

10. This was Mackie's opinion in the article cited above, n. 4. Greenfield (*op. cit., supra*, n. 3, pp. 455 f.) cited two examples in which *swa cwæð* precedes a quotation and held that Mackie's argument was therefore inconclusive. He chose to attribute lines 1–5 to the poet for the sake of what he thought was the most satisfactory structure. His view is supported by Erzgräber (*op. cit., supra*, n. 3, pp. 77 f.), who nevertheless calls attention (p. 75) to the link between *anhaga*, line 1, and *anhogan*, line 40.

Forþon ic geþencan ne mæg    geond þas woruld
for hwan modsefa    min ne gesweorce,
þonne ic eorla lif    eal geondþence,
hu hi færlice    flet ofgeafon,
modge maguþegnas.    Swa þes middangeard
ealra dogra gehwam    dreoseð ond fealleð.

[Verily[11] I cannot think, within the range of *this* world, why *my* mind should not grow dark, when I consider all the life of high-born men, how of a sudden they have relinquished the hall-floor, proud young retainers. So this world, each and every day, droops and falls.]

There are several ways in which this passage gains by being attributed to the second speaker. It was always a little puzzling to find the wanderer giving reasons for the darkening of his mind, as if it had not been darkened long ago by the death of his kinsmen. But the thinker, if he is to feel an answering sadness, must explain the ground for it. In the second line the possessive *min* now takes on the extra meaning that explains why it is carrying the alliteration: "why *my* mind should not grow dark," that is, "my mind also, like the wanderer's." But what chiefly strikes our attention is the sweeping generalization, so much greater in range and abstraction than the wanderer's, and so objective, as having nothing to do with the speaker's personal losses: "*all* the life of highborn men" (where, as the *modge maguþegnas* more clearly shows, it is men like the wanderer and his fellow-retainers that are in view, but collectively and by implication as representatives of mankind). And immediately after

11. This meaning of *forþon* was ably discussed by W. W. Lawrence in his influential though now largely superseded article, "*The Wanderer* and *The Sea-farer*," *JEGP*, IV (1902), 460–480; on *forþon*, pp. 463 ff. Fundamentally the word asserts that there is some sort of connection between what has been said and what follows. "As for that" is perhaps as close as one can come to the vague meaning paraphrased here by "verily." I find this vague meaning earlier in the poem at line 37 and probably also at line 64, though this last may be "therefore." The meaning is certainly "therefore" at line 17. The same meanings and another, "because" or "for," appear in *The Seafarer*. The case for an adversative sense, first suggested by Rieger for *The Seafarer*, is strongly supported by Marjorie Daunt, "Some Difficulties of *The Seafarer* Reconsidered," *MLR*, XIII (1918), 474 ff. Some of her examples are persuasive but a clearly adversative sense does not seem to be demanded in either of these poems. See further n. 28 below.

we encounter the image of the drooping and declining world, suggesting on the one hand that men are continually dying and disappearing from the world like leaves from some continually decadent tree, and on the other that the world is now in its sixth and final age, and resembles an old man on the brink of the grave.

We come next to some lines often blamed for irrelevance:

> Forþon ne mæg weorþan wis wer, ær he age
> wintra dæl in woruldrice. Wita sceal geþyldig,
> ne sceal no to hatheort ne to hrædwyrde,
> ne to wac wiga ne to wanhydig,
> ne to forht ne to fægen, ne to feohgifre,
> ne næfre gielpes to georn, ær he geare cunne.
> Beorn sceal gebidan, þonne he beot spriceð,
> oþþæt collenferð cunne gearwe
> hwider hreþra gehygd hweorfan wille.

[Verily {or therefore?} a man cannot become wise before he has a share of winters in the world. A wise man must be patient, must not be too hot of heart or too hasty of speech, nor too weak a fighter nor too reckless, nor too fearful nor too sanguine, nor too greedy for money, nor ever too eager to boast before he knows for certain. A fighting man must wait, when he is to speak his vow, until, bold of spirit, he knows for certain whither the purpose of (men's) breasts will turn.]

Surely this passage, though it is still a digression from the main course of the argument, looks a good deal more pertinent when it is recognized as part of the characterization of the second speaker. He is no *modig maguþegn* himself, though he may well belong to the warrior class for whose benefit he speaks, but a man schooled in prudential wisdom, and he seems to exhibit this practical aspect of his training at a point where his meditation brings it to mind, partly to show that he knows what is expected of a counselor.[12]

As now his thought carries him forward to the general doom, to its miniature yet impressive prototypes in the ruins that darken the landscape, and to his mournful realization that nothing earthly can endure, he reminds us further of the value he attaches to the intel-

12. A rhetorically similar passage in Blickling Homily X (ed. R. Morris, ⟨*The Blickling Homilies of the Tenth Century*, EETS 58, 63, 73 [London, 1880]⟩, p. 109, ll. 26–30), to which G. V. Smithers has called attention (*MÆ*, XXVI [1957], 140), is by contrast one-sidedly clerical in content.

lect. Thus at line 73 he says it is the *gleaw hæle* who must know how terrible it will be when the world is destroyed, and when he introduces his hypothetical elegist in lines 88–90 he defines him as one *frod in ferðe* and requires him to think deeply before uttering his lament. But I need not continue. From first to last he answers to the definition: he is *snottor on mode*.

Once we have made this distinction between the speakers it is difficult to resist it, for it so obviously matches the pattern of theme and image in the poem, and is so direct and simple an explanation for the poet's own words, the *swa cwæð eardstapa* and *swa cwæð snottor on mode*. But we may well hesitate momentarily in the face of the unfamiliarity of the form. Here we have two speeches complementing one another, the second a challenging extension of the first, yet the speakers are apparently not disputing with one another and the only direct indication that the second has been listening to the first is the vague implication of his opening *forþon* and the comparison implicit in his first sentence. This is certainly not an ordinary dialogue in which the speakers are addressing each other. What is the fundamental conception that can render such a juxtaposition of two speeches intelligible?

For a time I was inclined to believe that the poem was a meditative monologue by the thinker in which, after speaking lines 1–5 in his own character, he introduced the wanderer and quoted his words. Then, at line 58, the thinker resumed his meditation and proceeded to the end of it at line 110, after which the poet identified him as the principal speaker. This notion may need passing attention, because something very like it has already been suggested for *The Seafarer*; but it is surely mistaken. Once we recognize that the first five lines are much more appropriate to the wanderer than to the thinker, we are confronted by two consecutive speeches of almost the same length, and although the second is more inclusive than the first and comprehends it intellectually, there is no good reason why the second speaker should be made to quote the first. It is much simpler and more intelligible, as well as fairer, for the poet to quote each of them in turn, acting as a neutral reporter and letting us make up our own minds about the importance of each.

A much more satisfactory answer to the problem of the two speakers is suggested by the poet himself when he describes his second speaker, the *snottor on mode*, and says he was sitting apart at counsel, *gesæt him sundor æt rune*. Even if we take this expression with Bosworth-Toller as meaning primarily "sat apart communing with himself," it suggests that he would normally have been expected to be communing with others, taking his place *æt rune*. For example, in *Beowulf*, lines 171–172, we are told that many a man among the Danes *gesæt rice to rune*, and in *Andreas*, line 1161, that the counselors of the famished Mermedonians *gesæton sundor to rune*. The association of the word *run* with the consultations in hall by a king's trusted advisers is otherwise illustrated by the description in *Beowulf*, 1325, of the dead Æschere as having been Hrothgar's *runwita*. It seems possible, then, that the poet is not only describing the isolation of the thinker but at the same time implying that the scene is a nobleman's hall where a number of men are assembled to share experiences and ideas. The topic this time is bereavement, or more broadly, mutability, and two men of vastly different experience and training speak in turn. They are not disputing with one another but making their separate contributions to the discussion, the second, of course, speaking with full awareness of what the first has said and building upon it, but addressing himself, as the other had done, to the group.

Such, I believe, may well be the dramatic assumption behind these partly corroborative, partly antithetic speeches, though certainly the hall was not the only place where, in everyday life, men might have spoken successively on a topic without directly addressing one another, and it must be admitted that the poet has withheld all but the barest hint of a stage setting. The emphasis, beyond question, is on the speeches themselves, and whatever may be their relation to the patterns of actual discourse, it is clear that these dramatic voices are put in sequence for us in order that the poet may do justice to two different aspects of his theme.

At bottom, in fact, the poet reveals by the contrasting elements in these speeches his consciousness of the rival claims of two schools of thought, almost of two cultures. His love for the old Germanic poetical traditions and his mastery of them are amply revealed in the speech of the wanderer and are not altogether hidden in the speech of the wise man. The opposition between the two characters is by no means absolute. But some of the thinker's ideas in this speech and its whole purport reflect the influence of the Mediterranean learning that became available in the wake of the conversion. The fact that the poet preserves so much of the feeling of tradition in his imagery and his expressions suggests not only his unusual skill but the labor of predecessors in making poetry out of these new ideas and modes of feeling. The author of *The Wanderer*, in a more radical way than the author of *Beowulf*, seems deliberately to juxtapose the new mode and the old, to exhibit both the strength and the limitations of the old, and to suggest a synthesis dominated by the new.

As for the poem itself, it seems to me to gain greatly in precision and richness of meaning by the recognition of its duality. When we consider the relations of the two speeches we see that both characterization and theme have become sharper and have developed additional significance by their interaction in our minds. And the poet himself, in comprehending both his characters and the range of their thought and feeling, has displayed a breadth of understanding far beyond what we could see in the monologue we have grown accustomed to reading.

We must beware of oversimplifying the contrast between the two speakers. Both, we should assume, are nominally Christian, both preserve elements of old traditions, both show some interest in the world and its values. But the wanderer, as a typically loyal retainer, belongs to the conservative aristocratic world in both life and poetry; the thinker, though he recognizes a native tradition of wisdom, has moved into the sphere of Biblical and patristic learning, with some flavor of classical philosophy. And the darkness of spirit that has come over both these characters has different roots and leads to different conclusions. The wanderer's whole-souled devotion to his lord and his fellows of the comitatus is at once the sign of his nobility and the cause of his sorrow. This all-absorbing passion has been turned by the death of those he loves into the cold fetters of his loneliness. As the recurring images of confinement in the first half of the poem suggest, the wanderer is imprisoned by the sheer unchanging emptiness of his lordless, friendless environment. If he has found some alleviation of his misery it is not because he has learned to see it in a different light.

The thinker, in contrast, is not thus confined, nor has he suffered so personal a loss. His pensive melancholy, beautifully balanced against the other's sorrow, comes from the knowledge of other people's losses and the prospect of the general doom. His mind is constantly moving outward to survey men's history, to look on a landscape sprinkled with ruins, to look *through* life and the world. It is remarkable how often he uses *geond*, meaning variously "over, through, throughout," both as preposition and verbal prefix; it helps to emphasize the notions of penetration and range. The whole oppressive extent of the wanderer's suffering is diminished by his comprehensive view into the image of one disconsolate survivor of a battle saving a dead comrade from the birds and beasts of prey by burying him in the earth—quite uselessly, of course.[13] Thus, although he very movingly laments the passing of all things that seem of value in the world, there is a certain coolness in his attitude toward individual things and persons. His aloofness, as he sits apart, carries very different implications from the other's loneliness. For there is a balance in his thinking between sadness at the instability and waste of the world and the liberating energy of his thought. The elegy with which he concludes his speech expresses this balance with remarkable clarity and power. By its succession of images of good things that have perished it moves from a beginning full of regret and longing to deepening gloom and total disaster. But when, in the closing line, we find it said that "all this foundation of earth shall become void," we can hardly help recognizing that in the relentless completion of his thought the thinker has annihilated the very ground that breeds these vanishing satisfactions. Any expression of grief involves some release, but there is something almost triumphant in the sweep of this vision of dissolution.

13. Ll. 80–84. J. E. Cross has shown that at least the *sum*-formula of this passage, and possibly the enumeration of different ways by which the body may be destroyed, can be attributed to the influence of patristic writings. ("On *The Wanderer* Lines 80–84: A Study of a Figure and a Theme," *Vetenskaps-Societetens i Lund* [Årsbok, 1958–1959], pp. 75–110.) Yet whether this influence is admitted or not, I think we must recognize the basic sense of the passage as something rather different from what the fathers were concerned about. Here the distinction between the accusative plural in *Sume wig fornam* and the following instances of the accusative singular *sumne* should be observed. The thinker has just pictured a military host lying dead by a wall. He says, with understatement, that "some," meaning "many," had been carried off by war, and he now mentions what happened to the corpses: "One a bird carried off over the high sea, one the grey wolf shared with death, one a sad-faced earl hid in an earth-pit." A very similar interpretation is set forth by Erzgräber, *op. cit.*, *supra*, n. 3, p. 69.

Thus I am persuaded that there is more reason than ever to look upon this elegiac poem as having strong affinities with the literary consolation, as has recently been maintained afresh and very ably by J. E. Cross.[14] As Mr. Cross shows, the main reason for listing the poem as a member of this genre is not the brief acknowledgment of God's mercy at the beginning nor the assurance of steadfastness in heaven at the end, though certainly the latter is a significant way of closing the frame. The main reason is that the grounds for lamentation in the second half of the poem are also familiar medicines for a personal grief: in general, the contemplation of other people's distress tends to mitigate our own, and a panorama diminishes the importance of the foreground. With the separation of characters, it becomes evident that the entire speech of the thinker is at one and the same time a lament and an antidote against the sort of misery that had so long engulfed the wanderer. We need not be surprised at the bitterness of the medicine if we remember the methods of Dame Philosophy in Boethius, nor at the tendency toward consolation in a lament if we remember the funeral elegies of the poets.

But certainly what we have in *The Wanderer* is no reversal of mood, nor does the second speaker aim his speech at the first (or even at us) in the manner of a philosopher or a preacher, as if to inculcate a contempt for the world. Rather he assimilates his mood to the other's and seems, as the poet tells us, to be communing with himself though at counsel. He has been following a train of thought and it has ended in a bleak though strangely sublime vision of destruction. If we choose to find it instructive or consoling that is our affair.

Clearly our modern title for the poem does it less than justice. I shall not try to supplant it after more than a century of use, but perhaps I may be allowed to invent, for the sake of summary, one of those generous Elizabethan titles, borrowing a contradiction or two from Peter Quince: "The Wanderer's Lament and the Wise Man's Meditation: Being a Double Elegy and Most Doleful Consolation in Two Voices and an Epilogue, Wherein They that have

14. "On the Genre of *The Wanderer*," *Neophil*, XLV (1961), 63–75. The idea was suggested earlier, with apt comparison to Boethius, by R. M. Lumiansky, "The Dramatic Structure of the Old English *Wanderer*," *Neophil*, XXXIV (1950), 104–112. Erzgräber (*supra*, n. 3) presses still further the argument for Boethian influence.

Lost what they have Loved may Behold the Image of their Sorrow and may Feelingly Know that All Things Earthly Vanish into Night."

## II

The idea that there are two speakers in *The Seafarer* emerged early in the modern criticism of the poem and has recently, after a period of disfavor, been put forward again in a significantly modified form. It will appear once more in these pages, this time in a form strongly resembling that which has just been ascribed to *The Wanderer*. But along with many resemblances to *The Wanderer*, *The Seafarer* exhibits some important differences. It is a much harder poem to follow from passage to passage, so that the question of its dramatic form is seriously entangled with other problems of interpretation. We may profitably begin, therefore, by reminding ourselves of certain peculiarities of the poem and of some notable efforts to deal with them.

Under the scrutiny of two sharply opposed interpreters, Kluge and Anderson, who in this one matter agreed, the poem seemed to fall into three unequal sections, with one point of division after the first quarter and another in the middle.[15] I shall follow Anderson in calling the sections A1, A2, and B, although these symbols do not express the relationship that will ultimately emerge. The division in the middle between A and B (l. 64 or 66) is determined by a contrast in ostensible subject matter and style. The first half, A, is lyric and dramatic and contains frequent references to the sea, whereas the second, B, starts with a reasoned attack on the world and its values, ends with precepts and a sermon-like exhortation, and does not mention the sea. There is a transitional sentence (ll. 64b–66a) that preserves a bit of the imagery of A (the reference to *land* in contrast to sea) while it introduces the main theme of B, but otherwise the contrast is clearly marked. The division after the first quarter is determined by what has been interpreted by some as a change of speaker, by others as a shift to a new aspect of the same speaker's character, and to his present purposes as opposed to his past experience. The beginning, A1 (ll. 1–33a) tells in the first person of the hardships endured by a man who has made numerous voyages

15. F. Kluge, "Zu altenglischen Dichtungen, I, Der Seefahrer," *Englische Studien*, VI (1883), 322–327; O. S. Anderson, "The Seafarer: An Interpretation," *K. Humanistiska Vetenskapssamfundets i Lund Årsberättelse* (1937–1938), pp. 1–49.

and remembers the wintry ones with particular vividness. He contrasts his misery with the satisfactions of a landsman, his own knowledge of pain and anxiety and loneliness with the landsman's cheerful ignorance. The remainder of the first half, A2 (ll. 33b–64a), also predominantly in the first person, tells of the speaker's desire to make a voyage to a far country, denies that the satisfactions on land can distract a man from his voyage, and says that all the adornments of the land in its blossoming season urge a man to set out if he means to go far. The cuckoo urges him too and bodes sorrow. In confirmation of this note of sorrow and in accord with the earlier section, the speaker says that the prosperous man cannot know what is suffered by those who go farthest on the paths of exile. Yet the speaker is irresistibly impelled to set forth.

Before Kluge had distinguished these three sections Max Rieger had noted the signs of a change in line 33 and had concluded that there must be two speakers. He regarded the poem as a dialogue between an old man, full of bitter experience, and a young man who longed to make a voyage in spite of the other's warnings. The young man's first reply came at the beginning of A2 and there were further exchanges in the course of which no distinction was recognized between A and B.[16] Kluge, in the article already mentioned, accepted the dialogue theory but pointed out the weakness of the evidence for all the changes of speaker after the first and held that there were only two speeches, the old man's in A1 and the young man's after it. But he limited the young man's speech, as a significant piece of characterization, to A2, because he regarded B as a rather bungling addition to the original poem and was not concerned to reconcile it with A.

To Kluge himself and to other critics the separation of A and B seemed even more important than the question of dialogue within A. According to Kluge, if one accepted B as an integral part of the poem one might feel obliged to read A as an allegory, a reading that he thought incompatible with the internal evidence. By isolating A one could look on it as a purely imitative and secular piece, a lyric and dramatic treatment of men's relations with the sea. On this

16. Rieger's brief exposition forms part of the article cited *supra*, n. 2, *ZDP*, I (1869), 330–332. On pp. 334–339 he printed the entire poem as a dialogue according to his theory. The old man speaks ll. 1–33a, 39–47, 53–57, 72–124; the young man, ll. 33b–38, 48–52, 58–71.

matter he won the support of W. W. Lawrence, who was concurrently unwilling to accept the notion of a dialogue and tried to show that the contrast between A1 and A2 could be reconciled with the assumption that there was only one speaker.[17]

But Kluge's argument in dismissing B pointed to the means by which it was soon to be defended. Gustav Ehrismann was the first to present an allegorical interpretation.[18] He maintained that the poem was a loosely organized monologue setting forth the nature and claims of the monastic ideal of life. One set of symbols represented ascetic rigor and otherworldly aspiration in terms of a seafarer's life of toil and trouble on the sea and his concern to reach a far country, while another, contrasting set represented the aristocratic ideal of worldly success and pleasure in terms of the prosperous landsman and all the cherished satisfactions of life in the hall. In B the worldly satisfactions were disparaged as perishable, and the true end of a good Christian's endeavor was seen to be the attainment of the Lord's joys in heaven. There is no doubt that the contrasting images of A, when isolated, can be thus simply related to the main thesis of B; but if one considers them in the whole context provided by the formal elaboration of the poem a number of complications arise. Ehrismann made no attempt to explain the sequence of thought from passage to passage. He seems to have considered this a hopeless enterprise, for he described the author as a mere compiler, a clumsy arranger of appropriate passages out of the work of his predecessors, some of whom were skillful poets.

17. *Op. cit., supra,* n. 11. Lawrence's opinion has sometimes been misrepresented, as if he had accepted as original all but lines 103–124. On p. 462 he says, "I believe with Kluge that 64b–124 is an addition," and it is to this entire half of the poem (which Kluge had called homiletic) that he must be referring in his conclusion, p. 480: "There seems no reason to assume that the *Wanderer* and the *Seafarer* are not preserved in essentially their original form, with the exception of the homiletic addition to the latter poem." Doubting the originality of such a large part of *The Seafarer* could seem a small matter to Lawrence because his article was aimed chiefly at the fantastically disintegrative theory of R. C. Boer. It is a wholly different and subordinate problem that Lawrence takes up on p. 471, where he agrees with Thorpe that lines 103–124 may be, not an addition, but the end of another poem. See below, n. 29.

18. "Religionsgeschichtliche Beiträge zum germanischen Frühchristentum, II, Das Gedicht vom Seefahrer," *Beiträge zur Geschichte der deutschen Sprache und Literatur,* XXXV (1909), 213–218.

Thus it was left for O. S. Anderson, in the article cited above, to try to read the poem as a coherent and consistent allegory. Since he had followed a number of critics in rejecting the dialogue theories of Rieger and Kluge, he was obliged to explain the supposed allegory in A with respect to the life of its one speaker. He tried (as unsuccessfully, I think, as everyone else) to avoid the implication of a change of speakers at the start of A2, but in other respects he admitted a contrast between A1 and A2. A1, he maintained, was a presentation of the speaker's past life under the figure of voyaging along a dangerous coast in the winter. A2, then, presented the same speaker's longing to set out on a long summer voyage across the deep sea to a far distant country; that is, to take leave of this world altogether and make for the heavenly home.

There are several objections to this interpretation. For one thing, the meaning of the symbols shifts disconcertingly. In A1 the sea represents the vicissitudes of the world; in A2 it represents a passage to the hereafter at the point of death. If the shift were from literal to figurative meanings there would be no difficulty, but the literal meanings of sea and land are (for Anderson) an unregarded element in both sections: the shift is from one figurative meaning to another. Again, there is nothing in A1 to suggest that the speaker means anything beyond what he says. The account he gives of his sufferings at sea, though partly conventional, has seemed to contain so many imaginative touches and to mean so much when taken at face value that many readers are reluctant to take it otherwise. Unless as a secondary interpretation made in retrospect, an allegorical interpretation, having no power to make any of it more intelligible, is merely a nuisance.

It was this last objection that Dorothy Whitelock stressed when she proposed her ingenious and in many ways persuasive interpretation.[19] By assuming with her that the speaker is both a sailor and a religious zealot, a *peregrinus pro amore Dei* ⟨exile (or wanderer) for the love of God⟩, we can come very close to accepting everything in the poem at face value as spoken in character. For such a person would have had firsthand acquaintance with the actual sea (A1), would

19. "The Interpretation of *The Seafarer*," in *Early Cultures of North-West Europe: H. M. Chadwick Memorial Studies*, ed. Sir Cyril Fox and Bruce Dickins (Cambridge: Cambridge University Press, 1950), pp. 261–272.

have reason to plan another voyage, longer and more strenuous, perhaps, for religious ends (A2), and would be ready enough to philosophize and preach (B).

Certainly this interpretation much surpasses its predecessors in refinement and judgment. It does not foist allegory or religious overtones on verses that do not invite them, and yet it permits the positively religious implications of A2 and B to be recognized freely without the suspicion that they are the work of an interpolator. It also provides a historical context within which not only the seafaring *peregrini* but the age in which they flourished can be more clearly understood.

Yet it does not solve quite all the problems. For one thing it does not explain or condone (in terms of dramatic or poetic propriety) the absence of sea imagery in B. A pilgrim who was so deeply aware of the actual sea as to be capable of making the words of A1 his own might, in ordinary life, indulge in moral reflections such as we find in B without once mentioning the sea—in fact if the poem has one author, it is clear, no matter how we interpret it, that he has displayed this versatility. But a poetically conceived pilgrim ought not so to violate dramatic probability. For another thing, though as I have said this interpretation permits the religious implications of A2 and B to be recognized, its literalness nevertheless limits the meaning of A2. For, whereas A1 seems to gain by a literal interpretation, A2 seems to gain by an allegorical one. This peculiarity of A2 has been emphasized by studies more recent than Miss Whitelock's and will be considered in due course.[20]

Above all there is a stubbornly particular difficulty. Like all the theories that have treated the poem as a simple monologue, this theory does not give a satisfactory explanation for the language of the first sentence of A2:

> Forþon cnyssað nu
> heortan geþohtas þæt ic hean streamas,
> sealtyþa gelac sylf cunnige.[21]

20. Mrs. Gordon advances another objection in her excellent edition ⟨*The Seafarer* (London: Methuen and Co., 1960)⟩, p. 6. I do not make use of it here because (properly enough for Mrs. Gordon but disconcertingly here) it draws evidence for the speaker's character indiscriminately from A1 and A2.

21. Ll. 33b–35. My quotations are from Mrs. Gordon's text, though I have sometimes altered the punctuation, and for consistency I spell *forþon* as one word.

If one gives *sylf* the emphasis that its position in the verse demands, there is no good way to avoid the implication that the speaker has not been to sea before. This was pointed out specifically by Wülker,[22] and it was the one firm piece of evidence for the dialogue theories of Rieger and Kluge. If the experienced seafarer of A1 is still talking, why does he not say *eft cunnige* instead of *sylf cunnige*? In so crucial a matter the poet would hardly have sacrificed sense to a convenient alliteration. Those who have regarded the poem as a monologue have been obliged to believe that the poet was using *sylf* in a vacuous way and to find translations that would rob it of meaning. Lawrence, who made the first attempt to get around the difficulty, altered and weakened the *sylf* by a free paraphrase in which he inserted "again" for an *eft* that is not in the manuscript: "Even I myself, who have endured so much hardship, am impelled to make trial of the waves again."[23] Miss Whitelock, dealing more exactly with the rest of the sentence, simply leaves *sylf* untranslated: "Therefore my heart's thoughts constrain me to venture on the deep seas, the tumult of the salt waves."[24] One has only to reread the original after any of the translations given by the proponents of the monologue theory in order to feel that the evidence of the text at this point is flatly against them.[25] Yet if they found the older dialogue theories unsatisfactory on other grounds, what were they to do?

An answer of great interest, constituting what seems to me a signal advance, was made a few years ago by E. G. Stanley in the course of his article, "Old English Poetic Diction and the Interpretation

22. Richard Wülker, *Grundriss zur Geschichte der angelsächsischen Literatur* (Leipzig, 1885), p. 210.

23. *Op. cit., supra,* n. 11, p. 467.

24. *Op. cit., supra,* n. 19, p. 264.

25. Mrs. Gordon weakens *sylf* partly by a shift of emphasis and partly by a different interpretation of the clause in lines 34b and 35: "And so the thoughts trouble my heart now that I myself am to venture on the deep (or towering) seas." Here she gives partial recognition to *sylf* ("I in person" rather than "I also") but argues that the saving distinction is to be found in the emphasis on the *deep* seas, as if the speaker had made only coastal voyages before—a distinction that would be much clearer if only *sylf* were omitted. Her "now that" further weakens the effect. But this interpretation of *nu . . . þæt* is abnormal (the ordinary idiom being *nu . . . nu*) and is rendered very improbable by the seeming parallelism of the clause of purpose in the next sentence. (She is probably right, however, though this does not affect the argument, in taking *heortan* as object of *cnyssað*.)

of *The Wanderer*, *The Seafarer*, and *The Penitent's Prayer*."[26] He suggested that the poem, though not a dialogue, does in fact have two speakers, one of whom is quoting the other at the beginning. He regards A1 as a speech attributed to a typically conceived seafarer and quoted by the principal speaker as a basis and point of departure for his own discourse, which fills the rest of the poem. In order to emphasize the limited reality attributed to the person whose speech is quoted, and perhaps to suggest the direct influence of the rhetoricians, Mr. Stanley borrows the term *ethopoeia* from Mr. Huppé and gives it a more specialized sense than it normally conveyed:[27]

> There are two speakers speaking in the first person, the ethopoeic exile (lines 1–33a), and the wise, pious man eager to go on pilgrimage (33b to the end). The break comes (as it does in the various dialogue theories) in line 33; for the speaker who says (33b–35b) that he himself is now eager to make trial of seafaring cannot be the man who has just told of the hardships he has experienced in seafaring. The dialogue theories were advanced in the first place to overcome this difficulty, which is not explained satisfactorily by any of the later theories. The ethopoeic opening is the speech of a man whose imaginary exploits have led to a true view of this world; the poet has chosen this manner of conveying his message because it is the most vivid method of conveying it. The poet then expresses his wish to follow a way of life as contemptuous of the world as that of the ethopoeic Seafarer; he is speaking of himself, but he hopes to urge others to follow the same way of life, for his poem is didactic.

In spite of some dubious features that will be questioned presently, this interpretation marks a real advance because it deals more justly than previous interpretations with the natural implications and relationships of the text. The return to a strict interpretation of

---

26. *Anglia*, LXXIII (1955–1956), 413–466; especially 454 f.

27. Huppé discusses *ethopoeia* in the article cited above (n. 9), pp. 517 f. He took the term from Margaret Schlauch, "Prosopopoeia in *The Dream of the Rood*," in *Essays and Studies in Honor of Carleton Brown* (New York: New York University Press, 1940), pp. 30 f., who found it mentioned several times in *Rhetores Latini Minores*, ed. C. Halm (Leipzig, 1863). See especially the accounts of it by Emporius (Halm, pp. 561 ff.) and Isidore (Halm, p. 514). It applies properly to any imaginary speech so devised as to characterize the speaker, and therefore to almost all speeches in poetry, to which the rhetoricians resort for models. It seems hardly worth reviving, but it may have served as a catalyst for some good ideas of Mr. Stanley's.

*sylf* is only one of its merits. Even if Mr. Stanley is wrong, as I believe he is, in thinking that one speaker is quoting the other, he is right in feeling that the relation between the speakers is not that of an ordinary dialogue. The second speech is not so much a reply to the first as a major declaration of purpose and belief for which the first speech has given the stimulus. There are elements of contrast suggesting rejoinder as the second speech opens, but its main effect is to add another dimension to the imagery and transfer the discussion to another realm. Thus the notion that the second speaker quotes the first (however unsatisfactory in some respects) more nearly accords with the content of the speeches than would the notion of an ordinary balanced conversation or debate such as we usually find in a dialogue. More important, however, is Mr. Stanley's perception that if A1 is set apart, A2 and B can easily be joined together as the speech of a consistent character. For the talk of voyaging in A2 does not, like the talk in A1, reveal any direct experience of the sea, much less any deep subjection to its physical being. Even if we take the voyage literally, as Mr. Stanley, following Miss Whitelock, seems inclined to do, it is a voyage undertaken by the speaker as a part of his effort to disengage himself from the grip of the phenomenal world. With full dramatic propriety, therefore, though still perhaps to our regret, his thoughts move beyond images of the sea to their real center.

Kluge's version of the dialogue theory insisted on a completely secular and realistic interpretation of both A1 and A2, and treated B as essentially a separate, not properly relevant poem. But the allegorists and Miss Whitelock, defending the relevance of B, showed that A2 had strong signs of spiritual if not fully allegorical implications. Since they did not distinguish between the speakers of A1 and A2 they did not see the significance of what they nevertheless helped to establish, that A2 and B have much more in common than A1 and B. Hence Mr. Stanley's return to the notion of two speakers is not a return to Kluge's kind of poem. It involves the acceptance, with Kluge, of a literal and secular A1, but also, with the allegorists and Miss Whitelock, of a religious, possibly allegorical A2 and of a firm union between A2 and the thematically dominant B. In consequence there is opportunity for a more complete release of meaning in the various parts, and a more intelligible relationship between them than ever before.

Yet I think we can profitably modify Mr. Stanley's account of the structure and also his interpretation of the meaning. I shall begin with the structure, and first with the problem already mentioned, Mr. Stanley's notion that one speaker is quoting the other. An obvious objection is that the man alleged to be quoting does not say so. How can we understand what he is doing unless he introduces the other speaker with a *swa cwæð*? If the poem gives us two dramatic characters speaking in turn we can understand the omission of stage directions even if we have been sadly bewildered by their absence; but Mr. Stanley assumes a more or less autobiographical speech made by the poet himself in his own substantial character, at the start of which, without warning, he imitates a seafarer. It does not seem at all likely that the poet, in such a case, would not identify the subordinate speaker. Furthermore, the shadowy character attributed to the imaginary seafarer in contrast to the substantial poet is really not fair to the vividness and power of the speech. Why not accept the simpler view of the old dialogue theory and assume that the two speakers belong to the same plane of dramatic reality: that is, that they are equally fictitious and are speaking in turn? The second speech will still take the first as its point of departure, still overbalance it in length and scope, but will not disparage its authority in its own sphere.

Here at last *The Wanderer* may be called upon to lend its support and at the same time to suggest a further improvement in Mr. Stanley's view of the structure. *The Wanderer*, as described above, and *The Seafarer* show several very striking resemblances, some of which have already emerged and need only be called to mind: (1) Both begin with the speech of a fictitious character. (2) Both introduce a second fictitious character who builds on and enlarges what the first has said. (3) Both introduce the second character's speech with *forþon*.[28] (4) Both make use of the pronoun of the first person

28. At line 33b in *The Seafarer* the meaning of *forþon* may be exactly like that at line 58 in *The Wanderer*, an "as for that" which we may render as "verily" or "truly," or it may be "therefore," referring to the seafarer's statement that the landsman cannot believe what he has endured at sea: therefore the second speaker is impelled to make trial for himself. On the whole I prefer the vaguer sense. I also prefer not to take the *forþon's* at lines 33 and 39, or those at 58 and 64, as correlatives, as Miss Whitelock suggested in the article cited, pp. 264, 266, because the suspension created by the first *forþon* in the pair weakens the force of the sentence it

at the beginning of the second speech and imply a difference between the "I" now speaking and the "I" who has previously spoken, one of them giving alliterative prominence to *min*, the other to *(ic) sylf*. So much the reader will no doubt have observed for himself. But now there is a further resemblance, one that has often been noticed elsewhere but has not yet been brought to attention here: (5) Both have a passage at the end beginning with hypermetric verses. In *The Wanderer* this passage has already been taken to be an epilogue spoken by the poet. In *The Seafarer* the corresponding passage, though much longer, is probably the same thing.

Hitherto we have not paid attention to the internal structure of the second half of the poem, called B, since most of the problems could be treated by assuming its homogeneity. But in fact there is a noticeable difference between the part that extends to line 102 and the remainder, lines 103–124. As it happens, these verses begin a new page (actually a new gathering) in the Exeter Book, and Thorpe, the first editor of *The Seafarer*, suspected that a leaf was wanting and they were the end of another poem.[29] There is no supporting evidence for this conjecture and there are signs of relevance in the lines; but there is excellent reason for believing that they are not a part of the second speaker's discourse. In lines 66b–102 this speaker is explaining why he has said (64b–66a) that he prefers the joys of the Lord to this dead, transitory life on land, and parenthetically (72–80) maintaining the worth of virtuous action. He shows the instability of the world and the ultimate worthlessness of earthly

---

introduces. Elaborate logical structures are usually hostile to poetry. In both instances the first *forþon* (ll. 33 and 58) can be "verily" or "truly," the second (ll. 39 and 64) "for." See *supra*, n. 11.

29. *Codex Exoniensis*, p. 312 n. The idea was mentioned with at least tentative approval by others, e.g., Lawrence, *op. cit.*, *supra*, n. 11; N. Kershaw, *Anglo-Saxon and Norse Poems*, p. 18; Krapp and Dobbie (eds.), *The Exeter Book*, p. xxxviii. W. J. Sedgefield omitted these lines from his *Anglo-Saxon Verse-Book*, saying (p. 32), "We have omitted 22 or 23 lines with which the poem ends in the MS., as they are definitely religious rather than moralizing. It is possible that the latter part of this poem and of *The Wanderer* may have been later 'tailpieces' added by some monk for purposes of edification." Sweet, who first included the poem (as a monologue) in the seventh edition of his *Anglo-Saxon Reader* in 1894, accepted lines 103–108 as comparable to the last four lines of *The Wanderer* but relegated the rest to his notes. The problem is reviewed by Mrs. Gordon on p. 11 of her edition.

satisfactions, ending at line 102 with the worthlessness of gold. Then in lines 103–106 we encounter a series of precepts and gnomic observations that are vaguely pertinent but do not continue the argument. Six of the first eight of these lines are hypermetric, then the normal form returns. Finally, in lines 117–124, we have a lucid passage beginning like the closing exhortation of a sermon and ending with *Amen*.

> Utan we hycgan   hwær we ham agen,
> ond þonne geþencan   hu we þider cumen. . . .

Now the sermonizing conclusion, unlike the gnomic passage, is obviously relevant to the poem, but neither of them sounds like the second speaker. He impresses us in the early part of his speech as a man of intense feeling and compulsive purpose, full of the excitement attending a great personal decision. His reasoned pronouncements from 64b to 102 can readily be understood as his effort to justify the way of life he is choosing. The generality and loose sequence of the strongly worded gnomes form a contrasting boundary beyond which can follow the sermonizing conclusion with its gentle admonition and encouragement.

It is best, then, to take the precepts with their hypermetric opening and the cheerfully pious exhortation as an epilogue spoken by the poet as master of ceremonies. And this view is corroborated by the epilogue of *The Wanderer*, greatly though it differs in length. The first of its five neatly balanced hypermetric lines has no counterpart in *The Seafarer*, being an identification of the second speaker. But its next three and a half lines correspond in their gnomic style to the first fourteen of *The Seafarer*, and its last half-line, *þær us eal seo fæstnung stondeð*, corresponds in the use of the first person plural and in the blend of admonition and reassurance to the last eight of *The Seafarer*.

Thus it appears that in *The Seafarer*, as in *The Wanderer*, there are two complementary speeches by sharply differentiated persons, and that the poet, having presented these speeches, adds a conventional epilogue. This conception of the structure differs from Mr. Stanley's in that it sees both the persons who make use of the pronoun *ic* as dramatic characters clearly distinguished from the poet, and puts both speeches in the same plane of reality. This conception also entails a different analysis of the parts of the poem from that which is implied by the symbols A1, A2, and B. The first speech corresponds to A1, but the second, containing within itself the transition from talk of voyaging to ratiocination, combines A2 with two-thirds of B (ll. 33b–102), and leaves the end of B (ll. 103–124) to be set firmly apart as a mere epilogue to the poet's dramatic vision.

The main structural differences from *The Wanderer* are the absence of *swa cwæð* to identify either of the speakers and the different proportions of the speeches. The first difference may be due to faulty transmission of *The Seafarer* (though it is hard to find a good place in the first speech for an identifying aside), or, more probably, to an attempt to move one step closer to drama. The difference in proportion, however, is closely associated with the radical difference in theme and genre (as Mr. Cross has insisted)[30] between the two poems. For *The Seafarer* presents, in the central character of its second speaker, a man about to commit himself to a fateful course of action. In the early part of his speech he talks of his purpose and reveals the turbulent emotions that impel him toward it; in the later part, after stating the values that govern his choice, he defends it by a reasoned attack on the values he plans to reject. The first speech, insofar as it exists for a purpose beyond itself, is not something to be extended and counterbalanced like the speech of the wanderer, but something whose sensory vitality is to be transferred by the second speaker's thoughts to a different realm of meaning.

That the voyage this speaker contemplates has a spiritual end cannot well be doubted, since he says so clearly that the joys of the Lord are hotter to him than this dead, transitory life on land. And certainly his comparison invests the expression *lif on lande* with a figurative meaning, so that it comes to stand for the life of the worldling. I am not sure, even so, that there is a way to distinguish between the literal voyage that might be contemplated for spiritual ends by the sort of man Miss Whitelock has imagined and the allegorical voyage that might stand generally for the devout life amid the turbulent seas of the world. Yet for a number of reasons I am strongly inclined, now that the first speech in the poem does not have to be included in the same figurative pattern, to regard the voyage as allegorical.

30. *Op. cit., supra*, n. 14.

Thus, for one thing, if the voyage is allegorical, the speaker becomes more centrally representative of the religious life, so that both his voyage and his later rejection of worldly values acquire greater scope. Again, if he is not literally concerned with the sea, even as an instrument of purification, it is easier to understand why he never mentions it in the discursive part of his speech. His purpose, which demands a repudiation of the sensory world, merely declares itself openly after the images put into his mind by the vivid discourse of the veteran Seafarer have served their turn. And finally, I think the descriptive part of his speech has the character of the best allegorical composition, in that while it is lifelike and vivid and seems almost right as an imitation of a young man's eagerness for a voyage of ordinary adventure, it suggests, both by its extraordinary intensity and by certain expressions, that it ought to have some deeper import and a more general application. The prospective voyager, when he mentions the anxiety a man must have for his voyage, talks (though not quite explicitly in the negative sentence, ll. 39–43) as if every man that amounted to anything had a voyage to make. And at one or two points I am inclined to accept as secondary implications the meanings that have been proposed by a recent advocate of Anderson's theory.

One of these is *elpeodigra eard*, the destination of the prospective voyage according to line 38. This has usually been interpreted as "the land of foreigners (or strangers)" and taken as a description of a normal seafarer's destination abroad. But G. V. Smithers, in the first part of his study of *The Seafarer* and *The Wanderer*,[31] has argued that the word *elpeodig* here is used with reference to the idea that good Christians are exiles and aliens on earth, destined to travel as *peregrini* toward their *patria* in heaven (as in Hebrews 11:13–16, and in many passages in the church fathers) and that *elpeodigra eard* should therefore be taken as a reference to heaven, the future dwelling place of those who are now strangers on earth. So interpreted, *elpeodigra eard* anticipates and partially explains the speaker's enthusiasm for the joys of the Lord in lines 64b–66a, as Mrs. Gordon points out in accepting it in her edition (p. 9). It helps to explain,

31. "The Meaning of *The Seafarer* and *The Wanderer*," *MÆ*, XXVI (1957), 137–153; continued in XXVIII (1959), 1–22; Appendix, 99–104; the discussion of *elpeodigra eard* is in XXVI, 147–151.

too, the ravenous hunger of the speaker's soul (as described in lines 61–64a, a controversial passage of which I shall have more to say in a moment) at the sight of the far-off destination it has scouted on its preliminary flight. I think, therefore, that Mr. Smithers' interpretation, in spite of its riddle-like treatment of the expression, is probably correct. Yet I should prefer to regard *elþeodigra eard* as deliberately ambiguous, like certain expressions that have been pointed out elsewhere in the same speech.[32] The word *eðel* "homeland" is the usual and less equivocal term for the heavenly home when it is looked upon as the proper dwelling place of sojourners on earth, whereas *eard* is more neutrally taken as whatever country one lives in or is heading for.[33] Hence the ordinary translation, "land of foreigners," will naturally come to mind first, and it should be allowed to do so, for it fits the ordinary idea of a voyage that gives the figure its initial interest. But *eard* is also used for a dwelling place in heaven, and in one of Ælfric's homilies it is used pointedly in that sense, because Ælfric is developing the comparison between the promised land of the Israelites, *þone behatenan eard*, and the heavenly destination of the Christian journey.[34]

32. Earthly and heavenly meanings of *dryhten* in lines 41 and 43; *dream* in 65, 80, and 85; *blæd*, 79 and 88; *duguþ*, 80 and 85. See S. B. Greenfield, "Attitudes and Values in *The Seafarer*," *SP*, LI (1954), 15–20; also Mrs. Gordon's edition, pp. 26 f., and her discussion of "life on land," pp. 4 ff. and 42.

33. See the references under these words in Joseph Bosworth-T. N. Toller, *An Anglo-Saxon Dictionary* and *Supplement* (Oxford: Oxford University Press, 1898 and 1921). Mr. Smithers' most persuasive Old English illustration, from Blickling Homily II (ed. Morris, *op. cit.*, p. 23, ll. 1–7) has *eþel*: ". . . we synd on þisse worlde ælþeodige, . . . and nu eft sceolon oþerne eþel secan, swa wite, swa wuldor, swe we nu geearnian willaþ." Cf., also Ælfric, *Catholic Homilies*, ed. Thorpe ⟨*The Homilies of the Anglo-Saxon Church* (London, 1845)⟩, I, 162, ll. 16–20: "Nis ðeos woruld na ure eðel, ac is ure wræcsið; forði . . . we . . . sceolon efstan mid godum geearnungum to urum eðele, þær we to gesceapene wæron, þæt is to heofenan rice."

34. *Catholic Homilies*, ed. Thorpe, II, 214, ll. 25–27: "He gehælð his folc fram heora synnum, and gelæt to ðam ecan earde heofenan rices, swa swa se heretoga Iesus gelædde þone ealdan Israhel to ðam earde þe him behaten wæs." The word *eard* is repeated in the same sense at p. 222, lines 11 and 12; but at line 25 heaven is "ðone ecan eðel." I must add that the interpreters of the Bible did not feel obliged to adopt the same allegory for every mention of foreign travel. Thus Ælfric, expounding the parable of the talents (Matt. 24:14 ff.), translates "Homo quidam peregre proficiscens" ⟨a certain man setting out abroad⟩ as "sum rice man wolde faran on ælðeodigne eard" or, a little later, "on ælðeodignysse," and then

A second expression, less central but corroborative, occurs in the lines that describe the approach of summer, enumerating the signs that, as we learn immediately after, admonish the man who plans a long voyage to set forth:

> Bearwas blostmum nimað,    byrig fægriað,
> wongas wlitigað,    woruld onetteð.

The image of the hastening world can be explained, perhaps, as a mere reminder of the swift passage of the seasons provoked by the thought of the earth's activity and change as it bursts into bloom; and once again, as with *elþeodigra eard*, we can welcome this superficial meaning for its relevance to the figure of the voyage. But there seems to be an almost ominous urgency in the expression as it follows upon words so cheerfully evocative of springtime beauty, and the impression is strengthened when we find the cuckoo, as warden of summer, seconding the admonition with mournful speech and foreboding sorrow. The ominous urgency is very well explained if we accept the suggestion, made briefly by Mr. Smithers and more elaborately by Mr. Cross, that *woruld onetteð* is primarily an allusion to the impending though unpredictable end of this world.[35] Not only does the word *onettan* occur in several sermons with reference to the haste with which the world approaches its end, but Mr. Cross shows in detail how Gregory the Great, commenting on the image of the fig tree in Christ's prediction of the end of the world (Luke 21:29 ff.), turns a simple comparison into a paradox by leaving out the middle terms, making earth's fertility and growth into a direct prognostication of its ruin. Ælfric quotes the whole passage from

---

cites Gregory for the interpretation: "Hwæt is se man þe ferde on ælðeodignysse buton ure Drihten, seðe, mid þam lichaman ðe he on eorðan underfeng, ferde to heofenum? Witodlice flæsces wunung is eorðe, and Cristes lichama wæs gelæd swilce to ælðeodignysse ða ða he wæs ahafen to ðære heofenlican wununge, þær ðær næfre ær nan lichama ne becom." (Thorpe [ed.], II, 548, 550. Max Förster, *Anglia*, XVI [1894], 3, identifies Gregory's homily as the ninth of the series on the Gospel.) By this line of reasoning we could take *elþeodigra eard* as heaven because it is the land of spirits, who are strangers to the flesh; but certainly the interpretation offered by Mr. Smithers rests on a much more basic and widely diffused concept of the Christian's status on earth.

35. Smithers, *MÆ*, XXVIII (1959), 7; Cross, "On the Allegory in *The Seafarer*—Illustrative Notes," in *ibid.*, pp. 104–106.

Gregory in his sermon for the second Sunday in Advent,[36] stating the paradox as follows:

> Soðlice mid þisum wordum is geswutelod þæt ðises middangeardes wæstm is hryre. To ðam he wext þæt he fealle; to ðy he sprytt þæt he mid cwyldum fornyme swa hwæt swa he ær sprytte.

Immediately afterwards Gregory and Ælfric remind us that the world, having reached its sixth and last age, is like an old man about to die, and the same reminder occurs in lines 81b–90 of *The Seafarer*. I find it hard, therefore, to resist Mr. Cross's conclusion that *woruld onetteð* involves the threat of doom. Thus the prospective voyager has a reason beyond what is usual for setting out while the weather is propitious. No man can know whether there will be other summers after this one, and the voyage means the difference between life and death.

By no means, however, does my acceptance of these secondary meanings involve a commitment to the Andersonian view, now elaborated by Mr. Smithers, that the voyage represents merely the speaker's passage, at death, into the next world. Nor do I agree with Mr. Smithers' suggestion that we should return to the *wælweg* of the manuscript in line 63, with or without the extreme interpretation he has put upon the passage in which it occurs. The passage has caused trouble, however, and must receive some comment before I take up the larger problem of the speaker's death.

The six and a half lines beginning at line 58 form the climactic ending of the descriptive section of the speech. The speaker's soul leaves his breast, goes out over the sea, and comes back to him *gifre ond grædig*, as if hungering for what it has seen across the water.[37]

36. *Catholic Homilies*, ed. Thorpe, I, 614.

37. In his second article, *MÆ*, XXVIII (1959), 14 ff., Smithers cites evidence to show that behind this vivid passage is the widespread superstition that a man can send his soul out of his body and that it may appear to others in the form of an animal, often a bird. The same point has been made independently by Vivian Salmon, "*The Wanderer* and *The Seafarer*, and the Old English Conception of the Soul," *MLR*, LV (1960), 1–10. These illustrations seem decidedly pertinent, though there is no need to insist on taking the superstition literally here: it gives imaginative form to a universal psychological experience. Miss Salmon, however, has made it appear likely that related superstitions are responsible for some of the expressions in *The Wanderer*, ll. 52–55, notably the otherwise puzzlingly redundant combination, *secga geseldan*.

The passage concludes as follows according to the manuscript:

gielleð anfloga,<br>
hweteð on wælweg   hreþer unwearnum<br>
ofer holma gelagu.

In the first of his articles Mr. Smithers argues strongly for *wælweg* as "way to the abode of the dead" instead of Thorpe's almost universally accepted emendation, *hwælweg*. Neither compound occurs anywhere else in Old English, but *hwælweg* has the advantage of conforming to normal alliterative practice and of being obviously pertinent to the context. To make *wælweg* into a *durior lectio* ⟨more difficult reading⟩ instead of a simple piece of carelessness on the part of the scribe requires too great a strain on both versification and meaning—for although the notion of a violent death as a possible element in the voyage is not necessarily to be excluded even from my own reading of the passage, we must keep pagan associations with Valhalla very far in the background if we are to accept such a word as a description of a devout Christian's transit to heaven. There is an artistic difficulty, too, for such a blunt disclosure of the underlying meaning would shatter the illusion created by the richly figurative language of the passage. The time for disclosure is a moment later, when the images have done their work. Thus I think Mrs. Gordon has made the right choice in preferring the emendation.[38]

38. E. G. Stanley has renewed the plea for *wælweg* in his review of Mrs. Gordon's edition, *MÆ*, XXXI (1962), 54–60. He proposes (p. 58) a double meaning, both *wælweg* "oceanway," first adopted by Grein, and Smithers' *wælweg*. The meaning "oceanway" would certainly be acceptable if the alliance of *wæl* and *weg* could be shown to be probable (as I think it cannot), but the demands of alliteration would not be served, for crossed alliteration on *h* and *w* does not seem at all probable with this particular grammatical pattern. Stanley urges that a scribe would not be likely to change an easily understood compound such as *hwælweg* to anything so difficult as *wælweg*; but a scribe might very well drop an *h* without intending to change a meaning. The scribe of the Exeter Book has omitted initial *h* before a consonant at *Christ* 783 (*leotan* corrected to *hleotan*); *Azarias* 22 (*to worfne* corrected to *tohworfne*); *Phoenix* 126 (*remig*), 137 (*-leoþres*), 197 (*gewæs* corrected to *gehwæs*); *Juliana* 577 (*bi lænan*); *Widsith* 14 (*wala*); *Riddle* 15, 4 (*leorum*); 33, 3 (*leahtor*); 54, 5 (*rand*). Before vowels he has added it wrongly or omitted it on numerous occasions: e.g., *Christ* 615 (*is* for *his*), 885 (*healle* for *ealle*), 1412 (*ingonge* for *hingonge*); *Guthlac* 271 (*hus* for *us*), 950 (*hælmihtiga*), 1215 (*onhæfen* for *on æfen*); *Azarias* 61 (*hofne* corrected to *ofne*); *Phoenix* 477 (*eortan* for *heortan*), 650 (*elpe* for

Still more emphatically I must protest against a subordinate interpretation by which Mr. Smithers has sought to strengthen the idea that the speaker is about to die. He suggests that the *anfloga* of line 62b, instead of being the bird-like soul (*hyge*) that has been the subject of the preceding verbs, and can very appropriately be described as a "lone flier" (*ānfloga*), is a disease (\**andfloga*) ready to give the speaker a quick release into the next world.[39]

This last interpretation represents the extreme to which the Andersonian allegory has been pressed; but even the moderate interpretation of Anderson himself, by taking the prospective voyage as a voyage of death, runs counter to many of the implications of the poem even for those who, like Mrs. Gordon, take it as a monologue. Actually, as Mr. Smithers' own examples from the Bible, the fathers, and the Old English homilists abundantly demonstrate, the usual assumption about the return of the pilgrim to his heavenly home is that it is to be accomplished by a toilsome journey on earth in which death figures merely as a limit; and when the sea is introduced it is primarily associated with the tribulations of the world. Hence the closing sentences of Mrs. Gordon's rejoinder seem to me essentially right:

> The vain and fleeting pleasures and comforts of this world ('life on land') are to be left behind, and the suffering exacted by God from his followers (the *sorge* of the sea-journey) is to be

---

*helpe*); etc. My attention was called to this phenomenon by Miss Whitelock, to whom I am indebted for some very helpful criticism both at this point and elsewhere. I must add that Mr. Stanley says nothing in this review of his earlier interpretation of *The Seafarer* and seems inclined to favor that of Mr. Smithers.

39. *MÆ*, XXVIII (1959), 20–22. Mrs. Gordon's desire to identify the *ānfloga* with the cuckoo (*geac*) of line 53 (edition, p. 9) seems ill advised as soon as we are willing to grant that the soul itself resembles a bird in flight. The epithets of line 62a, *gifre ond grædig*, accord with the verb *gielleð* of 62b and should refer to the same creature. There is no need to identify the *hyge* with any particular bird, but these words would suit a bird of prey (*ful oft þæt earn begeal*, 24; [*ic*] *gielle swa hafoc*, *Riddle* 24, 3) at least as well as a sea gull, a bird that Mrs. Gordon understandably thinks inappropriate. Perhaps in the whole context the eagle supplies the greatest number of relevant characteristics, since he not only flies alone, screams, and has a voracious appetite, but is noted for his powerful flight and his sharp eyes. As a type of St. John the Evangelist he can look at the divine radiance by which others are blinded. But, of course, the speaker would hardly wish to claim for his soul more than a distant resemblance to so exalted a symbol.

undertaken with eagerness in the quest for eternity. The Seafarer [meaning the speaker of the whole poem, but we may
aptly think of the second speaker only] does not choose death;
he responds with eager longing to the challenge of that
suffering.[40]

An argument for this interpretation within the poem is the
passage (ll. 72–80) in which the second speaker concludes that a
man should earn the praise not only of those who live after him on
earth but of heavenly spirits by fighting against the devil before he
dies. This argument is all the stronger if we do not regard lines
1–33a as an account of the prospective voyager's earlier life. By
giving these lines to a different person we convert the voyage contemplated in lines 33b–64a into the major adventure of the second
speaker's life. We need not insist, with Rieger and Kluge, that he is
a very young man, but it is at least appropriate to think that he has
not passed the period of manly vigor. This accords well with the
imagery of the summer voyage as well as with his ardor, and likewise with his rejection (implicit in ll. 39–47, explicit in ll. 64b–102)
of the world and its satisfactions. An old man gains little credit by
renouncing what he is obliged to leave. The reasoning here is calculated to persuade those who can still make a choice, and the
speaker ought to be such a one himself. He must still *earn* the joys
of the Lord, however vividly he imagines them in advance.

The poem that has now taken shape is more complex than *The
Wanderer* in spite of the close similarity in structure. By its use of two
speakers it sets up a comparison between two kinds of seafaring, and
so not only shifts the focus from the natural to the supernatural order
but transfers the poignant immediacy of the poetry of sense to the
realm of spiritual action. This aspect of the design seems basic
enough to justify such a modified title as *The Two Seafarers*. But the
second seafarer is the principal character and the essential conflict
in the poem is the conflict that Ehrismann imperfectly discerned
between two ideals of conduct. It begins in the first speech as a mere
contrast between life on land and life at sea. It is transformed in the
second speech into a conflict between the secular ideal as defined by
aristocratic standards and the religious, not exclusively monastic,
ideal of a servant of God.

40. Mrs. Gordon's edition, *op. cit., supra*, n. 20, p. 10.

When we look at the second seafarer's speech as now established we see that it means most at several places if we assume that he himself, like many a man who took up the cross in those days, is a man of noble birth who can look forward to the successes and rewards of the comitatus, the *blæd* and *dream* of the *duguþ* with which he contrasts the heavenly counterparts in lines 79–80. When he says in the sentence starting at line 39 that no man on earth is so proud, so liberal (or so talented?), so youthfully keen, so valiant in his deeds, or so graciously treated by his lord that he will not always have anxiety for his voyage, as to what the Lord will bring him to, he is indirectly explaining his own anxiety and, therefore, implying that he himself has some share of the endowments he describes. The lures of life on land that he mentions in line 44, the harp and the receiving of rings, are foremost among the joys of the hall. He says they cannot keep a man from thinking about the surge of the waves, but later (ll. 80b–90) he encourages himself to forsake all such noble satisfactions by reflecting that the world is getting old and the glories of the heroic past have grown dim. It is relatively easy to scorn the soft and sheltered prosperity of the *sefteadig secg* of line 56 (according to Grein's emendation, which Mrs. Gordon accepts), but the aristocratic ideal includes heroic action as well, and this secular heroism must also be rejected or at least surpassed. That is what the speaker is trying to accomplish in lines 72–80. As we know from *Beowulf*, the military argument was very similar to the religious one: Since death is inevitable, its hazards must be ignored. *Dom ær deaðe* is all a man can hope to attain. The second seafarer does not deny this argument, but carries it a step farther in his effort to establish a new and superior heroism. By fighting against the devil instead of ordinary enemies he can hope to receive both the secular hero's reward, the praise of his successors on earth, and something much more valuable, because permanent, the praise of the angels.

I have tried to show that, by attending to the slight indications of the language and the major implications of the content, we can find ample evidence for repunctuating *The Wanderer* and *The Seafarer* and treating them as consisting, each in its way, of two dramatic speeches and an epilogue. The proof, as it seems to me, rests largely on the increased clarity, dramatic consistency, and richness of meaning in the poems when thus read. But I must not leave

wholly unanswered the objection that was often made to the old
proponents of dialogue in *The Seafarer*. Why is the point of change in
*The Wanderer* so weakly marked? Why has the change in *The Seafarer*, though not quite so unobtrusive in itself, been left so entirely
without the aid of stage directions? And why is the epilogue marked
by so slight a hint as a group of hypermetric lines and a change of
tone? How could any reader of the Exeter Book when it was new
have understood the form any better than a reader of today? To
this objection I can only say that I think there has indeed been a
mechanical failure in the written presentation of the poems. So
many scholars would not have gone wrong for such a long time if
there had been due warning of the changes I have mentioned. But
this is an easy mistake for a poet or an anthologist to make when he
is recording poems in an age that is accustomed to oral delivery. I
do not think, as the dual performance of Widsith and his fellow
Scilling might suggest, and as Rieger imagined for *The Seafarer*, that
there would normally have been two performers: the epilogues of
both poems render this doubtful, and the *swa cwæð*'s of *The Wanderer*
preclude it. But before an audience a single performer might have
indicated the change by shifting his position or by a change of tone
after a pause, and he might also have given warning of what was
coming by a revealing title and a few words of explanation before he
began. In the Edda we find dialogue poems introduced by explanations in prose, and it seems as if something of the sort might have
been general when poems were recited, though rarely included when
they were put on parchment. It is as if *The Wanderer* and *The Seafarer*
had been recorded in too nakedly poetical a form with only such
explanations (namely, the *swa cwæð* lines in *The Wanderer*) as had all
too inadequately been incorporated as orthodox verses. In the
dialogue of *Solomon and Saturn* the speakers are identified, but by
formulas that stand outside the verse. In the dialogue of Joseph and
Mary in the *Christ* there are no explicit identifications, and we must
judge, as in *The Seafarer*, entirely by what the speakers say (that is,
until Mary's carefully introduced speech at the end), though I must
add that I do not myself believe in the rapid interchange of speeches
ascribed to Joseph and Mary in our editions.

The form I have attributed to *The Wanderer* and *The Seafarer* has
no exact parallel either in Old English or elsewhere, so far as I know;
but the sharply differentiated dramatic speeches I have outlined, in

contrast to the loose and often inconsistent monologues we have been accustomed to reading, are of a sort that is by no means unusual in Old English poetry. From *Beowulf* to the Exeter Book *Riddles* there is abundant evidence that Old English poets took delight in inventing speeches for clearly imagined characters. We have wholly dramatic monologues in *The Wife's Lament, The Husband's Message*, the passionate little lyric *Wulf and Eadwacer*, and the brilliant *Deor*. All these poems have their obscurities, to be sure, but not in their dramatic aspect. We have a carefully framed dramatic monologue in *Widsith*. And in what is probably the finest of all the dramatically conceived poems, *The Dream of the Rood*, we have a speech within a speech; for the dreamer is as carefully conceived a character as the rood itself. Thus *The Wanderer* and *The Seafarer*, if we can attribute to them the form I have described, take their places even more securely than before as members of a vigorous dramatic tradition.

One may naturally ask whether these two poems are the work of the same poet or merely closely related products of the same poetic circle. The extraordinarily close resemblances in style, structure, and underlying ideas make it hard for me to resist the conclusion that they belong to the same poet, and the differences I have noted, important though they are, need not be considered an obstacle. Still, there is probably room for doubt. What appears certain is that each of these poems is the work of an accomplished and original poet, one who had full command of the traditional poetic idiom in combination with unusual powers of invention,[41] who understood the ancient feelings and attitudes of his people and also the intellectual and spiritual claims of the new age. If there were two such poets, the age was the richer.

Reprinted from Jess B. Bessinger, Jr., and Robert P. Creed (eds.), *Franciplegius: Medieval and Linguistic Studies in Honor of Francis Peabody Magoun, Jr.* (New York: New York University Press, 1965), pp. 164–193.

41. The traditional attitudes and expressions are naturally most abundant in the speeches of the two traditional characters, the wanderer and the veteran seafarer. That is probably the main reason for what J. J. Campbell has noted in his study of the distribution of verse formulas and poetic diction in *The Seafarer*: "Oral Poetry in *The Seafarer*," *Speculum*, XXXV (1960), 87–96. That there is a distinction between oral and written composition in different parts of the poem is unlikely on general grounds and is rendered still more unlikely by W. A. O'Neil, "Another Look at Oral Poetry in *The Seafarer*," *Speculum*, XXXV (1960), 596–600.

DOROTHY WHITELOCK

# The Interpretation of
# The Seafarer

THIS PAPER DOES not set out to solve the individual cruxes of the
Exeter Book poem known as *The Seafarer*, nor does it claim to be an
exhaustive survey of the views of former scholars.* O. S. Anderson's
careful study, *The Seafarer: An Interpretation*,[1] has rendered such a
survey unnecessary. In spite of the long preoccupation of scholars
with this poem, there is still no agreement on its meaning, and it is
perhaps worth while to suggest a solution along different lines. It
will be enough for my purpose to outline briefly the main positions
taken up by others.

There have been two main difficulties in the way of the general
interpretation of this poem: the one is the apparent vacillation in the
author's attitude to sea travel in the first part of the poem, the other
the complete absence of any reference to the sea in the latter part,[2]
which consists of moralizing reflections. The first difficulty led
Rieger in 1869[3] to formulate his theory that the first part is a dialogue in which an old man speaks of the hardships and a young man
of the attractions of seafaring. This view won considerable support,
though there has been difference of opinion as to the allotment of
lines to the postulated speakers. Strong arguments against it were
brought forward by Lawrence,[4] who held that the poem indicates
the shifting moods of a sailor, for whom the sea, in spite of its

---

* This paper owes much to the encouragement and helpful criticism of
Professor Dickins, Dr. K. Sisam, and Miss F. E. Harmer. I do not, however, wish
to imply that they are in complete agreement with the conclusions reached.

1. *K. Humanistiska Vetenskapssamfundets i Lund Årsberättelse* (1937–1938), I.
2. Usually assumed to begin at l. 64b.
3. "Der Seefahrer als Dialog hergestellt," *ZDP*, I (1869), 334–339.
4. "*The Wanderer* and *The Seafarer*," *JGP*, IV (1902), 460–471.

dangers and hardships, has an irresistible appeal. Schücking[5] has demonstrated that such an attitude would be anachronistic in these early times, and Anderson agrees with him.

Both of these interpretations left the second difficulty unsolved. The second part of the poem seemed to have no connection with what had gone before, and so the exponents of either opinion accepted the theory, first advocated by Kluge,[6] that the second part does not belong to the original poem, but is a later addition. This type of criticism of Old English poetry is less fashionable than it used to be,[7] and Anderson performs a useful service in demonstrating the weaknesses of the various attempts to divide the poem.[8] It is needless to re-examine such theories here, for all are based on the alleged lack of connection between the first and the second parts of the poem. If it can be established that a connected line of thought runs through the poem, the reason for dismembering it vanishes.

I share Anderson's conviction that the general reflections of the second part rise naturally from the references to sea travel in the first part, but not his belief that these references are to be interpreted allegorically. His view is, as he says, based in part on a suggestion of Ehrismann's[9] that the dangerous voyage is an allegorical representation of the afflictions of life, but he rejects Ehrismann's opinion that a contrast is being drawn between a winter and a summer voyage and that a materialistic view of life, represented by the nobleman living in luxury, is being opposed to the ascetic view of a monk, to whom the pleasures of the world are in themselves

5. Review of Sieper, *Die altenglische Elegie*, in *Englische Studien*, LI (1917), 107. Lawrence's view is defended briefly by E. Blackman, *MLR*, XXXIV (1939), 254 f.

6. "Zu altenglischen Dichtungen: I. Der Seefahrer," *Englische Studien*, VI (1883), 322–327. See other literature cited by Anderson, *op. cit.*, p. 2, note.

7. See, e.g., B. F. Huppé's defence of the unity of *The Wanderer* in "The *Wanderer*: Theme and Structure," *JEGP*, XLII (1943), 516–538.

8. *Op. cit.*, pp. 2–6.

9. "Religionsgeschichtliche Beiträge zum germanischen Frühchristentum," *Beiträge zur Geschichte der deutschen Sprache und Literatur*, XXXV (1909), 209–239. Kluge had in 1883 considered and rejected the possibility of allegorical interpretation (*Englische Studien*, VI, 324) and Sweet, in the seventh edition of his *Anglo-Saxon Reader* (Oxford: Oxford University Press, 1894), speaks of "a parallel between a seafarer's contempt for the luxuries of life on land . . . and the aspirations of a spiritual nature."

sinful. Anderson follows Schücking[10] in taking the voyage mentioned in l. 42, for which the Seafarer is longing, not only as "the life of the pious on earth" but as "life on the road to Eternity, and in this sense also death." While the hardships of the sea represent human life in the world, the poet "is longing to leave the cliffs and rocks of time and set out for the distant glories of eternity." This interpretation is worked out in detail with an ingenuity to which a brief summary cannot do justice. Either of these allegorical interpretations has the merit of establishing a sequence of thought between the references to sea travel and the remainder of the poem. I am not concerned to weigh their comparative merits as I do not think that the poem is an allegory. I shall try to defend its unity while clinging to a literal interpretation.

In passing, it may be noted that the theory that it is an allegory has failed to convince others. Doubt is implied by C. L. Wrenn[11] and clearly stated by S. B. Liljegren.[12] The main difficulty is that we are given no hint of any kind that the beginning of the poem is anything other than a realistic description. There is nothing equivalent to the expression "my life's bark" with which Anderson, though translating only the simple *ceol* "ship," warns us early on to be on our guard. It may be, as Anderson says, that "many of his phrases vividly recall venerable sentences used in every homily book; the rocks of life, the fetters of existence, the hunger for the life to come, the coldness and loneliness of life, etc.," but, unlike the homilists, the poet fails to give the slightest clue that he is using the terms rocks, fetters, etc., as images. The strongest argument brought forward against the dialogue theory, namely the absence of any indication in the text, seems to apply with equal force to the theory of allegorical interpretation.

I doubt whether a pious Englishman of the age of Bede and Boniface, or indeed much later, would have seen, as modern scholars have done, any inconsistency in a man's determination, or even eagerness, to venture forth on a journey whose perils and hardships

10. *Op. cit.*, p. 109.

11. *YWES*, 1938, XIX (1940), 48.

12. "Some Notes on the O.E. Poem *The Seafarer*," *SN*, XIV (1941–1942), 145–159.

he fully understands from his previous experience, in order to "seek the land of foreigners afar off." After all, was not this one of the recognized ways in which a man who did not "believe that earthly prosperity will last for ever" might earn his right to inherit the eternal joys?[13] It may be worth while to examine the poem with the thought of the voluntary exile, the *peregrinus*, in mind.

The poet declares that he will tell a true lay about himself, about his frequent sufferings at sea. With great vividness he describes the storm and the cold, the hunger, exhaustion and loneliness, pausing twice to point out that his sufferings lie beyond the conception of the happy dweller on land, of the man who, "proud and flushed with wine," knows the joy of life in the great houses. He contrasts the cry of the sea-birds with the sounds of revelry in the hall and he paints one of those winter scenes so dear to the Anglo-Saxon poet: "The shadow of night darkened, snow came from the north, frost bound the earth, hail, coldest of grains, fell on the ground." Then he continues:

> Forþon cnyssað nu
> heortan geþohtas, þæt ic hean streamas,
> sealtyþa gelac sylf cunnige;
> monað modes lust mæla gehwylce
> ferð to feran, þæt ic feor heonan
> elþeodigra eard gesece;
> forþon nis þæs modwlonc mon ofer eorþan,
> ne his gifena þæs god, ne in geoguþe to þæs hwæt,
> ne in his dædum to þæs deor, ne him his dryhten to þæs hold,
> þæt he a his sæfore sorge næbbe,
> to hwon hine dryhten gedon wille.
> Ne biþ him to hearpan hyge, ne to hringþege,
> ne to wife wyn, ne to worulde hyht,
> ne ymbe owiht elles, nefne ymb yða gewealc,
> ac a hafað longunge se þe on lagu fundað.         (33*b*–47)

13. See below, pp. 205 ff. A tenth-century Old English penitential includes among the twelve means of obtaining forgiveness of sins: "þæt gehwa his æhta 7 his bearn 7 his eard forlæte for Godes lufon, 7 on ælþeodignysse fare, 7 þær hys lif geendige" (B. Thorpe, *Ancient Laws and Institutes of England* [London, 1840], II, 224; R. Spindler, *Das altenglische Bussbuch* [Leipzig, 1934], p. 175). There is nothing to correspond to this passage in the Latin sources of this penitential.

[(Therefore)[14] my heart's thoughts constrain me to venture on
the deep seas, the tumult of the salt waves; at all times my heart's
desire urges my spirit to travel, that I may seek the land of
foreigners afar off; because there is no man on earth so high-
hearted, nor so liberal with his gifts, nor so bold in his youth,
nor so daring in his deeds, nor having so gracious a lord, that
he will not always feel anxiety over his voyage, as to what is the
Lord's purpose for him.[15] He will have no mind for the harp,
nor for the receiving of rings, no pleasure in woman nor delight
in the world, nor mind for anything else, except the tossing of
the waves, but he who puts out to sea has always yearning.[16]]

In other words, while earthly success may cause a man to forget

14. I think it possible that *forþon* here is correlative with the *forþon* of l. 39 and
redundant in a modern rendering, though S. O. Andrew (*Syntax and Style in Old
English* [Cambridge: Cambridge University Press, 1940], p. 33), who shares my
belief that the instances at ll. 58 and 64 are correlative, suggests that when the
principal sentence comes first the stress "is laid not so much on the action predi-
cated by the verb as on the reason for it." My general argument does not, however, depend on this interpretation of *forþon*, which is often rendered "assuredly" or
some other vague word. For discussion see Lawrence, *op. cit.*, pp. 463–466; M.
Daunt in *MLR*, XIII (1918), 474–478; E. A. Kock, *Lunds Universitets Årsskrift*,
N.F. Avd. I, Bd. 14, Nr. 26, p. 75; Anderson, *op. cit.*, pp. 7–9; Schücking, *Anglia-
Beiblatt*, XLIX (1938), 302 f.; Liljegren, *op. cit.*, pp. 152–155.

15. This passage has difficulties. Sisam doubts whether the *to hwon* clause can
be taken as an indirect question and points out that *dryhten* is used in two different
senses within three lines. He suggests that the line is interpolated, comparing the
almost identical line *Exhortation to Christian Living*, l. 61 (E. van K. Dobbie, *The
Anglo-Saxon Minor Poems* [New York: Columbia University Press, 1942], p. 69;
Grein-Wülker, *Bibliotek der angelsächischen Poesie*, [Kassel, 1883–1898], II, 276). In
this context the reference is undoubtedly to the fate of the soul after death, and I
interpret similarly the line in *The Seafarer*. A man crossing the dangerous seas will
have the thought of death constantly in his mind. What the poet wishes to shun is
the state of the man described in the Judgment Day poem in the Exeter Book:

> Lyt þæt geþenceð,
> se þe him wines glæd wilna bruceð,
> siteð him symbelgal, siþ ne bemurneð,
> hu him æfter þisse worulde weorðan mote.                              (77–80)

16. It is frequently assumed that *longung* means "a longing to be at sea," but
the word in Old English often means "grief" and could here apply to the voyager's
misery, which yet is safer for the soul than the life of pleasure on land. Kershaw
translates "there is never any peace of mind for him who goes to sea." Or the
"yearning" may refer to the longing for the security which only "the joys of the
Lord" can give.

the purpose of his being in the world, may lull him to a trust in material things,[17] the man at sea will be in no such danger, and the poet's heart urges him to leave his native land to seek a foreign country across the sea for this very reason. The coming of spring intensifies this impulse:

> Bearwas blostmum nimað, byrig fægriað,
> wongas wlitigað,[18] woruld onetteð;
> ealle þa gemoniað modes fusne,
> sefan to siþe, þam þe swa þenceð
> on flodwegas feor gewita*n*.[19]                    (48–52)

[The groves blossom, cities grow fair, the fields become beautiful, the world's astir. All these things urge on to his journey the man eager of heart, urge on the spirit of him who thus intends to depart far on the paths of the sea.]

Since he must leave all for dangerous paths, the cuckoo, though it is the herald of summer, can to him fortell nothing but sorrow. Once again he reiterates that a man who lives in luxury cannot even imagine the sufferings of an exile:

> Swylce geac monað geomran reorde,
> singeð sumeres weard, sorge beodeð
> bitter in breosthord. Þæt se beorn ne wat,
> esteadig secg, hwæt þa sume dreogað
> þe þa wræclastas widost lecgað.                    (53–57)

[Likewise the cuckoo with its mournful note[20] urges him, the herald of summer sings, forebodes bitter sorrow in his heart. The man living happily in luxury[21] does not know what some endure, those who journey furthest on the paths of exile.]

17. This is also the theme of Hrothgar's advice to Beowulf, *Bwf* 1724–1752. See also note 15 above.

18. MS *wlitigað* is usually emended to *wlitigiað*, but *-ig-* is a perfectly defensible late tenth-century spelling for [*iji*].

19. Reading, with most editors, *gewitan* for MS *gewitað*.

20. Anderson has a long discussion (*op. cit.*, pp. 22–26) on the cuckoo and its mournful note and concludes that the poet has in mind the cuckoo as the announcer of death, in accordance with his theory that the desired sea journey signifies death. This is, of course, unnecessary, and the similar reference to the mournful cuckoo in a happy context in *The Husband's Message* shows that the choice of the epithet need have no connection with the poet's mood.

21. Accepting *est-* for the manuscript *efteadig*. The sense *deliciae* for *est* is well evidenced. B. Thorpe's "favoured mortal," with *est* in a different sense, comes to much the same thing. But the emendation *seft-* improves the alliteration.

The *forþon* that introduces the next sentence could refer, not only to this last idea—the blind complacency of the prosperous man as a state of mind to be avoided—but also to the whole of the previous argument—but I prefer to take it as correlative with *forþon* of l. 64. The passage runs:

> Forþon nú min hyge hweorfeð ofer hreþerlocan;
> min modsefa mid mereflode
> ofer hwæles eþel hweorfeð wide
> eorþan sceatas, cymeð eft to me
> gifre ond grædig; gielleð anfloga,
> hweteð on *h*wælweg hreþer unwearnum
> ofer holma gelagu; forþon me hatran sind
> dryhtnes dreamas þonne þis deade lif,
> læne on londe: ic gelyfe no
> þæt him eorðwelan ece stond*a*ð.         (58–67).

[(Therefore) my thoughts are now roaming beyond the confines of my breast; with the ocean flood my spirit roams widely over the surface of the earth, over the whale's domain, and comes back to me eager and hungry; in its solitary flight it calls urgently, irresistibly impels my heart on the whale's path across the expanse of the seas; because dearer to me are the joys of the Lord than this dead life, transitory on earth: I do not believe that earthly happiness will endure for ever.]

Far from thinking that with l. 64b we begin the work of a continuator, I do not believe, with Anderson and others, that a new section commences here, nor even a new sentence.[22] The three and a half lines that begin here seem to me the culmination of what has gone before; for the first time the poet states unequivocally what it is that makes his restless spirit eager to embrace again the hardships he has described so forcibly. In my opinion these lines are the central lines of the poem, and all that follows is an elaboration of their theme. The mortality of man, the need to live so as to merit eternal life, the decay of the glory of mighty civilizations, in which each man can see a parallel to his own inescapable fate, the uselessness of hoarded wealth to the soul, the folly of forgetting the fear of the Lord—all are topics closely related to the theme of the first part of

22. Judged by his punctuation, Sweet, *op. cit.*, shared my view. See also S. O. Andrew, *op. cit.*, p. 33.

the poem as I interpret it. In the last twenty lines or so there are difficulties of interpretation which I do not propose to discuss here;[23] they do not affect materially my main thesis. The poem ends with a normal homiletic conclusion, on the note "Let us strive to reach our heavenly home," and I contend that the poet has shown us that for him the way lies through pilgrimage, with renunciation of worldly pleasures. He is not going seafaring for its own sake, but, as an islander, he cannot reach the land of foreigners except across the sea, and when we remember the conditions of early voyaging we need not wonder that this part of his journey should occupy so much of his thought.[24]

References to voluntary exile are common in historical sources of the early Anglo-Saxon period. We are told in the anonymous *Vita Ceolfridi Abbatis* that Ceolfrith's elder brother, Cynefrith, abbot of Gilling, withdrew to Ireland to study the scriptures and to serve the Lord more freely in tears and prayers,[25] and Bede's *Historia Ecclesiastica* has many such references. For example, Ecgberht, "qui in Hibernia diutius exulauerat pro Christo" ⟨who, for the sake of Christ, had exiled himself in Ireland for a rather long time⟩,[26] or "quem in Hibernia insula peregrinam ducere uitam pro adipiscenda in caelis patria retulimus" ⟨who, we have said, led a life as an exile on the island of Ireland in order to acquire a fatherland in Heaven⟩,[27] had made a vow, "quia adeo peregrinus uiuere uellet,

23. Reference must, however, be made to K. Sisam's note, "Seafarer, Lines 97–102," in *RES*, XXI (1945), 316–317, in which he shows that this much-disputed passage, at one time supposed to contain heathen reminiscences, is based on certain verses of Psalm XLVIII. The Psalter was, of course, one of the books most familiar to Irish and Anglo-Saxon *peregrini*.

24. The dangers of sea travel are mentioned many times in the correspondence of Boniface and Lul and also in other literature concerned with *peregrini*. See, e.g., Bede, *HE* I, 33; III, 15; V, 1; Eddius, *Vita Wilfridi*, cap. 13; *Vita Willibrordi*, p. 125; *Vita Willibaldi*, p. 90; and the Latin poem by Aedilwald in *MGH Auct. Antiq.*, XV, 528 ff., and also in *MGH Epistolae*, III, 242 ff.

25. Cap. 2. C. Plummer, *Baedae Opera Historica* (Oxford: Oxford University Press, 1896), I, 388.

26. *HE* III, 4. See also IV, 3: "ipse peregrinus pro Domino usque ad finem uitae permansit" ⟨he himself remained an exile for the Lord even to the end of life⟩.

27. *HE* V, 9. The Old English version is: "he in Hibernia þam ealonde in elþeodignesse lifde for þæm ecean eðle in heofenum to begytenne" (ed. J. Schipper, *Bibliothek der angelsächsischen Prosa*, IV, 589).

ut numquam in insulam, in qua natus est, id est Brittaniam, rediret" ⟨because he so wished to live as an exile that he would never return to the island, that is Britain, on which he was born⟩,[28] which the Old English translation renders: "þæt he â wolde for ʒôde his lîf on elðeodiʒnesse libban 7 næfre to Brytene ealonde hweorfan, þær he acenned wæs."[29]

*Peregrinus* had a wider meaning than our "pilgrim," often referring, to quote J. F. Kenney, to "the man who, for his soul's good, departed from his homeland to dwell for a space of years, or for the rest of his life, in strange countries."[30] Bede speaks in similar terms of Willibrord,[31] Wihtberht[32] and the two Hewalds,[33] all Englishmen living in Ireland. The presence of two Anglian runic inscriptions on the Isle of Man suggests that English *peregrini* went there also.[34] The Old English version normally renders Bede's various phrases "on elþeodignesse lifian." The Irishman Fursey came to England because "he wolde for Godes lufon on elþiodignesse lifian."[35] Many sought the Continent: Hild wished to lead the life of a pilgrim in the monastery of Chelles, "quo facilius perpetuam in caelis patriam posset mereri" ⟨in order to be able to merit more easily an eternal fatherland in heaven⟩;[36] but Rome was naturally the chief resort. Commenting on Ine of Wessex, who retired there "cupiens in uicinia sanctorum locorum ad tempus peregrinari in

28. *HE* III, 27.

29. Ed. J. Schipper, p. 320 (Corpus Christi College, Cambridge, MS. 41).

30. *Sources for the Early History of Ireland*, I: *Ecclesiastical* (New York: Columbia University Press, 1929), p. 488. See also W. Levison, *England and the Continent in the Eighth Century* (London: Oxford University Press, 1949), pp. 36, 44, 52, 55; Dom Louis Gougaud, *Christianity in Celtic Lands* (London: Sheet and Ward, 1932), pp. 129–131.

31. *HE* III, 13: "peregrinam pro aeterna patria duceret uitam" ⟨he led an exile's life for the sake of an eternal fatherland⟩.

32. *HE* V, 9: "peregrinus anchoreticam in magna perfectione uitam egerat" ⟨an exile, he led a hermit's life in great perfection⟩.

33. *HE* V, 10: "multo tempore pro aeterna patria exulauerant" ⟨for a long time they exiled themselves for the sake of an eternal fatherland⟩.

34. P. M. C. Kermode, *Manx Crosses* (London: Bemrose and Sons, 1907), nos. 25, 117, a reference which I owe to Professor Dickins.

35. Ed. J. Schipper, p. 276, translating *HE* III, 19: "cupiens pro Domino . . . peregrinam ducere uitam" ⟨desiring to lead an exile's life for the Lord's sake⟩.

36. *HE* IV, 23.

terris, quo familiarius a sanctis recipi mereretur in caelis" ⟨desiring to spend his exile at the time in the neighborhood of holy places in order to merit being received by the saints in heaven⟩, Bede adds that many of the English race, "nobiles, ignobiles, laici, clerici, uiri ac feminae" ⟨highborn, lowborn, laymen, clerics, men and women⟩, went to Rome for this end;[37] and when he records the similar act of Coenred of Mercia and Offa of Essex he tells how the latter "reliquit uxorem, agros, cognatos et patriam propter Christum et propter euangelium, ut in hac uita centuplum acciperet et in saeculo uenturo uitam aeternum" ⟨left his wife, family, and country for the sake of Christ and his Gospel, so that in this life he might get back a hundredfold, and eternal life in the age to come⟩.[38]

There is also no lack of references to pilgrimages in the normal modern sense; the visiting of the shrines of the apostles and martyrs was not the least important of the motives that took Benedict Biscop, like our Seafarer, many times across the sea;[39] on his first journey he was accompanied by the young Wilfrid, whose biographer Eddi makes him refer to the example of Abraham in order to explain his journey abroad and quote, in an abbreviated form, Matthew 19:29.[40] Many other examples of pilgrimages across the sea could be drawn from the writings of Bede, the correspondence of Boniface and Lul and other sources. It is unnecessary to attempt an exhaustive list.[41] The frequency of pilgrimages is shown not only by the well-known letter in which Boniface reveals his anxiety on account of the moral dangers to which the pilgrims may be exposed,[42] and by the arrangements made at Rome and elsewhere for their reception, but also incidentally by letters such as that in which between 719 and 722 the Abbess Eangyth, herself wishing to journey to

37. *HE* V, 7.

38. *HE* V, 19. This is based on Matt. 19:29, Mark 10:29–30, Luke 18:29–30. Cf., *Historia Abbatum* §I, and *Sermo in Natale S. Benedicti Abbatis*, §I.

39. Bede tells us in his *Sermo in Natale S. Benedicti Abbatis, loc. cit.*, that Benedict at one time intended to spend his whole life abroad, but that the Pope forbade this and ordered him to escort Archbishop Theodore to England.

40. Eddius, *Vita Wilfridi*, cap. 4. Matt. 19:29, had also been used by Bede (n. 38 above).

41. See, e.g., Levison, *op. cit.*, pp. 36–44; Gougaud, *op. cit.*, pp. 167–169.

42. Letter 78. M. Tangl, *Die Briefe des heiligen Bonifatius und Lullus* (*MGH Epistolae Selectae*, I), p. 169.

Rome "like most of her kindred and friends," complains of the unprotected position in which she has been left by lack of kinsmen,
many of whom have departed to visit the shrines of the Apostles
Peter and Paul and of the martyrs, virgins, and confessors.[43] The
*Vita Willibaldi* affords another example of several members of one
family becoming *peregrini*, and it is interesting to note that Willibald's father was at first reluctant, foreseeing the type of situation of
which the abbess complains.[44] Lul in one of his letters speaks of
leaving Britain with almost all his kindred when he crossed "the
threatening masses of the raging sea" in his longing to visit the
shrines of the Apostles.[45]

Pilgrimages are frequently mentioned in later records, though
the motive and purpose are not so fully stated and it is not always
clear whether what is intended is a visit to a shrine or a permanent
exile from one's native land. There is Continental evidence for an
English colony in Rome in the ninth century and later,[46] and several
English documents imply that there was a practice of retiring to
Rome or other Continental shrines late in life, in order to end one's
life there. Thus between 805 and 807, the reeve Æthelnoth and his
wife make arrangements for the permanent disposal of their estate
in the event of either or both of them going south,[47] and Abba, about
835, gives instructions for the disposal of land left to his wife, if
after his death she should enter a nunnery or go south.[48] The
ealdorman Alfred (871–889) similarly envisaged the possibility of
his widow's journeying to Rome after his death,[49] and about the

43. Letter 14. Tangl, *op. cit.*, p. 24.

44. *Vitae Willibaldi et Wynnebaldi* (*MGH Scriptores*, XV, 1), p. 90. This work,
written by an Anglo-Saxon nun of Heidenheim, called Hugeburc (Hygeburh),
towards the end of the eighth century, includes a most interesting account of
Willibald's pilgrimage to the Holy Land. See Levison, *op. cit.*, pp. 43 f., 294.

45. Letter 98. Tangl, *op. cit.*, p. 219.

46. See Cardinal F. A. Gasquet, *A History of the Venerable English College, Rome*
(London: Longmans and Co., 1920), pp. 11–19.

47. A. J. Robertson, *Anglo-Saxon Charters* (Cambridge: Cambridge University
Press, 1956), p. 6, l. 2: "gif hiora oðrum oððe bæm suðfor gelimpe." The term was
borrowed into Old Norse as suðrfǫr "pilgrimage."

48. F. E. Harmer, *Select English Historical Documents of the Ninth and Tenth
Centuries* (Cambridge: Cambridge University Press, 1914), p. 3, l. 20: "suð to
faranne."

49. *Ibid.*, p. 13, ll. 21 f.

same period the widow of a Mercian thane, desiring to go to Rome, sold an estate to a kinsman of her husband.[50] Again, between 929 and 939, a certain Weohstan sold an estate before going to Rome with his wife and son.[51] These may have been sales to raise money for the pilgrimage. Several wills have survived from the eleventh century made by persons about to "go over the sea"[52] or go to Rome,[53] or in one case to Jerusalem,[54] and the Exeter guild statutes suggest that pilgrimages were common, for they state what each member is to contribute "æt suþfore."[55] Flodoard's *Annales* record under 921 and 923 the slaughter by the Saracens of a great number of Anglo-Saxon pilgrims on the way to Rome.[56] In 1027, Cnut secured freedom from toll for his subjects travelling to Rome, whether merchants or "orandi causa viatores" ⟨travellers going to pray⟩.[57] Whether for a brief visit or a permanent stay, there is no doubt that pilgrimages across the sea were common throughout the Saxon period, and it would be possible to compile a fair-sized list of personages, from kings like Æthelwulf and Cnut downwards, who journeyed abroad for this purpose.

From their correspondence and the statements of their biographers, it is abundantly clear that the Anglo-Saxon missionaries to the Continent regarded their mission as a pilgrimage and trusted to win a heavenly home by relinquishing their native land. Boniface calls himself "exulem Germanicum" ⟨German exile⟩[58] and gives "timor Christi et amor peregrinationis" ⟨fear of Christ and love of pilgrimage⟩ as the cause of his separation from his friends,[59] and Archbishop Cuthberht uses the phrase "in tam periculosa ac ferocitate plena peregrinatione pro amore aeternae patriae" ⟨on a pilgrimage so dangerous and filled with ferocity for love of the

50. W. Birch, *Cartularium Saxonicum* (London: Whiting and Co., 1885–1899), no. 537.

51. *Ibid.*, no. 640. Cf. also nos. 192, 293, 313.

52. Whitelock, *Anglo-Saxon Wills* (Cambridge: Cambridge University Press, 1930), Nos. XXVIII, XXXVIII.

53. *Ibid.*, No. XXXIV.

54. *Ibid.*, No. XXXIX.

55. B. Thorpe, *Diplomatarium Anglicum AEvi Saxonici* (London, 1865), p. 614.

56. *MGH Scriptores*, III, pp. 369, 373.

57. F. Liebermann, *Die Gesetze der Angelsachsen*, I (Halle a.S.: 1903–1916), 276.

58. E.g., Letter 30. Tangl, *op. cit.*, p. 54.

59. Letter 94. Tangl, *op. cit.*, p. 214.

eternal fatherland⟩ with reference to his mission.[60] The biographers
refer frequently to the disregard for worldly goods and the contempt
for transitory pleasures of this world, often quoting the promise of
Matthew 19:29. A few quotations will suffice: of Wynnebald we are
told that, "propinquorum amicorumque suorum carnalium affec-
tum postponens, presertimque propria hereditatis patriam cum
noverca, fratrum sororumque suorum clientello contempnens,
ignotas peregrinationis predas probare penetrareque malluit quam
presentis vitae huius falsis divitiarum florere prosperibus" ⟨putting
aside the worldly love of his family and friends and especially his
heritage, his country and his stepmother's, refusing to be a petty
dependent on his own sisters and brothers, he preferred to prove and
investigate the unknown rewards of pilgrimaging than flourish in
the false prosperity of his present life⟩;[61] and Alcuin says of Willibrord: "patriam, cognationem et amicos, fervente fide, pro amore
Dei dereliquit; terrena contempsit, ut caelestia adquireret" ⟨father-
land, family and friends, with burning faith he left behind for the
love of God; he spurned the worldly in order to pursue the
heavenly⟩.[62] According to her life by Rudolf, Leoba was enjoined
by Boniface before his last journey never to desert the land of her
*peregrinatio*: "praesertim cum huius temporis spatia ad aeternitatem
comparata brevia sint et non condignae passiones praesentis saeculi
ad futuram gloriam quae revelabitur in sanctis" ⟨especially since the
duration of this time is brief compared with eternity, and the
passions of the present age are hardly worthy for the future glory
which is revealed in the saints⟩.[63] Instances could easily be multi-
plied, but enough have been given to show the prevalence of the
desire for pilgrimage and exile as a means of obtaining eternal life.[64]

The "peregrinatio pro amore Dei," or "propter nomen Domini,"
or "ob amorem Christi" ⟨exile for the love of God, or for the name
of God, or on account of the love of Christ⟩, plays, as is well known,
a very important part in the Irish Church,[65] and it occurs also in the

60. Letter 111. Tangl, *op. cit.*, p. 239.
61. *Vitae Willibaldi et Wynnebaldi*, p. 107.
62. *Vita Willibrordi* (*MGH Scriptores rer. Merov.*, VII), p. 140.
63. *Vita Leobae* (*MGH Scriptores*, XV, 1), p. 129. Cf., Rom. 8:18.
64. See also S. J. Crawford, *Anglo-Saxon Influence on Western Christendom, 600–800*
(London: Oxford University Press, 1933), pp. 32 f., 64–71.
65. See Kenney, *op. cit.*, pp. 487 ff.; Plummer, *op. cit.*, II, 170 f.

lives of Welsh saints.[66] In one of these Tatheus journeys from Ireland to Wales with eight companions in a ship "sine instrumentis naualibus" ⟨without navigational equipment⟩,[67] which at once reminds us of the three Irishmen who, according to annal 891 of the *Anglo-Saxon Chronicle*, came to King Alfred in a boat without any steering gear, "because they wished for the love of God to be on a pilgrimage, they cared not where." The wording "hi woldon for Godes lufan on elþiodignesse beon" is almost identical with phrases in the Old English translation of Bede. I submit that the poet of *The Seafarer* meant the same thing by "elþeodigra eard gesecan" and that he has given poetic expression to the impulse that sent numbers of his countrymen to the schools of Ireland, to the mission fields of Germany, and to the shrines of distant saints.[68]

Reprinted from Sir Cyril Fox and Bruce Dickins (eds.), *The Early Cultures of North-West Europe* (Cambridge: Cambridge University Press, 1950), pp. 261–272.

66. E.g., A. W. Wade-Evans, *Vitae Sanctorum Britanniae* (Cardiff: Board of Celtic Studies, University of Wales, 1944), pp. 2 f., where St. Brynach, "extra patriam se portans, patriam uoluit adquirere peregrinando" ⟨taking himself outside his fatherland, he wished to gain a fatherland through pilgrimage⟩; or pp. 24 f., where Petrocus began "mundana pro celestibus uilipendere" ⟨to spurn the worldly for the heavenly⟩, and became a *peregrinus* in Cornwall.

67. *Ibid.*, pp. 272 f. With this should also be compared the tradition related of the English *peregrinus* Bertuinus, that he crossed the Channel "sine remigandi auxilio" ⟨without the aid of rowing⟩. See *Vita Bertuini* (*MGH Scriptores rer. Merov.* VII), p. 180.

68. Only after this article was complete did I have access to J. A. W. Rosteutscher, "Germanischer Schicksalsglaube und angelsächsische Elegiendichtung," *Englische Studien*, LXXIII (1938–1939), 17–19. He realizes that the life of loneliness is regarded as having a positive value for the Christian, and he refers briefly in a footnote to the voluntary exiles mentioned by Bede, but, as he does not develop this thought nor draw the conclusions that I do, and as he takes the voyage in the first part of the poem merely to symbolize the sorrows of a life of loneliness, it seems best to let what I have written stand.

# *The Form of* Deor

THE OLD ENGLISH POEM *Deor* is preserved only in the Exeter Book (ff. 100ᵃ–100ᵇ) and its obscurities have given rise to a goodly number of speculations and emendations. As is proper, the main concern of scholarship has been to establish the literal meaning of its lines and the identity of the historical and semi-mythical characters to which direct allusion is made. Less attention has been paid for various reasons—at least in this century—to its overall signification: our ignorance of Germanic literary genres, our hesitancy to speculate until the certainty of the literal meaning can be established, positivistic biases, a lack of interest in this subject, a tendency to assume that there is no difficulty about understanding the poem's general aim or purpose.

This last has largely appeared in the form of what may be called the "romantic dramatic monologue" interpretation of the poem. *Deor* is assumed to be the psychological portrait of an unhappy or resigned man speaking of his misfortune and consoling himself by giving vent to his feelings and hopes. This Browningesque interpretation has been frequently expressed. Andreas Heusler speaks of the aseity of the poem which represents no genre but is a unique inspiration.[1] W. W. Lawrence describes the poem as a *"Consolatio philosophiæ* of minstrelsy."[2] Bernard F. Huppé speaks of the poem as a "consolatory lyric" on the subject of "The Lord giveth and the Lord taketh away." "Man must think not of his earthly but of his

---

1. *Die altgermanische Dichtung,* Handbuch der Literaturwissenschaft, ed. O. Wälzel (Berlin: Akademische Verlagsgesellschaft Athenaion, 1923), p. 140.
2. "The Song of Deor," *MP,* IX (1911), 23.

heavenly lot." [3] Winfred P. Lehmann writes, "In the south, Latin was generally preferred over the native languages for personal expression, as in the hymns; only from England do we have more than one sporadic poem, such as *Deor's Lament* which depicts the mood of the writer." [4] Ernst Sieper speaks of *Deor* as a unique Germanic "Selbstbekenntnis" ⟨self recognition⟩.[5] Many other scholars can be quoted to the same effect. There are differences of emphasis,[6] but the essential notion of a romantic personal lament remains more or less standard. And this notion is reflected in the title frequently given in the past to this titleless poem, "Deor's Lament" or a German favorite, "Des Sängers Trost" ⟨"The Consolation of the Singer"⟩.

Although there are still difficult philological problems to surmount in the study of the poem, it may not be amiss to attempt to identify its general form, not only because of its intrinsic and historical interest but also because a knowledge of the form and purpose of the poem may be of help in unravelling some of its knotty points. Usually a knowledge of the general aim of a poem is necessary before we can fully comprehend the rationale of its individual words and phrases. In understanding any literary work, but especially one of the past, we must continually move between its particulars and its overall purpose; but, when it can be determined, the latter, whether its metrical form, its genre, its general point,

3. *Doctrine and Poetry, Augustine's Influence on Old English Poetry* (New York: State University of New York, 1959), p. 236.

4. *The Development of Germanic Verse Form* (Austin, Texas: University of Texas Press, 1956), p. 26.

5. *Die altenglische Elegie* (Strassburg: Trübner, 1915), p. 163.

6. Leonard Forster, in "Die Assoziation in Deors Klage," *Anglia*, LXI (1937), 117–121, stresses the attempt of the speaker in the poem to surmount personal suffering through amalgamation with the sufferings of other, more notable, sufferers. E. E. Wardale (*Chapters on Old English Literature* [London: Routledge and Kegan Paul, 1935], pp. 29–30) sees a "fatalistic acquiescence" in the poem. P. J. Frankis, in a very recent and interesting article, "*Deor* and *Wulf and Eadwacer*: Some Conjectures," *MÆ*, XXXI (1962), 171, takes a similar stoic interpretation of the poem. George Anderson (*The Literature of the Anglo-Saxons* [Princeton: Princeton University Press, 1949], p. 155) says the poem purports to be the utterance of a cast-off bard "who is consoling himself by comparing his misfortunes with the greater woes of legendary and historical heroes, heroines and nations."

must provide the ultimate standard by which to judge the particulars. Just as in linguistic study, we need the utterances in order to determine the rules, ultimately it is the rules which control the utterances. Although a poem may not be an organic whole, it must have some purpose and arouse certain expectations which it attempts to satisfy if it is to give the sense of unity which is the essence of art.

*Deor* consists of 42 lines with a refrain *þæs ofereode; þisses swa mæg*, which occurs six times and which seems to divide the poem into six stanzas of unequal length. The capitals in the MS seem to bear out this stanzaic arrangement.[7] The only other lyric in OE literature which has a refrain, that which is now called *Eadwacer* or *Wulf and Eadwacer*, is a very puzzling work which follows *Deor* in the Exeter MS. Certain OE prose or semi-poetical charms, however, also have refrains.[8] Neither *Eadwacer* nor the charms use a refrain as frequently as *Deor* does. The parallel use of refrain in *Deor* and *Eadwacer* has suggested to a number of scholars a similarity of content.[9] This paper proposes to look rather in the other direction—at the

7. These stanzas of unequal length stimulated nineteenth-century "emenders" especially Müllenhoff to equalize ruthlessly the strophes. Needless to say, modern scholars eschew preconceived standards of this sort as justification for emendations or changes in the text and for branding lines as interpolations. It is furthermore true that the earliest preserved refrains do not divide poems into equal strophes at all. Catullus' poems nos. 61 and 62 and the *Pervigilium Veneris* all have refrains occurring at irregular positions. (I owe these references and those in nn. 34 and 35 below to my colleagues Professors Zeph Stewart and J. P. Elder). The notion of stanzas of equal length divided by refrains is of the later Middle Ages. Some, like Professor Kemp Malone, favor a seven stanza division, with ll. 28–42 (the portion from the end of the second-to-last refrain to the end of the poem) divided into ll. 28–34 and 35–42. See his valuable edition of *Deor*, Methuen's Old English Library (London: Methuen and Co., 1933; later editions 1949 and 1961), p. 17.

8. The most notable is the OE charm "Wið færstice" where the refrain "ut, lytel spere, gif her inne sie!" is found. Godfrid Storms (ed.), *Anglo-Saxon Magic* (The Hague: M. Nijhoff, 1948), pp. 140 ff. See below pp. 226–227.

9. Most recently by A. C. Bouman, "*Leodum is minum*: Beadohild's Complaint," reprinted from *Neophil*, XXXIII, in *Patterns in Old English and Old Icelandic Literature*, Leidse Germanistische en Anglistische Reeks I (Leiden: Universitaire Pers Leiden, 1962), pp. 95–106, and by Frankis (see n. 6 above). See also Kenneth Sisam, "The Arrangement of the Exeter Book," *Studies in the History of Old English Literature* (Oxford: Oxford University Press, 1953), p. 292. There are even occasional refrains—perhaps repetitions would be a better word—in ON poems.

charms to see whether we may find there some clues as to the overall form and purpose of *Deor*.

The stanzaic form of *Deor* is unusual enough to stimulate speculation, and ties with Old Norse literature have been suggested on this formal ground.[10] The alternation of prose narrative with lyric stanzaic poetry is found in Old Irish and Old Norse epic literature (e.g., *The Cattle Raid of Cooley, Bricriu's Feast, Gunnlaugs Saga Ormstungu*, etc.), and it is possible that *Deor* (and even *Eadwacer*) is merely a lyric relic from a longer narrative sequence. If so, it would help explain its epico-lyrical quality. However, if the argument I put forward here is correct, the relation between the lost prose and the poem is more complex than is usually assumed. We shall return to this point shortly. Any argument as to the form of *Deor* which I shall make should not be taken as necessarily denying the possibility of a lost narrative into which it once fitted.[11]

Before we look at *Deor* in the light of the charms, it will be necessary to summarize the poem once again. With a poem, however, in which a number of allusions are not clear and whose overall meaning has not been determined, any summary must to some extent

10. The ties, of course, would be due to a common ancestry among Germanic poetic procedures or possibly due to a common but independent borrowing from Old Irish literature. Henry Sweet in his "Sketch of the History of Anglo-Saxon Poetry" in the 1871 edition of Thomas Warton's *History of English Poetry . . .* , ed. W. Carew Hazlitt (London: Reeves and Turner, 1871), II, p. 8, pointed to Old Norse heroic lyrics as parallel in some regard to *Deor*. See also W. W. Lawrence, "The First Riddle of Cynewulf," *PMLA*, XVII (1902), 254–255, and Sieper (n. 5 above), p. 162, and Frankis, *op. cit.*, p. 165.

There have been some attempts to find parallels of content between some of these ON heroic lyrics and *Deor* (e.g., Bertha S. Phillpotts, *Edda and Saga*, The Home University Library [London: T. Butterworth, Ltd., 1931] p. 66), but because of the universality of misfortune, these parallels are singularly unconvincing.

11. Various Latin parallels with or even sources of *Deor* have been suggested. See Sieper (n. 5 above), p. 64 ("Commendationes animae" ⟨commendatory offices for the dead⟩ of liturgy), and Rudolf Imelmann, *Forschungen zur altenglischen Poesie* (Berlin, 1920), pp. 229 ff. (Ovid's *Heroides*, especially XVIII and XIX [cf., Helga Reuschel, "Ovid und die Ags. Elegien," *Beiträge zur Geschichte der deutschen Sprache und Literatur*, LXII (1938), 132–142], Virgil's *Ecologues* VIII and IX, and Alcuin's elegy *De cuculo*, etc.). Most of the similarities come down to the use of parallel clause structures (which incidentally can also be found in the Psalms), or of comparisons or of the general topic of consolation for misfortune. Influence is most problematical.

imply a position about its significance and be to some extent tendentious. My general assumption, which yet remains to be argued, is that *Deor* is either a sophisticated, Christianized charm against any kind of misfortune due to social or personal relations, particularly loss of property or rights of some sort, or against some particular unknown (to us) misfortune of a similar sort; or a poem influenced by the charm form and meant to suggest its prototype. Above all it is *not* a monologue by a minstrel Deor, hoping for alleviation of his sufferings. It rather attempts to do or to effect something which is not stated and which may have been stated in a lost prose introduction. It is true that the last misfortune mentioned in the poem overtakes a supposititious speaker, Deor, but it like the other misfortunes alluded to has passed.[12] This interpretation raises problems, it is true (such as why bring in Deor?), but it seems to me these are less troublesome than any others which alternative interpretations raise, and arise more naturally out of the text.

Each division, even if not stanza, as has been said, is objectively marked by the refrain, *þæs ofereode; þisses swa mæg*, the translation of which is crucial to the interpretation of the poem. There have been possibly over a hundred different translations—as has been estimated—for these lines. It seems hard to believe that these five words of rather simple OE should give rise to so many variant translations, but it is nevertheless true.

One of the traps is the word "mæg" whose normal meaning as the present of the preterite-present verb *magan* is "is able," "can" but *not* "may." Professor Malone says quite rightly that by litotes the word can mean "will."[13] My concern is, however, that it not be translated, as it often is, as "may," which is not its usual meaning in OE. "May" suits the romantic interpretation, for it expresses a pious wish; but our knowledge of OE gives little support for this translation.[14] Another trap lies in the absence of subject, for some-

12. My debt to Lawrence's fine article (see n. 2 above) on *Deor* in the interpretation of the last stanza of the poem is great in spite of his calling the poem a *consolatio philosophiæ* of minstrelsy.

13. In the Glossary (p. 34) to his edition (see n. 7 above) Professor Malone (p. 1) translates the refrain as "that passed; this will pass too."

14. I suppose "may" in the neutral sense of "introducing a hypothetical situation in future time" (Elliott Van Kirk Dobbie, *Beowulf and Judith*, The Anglo-Saxon Poetic Records IV [New York: Columbia University Press, 1953]

times *I* or *he* is assumed. Lawrence, for instance, translates these lines as "That he endured, so can I." However, the genitive forms *þæs* and *þisses* make it quite clear that the verbs are to be taken impersonally. Literally then the words mean "in respect to that it passed away; in respect to this it likewise can or will (pass away)." I am taking *þæs* and *þisses* as genitives of respect; however, *þæs* could have various meanings, e.g., "therefore," "accordingly," "afterwards."[15] I feel, however, that other translations will destroy the parallelism and contrast in the refrain. Hence, following Professor Malone, I render the whole refrain, polishing the literal translation, as "That passed away; so will ('shall' or 'can') this." The "may" translation of *mæg* and the assumption of a non-existent "I" or "he" support the romantic dramatic monologue interpretation of the poem, but they have no linguistic support.

I: Weland experienced suffering, sorrow, and misery after he had been bound by Niðhad. That passed away, so will this.

II: Beadohild [ravished by Weland through trickery] was more sorrowful over her pregnancy than over the deaths of her brothers; never could she face up to how that ought to be handled. That passed away, so will this.

---

p. lii) could be used to translate *mæg*, but this translation would be misleading unless the reader is expressly cautioned. Above all, it is not necessary to be so dangerously misleading when "can" is available.

15. Frankis, *op. cit.*, p. 171 n. 29, suggests *þæs ofereode* could mean "a time has passed since then." Lawrence later does translate the line "That passed over; this likewise may," avoiding personal subjects but using "may." Wardale (see n. 6 above), p. 33, translates the refrain as "The sorrow of that passed; so may the sorrow of this." M. G. Clarke, *Sidelights on Teutonic History During the Migration Period Being Studied from Beowulf and other Old English Poems* (Cambridge: Cambridge University Press, 1911), p. 7, translates the refrain as "That came to an end, this may likewise." Bruce Dickins (*Runic and Heroic Poems of the Old Teutonic Peoples* [Cambridge: Cambridge University Press, 1915]) offers "That was surmounted; so can this." "Surmounted" suggests an effort of the individual will. All these and many others are what Professor Malone calls "a formula of consolation" ("On *Deor* 14–17," *MP*, XL [1942], 2). Theodor Grienberger ("*Deor*," *Anglia*, XLV [1921], 397–399) will, however, have none of these translations, but assuming an elliptical *ic secgan* in the second part of the refrain, translates the line as "I can give information about that which has happened" and removes the whole poem from the category of consolations (or even of charms) by merely assuming the poet is referring to his command of his art. This suggestion has met with no favorable response and requires an unusual ellipsis in view of the fact that the first person does not appear in the poem until the last stanza.

III: Mæðhild was deprived of sleep because of the passionate love of Geat. That passed away, so will this.[16]

IV: Theodoric was ruler of the stronghold of the Mærings for thirty years. That passed away, so will this.[17]

V: Ermanaric was a savage king over the Goths and many a man wished for relief from tyranny which the overthrow of his rule would bring. That passed away, so will this.

VI: When sorrowful, an unhappy man can reflect on the fact that God distributes his gifts in different ways—some pleasant, some unpleasant. Concerning myself, I wish to say that I was formerly the minstrel of the Heodenings and dear to my lord. My name was Deor. I was well employed for a long time until Heorrenda, a skillful minstrel, received the landright [or rights of some sort] which my lord had given me. That passed away, and so will this.

This extremely sketchy summary, which bypasses most of the difficult matters of literal interpretation and meaning, is here given chiefly for convenience of reference. The chief problems of the overall interpretation of the poem lie in the meaning of 1) the refrain and particularly the word *þisses* and 2) the last stanza which purports to be autobiographical and uses the word I (*ic*). Let us look at both in turn.

In the refrain "That passed away, so will this," the reference of

16. This passage is a notorious crux. Mæðhild and Geat were probably a well-known pair of lovers, and their story may be preserved in some modern Scandinavian ballads as Professor Malone has argued (in *ELH*, III [1936], 253–256; *ES*, XIX [1937], 193–199; and *MP*, XL [1942], 1–18). This thesis has been attacked by F. Norman in *MLR*, XXXII (1937), 374–381, and *London Mediæval Studies*, I (1937–1939), 165–178. See also L. Whitbread, "The Third Section of *Deor*," *MP*, XXXVIII (1941), 371–384, for a history of some of the speculations on these lines.

17. What exactly this alludes to is not yet clear. Theodoric may be the Goth (Dietrich von Bern) or the Frankish king of that name. The city of the Mærings is a crux; if Theodoric is the Goth it may well be Ravenna, although why it should bear this name is not known. The question also is what misfortune is being alluded to, although the general picture of Theodoric among the Anglo-Saxons was that of a tyrant. The implication, at least, is that his reign was a misfortune to his subjects, notably Boethius. For a recent argument, see Frankis (see n. 6 above), pp. 162 ff. Professor Malone argues for Theodoric the Frank. See his edition (1949), pp. 9–13; "The Theodoric of the Rök Inscription," *Acta Philologica Scandinavica*, IX (1934), 76–84, and "Widsith, Beowulf and Brávellir," *Festgabe für L. L. Hammerich, aus Anlass seines siebzigsten Geburtstags*, Naturmetodens Sproginstitut (Copenhagen, 1962), pp. 161–167.

*that* presents no difficulty. It clearly refers, at least in the first five divisions, to the misfortune just described. *This*, however, raises problems. If we are to assume that the poem is a fictitious recounting of a present misfortune described by the minstrel Deor in division VI,[18] then the solution to the reference of *this* lies there. Deor is then consoling himself with the thought that other misfortunes well-known to his audience have disappeared and is being either hopeful or stoical. The reader of the poem cannot know what *this* refers to until he comes to the last stanza and then all is plain. He is being kept in artistic suspense until he is released by the knowledge division VI gives him.

However, with this interpretation, we immediately run into another difficulty. What do *þæs* and *þisses* mean at the end of the last stanza? "That passed away, so will this." The normal assumption would be that Deor has passed through his misfortune and is now happy or at least content. The only obvious way of avoiding this difficulty is to assume that *that* in the last refrain, unlike all the *that*'s of the earlier refrains, refers not to the immediately preceding misfortune but only to the first five; and that *this* refers for the only time in the poem to the immediately preceding misfortune. This assumption is obviously unsatisfactory.

Equally unsatisfactory is another way of avoiding the difficulty: to assume that the poet allowed the refrain to take over, so to speak. Refrains sometimes do have only a general connection with the content of a preceding verse, as in the Middle English poem "Blow, Northern Wind," and sometimes are nonsense lines, as in some of Shakespeare's songs. But these are regular refrains, that is, the scheme demands a refrain because of the regularity of the verse structure, whereas there is no such demand dictated by the structure

18. Frankis, *op. cit.*, argues that the misfortune is cryptically contained in the five misfortunes and refers to the elopement of Deor with the daughter of his lord, a story which appears in somewhat different form in ON and MHG versions concerning Hjarrandi, Heðinn, and Hild daughter of Hogni (to give the characters their ON names). This may be the case (my own argument does not depend in any way on the exact nature of Deor's misfortune), although this theory assumes a great deal of exact knowledge in the audience, an extremely allusive method of OE poetic composition (unparalleled in its complexity), and an ignoring of the fact that Deor complains only of his loss of "landright" because of the superior poetic ability of a rival. Frankis also seems to forget that the misfortune has passed.

of *Deor*. And none of them as far as I know uses demonstrative pronouns demanding a reference.[19] Unless the poet of *Deor* did not know what he was doing, we cannot accept this interpretation.

If we, on the other hand, assume, as W. W. Lawrence argued many years ago,[20] that the poet is using the last refrain in the same fashion as he has used the earlier ones, then the last misfortune has also passed by. Here the difficulty arises. What then does *this* in the refrain refer to? I assume it is being used to refer to any or a particular social misfortune unknown to us, and that the poem is meant either to have a practical and ritualistic purpose as a charm may have or, more likely, to suggest a charm.

The second main problem is created by division VI. We shall not be concerned with the historicity of the characters nor the exact nature of the misfortune, which are real enough difficulties, but the role of the division in the whole poem. If *Deor* is a kind of charm or meant to suggest a charm, why should it presumably be put in the mouth of a minstrel named Deor and why should one of the misfortunes listed in its homeopathic magical way suggest that the speaker of the poem is involved in a past misfortune? Before we can attempt an answer, we must look somewhat at charms and their form.

Charms in their narrow sense[21] are action literature created for the practical purpose of producing a desired effect through magic or

19. Professor J. B. Bessinger (to whom I am indebted for some suggestions incorporated into this paper) has suggested that the ME "Love in Spring" from MS. Harley 2253 (printed most recently in Bruce Dickins and R. M. Wilson, *Early Middle English Texts* [New York: Norton, 1951], p. 123) may also have been influenced by the charm form and that the last line "On wham þat hit ys on ylong" may be a refrain with at least a relative pronoun "demanding a reference." Inasmuch as this line does not recur in the poem, I cannot regard it as a refrain in the commonly accepted meaning of the term. Emily Doris Grubl claims that the last refrain of *Deor* is meaningless and that the poet used it mechanically at the end. See her *Studien zu den angelsächsischen Elegien* (Marburg: Elwert-Gräfe und Unzer, 1948), p. 116.

20. See n. 2 above. This interpretation has also been supported by Heusler (n. 1 above), p. 140, and Malone in his edition of the poem, p. 17.

21. The word *charm* is also used loosely to indicate any piece of literature which has a practical purpose of any sort and which rests upon a pseudo-scientific, magical, or religious base. A medical prescription or an address to plants to remind them of their powers (as in the famous OE *Nigon wyrta galdor*, ed. G. Storms [see below, n. 22], pp. 186 ff.) are often called charms. Certain types of prayer may also be called charms.

religion.[22] To use John Austin's term, they are a type of performative: they not only serve to communicate but to bring about what they deal with.[23] Their use is based on the primitive belief in the power of the word to control a world in which the supernatural continually intervenes. As Professor Butler writes, "The fundamental aim of all magic is to impose the human will on nature, on man or on the supersensual world in order to master them."[24] Charms make use of commands, invocations, requests, curses, and

22. The literature on charms is extensive. There is much similarity in their form in all countries of the world. For a recent general treatment of the subject (with emphasis on Germanic charms), see Irmgard Hampp, *Beschwörung, Segen, Gebet, Untersuchungen zum Zauberspruch aus dem Bereich der Volksheilkunde*, Veröffentlichungen des Staatl. Amtes für Denkmalpflege Stuttgart, Reihe C: Volkskunde 1 (Stuttgart: Silberburg Verlag, Jäckh, 1961). See also Oskar Ebermann, *Blut und Wundsegen in ihrer Entwickelung dargestellt*, Palaestra XXIV (Berlin: Mayer and Mueller, 1903); Friedrich Hälsig, *Der Zauberspruch bei den Germanen bis um die Mitte des XVI. Jahrhunderts*, Inaugural-Dissertation der Universität Leipzig (Leipzig: Seele, 1910); A. Kuhn, "Indische und germanische Segensprüche," *Zeitschrift für vergleichende Sprachforschung*, XIII (1864), 49–74, 113–157; John Abercromby, *The Pre- and Proto-historic Finns, Both Eastern and Western with the Magic Songs of the West Finns*, The Grimm Library, IX and X; 2 vols. (London, 1898), especially Vol. II; Reidar Th. Christiansen, *Die finnischen und nordischen Varianten des zweiten Merseburgerspruches, Eine vergleichende Studie*, FF Communications 18 (Hamina: Suomalaisen tiedeakatemian kunstama, 1914); W. H. Vogt, "Zum Problem der Merseburger Zaubersprüche," *ZDA*, LXV (1928), 97–130; George Wedding, *Die Merseburger Zaubersprüche und die Merseburger Abschwörungsformel* (Merseburg, 1930); Felix Genzmer, "Die Götter des zweiten Merseburger Zauberspruchs," *Arkiv för Nordisk Filologi*, LXIII (1948), 55–72; and J. Knight Bostock, *A Handbook on Old High German Literature* (Oxford: Oxford University Press, 1955), pp. 16 ff. On the OE charms in particular (although some of these place them in a wider context), see Felix Grendon in *Journal of American Folklore*, XXII (1909), 105–237 (also reprinted separately); Godfrid Storms, *Anglo-Saxon Magic*, Academisch Proefschrift . . . aan de R. K. Universiteit te Nijmegen . . . (The Hague: M. Nijoff, 1948); A. R. Skemp, "The Old English Charms," *MLR*, VI (1911), 289–301; F. P. Magoun, Jr., "Strophische Überreste in den altenglischen Zaubersprüchen," *Englische Studien*, LXXII (1937–1938), 1–6; Karl Schneider, "Die strophischen Strukturen und heidnisch-religiösen Elemente der ae. Zauberspruchgruppe 'wið þeofðe'," *Festschrift zum 75. Geburtstag von Theodor Spira*, ed. H. Viebrock and W. Erzgräber (Heidelberg: K. Winter, 1961), pp. 38–56. The above bibliography is selective.

23. See his *Philosophical Papers*, ed. ⟨J.O.⟩ Urmson and ⟨G.J.⟩ Warnock (Oxford: Oxford University Press, 1961), Chaps. III and X.

24. Eliza M. Butler, *Ritual Magic* (Cambridge: Cambridge University Press, 1949), p. 3. Cf., C. M. Bowra, *Primitive Song* (Cleveland and New York: World Publishing Co., 1962), pp. 116 ff., 277, *et passim*.

the great principle of homeopathic magic—that like can cause like.[25]

Abercromby lists the main elements in charms,[26] not all of which are by any means present in every charm: reciter invokes or desires help of stronger power—animate or inanimate; spirit of disease or helper is told what to do; origin or genealogy of disease or misfortune is described; reciter relates a short story or fact, the incidents of which are appropriate and have reference to what he wishes to do or obtain (sometimes followed by a wish or curse or some other formula); reciter orders, requests, advises, hints that the evil spirit remove itself; an inducement to depart is often given; the reciter invokes assistance from animals, birds, trees, stones, or rivers; disease or misfortune is told to go back where it came from; speaker boasts of his powers or relates what he has done or will do; something impossible is to happen before the particular evil dreaded is to be effected or removed.

The most basic elements in this somewhat disorganized list seem to be the story and the command or request (usually in formula form).[27] These are also the characteristics which interest us most. The story or epic part is homeopathic magic at its strongest. By words one can participate in a heroic or epic deed of an appropriate type and desire that its structure be repeated in the present. Probably originally the model deed was acted or danced out, before a narrative of the action was substituted for it. The happy outcome of the past event will, it is hoped, be transferred to the present dilemma. The model action of a hero or a god need not be close so long as it bears some resemblance to the present dilemma. It need not be any closer than the action which enables a saint to be considered a patron of an occupation or profession. St. Christopher

25. For a short introduction to homeopathic or imitative magic, see James G. Frazer, *The Golden Bough*, one vol. abridged ed. (New York: The Macmillan Co., 1941 reprint), pp. 11–37. See also Hutton Webster, *Magic, A Sociological Study* (Stanford: Stanford University Press, 1948), pp. 60 ff. and 92 ff.

26. *Op. cit.*, II, 40–44. If Abercromby were more interested in poetic structure, he could have listed repetitions and slight variant repetitions as another charm element.

27. See Ebermann (n. 22 above) and Hampp (n. 22 above), pp. 110 ff. Grendon (n. 22 above), p. 111, writes "charms with narrative passages in heroic style occur in nearly all Indo-European languages." It must, however, be stressed that all charms are not constructed in this way.

carried Christ over the river; hence he is an appropriate saint for taxi-drivers. The structural notion of the use of narrative in the charm as reflected in grammar is a kind of proportionate analogy: as X (the believed event or events in the past), so Y (the hope for similar outcome in the present). This kind of verbal participation, particularly in past heroic or divine deeds, is widespread in charms.

Among the OE charms, perhaps #13 and #15 come closest to the ideal form of story and command. Both are to be used against theft. #13 begins after some general directions:

> Bethlehem is the name of the town where Christ was born.
> It is well known throughout the whole world.
> So may this act [Swa ðeos dæd wyrþe] become known among men
> By the cross of Christ.

Then follow directions and several other commands. Then

> The cross of Christ was hidden and it is found.
> The Jews hanged Christ, they treated Him in a most evil way.
> So may this deed never be concealed.
> By the cross of Christ.

#15 is somewhat similar, with references to St. Helena and the crucifixion.[28]

Of a similar structure with narrative and command are the two famous OHG Merseburger charms of the tenth century. Here is the second:

> Phol and Wodan went to the forest. Then Balder's horse sprained its foot. Then Sinthgunt the sister of Sunna charmed it, then Frija the sister of Volla charmed it, then Wodan charmed it, as he was well able to do. Be it sprain of the bone, be it sprain of the blood, be it sprain of the limb: bone to bone, blood to blood, limb to limb, thus be they fitted together.[29]

28. Edited by G. Storms, pp. 206 ff. I use Storms' translation and numbering.
29. Bostock's translation (*op. cit.*, pp. 19–20). I am purposely avoiding the complicated problems of interpretation in this charm as they are not germane to my purpose. Cf. Storms, *op. cit.*, pp. 109–110.

After a brief introduction, a Highland charm for a bursting vein collected by Carmichael in the last century[30] reads:

> Christ went on a horse,
> A horse broke his leg,
> Christ went down,
> He made whole the leg.
> As Christ made whole that,
> May Christ make whole this . . .

A Syriac charm for a successful hunt, of recent centuries, links Noah and his collecting of animals for the ark with the hoped-for success.[31] Among the many incantations collected by Abercromby, many of which display the classic charm pattern, I quote one (#42b) in part.

> Kuume of old enclosed the moon, enclosed the moon, concealed the sun, Kapo released from its cell the moon, from the inside of an iron 'barn,' from the rock released the sun, from the mountain of steel. So I too now release this man from the spell-brought harm of villagers. . . . Just as the son of the sun escaped, when freed by Päivätär, so may this person too escape when freed by me.[32]

Moving back in time, we are told by Albrecht Dietrich that when an old Egyptian magician wishes to heal a snake bite, he tells a very long myth about Ra being bitten by a snake and healed by Isis.[33] A. Kuhn, a hundred years ago, pointed out the similarity of content structure between the German, especially the Merseburger, charms and some in the *Atharva-Veda*.[34]

30. Alexander Carmichael, ⟨tr.⟩ *Carmina Gadelica, Hymns and Incantations with Illustrative Notes* . . . , Collected in the Highlands and Islands of Scotland and translated into English (Edinburgh: Oliver and Boyd, 1900), II, 14–15.

31. Hermann Gollancz (ed.), *The Book of Protection, Being a Collection of Charms . . . from Syriac MSS* (London: H. Froode, 1912), p. lxxxiv. This book contains many other examples of similar analogical magic charms.

32. *Op. cit.*, II, pp. 133–134.

33. *Abraxas, Studien zur Religionsgeschichte des späteren Altertums*, Festschrift Hermann Usener zur Feier seiner 25-jährigen Lehrtätigkeit . . . (Leipzig, 1891), p. 136 n. 1.

34. See n. 22 above. In Maurice Bloomfield's translation of the *Atharva-Veda*, The Sacred Books of the East, XLII (Oxford: Oxford University Press, 1897), we

I have mentioned only a few examples out of many possible ones. Sometimes, too, the parallel is not to a semi-historical or mythical event, but to a natural one (e.g., "As the sun goes down, so may . . ."). However, I have selected only examples of the former as *Deor* does not use any parallels from nature.

If we look at *Deor* again, we can see that, with the possible exception of the reference to God's variable ways, it does fall into the frequent charm pattern of movement—suitable narrative episodes and a command or request and repetition. The reference to God seems to me to be an attempt to Christianize the structure of the poem by a poet who perhaps was aware of the original pagan form he was using. It is true, of course, that there is a clarity and elegance about *Deor* that we rarely find in extant charms, but an extremely common basic charm structure is visible. I think that *Deor* may well be a literary exercise or at least a very sophisticated version of a charm. It is hard to think of it in its present form as aimed at normal charm users, inasmuch as the kind of misfortune from which it seems to ask deliverance is not of the most pressing sort to people who live under constant exploitation and who are especially subject to disease, hunger, theft, the evil eye, and so forth.

The charm form in sophisticated poetry is by no means unknown. The famous fragment 1 of Sappho, a hymn to Aphrodite, is "constructed in accordance with the principle of the cult-song. This poem is, in form, an imitation of that type of ritual prayer which is rather a demand for a particular service than a general act of worship; the pattern of such prayers is immemorially old."[35] It uses the "as X, so Y" pattern. Catullus' poem to Diana (#34), although for the most part a direct address to the goddess, shows a similar

---

find a number of charms which begin with a short narrative or several narratives and are followed by a wish or command. See, e.g., VI, 11 (pp. 97–98), "Charm for Obtaining a Son"; IV, 4 (pp. 31–32), "Charm to Promote Virility"; IV, 12 (pp. 19–20), "Charm for Cure of Fractures"; IV, 37 (pp. 34–35); III, 13 (pp. 146–147); I, 25 (pp. 3–4); etc.

On classical charms of this form, see the article "Μαγεια" (by Hopfner) in Pauly-Wissowa, Neue Bearbeitung XXVII Halbband, 343.

35. Denys Page, *Sappho and Alcaeus, An Introduction to the Study of Ancient Lesbian Poetry* (Oxford: Oxford University Press, 1955), pp. 16–17.

form.[36] In fact, lyric poems were probably originally cult-songs and addressed to the gods. Lyric poetry has kept ties throughout much of its history with primitive incantation and prayer patterns.

How does all this help us to answer the question which gave rise to this discussion of charms? The answer can only be speculative, but it is possible that the singer Deor was well-known as an escaper of misfortune, and the poet assumed his mask to write his sophisticated charm or shifted into his role in only one stanza. As has been noted more than once, the speaker says his name *was* Deor. This may imply that the poet is taking on his personality, or it may indicate that it was the nickname of a well-known minstrel. This shifting to an "I," though rare, is not unknown in charms. In the second (in Storms' edition) OE charm, for example, a speaker of a charm assumes a mysterious and hard to explain first person role which indicates that he is taking up the mask of a mythological or heroic character. Although there are few or no charms in the *Poetic Edda*, we do find this role shifting in many of its poems.[37]

Let us look at this OE charm, or at least part of it, in translation.

### *Against Rheumatism* (or the *Stitch*)

Boil feverfew and the red nettle that grows through
the wall of a house and plantain in butter. Loud they
were, lo loud, when they rode over the mound,
they were fierce when they rode over the land.
Shield yourself now that you may survive their ill-will.
Out little spear, if you are in here!
I stood under linden-wood, under a light shield,
where the mighty women betrayed their power,
and screaming they sent forth their spears.
I will send them back another,
a flying arrow from in front against them,
Out little spear, if you are in here!
A smith was sitting, forging a little knife,

. . . . . . . . . . . . . . . . . . . . . . . . .

36. On the literary use of the prayer, see Friedrich Schwenn, *Gebet und Opfer, Studien zum griechischen Kultus*, Religionswissenschaftliche Bibliothek 8 (Heidelberg: K. Winter, 1927), pp. 53 ff., and Eduard Norden, *Agnostos Theos, Untersuchungen zur Formengeschichte religiöser Rede*, second printing (Leipzig and Berlin: B. G. Teubner, 1929), pp. 150 ff., *et passim*.

37. See F. P. Magoun, "Deors Klage und Guðrunarkviða I," *Anglia*, LXXV (1942), 1–5.

Out little spear, if you are in here!
Six smiths were sitting, making war-spears.
Out spear, not in, spear![38]

This is an obscure charm, but it obviously refers to supernatural or mythical creatures who may have caused the pain. It contains narrative suggestions rather than direct narrative and is given in a most allusive style. Like most of the preserved OE charms it does not use the "as X, so Y" structure, except perhaps by implication. It also contains much invective. What I am, however, primarily interested in (besides the refrain) is the use of the first person in the passage beginning "I stood under linden-wood," in which the magician identifies himself with some semi-historical or mythical episode which is not clear to us. This is exactly what we find in *Deor*. In all charms, of course, the speaker is an "I" which is implicit or explicit in the situation, but what is rare, though not unknown, is to find the "I" becoming a shape-shifter and assuming a role in some kind of epic or mythic narrative. Such a shift is to be found in *Deor* and in the second OE charm, whatever other differences there might be between them. This similarity at least shows that such historical or mythic "I" intrusions are not impossible in charms.

I do not claim that *Deor* is an ordinary charm. Its poetic power, the nature of the misfortune, the reference to God's mysterious ways would argue against such an interpretation. But it bears the major marks of a charm—short narratives referring to success in the past, an "as X, so Y" structure, commands or wishes, and repetitions. It can be seen then as a rather sophisticated poem in charm form either by a speaker assuming throughout the mask of Deor or by anyone who may for the last part of the last division be identifying himself completely with Deor. In this way we may perceive the underlying pattern of the poem.

It may, as has already been suggested, have been part of a longer narrative now lost. In this case, a specific but now unknown

38. Translated by Storms, *op. cit.*, p. 141. The dots indicate a gap in the MS. The last twelve lines are not reproduced here. See Elliott Van Kirk Dobbie, *The Anglo-Saxon Minor Poems*, The Anglo-Saxon Poetic Records VI (New York: Columbia University Press, 1942), pp. 122–123. For his valuable comments and notes on the OE poetical charms, see pp. cxxx ff. and 207 ff.

misfortune is being charmed away. Although I have found no charms in Old Norse and Irish prose-poetry saga, there are prophetic verse, riddles, and magic poems in these works.[39] The magic powers accredited to minstrels and bards would also make a figure like Deor suitable for incantation work.

Some twenty years ago, Margaret Schlauch spoke of scholars who are amazed at the "originality of form and the extraordinary emotional intensity"[40] of the OE lyric, a point of view still widespread. Much of this view is based on a very romantic interpretation of the OE elegies. While I should be the last to deny these poems great emotional intensity, it seems to me that the nature of this emotion needs to be understood. And I believe that I have shown that the form of at least one is not original. The uniqueness of this poem of which Heusler speaks does not lie in its form nor in its psychological realism, but must rather be sought elsewhere. The suggestions put forward here do not solve all the problems facing us in interpreting *Deor*, but they do attempt to answer the problem of its poetic genre and form, a knowledge of which in its turn can help us in tackling the many other difficulties still before us.

Reprinted from *PMLA*, LXXIX (1964), 534–541.

39. See the *Poetic Edda* (especially the stanzas about runes in the *Sigdrífumál*), *Njal's Saga*, *Bricriu's Feast* and *The Cattle Raid of Cooley*, etc.

40. "The *Dream of the Rood* as Prosopopoeia," *Essays and Studies in Honor of Carleton Brown* (New York: New York University Press, 1940), p. 23. It is possible that the charm form has influenced other poems besides *Deor*. See Professor Bessinger's suggestion in n. 19 above. It is a natural form for a request of any sort to take since it is to be found in the liturgy and prayers, even if the original magic aura is gone. See, for instance, Roland's prayer to God to save his soul (ll. 2384–2388, Alfons Hilka (ed.), ⟨*Das altfranzösische Rolandslied*⟩, third edition by Gerhard Rohlfs [⟨Tübingen: M. Niemeyer⟩, 1948], p. 65) and Charlemagne's prayer for protection while avenging Roland (ll. 3100–3109, *ibid.*, p. 85) in the *Chanson de Roland*. I should like to thank Professors Malone and Dobbie for suggestions in the composition of this paper.

Since writing and submitting this article, I have found one brief suggestion that the form of *Deor* resembles that of a charm. J. H. W. Rosteutscher, in his "Germanischer Schicksalsglaube und angelsächsische Elegiendichtung," *ES*, LXXIII (1938–1939), 11, writes of the refrain, "Er ähnelt stark einer Zauberformel, z.B. den magischen Sprüchen gegen Hexenstich, aber anderseits auch den christlichen 'preces commendaticiae'" ⟨"It strongly resembles a magic formula, e.g., the magic sayings against witchery, but in other respects also the Christian 'prayers of commendation'"⟩.

## RUDOLPH C. BAMBAS

# *Another View of the Old English*
# Wife's Lament

IT IS A COMMONPLACE observation that Old English secular poetry reflects the limited attitudes and interests of a primitive warrior culture. In such a culture, the only matters worth celebrating in verse are the affairs of heroic war chiefs and the brisk young men who follow them for gold and glory. The constant themes are the worth and dignity, the fortitude, loyalty, and generosity of the fighters who defend the tribe. Peaceable churls and slaves are hardly mentioned, and women are referred to so seldom and so briefly that the prominence given to the Danish queen, Wealhtheow, in *Beowulf* is considered remarkable.

Even more remarkable is a 53-line poem in the Exeter Book that is generally referred to as *The Wife's Lament, The Banished Wife's Lament*, or *The Maiden's Complaint*. According to the prevailing interpretation of this poem, it is a monologue by a woman who movingly expresses the sorrow of exile and the friendless state. The poem is difficult and obscure, but seemingly clear enough is the idea that the speaker's husband has been outlawed as the result of a feud. The outlawed man has gone overseas, leaving his wife to dwell, for some unexplained reason, in a cave beneath an oak tree in a desolate locale. Here the forsaken lady bewails her hardships and her separation from her husband. The poem concludes with gnomic comments on the need for stoicism under the stress of remembering better days in present wretchedness.

Recognizing the monologist of this poem as a woman has led to some interesting speculation. It supplied the basis for supposing that the idea of undying passion between a man and a woman existed among the early Teutons before the invention of courtly love and that the Anglo-Saxon audience was sufficiently ready to accept this idea to enable at least one poet to present it. The cruelly separated lovers languished like Tristram and Iseult; the lady was an "Anglo-Saxon Mariana . . . in the moated grange."[1] The need to explain the woman's isolation led to the suggestion that the poem was a version of the story of the calumniated wife, like Genoveva, Constance, or Desdemona. Like the highborn ladies of the sentimental romances of a later era, the wife of the Old English poem, though punished by a husband who wrongly disbelieved in her innocence, patiently loved him just the same.

However, understanding the speaker of the poem to be a woman presents difficulties. From what is known of the transmission of poetry among the early Teutons, poems were recited or chanted by male scops or minstrels at drinking festivities from which women had in good time withdrawn. Of entertainment by female minstrels nothing is known. This picture obliges us to suppose that when he recited *The Wife's Lament* the minstrel impersonated a woman, and so much mimetic capacity in the eighth or ninth century is difficult to believe in. It is true that women have speaking parts in some Old English poems: Wealhtheow speaks in *Beowulf*; in the religious poetry, Mary speaks in *Christ*, Eve in *Genesis B*, and Juliana, Elene, and Judith in the poems named after them. But in these instances the woman to be quoted is first carefully identified. By contrast, the situation in *The Wife's Lament* is not dramatic. There is no dialogue and no introduction identifying the matter that follows as utterance by a woman. The scop begins by reciting: "I sing this song of very wretched me, the adventure of myself." In the manuscript the words for "wretched" (*geomorre*) and "myself" (*minre sylfre*) have the feminine inflection, but without being better prepared for the situation, it is hardly credible that the audience would understand from the inflection of an adjective and two pronouns that the speaker was representing a woman. It seems necessary to suppose either that some introductory lines were omitted in the Exeter Book copy or that the feminine inflections of *geomorre* and *minre sylfre* are scribal errors.

The situation described in *The Wife's Lament* is difficult to associate with a woman narrator without assuming that the poem is a fragment of a larger poem whose lost parts explain why a woman was left to fend for herself in an uninhabited place. No reason for the narrator's exile being solitary is given. The poem merely says, "My

1. W. W. Lawrence, "The Banished Wife's Lament," *MP*, V (1908), 405.

lord bade me take shelter here" (l. 15) and "One bade me live in a wooded grove, under an oak tree in the cave" (ll. 27–28). That the isolation is temporary is implied by *abidan* in the last line of the poem:

> Wa bið þamþe sceal
> of langoðe    leofes abidan.

This expectation of reunion does not consort with the idea of the punitive exposure of a calumniated wife. If the poet is understood by his audience to be speaking of himself or of someone like him, a member of the entourage of a chief who is moving about in exile, then the situation is not unreasonable: the chief has undertaken a sea journey of some duration; in his selection of shipmates the narrator was not included, and he is consequently obliged to wait for the chief's return. The utter isolation of the narrator is the poet's imagined intensification of his sorrow at being deprived of the shelter of his patron. However, to understand on the literal level that the chief put his wife in unprotected isolation requires an explanation that the poem does not supply.

The vocabulary used to discuss the relationship between the narrator and the absent chief does not clearly signify a bisexual relationship. The absent man is called "lord" or "chief" (*hlaford, leodfruma, frea*) and "friend" (*freond, wine*). The relationship of husband to wife can be so expressed,[2] but these terms do not in themselves or ordinarily mean "spouse." The narrator speaks of "*freondscipe uncer*" (l. 25), and although "friendship" can mean "marriage" it does not often mean this in the extant literature. The only word in the poem that has a frequent conjugal sense is *gemaec* in "ic me ful gemaecne monnan funde" (l. 18), but *gemaec* is not exclusively conjugal. It may mean "congenial" or "companionable" and can be applied by one man to another.[3]

Lines 21–23a—

> Bliðe gebaero    ful oft wit beotedan,
> þaet unc ne gedaelde    nemne deað ana,
> owiht elles

---

2. In *Beowulf* Hrothgar is referred to as Wealhtheow's "frea" (l. 641), and she calls him "freodrihten min" (l. 1169); in *Genesis* Eve addresses Adam as "frea min" (l. 655) and "wine min" (l. 824).

3. As sailors use "mate," "shipmate" to refer to a congenial fellow.

—suit the fierce loyalty that existed between a chief and his follower. The sentiment is like that attributed to Offa in *The Battle of Maldon* (ll. 289–294), where *beotode* conveys the sense of a vaunting challenge to the forces of the world to test an unbreakable compact between a chief and his man. Applied to a sexual union, the lines in *The Wife's Lament* are appropriate to a courtly love situation of the thirteenth century, since courtly lovers are not bound to one another by marriage law and therefore have reason to give solemn affirmation of their loyalty. But for a wife in the Teutonic culture of the eighth century to boast of her intended fidelity would be gratuitous.

A severe crux occurs in line 9 of the poem, in the word *folgað*, which presumably means "service, followership, office," as it does in *Deor* (l. 38):

> Ahte ic fela wintra    folgað tilne,
> holdne hlaford. . . .

*The Wife's Lament* reads:

> Ða ic me feran gewat    folgað secan,
> wineleas wraecca,    for minre weaþearfe.

Thus, a woman is supposed to be saying that after her husband went into exile, "Then I, a friendless exile, went to look for service in my troubled need." "*Folgað secan*" is easy enough to understand if the phrase is associated with a landless man, a young warrior or a scop like Deor or the speaker in *The Wanderer*. But if the narrator is a woman who has just described her husband as a chief (*min leodfruma*, l. 8), it would be difficult for an Anglo-Saxon audience to understand her decline to a servant's level. Normally a wife would look after the conjugal property in her husband's absence, and normally she would have kin of her own to go to if her husband's enemies had seized his land and dispossessed his wife or if the hostility of his kin had obliged her to leave her home (if this is the sense of ll. 11–14). In the actual conditions of Anglo-Saxon life a decline in status from warrior to thrall no doubt occurred from time to time, through ill fortune or through ill conduct like that of the ten cowards in the dragon episode of *Beowulf*, but that such a social decline is a theme in *The Wife's Lament* is doubtful. The analogies from the much later romances suggested by Rickert[4] and others are not convincing. The romances are sentimental and sensational when they present Lancelot in a cart, a king's son in the kitchen, or an emperor's daughter and sultan's bride doing embroidery for a living or waiting on table or tending cows. These reversals of fortune and status are used for their shock value and are shocking because they depart widely from the actual and normal. But to find Byzantine sensationalism in a secular Old English poem is to have to struggle with an uneasy sense of anachronism. It is normal and actual for a landless young man to seek "*folgað*," to become a "*wineleas wraecca*," and even to take refuge in a cave and thereby become a kind of "last survivor" as in *The Wanderer* and in *Beowulf* (ll. 2236b ff.). For a woman to do these things in a poem that is in the early Germanic secular tradition in incredible.

To understand the speaker of the poem to be a man rather than a woman requires emendation of *geomorre* and *minre sylfre* in the first two lines of the poem. Thorpe[5] in his edition of the poem emended *minre sylfre* to *minne sylfes* to suit a masculine speaker. Schücking[6] suggested that the first two lines were added by a scribe and that the poem should begin in the third line with an exclamatory "*Hwaet!*" He was led to this hypothesis by the fact that the feminine forms make sense and are thus not obvious scribal errors. But the scribe of the Exeter Book committed errors in great number and of great variety, and it is not impossible that the feminine forms are simply the effect of chance rather than of the scribe's misunderstanding of the poem he was copying. Thorpe's emendation is preferable to Schücking's in that it does less violence to the text as it stands. If in the correct form of the poem *minne sylfes* was meant as a reflexive pronoun construction, then Thorpe's emendation is the correct one: the scribe mistook *sylfes* for *sylfre*. If, however, the words in question are adjectival intensives qualifying *sið*, then the scribe misread *minne sylfne* and in each word copied an *r* for an *n*. As to *geomorre* in the first

4. E. Rickert, "The Old English Offa Saga," *MP*, II (1905), 368, cites *Émaré*, *La Fille du Roi de France*, *Novella della Figlia del Re di Dacia* as analogous; Lawrence suggests the Cinderella story as an analogue; see also S. Stefanovic, "Das angelsächsische gedicht Die Klage der Frau," *Anglia*, XXXII (1909), 425–433.

5. B. Thorpe (ed.), *Codex Exoniensis* (London, 1842).

6. L. L. Schücking, "Das angelsächsische gedicht von der Klage der Frau," *ZDA*, XLVIII (1906), 447.

line of the poem, the scribe's copy may have read *geomorum* or *geomoru* (with or without a macron above the *u*[7]), and he mistook *u* or *um* for *re* and so copied it, not because he understood the subject of the poem to be a woman's lament, but because he was copying words and letters without a consistent effort to understand the sense of what he was copying. The emended first line and a half should then read:

> Ic þis giedd wrece    bi me ful geomorum,
> minne sylfne sið;

"I sing this song of very wretched me, my own adventure."

Another possible emendation would suppose the original text to have read "bi me ful geomore / minra sylfra siða," *geomore* being inflected as a substantive d. sg. m. and the following phrase a genitive plural construction. The sense of the line would then read: "I sing this song of me, (a) very wretched (man) in my own adventures." The scribe doubled the *r* in *geomore*, left off the *a* in *siða* and wrote *e*'s for *a*'s in *minra sylfra*, errors of a kind not infrequent in the Exeter Book.

Admittedly, the supposition that the scribe inadvertently gave feminine inflections to three successive words in his copy puts a strain on the laws of chance, but this strain is less to bear than that of understanding the poem to concern a woman. If it is truly a wife's lament, the poem is unique in several senses: it deals sympathetically with a woman's troubles in a warrior's world; it makes use of passionate bisexual love as a literary theme; it speaks of experience from a woman's point of view.[8] This uniqueness is interesting, of course, if we can believe that it is real, but it is difficult to believe in without a parallel in the literature of the time and without any support outside of the poem itself.

The view that the poem is a feminine monologue has been the prevailing opinion since Ettmüller proposed it in 1850.[9] Schücking

7. As in *Sumū* for *Sumum* in *Christ*, line 673 (G. P. Krapp and E. V. K. Dobbie (eds.), *The Exeter Book* [New York: Columbia University Press, 1936], p. 21), or *gewritu* for *gewritum* in *The Phoenix*, line 332 (Krapp and Dobbie, p. 103).

8. The fragment known as "Wulf and Eadwacer" or "First Riddle" may be a feminine monologue but is too cryptic to be clearly intelligible.

9. L. Ettmüller, *Engla and Seaxna Scopas and Boceras* (Quedlinburg and Leipzig, 1850).

argued cogently against the feminine theory in 1906, but his argument failed to unsettle confidence in the validity of the theory.[10] Since then, the only skeptical note has been sounded by the French scholar Legouis, who says that the poem "might be called the *Wife's* or *Maiden's Complaint*, were it certainly the utterance of a slandered woman who laments that she is banished from the neighbourhood of her love. Equally well, however, it may be the complaint of a young thegn kept from joining his dear and exiled lord." [11] The most recent studies of the poem proceed from the position that the feminine theory is established.[12]

The attractions of this view are considerable. It adds some range to a body of poetry that in theme is limited and monotonous and enables the modern mind to respond sympathetically to a culture in which women and a tender love story had a place after all, if only in a unique poem. The imagination is fired by the possibility that *The Wife's Lament* is a clue to a body of lost sagas and primitive romances that were deliberately not preserved by monkish compilers because of their amorous content.

However, the difficulties of accepting the view that the poem concerns a woman are in the end too great; the probability is that the poem concerns a man. From the evidence of the poem as it exists, it is too difficult to see how the minstrel's audience could understand that he was miming a woman. The poem must then be a fragment from which the poet's explanation has been lost. The poem must also be a fragment if it is a strangely early treatment of the romantic story of the calumniated but patiently loving wife. Too many pieces are missing. But if the poem concerns a man, a warrior

10. Schücking. Later, in his *Kleines angelsächsisches Dichterbuch* (Cöthen, 1919), he gave up his unorthodox view, and with H. Hecht (*Die Englische Literatur im Mittelalter* [Wildpark-Potsdam: Akademische verlagsgesellschaft Athenaion, 1927], p. 59), referring briefly to "The Wife's Lament," he agrees that the poem may be an early version of the Constance saga.

11. E. Legouis and L. Cazamian, *A History of English Literature*, trans. H. D. Irvine (New York: Macmillan, 1935), p. 26.

12. See, for example, E. D. Grubl, *Studien zu den angelsächsischen Elegien* (Marburg: Elwert-Gräfe und Unzer, 1948); S. B. Greenfield, "*The Wife's Lament* Reconsidered," *PMLA*, LXVIII (1953), 907–912; G. W. Dunleavy, "Possible Irish Analogues for *The Wife's Lament*," *PQ*, XXXV (1956), 208–213; R. D. Stevick, "Formal Aspects of *The Wife's Lament*," *JEGP*, LIX (1960), 21–25; J. A. Ward, "*The Wife's Lament*: An Interpretation," *JEGP*, LIX (1960), pp. 26–33.

or a minstrel like Deor or the speaker in *The Wanderer*, then it need not be a fragment. It still has its obscurities but is complete and understandable as it is.

To the emendation of Old English texts there will apparently never be an end. As much as possible, the copy of the Exeter Book should be allowed to stand, but the emendation of *geomorre* and *minre sylfre* to suit the masculine speaker intended by the poet is a necessity. The scholarly effort to sustain the concept of a feminine subject has been ingenious and learned but should yield to a simpler and more probable interpretation of the poem. For another title perhaps "The Exile's Lament" would do.

Reprinted from *JEGP*, LXII (1963), 303–309.

# J. B. BESSINGER, JR.

# Maldon *and the* Óláfsdrápa: *An Historical Caveat*

SINCE POETRY sometimes celebrates actual events (a siege of Troy, the death of Lincoln) and poets are effectively more interested in poetic events than in historical ones, a reader may go to an historical poem for its poetry, its history, or both together; in the last case perhaps not to his easy satisfaction. Should he decide to judge whether a poem's faithfulness to fact, where this can be ascertained, qualifies or defines its worth as a poem, he may suspect that his own literate and literary prejudices are weighted in favor of historicity, as those of earlier hearers and readers were freely conceded to have been. "And this is storyal soth, it is no fable," Chaucer in *The Legend of Good Women* assures his audience, whereupon the modern student, in an excellent humor about the legend (or fable) of Cleopatra, makes allowances for a medievalized battle of Actium, the fourteenth-century concreteness of which insures a very real kind of "storyal soth"; or conversely, in the case of a manifestly unhistorical poem, we strive to resolve the demands of realistic topography and inconsistent narrative design in the pilgrims' route to Canterbury. It is possible to be both gratified and discomfited to learn that the Sutton Hoo cenotaph documents the treasure burials in *Béowulf*, or that the epic-elegist's scattered account of a raid on the Rhine delta is no fable. Certainly a critic may and should sift verifiable detail from narratives otherwise traditional, fictional, or fantastic; but the present reader may decide from his response to the last three adjectives whether his valuation of *Béowulf* is at all conditioned by its narrow and incomplete historicity.

Judgment is harder when presumably historical poems from eras of scanty documentation are made of traditional forms, themes, and rhetoric, for these may have obscured historical outlines or grossly distorted them—witness the fate of Attila's character in North and

237

South Germanic legend. The makers of medieval historical poems can often be credited with reasonable accuracy, once their understandable temptations to overpraise a warrior-hero to his face, or to indulge in tribal or national pride, are taken into account; but when they had least cause to twist the truth, to magnify or diminish an action, their sources of knowledge still might fail them, or their traditional habits of narration confine them to a limited presentation of historical truth. We may consider two complementary and nearly contemporary poems whose authors can have had no reason to distort the truth for personal or patriotic reasons. Both candidly record disasters, one close to home, the other far away, that befell real and estimable persons. That *The Battle of Maldon* and Hallfreth's *Óláfsdrápa* are probably true in the main is not their virtue, however; they are no more truthful than they should be. As is clearer in the Norse piece than in the English one, they are historical poems from a markedly artificial tradition, poems which brilliantly demonstrate the virtues of their genre, the heroic panegyric, within the subtypes of narrative and court lyric. Let us examine them in turn and together.[1]

*Maldon* tells how a viking force invading the Blackwater estuary was engaged by an Essex fyrd under the earldorman Byrhtnoth. The English leader was killed, some of his troops fled, some of his loyal retainers were cut down—at which point the poem as it has come to us ends, without detailing the presumptive total victory of the Scandinavians. Much later documents give the anniversary of Byrhtnoth's death as 10 or 11 August; the Laud Chronicle (E), without mentioning day or month, and without specifying a

1. Parts of an earlier version of this paper were given as an illustrated lecture before the Mediaeval Academy of America in Chapel Hill, N. C., on April 20, 1961. Normalized Old English texts are quoted herein from editions by Francis P. Magoun, Jr., *Anglo-Saxon Poems* (Cambridge, Mass.: Department of English, Harvard University, 1960), *Béowulf and Judith* (Cambridge, Mass.: Department of English, Harvard University, 1959), *The Vercelli Book Poems* (Cambridge, Mass.: Department of English, Harvard University, 1960), with an additional few references normalized from *The Anglo-Saxon Poetic Records*, ed. George P. Krapp and E. V. K. Dobbie (New York: Columbia University Press, 1931–1953), Vols. I, III, V. Abbreviations for these poems are those given by Magoun in *EA*, VIII (1955), 138–146. The normalized Old Norse text is quoted from *Den Norsk-Isländska Skaldediktningen*, rev. Ernst A. Kock [ed. Elisabeth Kock and Ivar Lindquist] (Lund: C. W. K. Gleerup, 1946), Vol. I.

Scandinavian victory or naming the Scandinavian leaders, places Byrhtnoth's death in the year 991; the annals from Abington, Worcester, and Canterbury (CDF) do likewise; the Parker Chronicle (A), apparently by conflation of events from 991 and 994, and without mentioning day or month, names Unlaf (i.e., Olaf Tryggvason, the hero of Hallfreth's poem) as the viking leader of a ship-army victorious at Maldon over Byrhtnoth and his fyrd in 993.[2] Monastic histories of a decade to a century or more after 991 give differing accounts of a battle (or battles) at Maldon, when they describe one at all, but a general praise of Byrhtnoth's valor is found in them along with some details that may be derived from readings or recitals of the poem itself.[3] Our text of the poem derives probably from "a western copy of an eastern original" made some time in the eleventh century;[4] the opinion held by many that it was first composed shortly after the battle, possibly by an eyewitness, has no historical basis but springs from an impression of the vivid and minute detail found in the poem. The commentators are sometimes confusing on this point. Gordon believed that *Maldon* was composed when "memory of all that happened was still fresh, and the heroism of

2. Bruce Dickins, "The Day of Byrhtnoth's Death and Other Obits from a Twelfth-Century Ely Kalendar," *Leeds Studies in English*, VI (1937), 14–24. A Winchester kalendar of ca. 1023–1035 has August 11; the Ely kalendar has "10 August: Obiit ... brithnodus dux qui dedit huic ecclesie Spaldwic ... [et] plurima que in testamento eius memorantur" ⟨Byrhtnoth died, the general who gave Spaldwic to this church and many things which are mentioned in his will⟩. The latter kalendar is from 1173–1189, but Dickins believes "the monks of Ely, if anyone, should have known the day" (p. 23). For the other annals see E. V. Gordon (ed.), *The Battle of Maldon* (London: Methuen and Co., 1949), pp. 5–21, and references there cited.

3. Gordon, *op. cit.*, pp. 5–7, 17, 21–30, finds "love of rhetoric" and "exaggerations" in the *Vita Oswaldi*, but apparently not in the poem of *Maldon*: e.g., in the retainers' speeches "every detail is true and real: the conventionality of their sentiments only makes them ring truer . . . . *Maldon* has less ornament than any other Old English poem, and aims at severe simplicity and directness . . . . Even the undeniably rhetorical art of the retainers' speeches is little more than plain statement of heroic motives" (p. 27). Of two monastic histories he says further: "The account in *Liber Eliensis* [ca. 1130] of Byrhtnoð's stand is fuller, and in some respects nearer the tradition of the poem than the *Vita Oswaldi* [ca. 997–1005]; but it is much less accurate" (p. 7). Cf., Walter Sedgefield (ed.), *The Battle of Maldon* (New York: D. C. Heath and Company, 1904), pp. xi ff.

4. Gordon, *op. cit.*, p. 33.

individual deeds and speeches still seemed of primary importance. . . . The poet was probably not present at the battle" (pp. 21–22). The fresh urgency of the narrative, if rendered in traditional heroic style and founded on hearsay (whether once removed or handed on for years), proves that the poem is skillfully contrived, not that it is an accurate report. But modern scholars—Freeman, Liebermann, Laborde, Gordon, Stenton, Dobbie, and Bowra, among others— have accepted the poem as a more or less authentic record of the encounter.[5] It would appear that the poem has been an impressive witness in its own behalf; yet it makes no claims to the status of a chronicle.

It is not *prima facie* an historical poem like *The Battle of Brúnan-burh* or the other verse narratives found among the Old English annals. It does not date itself, as they do, with an introductory adverb, nor does it, like *Brúnanburh*, pointedly name a battle site, though it does incidentally mention a river name (*Pante*, the modern Pant, still applied to part of the Blackwater near its estuary). It is unlike *Brúnanburh* again in failing to name any figures on the enemy side, and in failing to call attention to its own historiographi-cal method with references to past warfare and to scholarly literature on that subject. To be sure, some lines at the beginning and end are lost, but what survives of *Maldon* provides very little journalistic information in the narrowest modern sense: it tells who and what, but not where, when, or why. It does not share with *Brúnanburh* the defining characteristics both of a panegyric and a chronicle. It celebrates heroism without the use of dates and (except for *Pante*) place names.

Since Freeman's *Norman Conquest*, however, the realism of place, of topography, attributed to the poem has figured prominently in

---

5. Edward A. Freeman, *The History of the Norman Conquest of England* (Oxford, 1876–1879), I, 271–277; Felix Liebermann, "Zur Geschichte Byrhtnoths, des Helden von Maldon," *Archiv*, CI (1898), 15–28, see especially p. 18; E. D. Laborde, "The Site of the Battle of Maldon," *EHR*, XL (1925), 161–173, and *Byrhtnoth and Maldon* (London: William Heinemann, 1936), pp. 1–8, 39–43; Gordon, *op. cit.*, pp. 1–30, and notes *passim*; Frank M. Stenton, *Anglo-Saxon England* (Oxford: Oxford University Press, 1947), pp. 371–372; E. V. K. Dobbie, *The Anglo-Saxon Minor Poems* (New York: Columbia University Press, 1942), pp. xxx–xxxi; C. M. Bowra, *Heroic Poetry* (London: Macmillan, 1952), pp. 122, 466–467, 510–511.

the historical, textual, and literary criticism of it, lending authority to an estimate of the poem as a realistic document—a different thing from recognizing historic value in the poem, which nobody would deny it. Freeman located the battle very near Maldon, at the western end of the estuary, on and around a bridge between the town and Heybridge, to the north. He imagined the vikings south of the bridge, in what is today reclaimed land, and the English opposite them on the north side. These compass directions can be deduced from the poem itself, which, as Freeman believed, describes a spear thrown by a viking from the south toward the English ("Sende þá se sæ-rinc súðerne gár," line 134), and earlier mentions the fact that the vikings, when Byrhtnoth and the tide allowed them to, advanced westward over the river ("west ofer Pantan," line 97). These topographical indications are, at first glance, contradictory, even if correctly interpreted individually, which is not certain. If the spear was thrown from the south, we should expect the vikings to advance soon afterward from the same direction; but it is possible to explain away the discrepancy by supposing a certain vanished topography.[6]

Since Laborde's studies of 1925 and 1936, historians, editors, and critics of the poem have accepted a different hypothesis, that the vikings landed their ships on Northey Island, located in the estuary about two miles east of Maldon, and that the *brycg* or *ford* of the poem was the causeway still connecting Northey and the flat fields south of it. This causeway is old (though it is not possible to show that it dates from Saxon times) and at high tide is still covered by water, as the structure defended against the vikings and later used in their crossing is said by the poem to have been. "Spear from the south" is now (except by the latest editor of the poem, who seems to reserve judgment[7]) generally taken to mean "spear made in the south, Frankish spear," rather than "spear thrown from the south"; and "west ofer Pantan" is taken to mean in effect "southwestward over the Pant," roughly the direction of part of the causeway at present. With *súðerne* thus perhaps removed as a difficulty, and also as a helpful locative indication, *west* remains something of a puzzle: first because the estuary runs east and west, so that a poet seeking authenticity but content with general indications would very likely

6. Sedgefield, *op. cit.*, p. xiv.
7. Dobbie, *op. cit.*, p. 144, note to line 134.

have described the viking advance to this mainland simply as "from the north"; second because, if he were a stickler for accuracy, the language and the formulas of his verse would have allowed him easily to say "southwest" or "from the northeast" if his topography so demanded.[8] Such puzzles will persist, however, only so long as the poet is imagined as a kind of battlefield correspondent.

No map is needed to follow Byrhtnoth's last fight, or his contemporary Olaf's, or before them Beowulf's, or after them Roland's. Indeed, the attempted use of a map might trick the modern imagination into the fallacy of misplaced concreteness, since heroic poets composed without the benefit of a cartographical sense that is second nature for a reader today. The bare literary topography along the Pant, at Swold, on a headland near Hronesness, or at Roncevals is enough to serve as setting for a traditional story (a fatal struggle against great odds) treating a stock theme (overconfident valor unconquered even in defeat), about characters shaped by tradition though bearing sometimes historical names, and using traditional verse forms. As W. P. Ker long ago observed, the spirit and theme of the poems about Byrhtnoth, Beowulf, Roland, and certain Norse heroes are part of a European tradition, and so is the "broadly indicated" landscape found in those works.[9] But if topographical minuteness plays only a small part in the traditional heroic poem, the words "southern" and "west" in *Maldon* are perhaps convenient poetic accidents, not reliable historical essences. The words should be scrutinized first in the Old English poem, rather than in the Blackwater estuary.

After an exchange of battle speeches too formal, balanced, and lengthy for realistic utterances, Byrhtnoth rashly allows the vikings to advance "west ofer Pantan," where they meet his troops on solid

8. A convenient *be-westan-súðan* "to the southwest" survives only in prose texts, but cf., *súðan-éastan* "from the southeast" (*Chr* 900); *súðan and westan* "from the southwest" (*MBo* 6.8); *norðan and éastan* "from the northeast" (*MBo* 6.12).

9. W. P. Ker, *Epic and Romance* (London: Macmillan, [1896–] 1931), p. 55, and cf., pp. 11–12, 69, 89, 95, 204 (on rhetoric used to express absolutes, not for "the immediate expression of the real life of an heroic age"); Kenneth Sisam, "Beowulf's Fight with the Dragon," *RES*, IX (1958), 129–140 (on the vagueness of historical and scenic background *vs.* the details of the fight); Arthur G. Brodeur, *The Art of Beowulf* (Berkeley: University of California Press, 1959), pp. 126–130 (on "spare," "stark" setting and traditional outlines).

ground. The sounds of this episode in the poem (lines 93–99) are extraordinary for Old English verse: a line-to-line alliteration in the sound of *w-* links a succession of five verse-pairs (of which three carry the *w-* sound in the main staves as well as in extra positions), and the sequence is climaxed by a cross-alliteration in *sc-* and *w-* before the secondary *l-* sounds of the three previous lines are resolved into the primary alliteration of the final line.[10] Thus the turning point in the encounter, which leads to disaster for the English, is underlined phonetically; the alliteration links Byrhtnoth's courageous resignation to the ominous, relentless advance of his enemy— on which simple movement the poet lavishes four verse-pairs of variation:

| | | | | |
|---|---|---|---|---|
| "Nú íow is ȝerýmed; gáþ recene to ús, | | r- | r- | |
| guman to gúðe. God ána wát | g- | g- | g- | w- |
| hwá þǽre wæl-stówe wealdan móte." | | | w-l | w-l |
| Wodon þá wæl-wulfas —for wætere ne | | | | |
| murnon— | w- | w-l:w-l | w- | |
| wíćinga weorod, west ofer Pantan, | w- | w- | w- | |
| ofer scír wæter scieldas wǽgon, | | sc- w- | sc-l | w- |
| lid-menn to lande linda bǽron. | l- | l- | l- | |

For historical and topographical critics these lines are perhaps the most important in the poem, because they seem to contain three vital clues—the place name, the direction "west" for some kind of tidal crossing, and the indication that until this moment Byrhtnoth's forces, perhaps with the water's help, had been able to defend some narrow passage. But in this densely-wrought sequence, which is further decorated (at least to modern eyes and ears) by special effects of assonance and consonance (*wǽgon* [MS *wegon*] / *bǽron;* *wæl* / *weal*[*dan*], *wæl* / *wul*[*fas*]; *land*[*e*] / *lind*[*a*]), it may be that the law was not given so much by topography as by the elaborate verse

10. It is here assumed that these and similar effects in the poem were desired and contrived; on cross-alliteration as a favorite device of the *Maldon* poet see Margaret Ashdown, *English and Norse Documents* (Cambridge: Cambridge University Press, 1930), p. 241; but cf., Robert B. Le Page, "Alliterative Patterns as a Test of Style in Old English Poetry," *JEGP*, LVIII (1959), 434–441, who on the basis of earlier poetry (*Bwf, Ele*) concludes that extra-alliteration was without stylistic significance and "that lack of it indicates a higher degree of conscious artistry."

tradition of Old West Germanic narrative. The vikings in the poem do not advance north or east or south over the stream (although along the winding approaches of the river close to its estuary there must have been places at which they actually could have found a crossing in one or more of these directions); they advance westward because the poet is causing them to advance in formulas and sets of formulas tuned, as one might say, to the key of *w-*; or to put the matter less fancifully, because he was reluctant or unable to interrupt, for a line or two more, his aurally intoxicating development of an alliterative pattern based upon that bilabial semivowel. As for stock verses involving "west" with contexts of aggressive movement, one might note examples in *Daniel* and *Riddle 29*, where further *weorod* ("troop, band") has affiliations in initial rime with still other poems whose formulas are grammatically and rhythmically similar to our poem's *wíćinga weorod*:

| | | |
|---|---|---|
| wæl-hréow weorod, | and west fóran. | (*Dan* 53) |
| worn þæs weorodes | west to-fǽran | (*Dan* 76) |
| wreććan ofer willan, | ʒewát hire west þanan | (*Rdl* 29.10) |

And compare:

| | | |
|---|---|---|
| wǽr-léasra weorod | wǽpnum cómon | (*And* 1069) |
| wǽr-léasra weorod, | and híe Wealdend ʒiefeþ | (*Chr* 1613) |
| wítenga weorod | wifmanna þréat | (*DHl* 48) |

When the crucial verse-pair "wíćinga weorod, west ofer Pantan" is seen within the poem as part of a specializing rhetorical complex, and both within and beyond the poem as a member of a generalizing formulaic association, its concrete historical significance becomes a little dubious. Formulas may of course occur in a journalistic poem, as they do in *Brúnanburh*, but it is not the formulas that make that poem journalistic; in the absence of definable journalistic properties, the formulas in *Maldon* are journalistically neutral.[11]

The same would hold true for the word "southern" if the phrase

11. Cf., William Whallon, "The Diction of *Beowulf*," *PMLA*, LXXVI (1961), 310: "Once many significant phrases are found in theory or in recurrent practice to provide for prosodic necessity, they are not to be defended for their semantic properties in isolated contexts."

*súðerne gár* could be shown to be directional rather than generic. The formulaic evidence is ambiguous, however.[12]

Another physical detail in the poem that has received close attention from the commentators occurs when the waters over the disputed crossing keep apart the two impatient bands of fighters. The poetic phrase describing this moment, "lucon lagu-stréamas" (line 66), if taken as a topographical reference, may be translated, "the tidal currents joined," that is, "the tidal currents (coming up-river around Northey Island) joined (at the western end of the island)," or, ". . . joined (and thus enclosed or trapped the vikings on the island)." Since the verb *lúcan* can also mean "to interlock, intertwine, weave together," it may have been used absolutely in this phrase, which would then mean "the tidal currents swirled together, mingled." The present topography of the site, in any case, would not suggest the phrase as understood by most historians (the areas involved are too broad and are in part hidden from the perspective of a supposed eyewitness at or near the supposed battle site), while tidal turbulence might easily suggest it. But if the phrase was not invented on the scene, it was modeled on similar formulaic expressions, and so is a precarious witness for physical, as opposed to poetic, topography; if it was meant to denote the isolation of the vikings, it resembles traditional expressions like:

| | |
|---|---|
| wæs . . . lagu-flódum belocen   líf-wynna dæl | (*Chr* 805–806) |
| wiþ wætre beléac . . . on lides bósme | (*Gen* 1409 f.) |

—the latter from a context of flood and ebb tide in the Deluge. If it was used absolutely, it then resembles the marine -ȝebland compounds in *Béowulf* (lines 1373, 1450): *ýþ-ȝebland* "wave-surging"; *sund-ȝebland* "turbulence of the water."

12. *Súðerne secg* "a southern (or foreign) man [?]" (*Rdl* 62.9) *vs. súðerne wind* (*MBo* 5.7); *éasterne wind* (*Gen* 315); *norðerne ýst* (*MBo* 6.14). The last three weather formulas are a reminder that OE *gár* "spear" could also possibly mean "storm, tempest" (see Kemp Malone in *ES*, XXVIII [1947], 42 ff.). If the *Maldon* poet was familiar with the directional storm formulas and also with the association *gár* "storm," is it possible that he here "conflated" *gár* "spear" with *súðerne*—"[hurled] from the south"? On *súðerne gár* "spear of southern make," see Gordon, *op. cit.*, note to line 134. That "weapons made in England and France were favoured by the vikings" may seem an unconvincing explanation for this usage in a patriotic English poem. The poet of course uses Norse loan words, but *súðerne* is not one of these; the point of view is odd.

Northey Island figures again in a recent study of the poem by Edward B. Irving, Jr., who seems to accept the topographical thesis and assumes that "the abundance of concrete historical detail in the poem and its accuracy, where it can be corroborated by contemporary documents, suggest strongly that the poem was composed shortly after the battle."[13] He therefore considers the poem "almost a news story" with a "powerful sense of verisimilitude," indeed as a "fragment of medieval journalism" (p. 458). But verifiable historical detail is not very abundant in the poem. As Gordon points out, "The poem is the important record of the battle: it is the only detailed account, and, except for the brief notice in Chronicles CDEF under 991, it is the only one that is generally trustworthy."[14] We have seen above that medieval journalism at its most annalystic is not always accurate. The "powerful sense of verisimilitude" rightly noted by Irving may derive more from our knowledge that some such event did happen, plus the emotional and stylistic competence of the poem as a whole,[15] rather than from any group of details like those he cites[16]: the flight of cowards, for instance, and the realistic infighting, can both be paralleled in the dragon episode of *Béowulf*, possibly the most unhistorical part of that poem. And here again the equation of poetic verisimilitude to historical verity leads to an unnecessary assumption about the action of *Maldon*. We are right to call Byrhtnoth's invitation to the vikings to cross the stream unwise and disastrous, for so the event proves. Moreover the poet has specified Byrhtnoth's reason for the invitation; it was *for his ofermóde* (line 89), a traditional heroic fault.[17] The poet does not give Irving's explanation for the invitation's rashness, that "presumably the English could have held the Vikings on the island until they

13. E. B. Irving, Jr., "The Heroic Style in *The Battle of Maldon*," *SP*, LVIII (1961), 457.

14. Gordon, *op. cit.*, p. 5.

15. See Irving's judicious defense of style and structure throughout his article; the structure has been criticized, as he notes, by Bertha S. Phillpotts in *MLR*, XXIV (1929), 172–190, and cf., Bowra, *op. cit.*, pp. 510–511: "Indeed the sequence of events carries conviction because there is no obvious artistic plan in it."

16. Irving, *op. cit.*, p. 458.

17. With Byrhtnoth's rashness compare Beowulf's in determining to go against the dragon without his comitatus (*Bwf* 2527–2535); on Roland's *desmesure* see Alain Renoir, "Roland's Lament: Its Meaning and Function in the *Chanson de Roland*," *Speculum*, XXXV (1960), 577.

starved them out."[18] We cannot know whether the poet presumed so, for he does not say, and the topography of the tenth-century site is unknown, but the present topography would allow the enemy to depart as Byrhtnoth tells us they arrived, namely by ship (line 56). What we may therefore provisionally assume is that the English could not have prevented the viking's departure any more than their arrival. Data external to the poem itself should be used very cautiously in the interpretation of an already self-sufficient narrative, especially where the narrative is grounded in part upon traditional features.

We may now more briefly notice the Old Norse exemplar of the same tradition. Of the two poems cited rather confusingly in some sources as the *Óláfsdrápa*,[19] the older (ca. 996) and shorter gives in its eighth stanza a short and undetailed confirmation of Olaf's campaigns around the British Isles, which according to the probably erroneous Parker Chronicle brought him to Maldon in 993. The latter and longer poem, the *Óláfsdrápa* or *Óláfs erfidrápa* (ca. 1001) is of more interest. It was included in Ashdown's *English and Norse Documents* "because the poem, like *Maldon*, is a poem on the fall of a hero, and the form, tone and style of the two poems, with all their general similarity, offer enough of contrast to emphasize the qualities of each."[20]

These poems from the same period differ in length and verse form (325 alliterative verse pairs, 29 *dróttkvétt* stanzas ⟨a *dróttkvétt* stanza consists of eight three-stress lines, with the last word invariably consisting of one accented and one unaccented syllable⟩) and also, more strikingly, in personal tone: *Maldon*'s stoic understatement is as eloquent as the outbursts of grief found especially in the last stanza of the dirge for Olaf. Hallfreth Ottarsson, nicknamed *vandréδaskáld* "the troublesome skald," was a poet at Olaf's court and his godson as well. The *drápa* laments the fall of Hallfreth's lord and of "other good friends" (stanza 5) in a bloody and confused defeat; one finds in his poem a literary and perhaps a biographical confirmation of Hallfreth's stunned bereavement as recorded in the

18. Irving, *op. cit.*, p. 462.
19. Kock (rev.), *Skaldediktningen*, I, "Óláfsdrápa," pp. 81–82; "Óláfs erfidrápa," pp. 82–85.
20. Ashdown, *op. cit.*, p. 109.

*Hallfreðar saga.*[21] Nothing could be more remote from the *Maldon* poet's impersonality than the self-consoling hyperbole of Hallfreth's *stef* (stanzas 19, 25),

> Allr glepsk friðr af falli
> flugstyggs sonar Tryggva,

[All peace is confounded by the death of the unflinching son of Tryggvi],[22]

or the intrusive autobiography (with which feature the poem's power is enhanced) of stanzas 26 and 27:

> Hlautk, þanns œztr vas einna
> —ek sanna þat—manna
> und niðbyrði Norðra
> norðr, goðfǫður orðinn.

[I assert that I got as godfather that one who was noblest of men in the north under the burden of dwarves, i.e., under heaven.]

> Illt's þats ulfa sultar
> optþverri stóðk ferri,
> mest þars malmar brustu,
> mein, þótt smátt sé und einum.
> Skiliðr em ek við skylja,
> skalmǫld hefr því valdit.

[It is a great shame that I was far from the king when the swords crashed, though there is little help in one man. Now I am parted from him; the tide of swords has caused this.]

The poet's sorrow at his absence from the battle inverts the theme that appears, with characteristic understatement, in *Maldon*, both in

---

21. *Islenzk Fornrit*, ed. Einar Ól. Sveinsson (Reykjavík: 1958), VIII, 192: "Hann spurði þá tíðenda, en þeir sǫgðu fall Óláfs konungs. Hallfreðr varð svá við sem hann væri steini lostinn ok gekk þegar heim til búðar með miklum harmi ok lagðisk þegar niðr í rúm sitt." [Then he asked for the latest news, and they told him of the death of King Olaf. Hallfreth reacted as if struck by a stone and went straight home to his booth in great sorrow and he immediately lay down in his bed.]

22. Editor's note ⟨S.B.G.⟩: Translations from the Old Icelandic were supplied by Wayne A. O'Neil.

Ælfwine's speech (lines 220–223) and, rephrased, in Leofsunu's (lines 249–251):

> Ne þurfon mé ymbe Stúr-mere    stede-fæste hæleþ
> wordum æt-wítan,    nu mín wine ʒecrang,
> þæt ić hláford-léas    hám siðie.

In *Maldon* the poet has imagined for his characters the traditional satisfactions of loyal self-sacrifice, providing expression for them with metrical formulas embodying a traditional theme: "My kinsmen will have no cause to reproach me that I fled leaving my lord."[23] Hallfreth can only reproach himself for having missed the battle, but his sense of chagrin is the reflex of shame to the Germanic commonplace, whereas the speakers in *Maldon* express the reflex of pride. In this subjective sense the poems are opposites. Objectively they tell similar stories in which the action at many points is parallel.

Olaf spurns flight and encourages his troops (stanzas 1–2). He must do without the help of those who should have been with him; some of his troops take flight (stanza 3). Details of individual combats are given; Olaf is always in the thick of the battle (stanzas 4–13). His bodyguard distinguishes itself (stanza 14). The location of the battle and simple compass directions are specified (*á viðu sundi . . . Holms; norðan, sunnan* ⟨toward the wide channel . . . of the Holm; from the north, from the south⟩) as opponents move together (stanzas 17–18). (Stanzas 19–28 tell of the grief caused by conflicting reports of Olaf's fate, a section that has no parallel in the English poem.) The *drápa* ends with the poet's prayer for the king's soul, as the first part of *Maldon* concludes with Byrhtnoth's prayer and death (lines 174–181).

The *Óláfsdrápa*, then, resembles *Maldon* in that it praises an historical figure and laments his death circumstantially. The poems share motifs common enough in Northern poetry and legend— leaders valiant to the point of rashness, comrades loyal to the death and cowardly deserters, bloody individual combats and general descriptions of battle. Each also gives passing reference to specific details of battle—place names and movements north, south, and

---

23. Gordon, *op. cit.*, note to line 315, cites examples of a variant theme, "He has cause to mourn ever." Another variant is, "He (or they, i.e., any enemy) had no cause to rejoice" (*Gen* 7–74; *Brb* 37–52; *Bwf* 2005–2009, 2363–2365).

west—that seem in part to represent fact and in part to be controlled by the needs of conventional verse (*Maldon*'s alliterative *west*; the *drápa*'s adverbs correspondingly fixed in the *aðalhending* rime ⟨perfect internal rime⟩: *orðsæll jǫfurr norðan* ⟨the celebrated king from the north⟩; *gunnr—Hǫkonar sunnan* ⟨battle—of Hákon from the south⟩). Both use the bardic formulas of narrative recitation (*hyrde ić; frá ek*), which in themselves do not prove or disprove historicity, or even absence from the source of the tidings, though in the case of Hallfreth this happens to be certain. It is probably due to a coincidence of the genre that both poems can be documented, though not precisely or entirely, from other sources; that the site of each battle has accordingly been disputed; and that each site involves, or may involve, an island in a tidal estuary. For Olaf's battle, "it is generally agreed that the site has to be looked for off Pomerania, not far from the island of Rügen. Since in the course of time the coast in this area has undergone great changes, the island itself may well have disappeared."[24] *Maldon* nowhere mentions an island, but, as we have seen, an island has been supplied from modern topography to explicate the poem's action. It may be that Northey or a nearby island figured in the scene of the real battle, but Northey itself, other islands close to it, the river's bed, banks, surrounding mud-flats, and adjacent man-made structures have all been substantially changed in the past thousand years, chiefly through the action of tides, storms, floods, and normal erosion and silting. It is difficult, therefore, to speak with any confidence about realistic topographical details in the poem about this battle. Nor would present-day tidal conditions allow the stated action of the poem to take place at Northey and its causeway even if a millenium of indeterminate topographical change could be ignored.[25]

Tests of specific realism, in other words, would appear to be largely beyond our reach for both poems, though the litmus of historical truth could perhaps be applied to them in other ways. For instance, if they had been intended patently as factual accounts, we

24. Ashdown, *op. cit.*, p. 215; see pp. 213–215 for a discussion of historical persons at Swold (Svǫlð) and for a summary of attempts to locate the battle.

25. If the date of the battle was August 10 or 11, 991, spring tides would have covered the area of the present causeway to a much greater width and depth than the high tides calculated by Laborde and Gordon.

might expect, given their obviously partisan authorship, to find them politically tendentious; but they are not. Short narrative or panegyric heroic poems like *Brúnanburh*, the Harley Manuscript's "Song of Lewes," or Tennyson's ballad of "The Revenge" can be identified as propagandistic by their stridency of tone and by their effort to flatter some broad partisan sentiment. They are crammed with names of persons, places, and the concrete details of struggle, which are worked up with some care, being frankly meant to convince some audience of their historical "truth." As a result they are at once too false and too true to be good as history. They can indeed be praised as vividly journalistic; they do indeed make concrete testimonials to historical events; but this is their defect when compared with *Maldon* and Hallfreth's poem, which triumphantly avoid the temptations of emotive historiography. The *drápa*, some may feel, barely does so, but the emotion in it is chiefly personal. Olaf's enemies are as brave and resourceful as he. In *Maldon* the hero's enemies are ciphers except for the herald, with his speech inviting appeasement. If the vikings are treacherous and bloodthirsty, good qualities in any enemy, the heroism of the English figures is understated and allowed to make its own effect, along with the cowardice of some of them. *Maldon* is patriotic without being propagandistic. One imagines the victorious invaders would have appreciated its thematic heroism. Olaf himself, evidently no poor judge either of poetry or of heroic action, would certainly have enjoyed it; he could have understood its language at least as well as the defenders and invaders of the poem understood each others' challenge "over the cold water."

A comparison of the *Óláfsdrápa* with *Maldon* thus suggests an historical awkwardness in the received interpretation of the latter poem. The impression it gives of historicity depends in some measure upon stock features, not always easy to identify as such, some of which it shares equally with historical and nonhistorical poems. The person of Byrhtnoth, and his death, along with the names of other men,[26] can be verified in extrapoetic sources, but few if any details of the battle can be; the topographical details especially cannot. These two poems are of the kind of poetry that

26. See Laborde, "Characters of the Poem," in *Byrhtnoth and Maldon*, pp. 9–38; Gordon, *op. cit.*, pp. 15–21.

deals with history without caring about history. Neither their general credibility nor their use of concrete detail (which with cor- roborating or conflicting historical evidence would seem equally convincing within the poems as they stand) need affect our estimate of their poetic value. Their excellence as poems is not an illusion, for it can be documented in other ways. Their resemblances, however, underline the potentially illusory nature of a limited kind of his- torical interpretation, for if credibly organized detail makes *Maldon* seem more historically true than it tries to be, the sum of similar detail in *Ólafsdrápa* (which is more easily recognized as a traditional and unjournalistic account) would compel one to rate it approxi- mately as high on a scale of truth.

Historical poems like these are only secondarily about events; they are rather about men seen and heard in typical heroic action, and on this subject they have much to tell us that a chronicle could not. *Maldon* describes honor that turns with swift fatality into an excess of honor—Byrhtnoth's *ofermód*, which is redeemed by his retainers' calmly sacrificial restoration of the balance. It is a stoical but affirmative poem which in its treatment of this theme deserves comparison with its analogue in the *Iliad*. Hallfreth's *drápa*, surely one of the liveliest dirges ever composed, breaks through its dense skaldic style with accents of real grief, and produces a sense of human waste totally lacking in *Maldon*. What is profoundly his- torical about the two poems is their (so to speak) antiphonal presentation of the heroic German ethos. For it is the affirmative *Maldon*, in the person of the enemy messenger, which says with dreadful plausibility before the slaughter begins, "Né þurfe wé ús spillan"—"We need not spend and destroy ourselves." It is the despairing Hallfreth who answers, not too confidently, for the ethos at large, "Frægr's til slíks at segja siðr"—"It is glorious to speak of such a deed in later times."

Reprinted from Stanley B. Greenfield (ed.), *Studies in Old English Literature in Honor of Arthur G. Brodeur* (Eugene, Oregon: University of Oregon Books, 1963), pp. 23–35.

J. A. BURROW

# An Approach to
# The Dream of the Rood

THE DREAM OF THE ROOD is one of the first and one of the most successful treatments in English of the theme of the Crucifixion. It is successful because it is more than just a biblical paraphrase in the Caedmonian tradition. For one thing, the biblical narrative is treated with a greater freedom of emphasis and selection; for another, it is integrated into a new, non-biblical form, involving dreamer, vision, and speaking Cross. The present essay attempts to analyze and illustrate these two aspects of the poem, and to suggest how its characteristic pattern of emphasis, its "point of view," emerges in both. For the poem seems to me remarkable among Old English poems in the closeness of its organization. The organizing principle is, partly, the point of view or religious sensibility characteristic of the early Middle Ages as against the late. I think, therefore, that comparison with some later medieval English poems of the Crucifixion throws light, by contrast, on the Old English poem. It will illustrate how strikingly treatments of the same traditional theme can reflect varieties of sensibility in author and audience in the distribution of emphasis and selection of detail, and how different narrative forms serve these varying emphases—as, for example, the "goût de la pathétique" ⟨taste of the pathetic⟩, which Mâle finds characteristic of fourteenth and fifteenth century treatments of the Crucifixion,[1] has its most representative literary expression at that period in the monologue of the "mater dolorosa" ⟨sorrowful mother⟩ by the Cross. I will quote one or two such Middle English examples in order to suggest what is significantly absent in the Old

1. E. Mâle, *L'art réligieux de la fin du Moyen Age en France* (Paris: A. Colin, 1925). See especially Part I, Chapter III, "L'art religieux traduit des sentiments nouveaux: le pathetique."

English poem, and to throw into relief its own peculiar unity of form and emphasis.

The form of the poem offers a suitable point of departure, in the striking use of the figure "prosopopoeia." Miss Schlauch has already pointed this out as a formal innovation in the tradition of Crucifixion literature, tracing its background in the poetic practice and rhetorical theory of classical and post-classical Latin writing.[2] I would like, here, to consider it from another point of view, as a controlling factor in the total meaning of the poem; for it seems to me that the identity and situation of the narrator, the "consciousness" through which the events of the Crucifixion are observed, is as significant here as—to draw a long comparison—in Henry James' *What Maisie Knew*, where Maisie's mind is made "the very field of the picture." It controls both what we see and how we see it, just as it does in the later Crucifixion lyric, where the same kind of device is frequently used, to different effect.

The use of prosopopoeia in descriptions of the Crucifixion is still to be found in the later Middle Ages (Miss Schlauch points out that Geoffrey of Vinsauf's most extensive illustration of the figure in his *Poetria Nova* consists of a speech by the Cross);[3] but the dramatic forms which are most frequent and characteristic in the Middle English Crucifixion lyric would, in rhetorical terms, be called "ethopoeia"—fictional dramatic speech not of an inanimate object but of a human being. This ethopoeia takes three main forms— monologue of the "mater dolorosa," dialogue between Mary and Christ on the Cross, and monologue by the crucified Christ. I will give a short passage to illustrate each, taken from Carleton Brown's collections. Dialogue between Mary and Christ:

> Ihesus:  Maiden and moder, cum and se,
> Þi child is nailed to a tre;
> Hand and fot he may nouth go,
> His bodi is wonden al in wo. . . .
>
> Maria:  Mi suete sone þat art me dere,
> Wat hast þu don, qui art þu here?

2. M. Schlauch, "The *Dream of the Rood* as Prosopopoeia," *Essays and Studies in Honor of Carleton Brown* (New York: New York University Press, 1940), pp. 23–34.

3. *Ibid.*, p. 34. The passage is *Poetria Nova*, 469–507.

> Þi suete bodi þat in me rest,
> Þat loueli mouth þat i haue kist—
> Nou is on rode mad þi nest.[4]

This passage illustrates how fully this form of ethopoeia lends itself to the humanizing pathos which is characteristic of late medieval religious feeling. The tone is set by the repetition of *child* and *sone*, by the nest image of the last line, and by the use of the characteristic epithet *suete*, which could even, at this period, be applied to the Cross itself:

> Swete be þe nalys,
> And swete be þe tre,
> And sweter be þe birdyn þat hangis uppon the.[5]

The same note is struck in the monologue form, the "lamentacio dolorosa" ⟨sorrowful lamentation⟩ of Mary, which is often only formally distinguishable from the true dialogue:

> Suete sone, þi faire face droppeþ al on blode,
> And þi bodi dounward is bounden to þe rode;
> Hou may þi modris herte þolen so suete a fode
> Þat blissed was of alle born and best of alle gode.[6]

In the monologue of Christ, by contrast, there is often a greater austerity of effect, as in this beautifully complete short lyric from the fifteenth century:

> I have laborede sore and suffered deyth
> And now I rest and draw my breyth;
> But I schall come and call ryght sone
> Hevene and erght and hell to dome;
> And thane schall know both devyll and mane
> What I was and what I ame.[7]

---

4. Carleton Brown, *Religious Lyrics of the XIVth Century*, 2nd ed. (Oxford: Oxford University Press, 1952), No. 67: *Dialogue between Jesus and the Blessed Virgin at the Cross*, pp. 1–4, 9–13.

5. *Ibid.*, No. 40: *Crux Fidelis*, pp. 5–7.

6. *Ibid.*, No. 64: *Lamentacio Dolorosa*, pp. 5–8.

7. Carleton Brown, *Religious Lyrics of the XVth Century* (Oxford: Oxford University Press, 1939), No. 111: *Christ Triumphant*, p. 177.

But this is strictly a post-Crucifixion lyric, spoken from the tomb. In the many monologues from the Cross, as in Herbert's *Sacrifice*, which follows this traditional medieval form, we find again the "goût de la pathétique," without, however, the peculiar resonance which comes from stressing the family relationship between Christ and Mary:

> Þi garland is of grene
> Of floures many one;
> Myn of sharpe þornes
> Myn hewe it makeþ won.
>
> Þyn hondes streite gloved
> White and clene kept;
> Myne wiþ nailes þorled
> On rode and eke my feet.[8]

In this, as in the other examples, the dramatic form serves directly to intensify the human immediacy of the Crucifixion scene, to excite "dolour" and "drede." In such poems, as Mâle puts it, speaking of the iconography of the Passion in the fourteenth and fifteenth centuries, "la sensibilité, jusque-là contenue, s'y exalte" ⟨the sensibility, up to that point contained, becomes exalted⟩.[9] I would like now to turn back to *The Dream of the Rood* with the previous quotations in mind, and consider how, there, the prosopopoeia serves, unlike the ethopoeia of the Middle English lyrics, to "contain" the human pathos and immediacy of the scene.

The vision opens, after a short introductory passage, with twenty lines introducing the Cross. Nothing in Middle English quite matches this passage. The Cross here is neither the *swete tre* of which the fourteenth-century poet speaks, nor the physical instrument of the Miracle plays, but a cosmic hieratic image of both. The *swete tre* becomes the *syllic treow*, raised to the sky, bathed in light, adorned with gold and jewels, worshipped by *eall þeos mære gesceaft*; the instrument of torture, alternating with it, soaked in blood—*mid wætan bestemed*—is correspondingly represented in non-naturalistic terms. Both forms of the *fuse beacen* recall liturgical practice, as Patch has

---

8. Brown, *Religious Lyrics of the XIVth Century*, No. 126: *Jesus Pleads with the Worldling*, pp. 3–10.

9. Mâle, *op. cit.*, p. 86.

shown;[10] neither makes any direct appeal to the human or the natural. The gap between the dreamer and the Cross, at this point in the poem, is absolute:

> Syllic wæs se sigebeam and ic synnum fah (13)
> Forht ic wæs for þære fægran gesyhþe (21)

With the opening of the speech of the Cross, however, there is a sudden shift in the tone and scale of the poem. The cosmic vision is left behind, and the Cross speaks as a natural tree:

> þæt wæs geara iu—ic þæt gyta geman—
> þæt ic wæs aheawen holtes on ende,
> astyred of stefne minum. (28–30)

The colloquial informality of this opening—without apostrophe or introduction—is in striking contrast to the impersonal liturgical grandeur of what has gone before. The congregation of worshippers, *halige gastas, menn ofer moldan, and eall þeos mære gesceaft,* is for the time being lost from sight, and there is nothing surprising when the Cross addresses the dreamer as if they were alone and on equal terms— *hæleþ min se leofa.* This sudden and unexplained transition from the public-hieratic to the private-colloquial would be possible only within the conventions of the vision form—it anticipates effects in *Piers Plowman.* It makes the mediating consciousness through which the action of the crucifixion is to be described a more complex thing than anything in the Middle English lyric. It is not a simple dramatic figure, but a double persona, strongly differentiated, belonging in its two forms to the two widely separate worlds (as they are presented at this point) of nature and the supernatural. The result in the narrative which follows is a kind of double focus, which I wish to consider next.

In the opening lines of its speech, already quoted, the Cross introduces itself in its natural environment, a wood, from which it is cut down to be used in executions for no other reason than that it stood *holtes on ende.* The tree is an ordinary one suddenly drawn into a world of violence. The suddenness and the violence, together with the passivity of the Cross itself, are conveyed in the compressed

10. H. R. Patch, "Liturgical Influence in the *Dream of the Rood*," *PMLA*, XXXIV (1919), 249–250.

paratactic syntax, the lengthened line, and the rapid sequence of
verbs of action in the passage immediately following:

> Genaman me þær strange feondas,
> geworhton him þær to wæfersyne, heton me heora wergas
>    hebban.
> Bæron me þær beornas on eaxlum, oþþæt hie me on beorg
>    asetton,
> gefæstnodon me þær feondas genoge.                    (30–33)

(The repetition of þær, to which Dickins and Ross tentatively assign
the meaning "then," seems rather intended to suggest the confused
telescoping of events at this point.)[11] These lines dramatically
establish the second, natural, persona of the Cross, and as such it
functions throughout its account of the crucifixion as a representative of common humanity and consequently of the dreamer himself.
Like the dreamer in face of his vision, the Cross is afraid:

> Bifode ic þa me se beorn ymbclypte; ne dorste ic hwæþre
>    bugan to eorþan.                                    (42)

and, again like the dreamer, with a verbal reminiscence of line 20, it
is "troubled with sorrows"—sare ic wæs mid sorgum gedrefed (line 59)—
just as, with the other crosses, it later stands weeping (70). In this
form, in fact, the Cross represents the common "crystyn creature" of
the Middle English Meditations on the Supper of our Lord:

> Now, crystyn creature, take goode hede,
> And do þyn herte for pyte to blede;
> Loþe þou nat hys sorowes to se
> Þe whych hym loþed nat to suffre for þe.[12]

But the Cross here does not only see with the dreamer—in its
second, non-natural persona it suffers with Christ:

> þurhdrifan hi me mid deorcan næglum; on me syndon þa
>    dolg gesiene,
> opene inwidhlemmas. Ne dorste ic hira ænigum sceþþan.
> Bysmeredon hie unc butu ætgædere.                     (46–48)

11. B. Dickins and A. S. C. Ross, The Dream of the Rood, 3rd ed. (London:
Methuen and Co., 1951), p. 24 n.

12. Meditations on the Supper of our Lord and the Hours of the Passion, ed. J. M.
Cowper (EETS, 1875), pp. 297–300.

Here the wounds of the Cross are carried over by transfer from Christ with whom it suffers (*unc butu ætgædere*). So, in 47b, there is an obscurer transfer which suggests a kind of "dream condensation" between Christ and the Cross. The motif which it states—that the Cross could strike down the crucifiers but dare not since Christ does not wish it—recurs elsewhere in the poem (36–37: *Ealle ic mihte feondas gefyllan, hwæpre ic fæste stod*); and it is linked with the idea, repeated three times, that the Cross could have refused to bear Christ by bending or breaking (35–36, 42–43, 45). These themes seem to me more than simply a natural extension of the animism implicit in prosopopoeia. They refer properly to Christ. It was Christ who could have struck down his enemies, and Christ who could have refused the ordeal, if he had not willed it otherwise (a theme to which we will return later).

Thus the Cross, in its own narrative, functions doubly as a surrogate both for the dreamer and for Christ; and these two functions correspond to the double transcendental-natural image of the Cross established at the beginning of the poem. The consequences of this in the poem are curious. It might be expected that the Cross would, as it were, bridge the gap between the natural and supernatural worlds by virtue of belonging to and speaking for both. One might look, that is, for the kind of naturalism which I have illustrated from the Middle English religious lyric, or even for the direct pathetic realism of the Miracle play. There is indeed a trace of such an effect—in the way the Germanic idea of comitatus loyalty is implied in the scene of the Deposition, where the *beornas* bury their *æpeling* and sing him a *sorhleop*—but the general impression is quite different. The gap between the natural and the supernatural is felt as absolute. There is here a striking difference of effect between the prosopopoeia of the Old English poem and the various ethopoeic forms of the Middle English lyrics. In the later poems the central scene is humanized through the speeches of Christ and Mary—the emphases fall on the physical suffering of Christ, his *won hewe*, his body *dounward bounden to þe rode*, and on his natural relation as the *suete sone* of Mary. In *The Dream of the Rood*, by contrast, the reader and the dreamer experience the human suffering and passive naturalness of Christ only in so far as these are transferred to the Cross itself, *blode bestemed*, and shared by it. For the Cross in its main role, as representative of the "crystyn creature," Christ remains completely opaque:

> Geseah ic þa frean mancynnes
> efstan elne mycle þæt he me wolde on gestigan.   (33–34)

These lines, in which Christ is for the first time introduced, follow immediately after the passage quoted above in which the *strange feondas* set up the tree as a cross. The passivity of the Cross in those lines throws into sharp relief the sudden dynamic appearance and mysteriously voluntary actions of Christ—he hastens *elne mycle*, *wishing* to ascend the Cross.

There is no concession here to circumstantial realism, no attempt to render the scene naturalistically in the late medieval way. The figure of Christ acts in absolute independence of its environment. The presence of the *feondas* is hardly felt at all from this point onwards in the poem—the moment of crucifixion itself is described in a series of non-realistic verbs which, as Patch has shown, recall the Latin hymns: *he me wolde on gestigan, gestah he on gealgan heanne* (*ascendere* ⟨to climb⟩), *me se beorn ymbclypte* (*amplexere* ⟨to embrace⟩).[13] There is no sense of the weight of the body dragging *dounward* such as we find in later plastic and literary works; Christ is presented ceremonially in positive deliberate action, just as a little later:

> he hine þær hwile reste,
> meþe æfter þam miclan gewinne.   (64–65)

The trope—death as sleep—was probably traditional in Old English verse (it is used of the dead Grendel, *guþwerig Grendel*, in *Beowulf* 1586); but it is characteristic of *The Dream of the Rood* that its use here should be fully meaningful, suggesting the willedness, and also the impermanence, of Christ's death. This emphasis harmonizes with the manner in which the crucifixion itself is described, and with those passages, already mentioned, in which it is Christ's will, *Dryhtnes word*, which controls the Cross itself.

The death-as-sleep trope is also used in the Middle English *Christ Triumphant*, quoted above; but, on the whole, the non-naturalistic mode which we have been illustrating in *The Dream of the Rood* is as alien to the Middle English lyric as it is to the Miracle plays. The nearest thing to *The Dream of the Rood* in Middle English

13. Patch, *op. cit.*, p. 253.

literature is to be found in Passus XVIII (in the B text, from which I will quote) of *Piers Plowman*. The differences both in form and approach are clear enough—there is nothing in the Old English poem which anticipates Langland's fluid allegorical method (except, possibly, in 52–54, where, if one follows Dickins and Ross in taking *scirne sciman* as parallel with *wealdendes hræw*, there is a suggestion of Langland's allegory of light and darkness—but the phrase may belong to the following clause).[14] Nevertheless, there is a striking similarity of emphasis between the two poets, for in some ways Langland stands outside the main Middle English tradition. There is little of pathos or passivity in his account of the crucifixion. Christ is a knight jousting with the powers of evil, who rides "pricking" to Jerusalem; or he is light conquering the darkness of hell. His death is described in words which recall the sleep metaphor, *the lorde of lyf and of lighte tho leyed his eyen togideres*. Correspondingly, there is little direct concession to the "goût de la pathétique"—the trial, the buffetings and the nailing to the Cross are treated sparely in less than twenty lines. We may recall the words of Repentance in his prayer to God earlier in the poem:

> And sith with þi self sone in owre sute deydest
> On godefryday for mannes sake at ful tyme of þe daye,
> Þere þiself ne þi sone no sorwe in deth feledest;
> But in owre secte was þe sorwe, and þi sone it ladde,
> *Captiuam duxit captiuitatem* ⟨he led captivity captive⟩.
>
> (V, 495–498)

These lines seem to me as relevant to *The Dream of the Rood* as they are irrelevant to the greater part of the lyric poety and drama which was being written in Langland's own day. The Old English Christ feels no sorrow in death; there too the sorrow is *in owre secte*, in the dreamer and in the Cross as his representative. For Langland, Christ at the Passion jousts in *Piers armes* (glossed as *humana natura* ⟨human nature⟩) *for no dynte shal hym dere as in deitate patris* ⟨in the divinity of (his) father⟩. This allegorical image stresses sharply, as Langland stresses throughout, the distinction between the natural and the supernatural Christ; in his poem the inviolable *deitas patris*

14. See the note on this passage in G. P. Krapp, *The Vercelli Book* (New York: Columbia University Press, 1932), p. 131.

⟨the divinity of the father⟩ is never for a moment lost sight of, just as in *The Dream of the Rood* it is continually recalled:

Ongyrede hine þa geong hæleþ, þæt wæs God ælmihtig.     (39)

Dickins and Ross are surely wrong in suggesting (Introduction, 17) that the second half of this line is an "addition" or an "expansion." The whole line, as it stands, stresses the dichotomy which, we have already seen, is stressed throughout the poem. It is perhaps significant, in this connection, that Christ is referred to as such only once in the account of the crucifixion—otherwise he is either on the one hand *geong hæleþ, beorn, guma, æþeling,* or on the other *Frea mancynnes, Dryhten, heofona Hlaford, Wealdend, rice Cyning, God ælmihtig.* The two sets of terms express the contrast between *humana natura* and *deitas patris,* the contrast which is summed up in line 39.

So far in this essay I have attempted, by considering the account of the crucifixion in the first part of *The Dream of the Rood* and comparing it with later treatments of the same subject, to define the point of view characteristic of the Old English poem, and to suggest how this point of view emerges both in the prosopopoeic form and in details of language and style. It is this overall unity of form and meaning which seems to me remarkable in the poem—not the point of view itself, which, abstractly stated, was by no means unusual at that period. In fact the contrast I have drawn with the Middle English lyric corresponds very closely to the well-established general lines of contrast between the religious art of the early and late Middle Ages. Visual representations of the crucifixion in the earlier period lay the emphases very much where *The Dream of the Rood* lays them, on the *deitas patris* of Christ on the Cross, and, again like the Old English poem, make little of the natural pathos. Similarly, the characteristics of the Middle English religious lyric extend to the visual art of the period. In the late Middle Ages, as Mâle has shown, painting, sculpture, lyric and drama "ont évidemment leur origine dans le même sentiment . . . la sensibilité, jusque-là contenue, s'y exalte" ⟨evidently have their origin in the same sentiment . . . the sensibility, up to that point contained, becomes exalted⟩.[15] They share the same naturalism, the same stress on the sufferings of Christ, the same "goût de la pathétique." Again, the contrasts with which I have been concerned have their parallels (perhaps even, to

15. Mâle, *op. cit.,* p. 86.

a certain extent, their explanations) outside the arts altogether, in the history of the philosophy and theology of the period. The pervasive Platonism in the religious thought of the early Middle Ages matches the supernaturalism implicit in *The Dream of the Rood*; and it is perhaps significant that traces of ultimately Aristotelian ideas are to be found in the most naturalistic of the Miracle cycles.[16] Perhaps, too, the strength of the Franciscan, anti-Aristotelian tradition in Langland's thought has something to do with the peculiarities of his passus on the crucifixion. But these are matters where "the bottom is a long way down," and it is enough here to point out that the attitudes and emphases which I have been discussing are not peculiar to *The Dream of the Rood*. For the purposes of the present essay there remains one further topic of more immediate relevance.

The account of the crucifixion in *The Dream of the Rood* ends with the burying of the crosses (line 75)—not quite half way through the poem as it stands in the Vercelli Book. The rest of the poem consists of a homiletic speech by the Cross to the dreamer (78–121), with which the vision ends, and a coda in which the dreamer describes his unhappy life on earth and his hope of a *heofonlic ham* (122–156). Dickins and Ross, who regard the Vercelli text as an expanded and composite version of an earlier work, are suspicious of this part of the poem. They argue that it "does not afford any metrical or linguistic evidence which necessitates the assumption of an early date," that "in quality it seems to us definitely inferior," and that "it is perhaps significant that the passages found on the Ruthwell Cross all correspond to passages in the first half of the Vercelli text."[17] The first of these arguments makes no claim to be conclusive, and the last is very weak—would it not, after all, be natural to choose passages from the speech of the Cross for inscription on a cross, rather than passages of a generally didactic or personally reminiscent kind? The case seems, therefore, to rest on the argument from inferiority, and this too is open to strong objection. The inferiority, to modern taste, of the latter part of the poem is hard to dispute; but the argument from this fact to an assumed composite

16. See the *Towneley Cycle*, ed. G. England (EETS, 1897), especially the play of Doubting Thomas (XXVIII), e.g., p. 342: My saull and my cors have knytt / A knott that last shall ay. This metaphor, which is representative of the play's argument, may be contrasted with Langland's allegory of Christ in "Piers armes."

17. Dickins and Ross, *op. cit.*, p. 18.

origin, although quite a common procedure in the criticism of Old English verse, begs so many questions that I feel justified in considering briefly the latter part of *The Dream of the Rood* as a legitimate component in the whole poem.

It is, as I have admitted, inferior; but, despite some laxness of rhythm and diffuseness of expression, it is not difficult to see that the themes of the earlier part are developed consistently and meaningfully. With the conclusion of the account of the crucifixion (75), the tone of the speech of the Cross begins to change. It no longer speaks as a representative of common humanity to which the supernatural world is opaque (part, as we have seen, of the effect of the earlier passages), becoming again unambiguously an initiated member of that world, as it was in the opening vision, honored above natural trees as Mary is honored above women (90–94). The Cross reassumes its original persona, and, as it does so, the themes and images of the opening lines return—first in a brief reference to the Invention:

> Hwæþre me þær Dryhtnes þegnas
> freondas gefrunon,
> gyredon me golde and seolfre.                    (75–77)

and then, almost immediately, in full restatement:

> Is nu sæl cumen
> þæt me weorþiaþ wide and side
> menn ofer moldan and eall þeos mære gesceaft,
> gebiddaþ him to þyssum beacne              (80–83)

where the verbal reminiscences seem deliberately to stress the recapitulation (line 82 is identical with line 12, for example). The Cross, thus reestablished in its original transcendent form, ends its speech appropriately enough by explaining to the dreamer the mysteries of salvation.

The poem, however, does not end here; there is a further thematic development, which appears in the closing soliloquy of the dreamer. In order to appreciate this, the reader must recall the opening section of the poem, as the poet himself recalls it in lines 75–83. That section, as we have seen, turned on the sharply marked contrast between the natural and the supernatural:

> Syllic wæs se sigebeam and ic synnum fah

and it is only in terms of this contrast that the dreamer's identity is defined at this point. He appears as a generalized, passive figure, prostrate in face of his vision, which in its turn is static, though brilliantly decorative, like a tableau:

> Hine þær beheoldon halige gastas,
> menn ofer moldan and eall þeos mære gesceaft.  (11–12)

The last part of the poem offers a deliberate contrast to these effects. The dreamer takes on an independent personal identity, with a past in which he has suffered *feala ealra langunghwila* and the death of powerful friends; and it is these snatches of elegiac autobiography which provide the personal background for a new dynamic religious feeling:

> ic wene me
> daga gehwylce hwænne me Dryhtnes rod
> þe ic her on eorþan ær sceawode
> on þysson lænan life gefetige
> and me þonne gebringe þær is blis mycel.  (135–139)

Instead of gazing at the Cross, he prays to it:

> Gebæd ic me þa to þan beame bliþe mode
> elne mycle.  (122–123)

It is in keeping with this development in the dreamer's attitude that the last lines of the poem should be crowded with verbs expressing *movement* (the only movements in the opening vision are the symbolic transformations of the Cross):

> . . . ic þone sigebeam *secan* mote  (127)

> . . . hie forþ heonon
> *gewiton* of worulde dreamum, *sohton* him wuldres
> Cyning  (132–133)

> . . . ic wene me
> daga gehwylce hwænne me Dryhtnes rod
> þe ic her on eorþan ær sceawode
> on þysson lænan life *gefetige*
> and me þonne *gebringe* þær is blis mycel  (135–139)

> . . . þa he mid manigeo *com*
> gasta weorode on Godes rice  (151–152)

These passages contrast sharply with the static, hieratic imagery of
the opening vision, for they represent the third and last stage in the
development of the poem, where the opening tableau takes on life
and motion after the central scene of the Crucifixion. The theme is
the activity of Grace, released through the death of Christ; the
language is the abstract language of motion—seeking, travelling,
fetching, coming, bringing—abstract, that is, in the sense that it has
little to offer in the way of visual "imagery." Perhaps it is for this
reason that the last part of the poem is the least memorable, at any
rate for most modern readers. It has to compete on unequal terms
with the visual and dramatic concreteness of the visions of the Cross
and of the Crucifixion.

The poet himself may have felt this, for at the very end of the
poem (148–156) he attempts, as it were, to dramatize the personal
religious themes of the last part in an account of Christ's Harrowing
of Hell. There seems no reason to accept Cook's contention that this
is an addition. The transition from the personal present to the
historic past is skillfully managed, and it is hard to see where the
supposed addition might begin:

> Si me Dryhten freond,
> se þe her on eorþan ær þrowode
> on þam gealgtreowe for guman synnum     (144–146)

The relative clause effects the shift in tense and person, from the
present to the past and from the dreamer to mankind (*guman*) which
is confirmed in the following lines:

> He us onlysde and us lif forgeaf,
> heofonlicne ham

The further transition to the Harrowing of Hell (*Hiht wæs geni-
wad . . .*) is natural at this point as an amplification of Christ's
"releasing" power. It is also convincing in the general economy of
the poem. The last lines are not vivid, as is the treatment of the
same theme by Langland (who draws on the Miracle play tradition)
—though there is a compensating syntactic effect in the sequence of
parallel clauses leading up to *þær his eþel wæs*—but they do have a
specific relevance. This lies not so much in the traditional doctrinal
association between the Harrowing and the Crucifixion, as in the

story's tropological significance at this point in the poem, its relevance to the dreamer's "moral state"—his personal *hiht* (see line 126) which is the distinguishing theme of the closing soliloquy.

This personal theme is implicit in *The Dream of the Rood* from the first. The essential principle of development lies here, in the dreamer himself, just as it does in *Piers Plowman*. At the beginning of Langland's Eighteenth Passus, before the vision of the Crucifixion, the dreamer is *wolleward and wete-shoed* and *wery of the worlde*; when it is over he wakes joyfully calling to his wife and daughter to pray to the Cross:

> Crepeth to the crosse on knees & kisseth it for a iuwel,
> For goddes blissed body it bar for owre bote.

So the dreamer in the Old English poem moves from fear and sorrow to hope, and it is this simple emotional sequence which links the closing soliloquy with the opening vision and sets the tone of the central Crucifixion scene.

Reprinted from *Neophilologus*, XLIII (1959), 123–133.

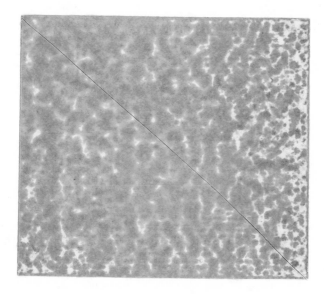

# N. F. BLAKE

# *The Form of* The Phoenix

THOUGH THE POET of *The Phoenix* was following a Christian tradition in reading the *Carmen* ⟨*de ave phoenice*, attributed to Lactantius (ca. 260–ca. 340)⟩ allegorically, and an Old English tradition in translating and adapting a Latin original, we should not belittle his achievement, for not only has he had to combine and adapt different sources in order to present his allegory, but also these sources vary considerably in both content and intention. It is a tribute to the poet that he has been able to construct a homogeneous poem out of this diverse material. We must now consider how he has managed to accomplish this, and first we must see how the poet treated the *Carmen*, his principal source.

The first 380 lines of *The Phoenix* correspond to the *Carmen*'s 170 lines.[1] But the English poet was by no means a slavish imitator and he adapted the original to suit his own ends. He omits, adds to, or develops many of the details found in his Latin source. A typical example of how he went to work can be found in the opening lines of the poem. The *Carmen* opens: *Est locus in primo felix oriente remotus* ⟨There is a blessed place, remote, in the far east⟩, and this line corresponds to the opening six lines of *The Phoenix*:

> Hæbbe ic gefrugnen    þætte is feor heonan
> ēastdǣlum on    æþelast londa
> fīrum gefrǣge.    Nis se foldan scēat

---

1. O. F. Emerson, "Originality in Old English Poetry," *RES*, II (1926), 19, has noted that of the first 380 lines in the English poem, only 148 lines can be said to follow the Latin. But this total is hardly a fair indication of the use of the *Carmen* in *The Phoenix*, as Emerson does not include in it phrases which are parallel to or expansions of those expressions which do translate something from the Latin. Furthermore, it is often possible that the Latin suggested something to the Old English poet, even though he did not translate the Latin literally. Emerson claimed that approximately 63 lines of the *Carmen* were not used by the English poet.

> ofer middangeard    mongum gefēre
> folcāgendra,    ac hē āfyrred is
> þurh Meotudes meaht    mānfremmendum.

*The Phoenix* is verbose, and one might almost say diffuse, whereas the *Carmen* is precise and compact. The Latin poem states briefly that a blessed spot is to be found in the far east. But the English poet is not content with this unassumingness: he opens his poem with a flourish. He uses the typical epic formula of Old English poetry: *Hæbbe ic gefrugnen.* Similar openings are found in *Andreas* and *Beowulf,* and we can tell immediately that the poem is firmly placed in the Old English poetic tradition. The next two lines of *The Phoenix* relate what the first line of the *Carmen* has, but with some significant differences. The Latin *felix locus* ⟨blessed place⟩ appears as *æpelast londa,* and this land is further described as being *firum gefrǣge.* There is a constant attempt by the English poet to make his landscape noble and impressive, and the word *æpele* is used four times in the first fifty lines to describe the paradise where the phoenix lives. He is not so much interested in the land's beauty as in its attributes. It is not merely beautiful; it has a deeper, more significant meaning; and the English poet's descriptions are always affected by the allegorical implications. The home of the phoenix is *æpele, wlitig,* and *ænlic,* though none of these attributes is mentioned in the Latin. In this way the poet paves the way for the allegorical interpretation which is to follow. What is implicit in the first half is made explicit in the second. The second half is thus the logical continuation of the first.

Yet the English poet does not leave his translation of the first line at that, for the *remotus* ⟨remote⟩ has suggested something further to him. Because the land is far away, it is not accessible to man. The poet expresses this idea within the framework of the *nis (ne) . . . ac* construction, one of the most characteristic rhetorical devices used in the poem. The poet first states a negative and then its opposite: paradise is not accessible to any man, but it is barred to all sinners. The frequency of this construction is one of the principal reasons for the poem's verbosity, for it is fatally easy to multiply the negatives in the first half of the construction. Thus, in a second example of this construction a few lines later, the *Carmen*'s statement that the land was not visited by summer's heat or winter's cold is extended by the

English poet to include among other things rain, snow, frost, fire, and hail. Consequently, although the poet is able to achieve a fine effect as of incantation, the length of the first clause destroys the balance of the construction as a whole. The last clause too often comes as an anticlimax. It is partly for this reason that we get the impression from the poem that paradise is described in negative rather than positive terms.

But to return to our consideration of the opening lines of the poem, a further difference between *The Phoenix* and its source should be noted. In *The Phoenix* we learn that it is God who has ordained that this land should be far removed from sinners. God dominates the poem which is firmly and unashamedly Christian. In the *Carmen*, however, there are references only to heathen gods and goddesses, and these are included for rhetorical purposes alone. There is no suggestion in the *Carmen* that there is one deity who guides and governs all. In *The Phoenix*, on the other hand, this wonderful land is under God's strict surveillance and care (cf. 43–46).

It is not, of course, possible here to compare in detail all of the first part of *The Phoenix* with the *Carmen*. But the following general principles are characteristic of the Old English poet's approach to the *Carmen*. He made his work explicitly Christian and he tried to relate it to the Old English heroic background, as exemplified in the earlier poetry. Consequently, anything that was alien to either of these two aims was omitted. The classical gods, goddesses, and heroes are all banished. Instead of Phaeton, Deucalion, Phoebus, Aurora, and Aeolus we have the Christian God, who is alone said to guide and direct all things. Other classical references to such things as Olympus and the constellation Cancer are likewise omitted. The English poet has not attempted, however, to shift the scene of action from the far and the near east. The phoenix is said to visit *Syrwara lond* (166). The English poet has also rejected the *Carmen*'s list of precious spices, which are gathered by the phoenix as it prepares for death. Although their names were possibly familiar to educated Englishmen who would be able to read Latin, there were no English words for many of them and the English poet no doubt felt that they were not sufficiently naturalized for inclusion in his poem. As a result, the poem has lost some of the richness and ornateness of the Latin. Nevertheless, it can hardly be doubted that it was right to exclude those terms, for they would have been out of place in the reworking of the story.

In order to fill the vacuum created by leaving out all that might be considered classical, the English poet has set his poem against a Christian Germanic background. Instead of classical gods and heroes we have a Christian God with copious references to such events as the Day of Judgment. This event was introduced as a result of the allegorical interpretation: the fire of the phoenix symbolizes the fire of judgment in which the souls are tested and the good souls purified, and the rebirth of the phoenix symbolizes the resurrection of man on that fatal day. There are many other instances like this where the allegory intrudes into the first half * * *. In order not to misunderstand this feature it is necessary to bear in mind the nature of medieval allegory. The world to medieval man was the creation of the divine logos. Consequently every created thing was an expression of the divine thought; the world in fact was a book written by the hand of God in which every creature is a word charged with meaning. By reading nature aright, the wise man can look beyond the material form and penetrate to the divine thought of which it is the material expression. In a word the whole world is a symbol. Consequently, for the Old English Christian poet of *The Phoenix* the bird is merely a symbol of a divine truth. The poem was written in order that we might realize what this truth was. The poet probes the meaning of the natural symbol. It must be emphasized, therefore, that for the poet the most important fact is the allegorical interpretation of the symbol. The phoenix in itself is merely one of the many natural ways in which this Christian truth finds expression, and as such is neither more nor less important than the story of the seed (242 ff.) which is a symbol for the same Christian truth. So it need not surprise us that the allegory keeps on appearing in the first half, for the symbol and the interpretation are one and the same thing. One is the divine thought and the other is the expression of that thought in a material form. We today may perhaps find the story of the phoenix more enjoyable than the allegorical interpretation. Many modern critical works stress the great beauty of the descriptions in the first half of this poem. But we must not forget that for the poet these were subservient to his real purpose, the revelation of the Christian message to be found in a created being. But as the phoenix was only a symbol for the poet, this was bound to affect his attitude to his source. He would take only that which served his purpose.

It is interesting to note how the poet sets his poem against a Germanic background. We have already seen how he uses the Old English epic opening. There are also many descriptive touches which are clearly influenced by earlier descriptions. Thus the *Carmen*'s *Atque ubi Sol pepulit fulgentis limina portae* ⟨And when the sun struck the threshold of the glittering gate⟩ (43) appears in *The Phoenix* as:

> Sōna swā sēo sunne    sealte strēamas
> hēa oferhlīfað.                       (120–121)

Instead of the classical gates of heaven, the sea which appears so often in Old English poetry is introduced. And there is in *The Phoenix* frequent reference to both sun and sea. But one should pay particular attention to the poet's use of words drawn from the Old English heroic vocabulary, such as *wælrēaf*, *beaducræftig*, *heaporōf*, and *ānhaga*. These words which are reminiscent of more vigorous and bloodthirsty exploits appear at first to be incongruous in a poem which portrays a peaceful idyll of happiness and joy. But they are included to make plain the correspondence between the life of the phoenix and that of man, the symbol and the thing symbolized. The phoenix's life, death, and rebirth stand for the life, death, and future resurrection of man. In order to make this plain the poet tends to anthropomorphize the phoenix. Thus the bird is described in terms like those above which would be more appropriate to Old English heroes; its nest is described as a *hūs*, a *willsele*, and a *hof*; the bird collects its ashes and bones "from the grave" (267) as men will do on the Day of Judgment; and the bird emerges from the fire "purged of sins" (242). This last phrase reminds us of the blessed who will come through the purgatorial fire purged of their sins. One cannot deny that to us the result is sometimes jarring, but in this way the poet has cleverly linked the symbol to the thing symbolized and he has thus prevented the poem from falling into two halves.[2]

*The Phoenix* differs considerably from the earlier poems in the

2. See further N. F. Blake, "Some Problems of Interpretation and Translation in the OE *Phoenix*," *Anglia*, LXXX (1962), 50–62.

mood created by the natural descriptions. The earlier poets portrayed nature in its sternest moods and their descriptions are both
vigorous and positive. The poet of *The Phoenix*, however, portrays an
imaginary, ideal landscape. Everything is pleasant, nothing is
harmful. His descriptions therefore have none of the reality of those
in the earlier poetry, and he portrays the land in very negative
terms. This does not mean that we should agree with Moorman, who
claims that "the poem marks the decadence of the descriptive
powers of pre-conquest poetry."[3] The poet is not trying to create
the same effect as the earlier poets, and their descriptions are hardly
comparable. In *The Phoenix* we are to imagine at one and the same
time a real garden and a spiritual haven, a terrestrial and a heavenly
paradise. To have concentrated too much on the material side of the
garden might have lessened our appreciation of its more spiritual
qualities. The essential unity of the poem would also have been
endangered, as the two halves would have become two separate
entities: the first, the story; the second, the interpretation. Therefore
the descriptions tend not to be visual, and when we compare *The
Phoenix* with the *Carmen* we see that the English descriptions have
lost much of that precision and detail which are to be found in the
Latin. An example of this is the description of the *fons* in the garden.
In the *Carmen* this is described as *perspicuus, lenis, dulcibus uber aquis*
⟨clear, mild, abreast with sweet waters⟩ (26), whereas in *The Phoenix*
it is merely mentioned as *wæter wynsumu* (65). It could be said that
*wynsumu* here means hardly more than "pleasant," but yet it carries
with it overtones of that unalloyed pleasure which one experiences
not only in this pleasant land but also in heaven. For *wyn* as either a
simplex or an element of a compound is one of the poet's favorite
words, and apart from *wyn* itself we find *wynlīc, wynlond,* and *wynsum.*
The difficulty the poet came up against was how to express in
positive terms what heaven means to the soul, a difficulty he tried
to solve by a heavy reliance on adjectives expressive of joy, majesty,
light, and bliss. These adjectives are in one sense more fitting in the
allegorical interpretation than in the story of the phoenix. But this
is to make a distinction between the story and its meaning, a distinction which, as we have seen, the poet did not make, for to him

3. F. W. Moorman, *The Interpretation of Nature in English Poetry from Beowulf to
Shakespeare* (Strassburg: K. J. Trübner, 1905), p. 43.

they were one. He naturally painted the garden in more symbolic terms than those found in his source. So *wynsumu* in line 65 also implies the pleasantness of the heavenly home. Thus in order to appreciate the poem we must look through the actual material objects to what they represent; we can read the phoenix story in the first half only in the light of the allegorical interpretation. It has no existence in its own right.

So far we have been considering the way in which the poet of *The Phoenix* handled his principal source, the *Carmen*, in the first half of the poem. It is time now to turn to a brief consideration of his treatment of Ambrose's *Hexameron*, which he used in the second half. Not unnaturally the problems here were different, for the source was both Christian and allegorical already. The poet's task was to relate the material found in Ambrose to the story he had told earlier and to work Ambrose's allegorical interpretation into the general allegory which he was drawing in the second half. Ambrose for his part when he wrote the *Hexameron* had not been interested in presenting a complete account of the phoenix. He was able to select those details of the story which would help to illustrate the moral he was drawing. His use of the phoenix story was therefore limited. But the English poet chose to base his poem on the complete phoenix story, which is then used as the basis for the allegory. So, though the story can to some extent be altered to suit the allegory, it must in itself be logical and coherent. Not only had the poet to take the demands of his story into consideration, but he had also to relate the allegory found in Ambrose to other allegorical interpretations of that story. Ambrose provided him with only one way of reading the phoenix story. He clearly, however, knew many other ways of reading it, even though it is not certain whether he had learned of these from written or oral sources. Consequently, the interpretation in the *Hexameron* was altered somewhat to meet these requirements. Even so the poet has not managed to present a unified allegory. But in order to show this it might be best to glance briefly at the development of the allegory.

The allegory opens with the description of the expulsion of our forefathers from Eden after they had tasted the apple (393 ff.). They were forced to leave that blessed plain (418) which was then barred to them until Christ by his death here on earth reopened it. The expulsion of Adam and Eve from Eden resembles the flight of the phoenix from its home when it is old (428 ff.). But whereas the phoenix leaves to become rejuvenated and then returns home, man wanders in the world afflicted by the powers of evil. Nevertheless, some men in this world obey the commands of Christ (443 ff.). The allegory is now developed by comparing the tree in which the phoenix built its nest with Christ. If a man shelters in Christ nothing can harm him, as nothing could harm the phoenix in its nest (cf. 179–181). To shelter in Christ man must build a nest by means of his good works, which correspond to the spices used by the phoenix to construct its nest. By these good deeds a man earns admission to the heavenly home. But first at his death he is buried and waits in his grave till Doomsday (489–490). At Doomsday all are led before God in judgment and the world is consumed by fire (491 ff.). Then the sign of the phoenix, by which we are to understand God, or more likely Christ (cf. 646–647), will be revealed to men when all the dead take on a new body and come to judgment. The blessed are happy, for they have won salvation by their good works and they rise to glory having been purged by fire (518 ff.). At this point the poet includes the metrical paraphrase of Job (546 ff.). Job is certain he will rise again at the Day of Judgment, just as the phoenix rose again from its ashes. This leads to a restatement of the allegory with a slightly different emphasis; as the phoenix is reborn, so will the souls of good men be reunited with their bodies and together they will rise to heaven (570 ff.). In heaven the blessed follow Christ around in a great company, as the birds had followed the phoenix (589 ff.). Yet, like the phoenix, the blessed live in glory and are clothed in shining garments. In heaven there is no sorrow, pain or anything harmful, just as all these hurtful things had been excluded from the home of the phoenix (611 ff., cf. 50 ff.). The blessed sing the praises of Christ in heaven. The poet then briefly introduces the story of the Resurrection, and the rebirth of the phoenix is now compared with the death and resurrection of Christ (638 ff.). As the phoenix gathers spices in his wings when he is eager for rebirth, so Christ gave us eternal life by his death here on earth (642–654). The poem then concludes with praises to God.

This synopsis of the second half reveals that the poet has not confined himself to simple allegory, for the details of the story can be interpreted in several different ways. Thus the phoenix represents at first all men who will rise again at Doomsday, then more narrowly all good men who will go to heaven, and finally Christ himself. The phoenix's rebirth foreshadows man's future resurrection, but is also a symbol of Christ's past resurrection. Consequently, a certain amount of confusion can arise, for the blessed are sometimes compared with the phoenix and sometimes with the birds which follow the phoenix. Likewise Christ is represented in the original story either by the tree or by the phoenix itself. The poet has failed to select and arrange his material satisfactorily, for the overlapping interpretations sometimes confuse the reader. One should not of course expect a perfect concordance between the story and the allegory, though the method the poet has chosen of presenting first the story and then the allegory invites one to extend the allegory to the entire story. But this is impossible, for though the poet has chosen to present the entire phoenix story, he has used only individual scenes from that story to illustrate the various Christian themes which he wished to exemplify. The allegory is fragmentary and this tends to prevent a proper fusion of the two halves, as they are not satisfactorily balanced against each other. One can agree that by refusing to confine himself to one allegory the poet has given his work greater significance and depth; but nevertheless one cannot help feeling that a greater poet would have been able to order the various allegorical strands into an organic unity. The interweaving of the different interpretations in *The Phoenix* has not been carried out with sufficient subtlety. They are too isolated and too fragmentary. The poet is never able to suggest that the phoenix story symbolizes all these Christian themes at one and the same time. The fault may well be that the poet knew too many different interpretations of the phoenix and attempted to include them all without, however, being able to combine them into a comprehensive pattern.

The failure to provide a comprehensive allegory undermines to some extent the poet's attempt to unify the two halves of the poem, which consists in constantly anticipating the allegory in the first half and by constantly looking back to the phoenix story in the second half. Thus the details of the phoenix story are often colored by their allegorical attributes. The phoenix in the first half is described as *se tīrēadga, þēodne mǣrum, se clǣna, se mōdga, þone hālgan, se gesǣliga,* and *se ēadga,* all of which appellations clearly look forward to the Christian interpretation, particularly as many of them are later applied to Christ or the blessed. We have already seen that the same applies to *wlitig* and adjectives like it. But there are, furthermore, many verbal parallels between the two halves which serve to link them even more closely. Even the opening of the phoenix story, *Hæbbe ic gefrugnen,* is echoed by that of the opening of the allegory *Habbaþ wē geascad* (393). More important echoes are such verbal parallels as

> Ne mæg him bitres wiht
> scyldum sceððan          (179–180)

> þær him wihte ne mæg
> ealdfēonda nān    ātre sceþþan,
> fācnes tācne   on þā frēcnan tīd.      (448–450)

And passages with the *nis (ne)* . . . *ac* construction are found in both halves to describe paradise (cf. 611 ff., 50 ff.).[4] Sometimes, however, the allegory intrudes too forcefully in the first half and sometimes an incomplete fusion of story and allegory leads to confusion and uncertainty.

*The Phoenix* then represents a valiant attempt by a sensitive poet to produce an Old English poem out of a mixture of a late classical Latin poem and some Christian themes. The attempt is not altogether successful for the poet has not been ruthless enough in selecting and arranging his material. Though he has substantially altered the *Carmen,* he has not tailored the allegorical interpretations adequately to the measure of the story that he adapted from the *Carmen.* The poem is composed in a simple, fairly plain style, the major fault of which is a tendency to repetition. The poet repeats too many of his favorite phrases, he overworks the *nis (ne)* . . . *ac* construction, and he starts far too many of his sentences with *þonne.* He can, however, at times make use of striking similes and words. The poem's beauty

---

4. A list of the major correspondences between the two halves can be found in A. S. Cook and C. B. Tinker, *Select Translations from Old English Poetry* (Boston: Ginn and Company, 1935), p. 144.

lies in its idyllic tone, in the picture of a terrestrial-heavenly paradise, and in the gracefulness with which some of the allegorical interpretations are linked with the story of the phoenix. It has indeed a quiet charm and simple dignity which are not found elsewhere in the whole of Old English poetry.

Reprinted from N. F. Blake (ed.), *The Phoenix* (Manchester: Manchester University Press, 1964), pp. 24–35. One footnote has been deleted.

DOROTHY WHITELOCK

# The Audience of Beowulf

FROM TIME to time in *Beowulf* studies it is desirable to do a sort of stock-taking, to see if received opinions have stood the test of time and the impact of new evidence. It is a salutary undertaking even if, at the end, we should find ourselves very much where we were before; for we can then go on to build on the old foundations with increased confidence. It may be that more positive results will be forthcoming from the investigation, that new matter can be added to that kernel of material which it is safe to regard as the established fact of *Beowulf* scholarship; or, on the other hand, that some material can be shown to be masquerading as established fact when it should still be regarded as open to doubt. It sometimes happens that a well-argued theory, with the authority of a great scholar behind it, will, after a series of progressive repetitions by others who ignore the safeguards and reservations of the original propounder, acquire an axiomatic quality which that propounder would have been the first to deplore; and then, being handed on as incontrovertible fact, which it is not, it may block the line of advance and stand in the way of the true assessment of new evidence as this comes to light. It is in no mood of disparagement of the work of any scholars of the past, that I propose to re-examine a few of the basic problems of *Beowulf* scholarship, in relation to any available new factors. Such factors may be the product of work in other fields of learning, and there is sometimes a time-lag before it is realized that their reverberations reach our poem.

And why my title? It will seem very trite and obvious to say that the effect of any work of art depends not only on the author's power and skill, but also on what is already present in the minds of its hearers, or readers, or—in the case of the visual arts—its beholders. Nevertheless, this consideration is particularly pertinent to the poem of *Beowulf,* partly because it is far removed from us in time, so that we are not entitled to assume without investigation that an audience of the poet's day would be moved by the same things as we are, or, if by the same things, in the same way; but still more, because much of the poem is composed with a subtle technique of allusion, reminder, and suggestion, so that we cannot guess at the effect the poet was hoping to obtain unless we know something of the meaning and associations his hints and allusions carried to those for whom he composed his poem. This is, of course, no new idea: it is implicit in most *Beowulf* scholarship, though occasionally writers have lost sight of it. Yet it seems to me that the contribution of the audience to the full understanding of the poem is so important that it is time that for once it should be allowed to get on to a title-page. I propose, in these three chapters ⟨only the first of which is reprinted here⟩, to focus attention on to it.

There may be persons who are content to study the impression that the poem makes now, concerning themselves only with what has survived the changes in our civilization and methods of thought, and caring little that ignorance of what the author counted on his audience knowing robs many of his remarks of their point. The poet has perhaps conveyed something of permanent value that is above the accidents of time and place and has survived the ravages of the centuries. I think he has. It is not for me to discuss the legitimacy of such an approach, but it is not such persons that I am addressing. For my own part, I should like to know what effect the poet was consciously striving to produce on the men of his own time; I want to see if by studying these men we can get any nearer to that knowledge. It will be necessary in the first place to gather what we can about them from the poem's statements and implications; but this does not mean that I wish to use the poem merely as a quarry for social history. I propose to use the poem of *Beowulf* to elucidate the poem of *Beowulf.*

First, however, I must define what I mean by the "poet" and the "audience" of *Beowulf.* By the "poet" I designate the Christian author who was responsible for giving the poem the general shape and tone in which it has survived, and by the "audience" the people whom he had in mind. It is as well to admit that one cannot prove beyond question that there never was a heathen poem on *Beowulf.*

It is difficult to prove a negative, and we cannot know in what form the older materials which the Christian author undoubtedly used were available to him. But one can show that, if a heathen poem on this subject once existed, it must have been very different from the work that has come down to us. As has often been pointed out, the Christian element is not merely superimposed; it permeates the poem. It is not confined to a few—or even to a number—of pious ejaculations in the author's own person or in the mouths of his characters; an acceptance of the Christian order of things is implicit throughout the poem. It pervades the very imagery: the sun is "heaven's candle" or "the bright beacon of God," the spring thaw comes when "the Father unbinds the fetters of the pool." If there once was an original *Beowulf* from which all this was lacking, a poet —no mere scribe—has gone to the trouble of completely re-thinking and revising the work, and it is with the audience for whose benefit he did this that I am concerned, not with the hypothetical audience of a postulated earlier work. I do not, however, wish to maintain that the poem has been immune from modification during the period that separates this Christian author from the date of the extant manuscript. It is hardly likely that it should have become so stereotyped that any change was impossible; nevertheless the work makes on me, as it has on others, so strong an impression of homogeneity that I believe that later alterations have not materially changed the general conception and purpose of the man whom I call "the *Beowulf* poet."

My task would be easier if it were possible to state categorically when and for whom the author was working; but both these are problematic matters, and it will be in place to begin with them. It will first be necessary to examine the attitude to the Christian faith of the audience the poet had in mind.

He was composing for Christians whose conversion was neither partial nor superficial. He expects them to understand his allusions to biblical events without his troubling to be explicit about them. He does not think it necessary to tell them anything of the circumstances in which Cain slew Abel, or when, and why, "the flood, the pouring ocean, slew the race of giants." [1] He assumes their familiarity

1. Ll 1689 f. ⟨Unless it is otherwise stated, references in the footnotes by line refer to *Beowulf* in the Klaeber edition (Boston: D. C. Heath and Co., 1950)⟩.

not merely with the biblical story, but with the interpretation in the commentaries—not, of course, necessarily at first hand, but through the teaching of the Church. His hearers would not have understood why it was "the race of giants" that were destroyed by the flood, unless they were aware of the identification of the giants of Genesis 6:4 ("There were giants in the earth in those days") with the progeny of the union of the descendants of Seth with those of Cain, a union thought to be implied in Genesis 6:2 ("The sons of God saw the daughters of men, that they were fair").[2] The passing reference earlier in the poem to "giants, that fought against God for a long time; He paid them out for it"[3] would have been altogether cryptic and obscure to a newly converted audience. In fact, it is unlikely that a recently converted people would have known the word the poet uses for giants, for it is a Latin loan-word coming most probably from the Latin Bible, and the poet gives no explanatory gloss. It is not the only ecclesiastical Latin loan-word which he uses; *candel*, used only in a metaphorical sense, applied to the sun, *forscrifan*, a formation from the Latin *proscribere* ⟨to proscribe, condemn⟩, are other instances; and, most significant of all, as Professor Girvan has pointed out, the word *non* has had time to be generalized from its original application to a church service at the ninth hour till it indicates merely a certain time of the day. It is interesting to contrast the practice of the poet of the *Heliand* with that of the *Beowulf* poet in this respect, for while the latter says casually in a secular context "Then came noon of the day"[4] the former normally glosses the term; for example, he says: "the noon of the day at the ninth hour"[5] and "at noon, when it was the ninth hour of the summer-long day."[6] It is only when he uses the term for the third time that he allows it to stand unsupported. The poet of *Beowulf* expects the word to be understood; more than that, the context in which he uses it suggests that it no longer even had an ecclesiastical flavor.

It is quite true, as has frequently been commented on, that the biblical references are confined to Old Testament events. But it

2. See O. F. Emerson, "Legends of Cain, especially in Old and Middle English," *PMLA*, XXI (1906), 878–929.

3. Ll. 113 f.

4. L. 1600.

5. *Heliand*, l. 3491.

6. *Ibid.*, ll. 3420 f.

would be absurd to assume from that that the poet is composing for a partially converted audience who have been taught about Cain and Noah's flood, but have not yet got as far as the events of the New Testament. That is not how missionaries teach the faith of Christ. The missionaries to the Anglo-Saxons were not exceptional in this respect. They preached first of the major doctrines; they spoke of the Redemption of the world by Christ's Passion; the detailed stories of the Old Testament could be left till later, special emphasis being laid on such events as were held to foreshadow those of the New. When Benedict Biscop brought back from Rome pictures to adorn the churches of Wearmouth and Jarrow, with the express intent of influencing people who could not read, among those first chosen were pictures from the gospels and the Apocalypse; on a later visit he brought back a series to illustrate the connexion of the Old and the New Testament.[7] Any set of persons in Anglo-Saxon times that is well-informed on the Old Testament can be assumed to be cognizant of the Christian faith as a whole. The absence from our poem of allusions to the New Testament must receive some other explanation than one which supposes that such allusions would be unintelligible to an audience that knows about Cain and Abel. Nor is it difficult to provide another explanation; the theme which the poet has chosen, the ravages of monsters among mankind, leads him naturally to think of the giants of Genesis, and, indeed, forces him to find a place for his monsters in the scheme of Creation, as set out in Genesis. It is his theme, not his inclination, still less any doubt of his audience's knowledge of Christianity, that limits his allusions to Old Testament history.

An audience which understands biblical references will also be familiar with the stock metaphors of the homiletic tradition, themselves often of biblical origin. The poet is not afraid of being misunderstood when he speaks of "the slayer . . . who shoots wickedly from his bow"[8] or of the man who, when the "guardian of the soul" sleeps, "is struck under his helmet with a sharp arrow."[9] The metaphors of the spiritual armor against the arrows of the devil are too much the common property of sermon literature for it to be

7. Bede, *Historia Abbatum*, ed. C. Plummer, *Baedae Opera Historica* (Oxford: Oxford University Press, 1896), I, 369 f., 373.

8. Ll. 1743 f.

9. Ll. 1742, 1745 f.

worth while to look for a specific source for their use in *Beowulf*.
They occur, for example, in Vercelli homily No. IV.[10] The poet
need not have been conscious of passages like Ephesians 6:16. What
is important is that he regards such metaphors as instantly intelligible to his hearers, and this could not have been the position in the
earliest days after the conversion of the English.

It is in keeping with all this that the poet assumes that the conception of a last judgment, of retribution after death for sins, of
eternal life for the righteous, will be accepted without question. He
does not labor these matters; he does not need to; he is not asserting
them against a different point of view. His audience accept the
Christian dogmas and the poem is free from religious polemic.

I would go further than claiming that the audience of *Beowulf*
was thoroughly acquainted with the Christian religion. I believe
that it was also accustomed to listen to Christian poetry. There is no
general difficulty in the way of such an assumption, unless one
wishes to date the poem very early indeed. Already when Bede was
writing his *Historia Ecclesiastica*, which he tells us he finished in 731,
there had been a number of poets who had followed Caedmon's
example and composed religious poems in the traditional native
meter;[11] and from *Beowulf* itself it can legitimately be gathered that
it was not only ecclesiastics who listened to poems on religious
themes. Whatever may have been the poet's reason for making
Hrothgar's minstrel sing in Heorot of the Creation, * * * the picture
he draws would surely have been incongruous, or even ludicrous, if
minstrels never sang on such themes to lay audiences. To depict the
heathen retainers of a Danish king as listening to Christian poetry
would have been impossible if such a procedure had been abnormal
at the courts of the Christian kings of his own day.

It is not, however, simply on general probability that I am basing
this claim. I have committed myself elsewhere[12] to the view that the
poet did not himself invent all his poetic expressions for Christian
conceptions, but drew them from a common store that had gradually

10. *Die Vercelli-Homilien*, ed. M. Förster (*Bibliothek der angelsächsischen Prosa*, XII
[Hamburg, 1932]), pp. 103–106.

11. Bede, *HE*, Book IV, chap. 22 (24), ed. Plummer, *op. cit.*, p. 259.

12. "Anglo-Saxon Poetry and the Historian," *Transactions of the Royal Historical
Society*, Series, XXXI (1949), 83.

grown up among poets dealing with religious subjects. I will elaborate a little on this opinion. The poet uses a great number of Christian expressions that are also to be found in surviving religious verse. This verse shares with *Beowulf* not only many of the poetic periphrases for the divinity, such as *wuldres wealdend, lif-frea, wuldor-cyning, sigora waldend, heofena helm, dæda demend,* but many other expressions also: e.g., *miclan domes* "of the great judgment," *werhðo dreogan* "suffer damnation," *ece rædas* "eternal benefits," *lænan lifes* "of this transitory life"—all of them complete half-lines—*God eaðe mæg* "God can easily," always used as a second half-line with its object in the following line. Much of the verse in which these expressions occur is probably later than *Beowulf*, none can be proved to be earlier, for I consider the expression *ece Dryhten* "eternal Lord," shared by *Beowulf* and Caedmon's *Hymn*, to be too obvious an epithet for the divinity for it to carry any weight in this argument. It would therefore be possible to claim that the other poets who use these expressions were borrowing them from *Beowulf*. But is it likely? It would indeed be odd if it first occurred to a poet whose theme is not primarily religious to invent so much new phraseology for Christian conceptions, sometimes apparently by translating expressions in the Vulgate or the early Christian hymns, and if subsequent poets, composing on religious themes, used this predominantly secular work as a store-house of Christian phrases. It is easier to imagine the *Beowulf* poet and these religious poets deriving the diction they have in common from the same source, earlier religious verse which has not survived.

That this is the true explanation is supported by the impression which some of the Christian phrases in *Beowulf* make, of not having been invented for their present context. For example, some expressions used of Grendel and the dragon are applied to the devil elsewhere, and this sometimes is their more original use. Some of them are, as Klaeber has shown,[13] translations of Latin periphrases for the devil, e.g., *captivus inferni* ⟨prisoner of hell⟩ rendered as *helle hæfta,* *hostis antiquus* ⟨ancient enemy⟩ as *ealdgewinna, hostis humani generis* ⟨enemy of the human race⟩ as *feond mancynnes.* Probably the audience was familiar with these descriptions of the archfiend and accustomed

13. "Die christlichen Elemente im Beowulf," *Anglia*, XXXV (1911–1912), 249–259.

to hear them used in a more general sense to emphasize the evil malignity of other beings. The phrase "to seek the concourse of devils" [14] does not sound as if it were first coined to describe Grendel's wish to reach the lair which he inhabits alone with his mother; and would the poet have gone out of his way to invent the periphrasis for death "he chose God's light" [15] in order to describe the passing of a heathen king, however anxious he may be to ignore the heathenism of his characters? But if it were already a recognized poetic circumlocution for "he died," the poet might well employ a ready-made half-line without thinking too much about its implications. Surely, however, he could do so only if his hearers were likely to understand it in the same weakened connotation as he did. If to them it were a new and unfamiliar expression, they would give it its full meaning, and might well have felt it incongruous. The poet is free to use Christian poetic phraseology somewhat inexactly if it has come to be an accepted convention. But whether it be conceded or not that the poet's first hearers were familiar with much of his Christian phraseology in a different kind of setting, it seems clear enough that their religious education was too thorough for them to be recent converts.

It is not necessarily a sign of very early date that the poet should expect his audience to be interested in the vivid and impressive funeral rites of the heathen period, and should therefore describe at length the ship-burial of Scyld and the cremation of Beowulf. It would be a different matter if it could be proved that these descriptions were based on eye-witness accounts. * * * ⟨But⟩ as long as it is open to us to believe that these descriptions were drawn from earlier accounts, in poetry or otherwise, we need not date the poem within living memory of these ceremonies. The poet may have found similar scenes described in the sources from which not only he, but his hearers also, had gained their knowledge of the heroic stories alluded to in the poem. I have suggested elsewhere [16] that before so Christian a poet—and here I would add so Christian an audience— can take pleasure in detailed accounts of heathen burial rites, those rites must be so far in the past as to have lost much of their association with other, more obnoxious, heathen ceremonies. As long as the

14. L. 756.
15. L. 2469.
16. "Anglo-Saxon Poetry and the Historian," *op. cit.*, p. 83.

fate of Christianity in England was in any way insecure, its more pious adherents could hardly enjoy hearing of the practices of a heathenism from which they had only recently been released, even if purely heathen poems were still being listened to by their less religiously minded contemporaries.

Neither is it a sign of early date that the audience is assumed to be interested in the blood-feud, to judge by the frequent references to stories which turn on this motive. If this implies a people not fully weaned from heathen ethics, the same could be said with equal justice of the Anglo-Saxons throughout their history. For the duty of protecting one's kindred, or one's lord, or one's man, and of exacting retribution from the slayer and his kindred if any of these were killed, was not superseded by Christianity. Action by the kindred, or, in special circumstances, by other persons empowered to act in their place, was the only means by which Anglo-Saxon law dealt with homicide until after the Norman Conquest. It is true that the Church threw the weight of its authority to support the practice of settling feuds by the payment of wergilds instead of by the actual taking of vengeance, and that the law tried to put some pressure on the offender to make him pay composition for his deed. But even if the combined efforts of Church and State had been completely effective, there would remain the problem of the poor man of a poor kindred, who could not pay the wergild. Was such a person to be allowed to kill with impunity? In such cases, and also when, as frequently happened, passions were too enraged for peaceful settlement to be acceptable, the vengeance was allowed to take its course. A few examples will show that killing for the sake of vengeance was not felt to be incompatible with Christian ethics at any period in Anglo-Saxon times.

In 801 no less prominent a churchman than Alcuin himself wrote to Charles the Great in recommendation of a Northumbrian nobleman called Torhtmund that he had "boldly avenged the blood of his lord."[17] Towards the end of the tenth century, the Cambridge Thanes' Guild, an association of a semi-religious, semi-social character, had its statutes entered on what was most probably a fly-leaf of a gospel-book once belonging to the monastery of Ely. These statutes pronounce: "If any guild-brother slays a man, and does so as an avenger by necessity, and to remedy the insult to him

17. *Alcuini Epistolae*, ed. Dümmler (*MGH*, Epist. Karolini Aevi, II), p. 376.

... each guild-brother is to supply half a mark to his aid. ... If, however, the guild-brother slay anyone foolishly and wantonly, he is to be himself responsible for what he has done." [18] These men were loyal sons of the Church; they rendered their alms to St. Audrey at Ely, they made arrangements for due Christian ceremony at their burial; but they recognized that any one of them might find himself an avenger by necessity, and they saw nothing blameworthy in such an act. So when the *Beowulf* poet lets his hero speak those famous words: "Better it is for each that he avenge his friend than mourn much" [19]—in a situation, we may notice, where no question of compensation could arise, since this type of foe "did not wish to remove the deadly enmity, to compound with money" [20]—it is no mere reminiscence of heathen times, but a sentiment that all present could applaud. Feeling could still run strong on this matter even as late as the episcopate of Wulfstan II of Worcester (1062–1095), when, we are told, the brothers of a slain man declared that they would rather be utterly (*omnino*) excommunicated than fail to avenge the death of their brother. On this occasion both ecclesiastical and popular opinion felt the attitude to be unreasonable, but this was because the slaying had been accidental and the slayer was willing to pay full reparation. Divine vengeance afflicted one brother with madness, and the others came to a better frame of mind. [21] The *Life of St. Wulfstan*, which records this incident, has another, slighter reference to the continuance of feuds at this time: a rich priest was set on by his foes and killed, and since he had been scornful of St. Wulfstan's advice, the biographer makes no adverse comment on this act of violence. [22] The first of these incidents took place in the diocese of Worcester and thus proves that it was not only in the Scandinavianized North and East of the country that the blood-feud was current in late Saxon times.

Beowulf's sage remark: "Rarely anywhere does the slaughtering

18. *Diplomatarium Anglicum Ævi Saxonici*, ed. B. Thorpe (London, 1865), pp. 611 f.

19. Ll. 1384 f.

20. Ll. 154, 156.

21. *The Vita Wulfstani of William of Malmesbury*, ed. R. R. Darlington (London: Offices of the [Royal Historical] Society [by Butler and Tanner, Ltd.], 1928), pp. 38 f.

22. *Ibid.*, pp. 92 f.

spear remain at rest even a little while after the fall of men,"[23] was true not only in the days of an heroic past. One of the codes of King Edmund (939–946) attempted to curb the blood-feud,[24] and it reveals the tremendous care necessary to prevent the flaring up afresh of emotions while the feud was being settled. The slayer and the kindred of the slain man must each have an advocate, and the slayer is not to approach in order to pledge himself to pay the wergild until the kin of the slain man have given security to his advocate that he may do so under safe-conduct. When this has been done and the slayer has found surety for the payment of the wergild, the king's *mund* is to be established, that is to say, any act of violence committed by either party will be regarded as a breach of the king's own right of affording protection, and make the offender liable to a very heavy fine, over and above the other consequences of his act. There is an interesting account of how in the eleventh century a feud broke out again after settlement, and, though it comes from a rather late source, there is no reason to reject its general accuracy.[25] When Earl Aldred of Northumbria had taken vengeance for his father's murder by killing the murderer, Thurbrand, there was a deadly feud between him and Carl, Thurbrand's son. But eventually, by the agency of friends, reparations were made and the feud was so completely settled that the two protagonists became sworn brothers. We are not told what renewed the quarrel, but it underlines my point—that it was not only men hostile or indifferent to the teachings of the Church who admitted the duty of vengeance—to note that Carl killed Aldred at the very moment when they were waiting for a favorable wind for them to start on a pilgrimage to Rome together. Aldred lay long unavenged, but in 1073 his grandson sent a band of assassins who took the sons and grandsons of Carl by surprise as they were feasting at Settrington, and slew all but one, whom they spared for his goodness of disposition. Aldred's grandson who organized this massacre was Earl Waltheof, who was

23. Ll. 2029–2031.

24. II Edmund. See especially chaps. 7–7.3.

25. It is the tract known as "De obsessione Dunelmi," in *Symeonis Monachi Opera Omnia*, ed. T. Arnold, *R.S.*, I, (London: Longman & Co., 1882), pp. 215–220. It was written at Durham at the end of the eleventh century, and I suspect the author to be drawing on an oral narrative. Even if the details of the story cannot be vouched for, it still reveals how the blood-feud was regarded.

regarded in some quarters as a martyr after his execution by William the Conqueror.

I think it is important, if we wish to estimate the effect of our poem on its contemporaries, to realize that there is no period in Anglo-Saxon history when the interest taken in the carrying out of vengeance would be merely antiquarian. The tales referred to in the poem would not be regarded simply as violent, dramatic tales of the bad old days, or, in nostalgic mood, the good old days. Like the thegns of the Cambridge Guild mentioned above, any man of the audience might find himself suddenly forced to become an avenger by necessity, perhaps in circumstances that involved his acting counter to his inclination and affections. The dilemma of an Ingeld or a Hengest might one day be his own. The poet's allusions to characters such as these give his poem more than an "historical" background; they hint at a problem that was real to the poet's contemporaries.

Some years ago, I suggested that a puzzling passage in the poem became clear enough if one looked for its interpretation to Anglo-Saxon law instead of to remote legends.[26] When the poet wishes to bring home to his audience the utter desolation of the old King Hrethel when one of his sons has been accidentally killed by another, he compares his situation to that of a man whose son is hanging on the gallows,[27] for it was a principle of Anglo-Saxon law that no vengeance could be taken for an executed criminal, and Hrethel is just as effectively cut off from the consolation of exacting a great reparation or taking vengeance, though for very different reasons. Similarly, the story of how Carl slew Earl Aldred, which is certainly based on history, may help us to understand how Hengest in the Finn story could turn against Finn, in spite of his having accepted a settlement with him. Like Carl, Hengest could not refrain from brooding on his loss, even though he had come to terms. Carl had accepted a wergild, and I do not understand why Klaeber should pronounce so categorically that in the Finn episode the gold brought from the hoard after the oath was performed[28] could not have been for the payment of wergild. It is difficult to see how

26. *MÆ*, VIII (1939), 198–204.

27. Ll. 2444–2462.

28. Keeping the manuscript reading *að* "oath," instead of the common emendation to *ad* "pyre."

Hengest and his party could have come to terms with Finn without a settlement being paid for Hnæf.[29] We are not expressly told so, in this very summarized and selective account, but this is as likely to be because it would have been so obvious in the poet's day as because it did not take place. However, unless fresh evidence should come to light, we shall never reach certainty in interpreting this part of *Beowulf*, and too much brooding over our inadequate scraps of evidence for the Finn tale has been one of the most unprofitable and time-consuming occupations of *Beowulf* scholars.[30]

One may reach the conclusion that the audience of *Beowulf* was a Christian company, and one which admitted that vengeance, in unavoidable circumstances and carried out in accordance with the law, was a binding duty. This second consideration is of no help at all in our dating of the poem; but the first, its Christianity, is. The depth of its Christian knowledge is for this purpose far more important than that of the poet himself, for his Christian education might be exceptional; it would be unsafe to argue from it to the general conditions of his day. Nor would the extent of the audience's Christianity be of much assistance in dating the poem if there were any reason to suppose that the poet was addressing himself to ecclesiastics alone. My choice of the term "audience" has already indicated that I do not believe that *Beowulf* was composed merely for people who could read, which is almost equivalent to saying, for the clergy. Nothing that is recorded of the ecclesiastics of Anglo-Saxon England lends countenance to a view that they were in the habit of composing long poems on secular themes solely for circulation among themselves. It is difficult to imagine any bishop or abbot approving the use of so much expensive parchment for a work which he would not regard as directly edifying to men of religion. Some of these were interested in the tales of the Germanic heroes, and scandalized Alcuin in 797, but nothing in the letter in which he reproved the monks of Lindisfarne for their interest in songs about Ingeld[31] suggests that this taste was pandered to in monastic scriptoria. *Beowulf*, though it may contain elements intended for

29. Ll. 1107 f. Cf., Klaeber, *op. cit.*, p. 173: "The payment of *wergild* seems out of the question."

30. Cf., Bruce Dickins, Review of Chambers, *Beowulf: An Introduction*, in *TLS* (Jan. 12, 1922), p. 26.

31. *Alcuini Epistolae*, p. 183.

edification, is surely first and foremost literature of entertainment, and as such, intended mainly for laymen. The scholarly tastes of King Aldfrith of Northumbria should not lead us to suppose that literacy was very common among the upper classes of the laity. Aldfrith, an illegitimate son who had spent his youth in exile in Celtic lands, with little hope of succeeding to the throne or to high preferment at home, received an education that was certainly not typical among men of rank. It would be hazardous to postulate a considerable reading public of laymen, and I do not consider the length of *Beowulf* an insuperable obstacle to the view that it was intended for oral recital. It could easily have been delivered in three sittings. It is perhaps not by accident that the second episode, the fight with Grendel's mother, begins with a neat synopsis of what has gone before;[32] this may be intended to inform newcomers and remind the previous audience of what has happened in the first part. The third episode, the dragon fight, is intelligible by itself. The ease with which the work divides in this way does not force us to suppose that it was intended for oral performance, but it supports such a view if this is probable on other grounds.

For a lay company to be so steeped in Christian doctrines, a considerable time must have elapsed since the acceptance of Christianity. This is still more certain if the terminology of Christian vernacular poetry has become so familiar that it can be used in a generalized and weakened sense; for, if we are to believe Bede, it was not until late in the seventh century that the native poetic technique was first applied to religious subjects. One must allow no short time for the spread of this habit till the point is reached when a poet could take for granted his audience's familiarity with the conventions of Christian poetry. But even apart from this consideration, it is doubtful whether the attitude of Christianity and the knowledge of it, which are implied by the poem, could be as early as the seventh century, and perhaps not even early in the eighth. The spread of the new faith was not so rapid as all that. A hundred years after Augustine's landing, a king of Kent finds it necessary to legislate against the worship of "devils,"[33] and about the same period there are parts of England in which Christianity had only

32. Ll. 1251–1276.
33. Wihtred, chaps. 12 f.

recently been accepted as an official religion.[34] Bede, writing in 734, is of the opinion that the Church in Northumbria is far too understaffed for effective instruction in the Christian faith to be given to the laity throughout the kingdom. If, then, it is desired to date *Beowulf* in Bede's lifetime, it must be assumed that it was intended for a section of the community with a degree of religious education far above that of the average layman; or, alternatively, that it was composed outside Northumbria, and that this kingdom was worse off than other parts of England in this matter of religious education. If this were so, one would have to attribute this backwardness to the particular difficulties of communication in this kingdom, and perhaps also to Wilfrid's long resistance to the subdivision of his see; but all our available evidence suggests that Northumbria in the eighth century was in advance of other kingdoms, many of which had been converted later, and not behind them.

In view of these difficulties, it might be as well to consider if we really are forced to date *Beowulf* in the age of Bede (*c.* 672–735). Of late years, it seems to have become widely accepted as a dogma that that is where the poem must be placed. For example, Berendsohn works on the assumption that it was written by an Anglian poet about 700,[35] while a Swedish archaeologist wrote in 1948: "It is generally accepted that *Beowulf* was composed in about A.D. 700, that is to say, while many of those who had witnessed the burial at Sutton Hoo were still alive."[36] * * * But this quotation shows that so confident a dating, if there are no strong grounds for it, may be misleading a scholar in another field and causing him to draw some false conclusions. The interests of scholars other than those whose primary concern is with *Beowulf* may therefore be served by a re-examination of the evidence for dating the poem.

There have been many advocates for a date in "the age of Bede." To quote only more recent writers, Lawrence wrote in 1928: "The commonly accepted dating in the age of Bede remains unshaken"[37] and Professor Tolkien said in 1936: "I accept without

34. The conversion of Sussex dates from 680, that of the Isle of Wight from 686.

35. W. A. Berendsohn, *Zur Vorgeschichte des "Beowulf"* (Copenhagen: Levin and Munksgaard, Ejnar Munksgaard, 1935), p. 233.

36. Sune Lindqvist, "Sutton Hoo and Beowulf," *Antiquity*, XXII (1948), 131.

37. W. W. Lawrence, *Beowulf and Epic Tradition* (Cambridge, Mass.: Harvard University Press, 1928), p. 263.

argument throughout the attribution of *Beowulf* to the 'age of Bede' —one of the firmer conclusions of a department of research most clearly serviceable to criticism: inquiry into the probable date of the effective composition of the poem as we have it."[38] Chambers in 1932, though still clinging to "the age of Bede," seemed willing to interpret this somewhat widely, to cover a period from 650 to 750.[39] Crawford wrote in 1931: "There is a general consensus of opinion that *Beowulf* was written about the middle of the eighth century,"[40] a date a little late for the age of Bede, if we take that literally. Klaeber favored in 1922 a date in the first half of the eighth century, "perhaps not far from the middle of it."[41] In the third edition of his work (1936), he cut out this last remark. The claim of the more recent writers mentioned above to a general acceptance of a date about 700 is no doubt to be attributed to Professor Girvan's *Beowulf and the Seventh Century*, which was published in 1935 ⟨see note 43 below⟩; but, though this work argues convincingly that the poem is not earlier than the late seventh century, the evidence brought forward does not, in my opinion, prove that it is not later than this time. Finally, Schücking has never, to my knowledge, retracted his view that the poem belongs to about 900,[42] and, though he has won little support in England, recent correspondence and conversation with German scholars has shown me that some are still inclined to regard so late a date as a possibility with which one must reckon.

So late a date seems highly unlikely. The poem is surely pre-Viking Age. It may be true that we should not attach an exaggerated importance to the high terms of praise and respect with which the poet speaks of the Danes and their rulers. Heroic poetry shows respect to kings and chieftains as such; the poet would probably have used similar terms of the Goths, the Lombards, or the Burgundians, or any other nation, if the story he was telling had

38. J. R. R. Tolkien, "Beowulf: the Monsters and the Critics," *PBA*, XXII (1936), 262.

39. R. W. Chambers, *Beowulf: An Introduction* (Cambridge: Cambridge University Press, 1932), p. 393.

40. "Beowulfiana," *RES*, VII (1931), 448.

41. *Beowulf and the Fight at Finnsburg* (Boston: D. C. Heath and Co., 1922), p. cxvi.

42. "Wann entstand der Beowulf? Glossen, Zweifel und Fragen," *Beiträge zur Geschichte der deutschen Sprache und Literatur*, XLII (1917), 347–410.

happened to be located in their courts. It is not in order to pay honor to the Danes, but to heighten the dignity of his subject, that the poet lays such stress on the might and splendor of the court where his monsters' ravages take place. All this I would readily yield. Yet, I doubt whether he would have spoken in these terms during the Viking Age, or whether his audience would have given him a patient hearing if he had. It is not how men like to hear the people described who are burning their homes, pillaging their churches, ravaging their cattle and crops, killing their countrymen or carrying them off into slavery. So, if the poem is later than the time when viking invasions began in earnest, about 835, it can hardly be placed before the tenth century, and even then it would have to be put, as Schücking puts it, in the court of an Anglo-Danish king in the Danelaw. It could hardly be located in English England until the reign of Cnut, and that is later than our surviving manuscript.

When Schücking defends his late dating of the poem, he makes several penetrating observations about the advanced civilization portrayed in the poem which deserve general acceptance; but I do not understand why he should disallow such a civilization to the England of the days of Boniface or of Alcuin. There is certainly no sign that the Danelaw of the petty Scandinavian kings, Eohric, Siefred, Rægnold, Sihtric, the two Anlafs, Eric Blood-Axe, etc., was a more civilized land than England in the eighth century. There is also a linguistic difficulty about attributing *Beowulf* to their courts: these men spoke Norse. Schücking gets round these difficulties by his suggestion that an English poet was commissioned by a Danelaw prince to produce the poem for the education of his sons. I should be sorry to believe that the poem was from the beginning what it has since too often become, a work studied by young people to whom the language is unfamiliar, and it would need positive evidence of a late date to force this conception on me. Beyond the respect paid to the Danes, which can be accounted for otherwise, there seems to be none. Alcuin's reference to Ingeld shows that one Scandinavian story, at any rate, was popular in eighth-century England, so it cannot be argued that the interest in Scandinavian tales began with the Danish settlement. Linguistically and metrically the poem differs from datable tenth-century poems, and the proper names show no influence of the forms that would be in use in Scandinavian versions of these tales in the Viking Age and later. For example, it does not use *Sconeg*, as Alfred does, but retains *Scedenig*. The tone of the poem's Christianity does not suggest a period when the Church was fighting the fresh wave of heathenism introduced by the Danish and Norwegian settlers, and the Christian knowledge the poet assumes in his audience would not be possessed by the followers of the recently and imperfectly converted monarchs of the Danelaw.

Though I cannot concur in so late a date for our poem, I think it desirable to reconsider the evidence on which so many scholars put their final limit about 750. Why do they so firmly exclude the second half of the eighth century? The evidence they depend on is partly linguistic, partly historical. Meter shows that the poem contained some early linguistic features which do not occur in the poetry of Cynewulf and his school. But there is very little contemporary evidence to help us to put an absolute date to the sound changes involved, and even the arranging of the various poems in a relative chronology is completely valid only if there is reason to suppose that they come from approximately the same part of the country. The rate of development need not have been uniform in the various dialects. The most definite of the early linguistic features is the presence, proved by meter, of uncontracted forms, mainly where later contracted forms arose from the loss of an intervocalic *h*.[43] How unsafe it would be to date *Beowulf* about 700 for this reason is shown by the presence of *Guthlac A* in Professor Girvan's list of poems in which a similar condition is found, for this poem is almost certainly based on Felix's Latin *Life of St. Guthlac*, for which 730 seems about the earliest likely date. In glosses, which are assumed (by no means certainly) to go back to an original of about 680–720, the intervocalic *h* is sometimes still preserved. A Kentish charter of 679 affords an instance of its loss, but this occurs in the second element of a compound place-name, and not in stressed position.[44] It has not hitherto been noticed in this connection that a

43. See, e.g., R. Girvan, *Beowulf and the Seventh Century* (London: Methuen's Old English Library, 1935), pp. 16–18; Klaeber, *op. cit.*, 3rd ed., pp. cviii–cx; Chambers, *op. cit.*, p. 111.

44. *British Museum Facsimiles*, I. Pl. 1; Walter deGray Birch (ed.), *Cartularium Saxonicum*, I (London: Whiting and Co., 1885), No. 45 ⟨pp. 70–71⟩.

questionable charter from Malmesbury Abbey, which nevertheless contains a genuine list of witnesses of 705–709,[45] has in this list the name *Heaha* for an abbot whom later sources, mistaking the oblique case for the nominative, refer to as *Hean*; and, if the *h* could be preserved as late as the beginning of the eighth century, it would be rash to assume that its loss, and the later development by which the resulting hiatus was got rid of by contraction, were all over and done with so long before the second half of the eighth century that even poetry—archaic and conservative as this so frequently is—could not avail itself of the dissyllabic forms after about 750.[46] I suspect that the belief that linguistic evidence forbids a later date than 750 for *Beowulf* is to a great extent based on too early a dating of the work of Cynewulf, and that scholars have been slow to realize that, when Dr. Sisam showed that no valid reason prevents our assigning Cynewulf's work to the ninth century,[47] he was also giving us a much longer maneuvering space in relation to *Beowulf*.

As for historical reasons for fixing the date of the poem, I have tried elsewhere[48] to indicate that it is not enough to show, however convincingly, that the poem fits into a certain historical context, unless one can also show that no other historical context exists into which it could equally well be fitted; and, as our evidence is fragmentary and unequally distributed, there may well have been contexts about which we know little or nothing which would have suited our requirements very well. The fullness of the records for the age of Bede has made it possible for a case to be made out for the court of Aldfrith of Northumbria (685–705) as the place where *Beowulf* was first produced;[49] but enough is known about Eadberht Eating, king of Northumbria from 737 to 758, to show that he could have sponsored such a poem, while quite a number of rulers about whom, by accident, less is known may be eligible for the position of

45. See H. M. Chadwick, *Studies on Anglo-Saxon Institutions* (Cambridge: Cambridge University Press, 1905), p. 286; F. M. Stenton, *The Early History of the Abbey of Abingdon* (Reading: University College, 1913), pp. 16 f.

46. See also the recent article by R. Quirk in *MLR*, XLV (1950), 1–5.

47. K. Sisam, "Cynewulf and his Poetry," *PBA*, XVIII (1932), 304–308.

48. D. Whitelock, "Anglo-Saxon Poetry and the Historian," *op. cit.*, pp. 78, 85–88.

49. A. S. Cook, "The Possible Begetter of the O.E. Beowulf and Widsith," *Transactions of the Connecticut Academy of Arts and Science*, XXV (1922), 281–346.

patron to our poet. On historic grounds alone, one could not reject the great Mercian kings, Æthelbald and Offa, or Ælfwald of East Anglia, to whom Felix dedicated his *Life of St. Guthlac*, or Alhred and Ælfwald of Northumbria, or Ine and Cynewulf of Wessex, or various Kentish kings. One can sympathize with a desire to assign *Beowulf* to the age of Bede, and thus make it contemporary with the masterpieces of Northumbrian art, such as the best Anglian crosses and the Lindisfarne Gospels; and I should like to make it clear that I do not wish to argue that the poem *could* not have been composed then, but merely that it *need* not have been. It is not that I wish to substitute a different date from that so commonly held, but rather to extend the later limit to include the later eighth century within the range of possibility, because I believe that the interests of Beowulfian scholarship will be best served by a refusal to settle securely into too definite a dating at present. The age of Bede may seem to supply so suitable a background to the poem merely by the accidental circumstance that it happens to be a period that is well recorded. * * *

It is normally accepted as dogma that the poet was an Anglian, but opinions differ as to whether he belonged to the Mercian or Northumbrian branch of that people. Like most Old English poetry, the poem contains in its present form some Anglian forms and some that are held to be specifically Mercian; but these forms are not proved to go back to the poet himself by their occurrence in rhyme, as are some of the Anglian forms in Cynewulf's poetry.[50] There has of late been some restiveness against the assumption that Anglian forms in our extant manuscripts always, of necessity, indicate that the authors were of Anglian origin, an assumption which robs Wessex of poetry almost altogether, though there is plenty of evidence for its cultivation there. Doubt is most clearly expressed by Dr. Sisam, who says: "A consideration of dialect conventions in Greek literature must raise doubts." He points out also that "without early Southern texts, there is no sure distinction between words, forms, and constructions unknown to Southern poets in early times, and those, once general, that survived in Anglian only."[51] Professor Girvan has suggested that the Northumbrian origin of the earliest

50. K. Sisam, *op. cit.*, p. 304.

51. Review of Menner, "The Poetical Dialogues of Salomon and Saturn," in *MÆ*, XIII (1944), 32.

vernacular Christian poetry may have given Anglian forms a prestige and caused them to be used by poets of other areas.[52] Chambers also felt dubious about establishing the locality of the poem solely on linguistic grounds and repeated Sedgefield's argument that the same scriptorium could contain men from various areas which might lead to some dialect admixture.[53] We may note that Peterborough has been shown to possess daughter houses in the eighth century in places as far apart as Breedon in Leicestershire, Woking and Bermondsey in Surrey, Hoo in Kent, and perhaps Brixworth in Northamptonshire.[54] Nor was it only ecclesiastics who moved from kingdom to kingdom. It was common for men to take service under alien lords, and youths were sometimes brought up, as fosterlings or hostages, at courts outside their native kingdom. Minstrels were a peripatetic class. One could not even be certain that the *Beowulf* poet composed his poem for men of his own kingdom. What swayed Chambers more than the dialect forms in his location of the poem was the introduction of Offa, a king in ancient Angel, as the only "English" character of the poem. * * *

Meanwhile, one must reckon with another possibility when assessing the significance of the Anglian forms in our manuscript. Sir Frank Stenton's work has made it clear how real and important was the authority wielded by the overlord of all the lands south of the Humber, the supremacy of which carried with it, according to a ninth-century authority, the title of *Bretwalda*. Sir Frank says: "Before the end of the seventh century the overlord was dealing with his subject kings very much as he dealt with the hereditary nobility of his own country. His safe-conduct ran throughout their lands and he could transfer provinces from one of them to another. It was always wise for an under-king to obtain the overlord's consent to important grants of land."[55] The overlord took tribute, and he required subject kings to attend his court and to fight under him in time of war, along with their following. From about 730 until 796,

52. Girvan, *op. cit.*, pp. 13 f.

53. Chambers, *op. cit.*, pp. 104 f. Compare *Beowulf*, ed. W. J. Sedgefield (Manchester: Manchester University Press, 1910), pp. 4 f.

54. F. M. Stenton, "Medeshamstede and its Colonies" in *Historical Essays in Honour of James Tait* (Manchester: Printed for the Subscribers, 1933); *idem*, *Anglo-Saxon England* (Oxford: Oxford University Press, 1943), p. 160.

55. *Anglo-Saxon England*, p. 35; cf., "The Supremacy of the Mercian Kings," *EHR*, XXXIII (1918), 433–452.

under two successive powerful kings, Æthelbald and Offa, this supremacy was held by Mercia, and the power of the overlord steadily increased. Offa treats with Charles the Great as if empowered to speak for the whole country. To Alcuin, writing to Offa, the whole of England is covered by the terms "my country" (Northumbria) and "your country" (the rest of England). The papal legates in 786 met a southern gathering convened by Offa, at which the West Saxon king Cynewulf was present, and a northern council. They clearly saw no necessity to consult any other rulers. Offa held councils attended by all the episcopate of southern England, but by Mercian laymen alone. He interfered in the affairs of other southern English kingdoms. Can we then be so certain, in view of all the evidence for Mercian influence and prestige, that the presence of Anglian linguistic forms in our poetic texts proves that the authors were Anglians? Is it not possible that the Mercian official language during the heyday of Mercian power was influential outside the area in which it was spoken? There is evidence of "Mercian" forms in West Saxon before the time of Alfred's Mercian helpers.[56] Even if this possibility is rejected, there remains the likelihood that many works would be copied in Mercia during these days of its prosperity, and hence be available to subsequent copyists in an Anglian spelling.

It may be as well, therefore, to leave the question of original provenance just as open as that of exact date, even though this will put us to the trouble of looking for evidence of conditions in all the kingdoms of the Heptarchy. It is not that I have an axe to grind; I am not leading up to a suggestion that St. Aldhelm was the author of *Beowulf*, for example; but, if anyone were to put forward such a suggestion (and there have been wilder), it could not in my opinion be refuted on linguistic grounds alone.

Reprinted from Dorothy Whitelock, *The Audience of* Beowulf (Oxford: The Clarendon Press, 1964), pp. 1–30. A little more than five sentences, in which Miss Whitelock points toward material that she discusses more fully in subsequent chapters (not reprinted here), have been deleted.

56. See Birch (ed.), *Cartularium Saxonicum*, I, No. 225, a charter of Cynewulf, dated 778 (*British Museum Facsimiles*, II, Pl. 3); and II, No. 451, a charter of Æthelwulf, relating to lands in Devonshire, dated 847 (*British Museum Facsimiles*, II, Pl. 30).

## G. STORMS

# The Subjectivity of the
# Style of Beowulf

THE OLD ENGLISH epic poem *Beowulf* has been praised, and rightly praised, for its diction. Much of it must be called traditional and a large part is even formulaic, as Magoun[1] has shown, but the influence of tradition does not prevent the poet from expressing the particular meaning and the special tone demanded by the occasion. The words *tradition* and *formula* are often accompanied by qualifications such as *fixed* or *established*, implying emptiness of emotional connotation and meaninglessness of reference. A traditional and formulaic style is of great technical assistance to less gifted poets, not to say poetasters, and by keeping to the external form they seemingly continue established standards. The dangers of tradition can be witnessed in all periods and in all arts. Eloquence develops into rhetoric, grandeur gives way to pomposity. Whenever it is said that an artist was a follower of some one else, the statement rarely denotes a compliment. In Old English literature the Cynewulfian poems provide numerous instances where the old poetic vocabulary is losing its vigor and significance, where the diction is merely traditional and formulaic, and where the earlier contextual freshness is absent.

Thus when in *Juliana* the maiden has rejected Heliseus' proposal of marriage, and he has summoned her father to talk to him about the unexpected refusal, the poet says:

> Reord up astag,
> siþþan hy togædre   garas hlændon,
> hildeþremman.                                         (62–64)

[The sound of their voices rose after they, the warriors, leant their spears together.]

1. Francis P. Magoun, Jr., "Oral-Formulaic Character of Anglo-Saxon Narrative Poetry," *Speculum*, XXVIII (1953), 446–467.

The epithet *hildepremman* lends incongruous importance to the conversation. It is true, the martyrdom of Juliana is presented as a battle between the forces of heaven and those of hell, and though the literal meaning of *hildepremman*, "men strong in battle," is not entirely unwarranted, the introduction of battle terminology is too conventional to carry conviction.

The style of *Beowulf* is different. It we turn, for instance, to the passage in which the Danes and Geats go out to look for the lair of Grendel's mother, we find many conventional elements but each word fits exactly into the context and adds something new to the description of the expedition.

> Þa wæs Hroðgare    hors gebæted,
> wicg wundenfeax.    Wisa fengel
> geatolic gende;    gumfeþa stop
> lindhæbbendra.    Lastas wæron
> æfter waldswaþum    wide gesyne,
> gang ofer grundas,    swa gegnum for
> ofer myrcan mor,    magoþegna bær
> þone selestan    sawolleasne
> þara þe mid Hroðgare    ham eahtode.
> Ofereode þa    æþelinga bearn
> steap stanhliðo,    stige nearwe,
> enge anpaðas,    uncuð gelad,
> neowle næssas,    nicorhusa fela;
> he feara sum    beforan gengde
> wisra monna    wong sceawian,
> oþ þæt he færinga    fyrgenbeamas
> ofer harne stan    hleonian funde,
> wynleasne wudu;    wæter under stod
> dreorig ond gedrefed.              (1399–1417)[2]

[The bridle was put on Hrothgar's horse, a steed with plaited mane. Splendidly equipped, the wise prince set out; the band of shieldbearers marched on foot. The tracks were clearly visible, where the undergrowth of the forest had been trodden down, her passing along the earth, as she returned across the dark moor, carrying away lifeless the best of young retainers, of those who guarded the home together with Hrothgar. Then the son of noblemen went across steep, rocky slopes, along roads that

2. My quotations are from *Beowulf*, ed. F. Klaeber (Boston: D. C. Heath and Co., 1941).

became less wide, on to narrow paths on which only one man could walk (and finally) they came to an unknown region, to precipitous headlands, the abodes of many water-monsters; he (Beowulf) went forward, with a few wise men only, to explore the district, until suddenly he found mountain trees hanging down over greyish rock, a joyless wood; below was a pool, bloodstained and turbulent.]

It was no doubt a convention to call a king wise and to speak of warriors as shieldbearers; it was an epic formula to refer to a man as so and so's son; it was part of a poetic tradition to make use of variation. Such devices are not meaningless, however, though their poetic value may be low at times. Here the adjective "wise" is applied to Hrothgar, who throughout the poem is praised as a good king and whose excellence serves as a gold frame to set off Beowulf's qualities as hero, friend, and king. "Wise" has a general not a particular value. So has *lindhæbbendra*. The Danes accompany Beowulf on a dangerous enterprise and they may have to defend themselves.

After deducting these traditional elements we come to the positive characteristics of the passage. The narrative moves on swiftly and the tension, caused by a frightening creature that is felt rather than seen, grows with each line. The Danes follow the tracks of the monster from the residential hall of their king to the place where it presumably lives. It is worth calling attention to each successive stage. First through the forest, which was probably well known to them, then across a dark moor; as they approach steep rocky cliffs, the road narrows until they can only move on in single file and finally they come to unknown territory, a region into which nobody had ever ventured to go before. The sequence is no ordinary variation of the concept "road"; it is a highly poetic description of the movements of an expedition that may end in disaster to its members, as suggested by *sawolleasne* in line 1406. Hrothgar and his men do not know what to expect, and the omission of any mention of Grendel's mother, the slayer of Æschere, is significant. She will be there when they come to the end of their march, but who or what else will be there? The *nicorhusa fela* are not unoccupied. Apparently the trail of the monster is less clear on the rocky cliffs, and when Beowulf moves forward with a few experienced men to spy out the land, he suddenly sees some trees hanging down from a mountainous rock and under them a bloodstained and turbulent pool. The Danes are not long in doubt concerning the origin of the blood; their gloomy forebodings are soon realized when they come upon the severed head of Hrothgar's favorite thane, Æschere.

The literary craftsmanship of the Anglo-Saxon poet is proved by his handling of the progress of the Danes and the suggestive use of emotive elements. At the beginning of the passage the horse is described as *wicg wundenfeax* "a steed with plaited mane" and of Hrothgar it is said that he set out *geatolic* "equipped, adorned, splendid, stately," derived from *geatwa* "equipment, splendid objects." Both qualifications suggest beauty and gaiety, heightening by contrast the somber purpose of the march. As we have just seen, the monster itself is not directly mentioned, but instead we find a reference to its tracks through the woods and across a *dark* moor. The emotive connotation of OE words is not always easy to establish. Nearly all the OED ⟨Oxford English Dictionary⟩ quotations of the related "murky" are definitely emotional and intensive, but those of "murk" are less clear. The earliest figurative use has the sense of "atrociously wicked" (OED) and it is used several times to refer to the lack of light during an eclipse, which again makes it plausible that it had a special emotional connotation. In the present instance the emotional coloring, whether objective or subjective, is obvious.

By objective emotional meaning, I understand the emotive sense that is directly conveyed and that is always present with the word. Happy, cheerful, sad, grievous, fearful, horrible, angry, etc., have as reference a particular emotion; they have an objective coloring. A word like *dark* on the other hand has no objective, no permanent and inherent emotional coloring, but it may assume an emotional connotation by the context or the situation in which it occurs. The so-called figurative meaning is frequently characterized by an added emotional sense: dark prospects, dark looks, the powers of darkness, etc. In many instances both an objective referential sense and an emotive sense may be present and the borderline is often difficult to draw.

By subjective emotional coloring I mean those senses that are not permanent or inherent in the word but that are added by the contextual situation or produced by an emotional tone. The intensity of the emotive element is usually subjective. "Darling" has an objective emotional quality, but it has also a wide subjective range, dependent on the person who uses it, the tone of the speaker, the situation that evokes it, etc. An incongruous situation, or an incongruous tone, may even change the objective quality, as happens, for instance, when it is applied in sarcasm.

*Ofer mycran mor* presumably has both an objective and a subjective emotional connotation. The dark color of the moor and its concomitants: the danger run in hunting a ferocious monster, the death of a good man, and the uncertainty as to the outcome of the expedition, bring gloomy implications into the picture. *Myrce* intensifies the gloom without particularizing a specific aspect. Subjective emotional coloring is present in the word *lastas*, because the reference is to the tracks of a fearful monster, which only a few hours before had killed a man in the hall and carried him off.

Strong emotional coloring is also conveyed by another word in the same sentence, namely *sawolleasne*. Adjectives in "-less" objectively denote the absence of something expressed by the first part of the compound, or, with verbs as their first component element, they denote something "not to be -ed." For instance, hopeless, fearless, merciless, friendless, etc.; or countless, numberless, tireless. We cannot always tell whether we have a nominal or a verbal derivative, as in "blameless behavior," "a blameless person." What is not commented upon by the OED is that these adjectives have an emotional and/or intensifying function in that they give expression to a pronounced subjective, personal point of view: a hopeless situation, merciless punishment, tireless efforts, careless conduct, endless negotiations, speechless astonishment, needless fuss, a childless marriage, etc. They are frequently, though not invariably, formed from nouns with emotive connotations, such as hope, fear, mercy, and often also the noun qualified has an emotional connotation, as in speechless astonishment and needless fuss. In "I was speechless" or in "a needless remark" the adjective only is emotional. This emotional character must be very old, for we find it likewise in Dutch and German.

The emotional character of *sawolleasne* (lifeless) in the passage under discussion can be ascertained from its particular meaning—anything connected with life and death is bound to strike us emotionally, from the fact that it says something about a favorite thane, and from the fact that all the *-leas* compounds in *Beowulf* are emotional. As it is important for an analysis of the sensitivity of the poet, the various occurrences of these compounds are worth investigating.

(1) *aldorleas* (line 15)

> Ðæm eafera wæs    æfter cenned
> geong in geardum,    þone God sende
> folce to frofre;    fyrenðearfe ongeat,
> þe hie ær drugon    aldorlease
> lange hwile.

[Afterwards a son was born to him, young life at court, whom God sent as a help to the people; He had observed the sore distress they had suffered because before they had been without a leader for such a long time.]

The emotional connotation of *aldorleas* will hardly need any comment, because the situational context is sufficient evidence. Both in Germanic and in modern times the lack of a leader has provoked disaster.

(2) *sigeleas* (line 787)

> Sweg up astag
> niwe geneahhe:    Norð-Denum stod
> atelic egesa,    anra gehwylcum
> þara þe of wealle    wop gehyrdon,
> gryreleoð galan    Godes andsacan,
> sigeleasne sang,    sar wanigean
> helle hæfton.

[A sound arose which was absolutely new: a terrible fear seized the Danes in the North,[3] each of them that heard the wailing from the wall heard the adversary of God sing a horrible lay—it was not a song of victory—heard the captive of hell lament his distress.]

Although the poet had dropped some hints that this time Grendel would not be successful in his raid on Heorot, the ease with which he had penetrated into the hall and the cruelty and speed

---

3. For the significance of *Norð-Denum*, see my *Compounded Names of Peoples in Beowulf* (Nijmegen: Dekker en Van de Vegt, 1957).

with which he had killed and devoured a Geat manifested the super-human strength and the fiendish ferocity of the monster. Those hints at Grendel's defeat serve the artistic purpose of bringing in an element of uncertainty as to the outcome of the fight, which other-wise would not have been created in the audience. The fight itself is only described in its initial stage, when the two contestants come to grips; after that the poet reverts to indirect means, which by their suggestiveness are all the more effective. It was a great wonder that the hall held out against the violence of the struggling opponents, that it did not fall to the ground, though many a meadbench was wrenched loose and thrown aside. The first real indication that Beowulf is having the upper hand is this reference to the *sigeleasne sang* of the fiend. This time its song is not meant to herald another victory, and now Beowulf's companions enter the struggle and try to cut down Grendel with their swords. The tension mounts once more when iron weapons prove unable to pierce the monster's skin. The final decision is not reached until line 815, when we are told that the horrible monster suffered a wound in its body. Near the shoulder a gaping wound began to show, the sinews sprang apart and the joints burst.

In the context *sigeleas* gives a strong hint as regards the course of the fight, without removing entirely the anxiety of the audience. Hope and fear are successively evoked by the poet's sense of its emotional possibilities.

(3) *wynleas* (line 821)

> Beowulfe wearð
> guðhreð gyfeðe; scolde Grendel þonan
> feorhseoc fleon under fenhleoðu,
> secean wynleas wic; wiste þe geornor,
> þæt his aldres wæs ende gegongen,
> dogora dægrim.

[Beowulf was given glory in battle; Grendel had to flee from there mortally hurt to try and find a joyless abode under marshy slopes; he knew but too well that he had reached the end of his life, the full number of his days.]

Having lost an arm, Grendel had to give up the struggle. The marshy slopes to which he made his escape are called joyless, partly in allusion to its associations with hell. Grendel is called God's adversary and a captive of hell, while earlier in the poem his ancestry had been traced back to Cain. In the eyes of the Christian poet the place of the doomed was naturally devoid of all joy and happiness. Besides having this general meaning, the word aptly describes Grendel's state of mind on being defeated. He had found some sort of pleasure in destroying the happiness of the Danes and now that he has run up against a more powerful antagonist, even this *Schadenfreude* is taken away from him. A contextual connotation of *wynleas wic*, the joyless abode, is that he knows he is going to die. Etymologically there does not seem to be any connection between *wic* and OE *wican*, Dutch *wijken* "to yield, to give way," and Dutch *de wijk nemen* "to seek refuge," but as they are similar in form, they may have become associated in the thoughts of the Anglo-Saxons. There is not a safe spot, a place of refuge for him anywhere; his days are numbered.

A second instance of *wynleas* occurs in the passage (line 1416) we are discussing.

(4)  *tirleas* (line 843)

> No his lifgedal
> sarlic þuhte     secga ænegum
> þara þe tirleases     trode sceawode,
> hu he werigmod     on weg þanon,
> niða ofercumen,     on nicera mere
> fæge ond geflymed     feorhlastas bær.

[His separation from life did not seem grievous to any of the men who observed the track of one that had lost all claim to glory, how, on his way thence, to the pool of the monsters, weary in mind, vanquished in battle, fated to die and put to flight, he had left a bloody trail.]

Every part in the description has its own special significance and all parts cooperate as a structural unit to stress that the unbelievable had actually happened. Many war-veterans, leaders of the people from far and near, flocked together to see the "wonder," the tracks of the hated enemy. *Wundor* in line 840 may refer to the arm of the monster, put down by the hero under the vaulted roof, but it certainly refers to what the tracks make clear, namely, that the monster had lost so much blood that it could not possibly survive. What had not seemed possible to the Danes, this wonder, had been accomplished by Beowulf. The persecution by Grendel was over and the general relief finds expression in words of praise of the hero and the horse races that are spontaneously organized to give vent to their feelings.

*Tir* means "glory, honor, decoration"; it is also the name of a Germanic god, the counterpart of the Roman Mars, and as such it stands for victory. Its religious connotations were probably still felt when *Beowulf* was composed. *Tirleas* means "inglorious, undecorated"—with several of the modern senses—"forsaken by *Tir*, vanquished, defeated"; its emotional overtones are manifest, particularly in the context.

(5) *ðeodenleas* (line 1103)

> Fin Hengeste
> elne unflitme    aðum benemde,
> þæt he þa wealafe    weotena dome
> arum heolde,    þæt ðær ænig mon
> wordum ne worcum    wære ne bræce,
> ne þurh inwitsearo    æfre gemænden,
> ðeah hie hira beaggyfan    banan folgedon
> ðeodenlease,    þa him swa geþearfod wæs.

[Firmly and unquestionably Finn confirmed on oath to Hengest that in agreement with the judgment of his councillors, he should treat the survivors of the calamity honorably, that neither by word nor by deed any man should break the compact, nor ever make maliciously ambiguous songs, although they (the Danes) now followed the murderer of their treasure-giver and were without a leader from among their own people, for it had been forced upon them by necessity.]

*Ðeodenlease* has a greater suggestive significance than *aldorlease*, for young men might seek their fortunes with a prince abroad. *Ðeoden*, derived from *ðeod* "people, tribe," indicates a blood relationship, so that the necessity to follow a foreign king, a Frisian, was all the more goring to Hengest and the Danes. In line 15 *aldorlease* simply means lack of leadership and the general misery accompanying such a state; in line 1103 *ðeodenlease* expresses the general feeling of distress of the Danes and at the same time the personal, individual implications for each of them. In the preceding line *beaggyfan* "ring giver" states that their former lord had paid them, that he had carried out his obligations, that he had done what was expected of a good king. So the rules of the Germanic code of honor were broken by the Danes in accepting Finn as king, and the poet takes care to stress the *force majeure* which, for the time being, compelled them to agree to the compact.

(6) *sawolleas* (line 3033)

> Fundon ða on sande    sawulleasne
> hlimbed healdan    þone þe him hringas geaf
> ærran mælum.

[On the sand they found bereft of life and lying on his last resting-place the man who up till then had given them rings.]

*Sawol* is the principle of life and also that of the intellect. Following on the story of the messenger who had predicted the disasters that were going to befall the Geats, the function of *sawulleas* may be to suggest the loss of the king who had fought and thought for them. It indicates the utter uselessness of the bodily remains, an association that may also be present in *hlimbed*. Connected as it is with *hlinian* "to lean, to recline," this word too can have the connotation "stretched out on his back like the lifeless body of a bird or a fish."

In line 1406, *sawolleas* can have the same connotation in connection with Æschere, for the "soulless" body of a human being is more gruesome to look at than that of an animal.

(7) *sorhleas* (line 1672)

> Ic hit þe þonne gehate,    þæt þu on Heorote most
> sorhleas swefan    mid þinra secga gedryht,
> ond þegna gehwylc    þinra leoda,
> duguðe ond iogoþe,    þæt þu him ondrædan ne þearft,
> þeoden Scyldinga,    on þa healfe,
> aldorbealu eorlum,    swa þu ær dydest.

[I declare to you solemnly that you may sleep free from all cares in Heorot with the entire company of your men and all the thanes of your people, the veterans as well as the young retainers,

that you, prince of the Scyldings, need not have any more fear
on that side, have expectation of deadly evil for your warriors,
as you have had till now.]

The primary function of *sorhleas* is emotional. It denotes the sudden
liberation from the oppressive threats of the visitations of Grendel
and his dam. As the first part of the story opened with the carefree
happiness of the Danes in Heorot, so now again they can live and
sleep in the hall and enjoy themselves.

(8) *dreamleas* (line 1720)

> Hwæþere him on ferhþe greow
> breosthord blodreow;   nalles beagas geaf
> Denum æfter dome;   dreamleas gebad,
> þæt he þæs gewinnes   weorc þrowade,
> leodbealu longsum.

[However, a bloodthirsty spirit grew in his heart; he did not at
all give costly rings to the Danes according to the meritorious
deeds they had done; unsurrounded by happy mirth he lived,
until he suffered the troublous end of the struggle, long-lasting
national evil.]

*Dream* has for its reference the merry rejoicing at a party, the
melody and music of song. Heremod has killed his closest companions, his *beodgeneatas* and *eaxlgesteallan*, the men with whom he
took his meals and those who fought beside him when he went to
war; now he sits down in gloomy, lonely silence, he is *dreamleas*, he is
without the pleasures found in the presence of happy friends.

(9) *feohleas* (line 2441)

> Þæt wæs feohleas gefeoht,   fyrenum gesyngad,
> hreðre hygemeðe;   sceolde hwæðre swa þeah
> æðeling unwrecan   ealdres linnan.

[It was a fight which was not to be atoned for by paying a sum
of money; it was a criminal wrong, distressing to the heart and
the mind; nevertheless a king's son had to die unavenged.]

The death of the young prince had not occurred in an honest,
man-to-man fight; the victim had had no chance of defending himself, nor had there been any reasonable cause or occasion for it. It

was a horrible crime, which could not be expiated by paying the *wergeld*. Under the circumstances a feud would follow to save the honor of the family and the tribe. Yet the father is powerless to relieve his feelings by taking action against the murderer.

(10) *wineleas* (line 2613)

Þæt wæs mid eldum   Eanmundes laf,
suna Ohteres;   þam æt sæcce wearð,
wræccan wineleasum   Weohstan bana
meces ecgum,   ond his magum ætbær
brunfagne helm,   hringde byrnan,
ealdsweord etonisc;   þæt him Onela forgeaf,
his gædelinges   guðgewædu,
fyrdsearo fuslic,   —no ymbe ða fæhðe spræc,
þeah ðe he his broðor bearn   abredwade.

[It (a sword) was known among men as the heirloom of Eanmund, the son of Ohthere; he had been killed by Weohstan with a sharp cutting sword in a quarrel, when he was an exile, forsaken by his friends; he (Weohstan) had robbed his relations of the burnished helmet, the ringed mailcoat, the ancient giantmade sword; all this had Onela granted him, the war-dress of his relative, the complete equipment to undertake an expedition —he did not speak at all about the feud, though he had killed the son of his brother.]

In a society in which a man's safety depended on his being a member of a larger organization, the consequences of being *wineleas* could be terrible, as they actually were for Eanmund, the exile. Away from the protection provided by his own people and living without friends in a foreign country, he was killed in a quarrel, and his splendid war equipment was taken by his adversary. Nobody went to the trouble of demanding *wergeld* or of avenging him. His uncle Onela ought to have stood up for him, but the dynastic quarrels between him and his nephews made him overlook this death and prompted him, if not to reward the murderer, at any rate to allow him to keep the possessions of Eanmund. *Feohleas* and *wineleas* have parallel emotional connotations, partly based on the referential meaning of their first elements, partly on the contextual situation and partly on the organization of society in Germanic times.

(11) *domleas* (line 2890)

> Nu sceal sincþego    ond swyrdgifu,
> eal eðelwyn    eowrum cynne,
> lufen alicgean;    londrihtes mot
> þære mægburge    monna æghwylc
> idel hweorfan,    syððan æðelingas
> feorran gefricgean    fleam owerne,
> domleasan dæd.

[Now the handing out of treasure and the rewarding of swords, the happy possession of lands and homes for your families, all favors shall cease for you; each man of your tribe must wander about, deprived of the privileges of the owner of land, when princes abroad hear of your flight, your inglorious behavior.]

The ignominy attached to the cowardly conduct of the Geats can only be fully understood when seen against the background of the Germanic code of honor, and against the standard depicted by the poet of *Beowulf*. *Dom*, the judgment pronounced by following generations on the actions and the character of a man, is the ultimate aim of every warrior; it is all that will remain of him after his death; it is glory, fame, and a kind of immortality. In the words of the hero:

> Ure æghwylc sceal    ende gebidan
> worolde lifes,    wyrce se þe mote
> domes ær deaþe;    þæt bið drihtguman
> unlifgendum    æfter selest.          (1386–1389)

[Each of us must expect the end of his life in this world; let the man who has a chance attain a position of lasting fame before his death; that is best for a warrior, when he is no longer alive.]

The men who ran away when they should have stood by Beowulf are without *dom*, and their shame is so great that all the members of their families and their tribe will have to suffer with them. As a people the Geats will be wiped out. Courage will last, cowardice will find its own punishment. By the time the *Beowulf* poet sang his song in the royal halls of Anglo-Saxon England, the Geats had disappeared from history and he could charge the word *domleas* with a significance that was all the greater, because he had created it himself in the course of an evening's singing.

(12) *hlafordleas* (line 2935)

> Sona him se froda    fæder Ohtheres,
> eald ond egesfull    ondslyht ageaf,
> abreot brimwisan,    bryd ahredde,
> gomela iomeowlan    golde berofene,
> Onelan modor    ond Ohtheres;
> ond ða folgode    feorhgeniðlan,
> oð ðæt hi oðeodon    earfodlice
> in Hrefnesholt    hlafordlease.

[Immediately the experienced father of Ohthere, old and fear-inspiring, launched a counter-attack, dealt a destructive blow to the sea-leader, rescued his bride, the beloved maid of early days, now old and deprived of her gold, the mother of Onela and Ohthere; and then he pursued his deadly foes, until with great difficulty and without a lord to protect them they sought refuge in Ravenswood.]

*Hlafordlease* pictures the complete defeat and the utter discomfiture of the Geats after their initial successes. They had crossed the great lakes dividing the territory of the *Sweonas* and the *Geatas*, as is suggested by the epithet *brimwisan* "sea-leader," and in doing so had caught their hereditary enemies by surprise, even capturing the wife of Ongentheow. The old king, however, had rallied his forces, before the Geats had had time to load their booty into the ships, and, attacking the routing Hæðcyn and his men, he probably captured or destroyed the ships. The remainder of the Geatish force must have tried to return to their country by land, but they were pursued and harassed by Ongentheow's men and finally took refuge in Ravenswood, unable to plan or manage an escape. The special connotation of *hlaford* is that of lord and protector as against man and protégé, and *hlafordlease* describes the state of the Geats in Ravenswood, where they had no one to protect them against the rage of Ongentheow, threatening to hang "a few" of them on the gallows and to give their bodies to the ravens croaking in the trees above their heads. The wood may well have received its name on this occasion. The emotional sense of *hlafordleas* is stated explicitly and objectively in the expression *earmre teohhe* "the miserable band" in line 2938 and *sarigmodum* "distressed in mind" in line 2942. The episode should be read as a whole, of course, to allow the full significance of the position of the Geats to sink into the mind. On that occasion, at the moment of their greatest need, there was another king to take over and save them, because, although defeated, they had shown courage and endurance. In their present predicament, and this is the subjective, secondary meaning of *hlafordlease* as well as the reason for the insertion of the episode, they are again without a protecting lord and, instead of conducting themselves bravely, they had shown the basest cowardice; they had, in the etymological sense of the word, put their tails between their legs and run at the very moment when their king was being killed. Beowulf has no heir, as he complains himself before he dies, and, on hearing of the cowardice of the Geats, the Swedes will soon fall upon them and put an end to their independence. Now, however, they have to blame themselves for being lordless.

We may now return to the passage we are discussing (lines 1399–1417). The analysis of the adjectives in -*leas* has provided evidence that the poet of *Beowulf* selected his words carefully and purposively and that the exigencies of alliteration did not hamper his creative artistry. I do not mean to say that he never picked a word for the sake of alliteration; he certainly did and he also made use of a number of formulaic expressions to fill out a half-line or even a full line. The *maðelode* combinations and the device to name a person by calling him "X's son" are comparatively meaningless, though the *maðelode* formula imparts dignity to the words of the speaker, and it is sometimes important to know a man's descent.

Klaeber's observations on the style of *Beowulf* are a curious mixture of sensitive appreciation and lack of full understanding (p. lxiii). His remarks on the emotional character of the style are perfectly true, but when he says that characterizing adjectives are less prominent, at any rate less striking, we must disagree: the -*leas* adjectives appeal as much to the imagination as to sentiment and moral sense. Nor do we regard the device of variation as a retarding element, as Klaeber does (p. lxv). In nearly all cases the variations have a semantically important function. Klaeber was probably misled by Paetzel's work on the variations in Old Germanic poetry, a work which is based on too much mechanical collection of material and founded on a wrong definition: a concept which is already sufficiently known is once more placed before the mind of the hearer or reader, often accompanied by a break in the syntactical connection, and in contrast to what is customary in prose.[4] The definition eminently suits the purpose of card-indexing the various occurrences of variations in Germanic poetry, but it denies and discards their poetic significance. The purpose of the variations is to introduce a new aspect of the person or thing referred to, or to add an emotional element. The reference of *þeoden*, *ealdor*, *beaggyfa*, *helm*, etc., may be identical; the meaning is not the same.

A better example than our passage to prove how exactly and with how fine distinctions the poet handles his language need not be looked for. Note how he describes the track of the monster: "Lastas wæron æfter waldswaþum wide gesyne." ("The tracks were visible in many places [*wide*] where the undergrowth had been trodden down [*æfter waldswaþum*].") The Anglo-Saxons were accustomed to hunt wild animals and they could not afford to play a game of blindman's-buff with bears and *Auerochsen*. They carefully scrutinized the tracks they saw while hunting, and they study the tracks of Grendel's dam. All editors, except Else von Schaubert, connect the second element of *waldswaþum* with *swæþ* "track." Von Schaubert rightly gives the nominative as *wald-swaðu*, *Waldspur*, *im Walde ausgetretener Weg*, *Steg im Walde* ⟨footprints in the forest, trodden path in the forest, footpath in the forest⟩, without realizing the full implications of her translation. *Swaþu*, MnE "swath(e)," means "the space left clear after one passage of the mower." Instead of the grass lowered by the scythe we have here the wood, the bushes and young trees lowered, trodden down by the monster. It is a concrete image to make us feel its size, weight, and strength. As a so-called variation we have *gang ofer grundas* "its passing across the earth." *Grund* is a fairly vague word, meaning "ground, earth, bottom"; Klaeber (in his Glossary) adds "plain," Chambers "floor." As a translation in this particular context Klaeber and

---

4. ⟨The source of this statement is the following quotation:⟩ "Ein für das Verständis genügend gekennzeichneter Begriff wird, entgegen dem Gebrauch der Prosa, noch einmal und zwar oft mit Unterbrechung des syntaktischen Zusammenhanges dem Hörer oder Leser vor die Seele gerückt. Diese Ausdrucksform nenne ich Variation." Walther Paetzel, *Die Variationen in der altgermanischen Alliterationspoesie*, *Palaestra*, XLVIII (Berlin, 1913), p. 3.

Sedgefield give "plain," Clark-Hall–Wrenn "lands," words whose particular sense is not very clear. Keeping to the literal meaning, I take it as "ground in contrast to the sky," just as we find it several times as "ground in contrast to the water of the sea or of a pool." When the Anglo-Saxons thought of monsters, they would associate them in their minds with dragons; but dragons have wings and fly: *her draca ne fleogeð* "here no dragon flies," says the singer of *Finnsburh*. Grendel's dam does not fly either; it moves across the earth, trampling down the wood as it passes. We can imagine the sensations of wonder and fear of the Danes following the track. Nevertheless they push on, emboldened by the presence of Beowulf, across steep, rocky slopes—and these *stanhliðo* will have suggested "plains" for *grundas*; they would naturally rely on numbers in their pursuit of the monster, and now the road narrows and becomes a path on which only one man could walk at a time and where he would lack the comforting company of a "shoulder-companion." No wonder we find the emotional adjective *enge*! Brodeur[5] has already called attention to the admirably chosen adjectives at this point in the narrative. *Enge* is an excellent example. It is etymologically connected with Dutch and German *angst*, Latin *angor* and *angustus*; its root means "to press together, to choke." Modern English equivalents of *enge* are "narrow, horrible, oppressive, fearful, cramped, creepy, weird"; the emotional character is definitely predominant. What would they do, if the monster suddenly showed up on the *enge anpæð*?

At this moment what path was left peters out and they find themselves in completely unknown territory. My translation of *gelad* "territory, district, region" again differs from the usual interpretation "road, path, course." In line 1359, in the course of Hrothgar's description of the haunt of the monsters, we have the compound *fen-gelad*, and in combination with "wolf-haunted slopes and windy headlands" there can be little doubt about the meaning "fen region." As the slopes and the headlands are also mentioned again in our passage, we must infer that *gelad* in line 1410 is the *fen-gelad* of line 1359. Corroborating evidence is the meaning "ocean, sea" in

5. A. G. Brodeur, *The Art of Beowulf* (Berkeley: The University of California Press, 1959), pp. 25 ff.

*ofer deop gelad* in *Guðlac*, line 1292[6] and *Andreas*, line 190.[7] The subjective, emotional sense of *uncuð* is based on the contextual situation and the associative echo of *frecne fen-gelad* "the dangerous fen region" of line 1359. Artistically, the Beowulfian line is so much superior to the parallel *enge anpaðas, uncuð gelad* of *Exodus*, line 58, that this cannot but be an imitation of *Beowulf*.

*Neowle næssas, nicorhusa fela* "precipitous headlands, many dwelling-places of monsters" form, with their concrete descriptions of tangible dangers and attacks from the heights by the monsters round about them, a kind of relief almost from the horrors imagined on the way. The party makes a halt and Beowulf, with a few experienced men, men who can read a track, goes on to spy out the region. And then all of a sudden they come upon the place which must be the abode of the troll. They see mountain trees hanging down over grey rocks; it is a joyless wood, with underneath a blood-stained and turbulent pool. *Wynleas* "joyless" evokes the atmosphere of the place. How weird it really was, had been told by Hrothgar. It was a place which the hart did not dare to enter, though brought to bay by the hounds; it would give up its life rather than meet the horrors to be found there. Every night a mysterious fire burns in the water and black surging waves spout up into the sky. Indeed, it is not a pleasant place (lines 1365 ff.).

The Anglo-Saxons themselves must have appreciated *Beowulf*, for the tenth-century text that has come down to us shows evidence of having passed through several copyings, and linguistic research has pointed out Northumbrian, Mercian, Kentish, and West Saxon elements. In our own days the front position of *Beowulf* among other OE poems is secure; what is not yet established is its position in English literature as a whole. Before this can be done with any amount of objectivity, the associative richness of its language must be investigated throughout the poem. How rewarding such a study can be, will be apparent from the above preliminary attempt at a literary commentary on the poem.

Reprinted from Stanley B. Greenfield (ed.), *Studies in Old English Literature in Honor of Arthur G. Brodeur* (Eugene, Oregon: University of Oregon Books, 1963), pp. 171–186.

6. G. P. Krapp and E. V. K. Dobbie (eds.), *The Exeter Book* (New York: Columbia University Press, 1936).

7. G. P. Krapp, *The Vercelli Book* (New York: Columbia University Press, 1932).

ADRIEN BONJOUR

# The Digressions in Beowulf:
# The Finn and
# Heathobards Episodes

### The Finn Episode

IN THE COURSE of a brilliant ceremony at Heorot in honor of Beowulf's victory, the hero has been offered rich presents by the King. The festivities are carried on and then the court poet recites the Tale of Finnsburg. We here give Klaeber's brief summary of the Finn legend:

> A band of sixty Danes under their chief, Hnæf, find themselves attacked before daybreak in the hall of the Frisian King Finn, whom they have come to visit. . . . Five days they fight without loss against the Frisians, but (here the Episode sets in) at the end Hnæf and many of his men, as well as of the Frisians, are counted among the dead. In this state of exhaustion Finn concludes a treaty with Hengest, who has assumed command over the Danes. The fallen warriors of both tribes are burned together amid appropriate ceremonies. Hengest with his men stays in Friesland during the winter. But deep in his heart burns the thought of revenge. The day of reckoning comes when the Danes Gūðlāf and Oslāf, unable to keep any longer the silence imposed upon them by the terms of the treaty, openly rebuke their old foes. Finn is set upon and slain, and Hildeburh together with the royal treasure of the Frisians carried home to the land of the Danes.[1]  (1066–1159)

### The Ingeld Episode

In his report to Hygelac Beowulf describes his reception at Heorot and alludes to the king's daughter Freawaru, who distributed the ale-cups to the *duguðe*.

The young princess is engaged to Froda's son (Ingeld). The match was destined to put an end to the endless feud between Danes

---

1. Klaeber, *Beowulf and The Fight at Finnsburg* (Boston: D. C. Heath and Co., 1950), pp. 231–232.

and Heathobards. Beowulf then intimates that such a settlement is
bound to be transient: the followers of Freawaru will carry swords
that once belonged to Heathobard warriors who had been killed in
battle (by the Danes), and the Heathobards will resent it. Then an
"old grim warrior, chafing under the trying situation" and remembering the death of those men, incites a young comrade, whose
father's sword is now carried by a Dane in the hall of the Heathobards, to an act of revenge. Again and again he spurs him on with
bitter words until the young man kills Freawaru's thane. Retaliation
will follow on the part of the Danes and this will kindle Ingeld's
*wælnīðas* whereas his love for his wife will grow cold. Therefore,
concludes Beowulf,

> "ic Heaðo-Bear[d]na hyldo ne telge,
> dryhtsibbe dǽl Denum unfǽcne,
> frēondscipe fæstne."                    (2024–2069)

The most interesting glimpses we get of events underlying
Danish history are no doubt the Finnsburg tale and the Heathobards episode. Both are characteristic by their dramatic intensity,
and the latter is generally acknowledged one of the finest passages
in the poem. Yet it is not so much their intrinsic qualities which we
shall try to investigate as, again, their actual value in the organic
structure of the poem.

What the themes of these two episodes imply can only be properly understood when viewed in connection with the Dragon part.
To put it in other words, the Dragon part, or, to be more accurate,
its background alone, can give the ultimate justification of the
presence of these episodes in the poem viewed as an organic whole.
They indirectly but palpably help to bring to its highest pitch the
tragic keynote of that dramatic background. But let us first examine
the dominating themes.

Speaking of the allusions to Danish history and the events to
which they refer, Professor Klaeber writes: "Thus the two tragic
motives of this epic tradition are the implacable enmity between the
two tribes, dominated by the idea of revenge which no human bonds
of affection can restrain, and the struggle for the crown among
members of a royal family."[2] Whatever the divergences of critics

2. *Ibid.*, p. xxxvi.

concerning the reconstruction of the "Finn legend," the one settled point which has never been open to doubt is indeed the central theme of the story, i.e., how the irresistible force of tribal enmity sooner or later sweeps aside with its imperative all human attempts at a compromise. This can best be realized if we compare the Finn episode with the "Fragment."

The *Fight at Finnsburg* is, of course, of special interest as it presents an independent treatment of the Finn legend which allows us, by comparison, to catch a glimpse of the *Beowulf* poet at work on one point at least of the poem. Critics have shown that there is a fair amount of agreement between the two versions,[3] especially if allowance is made for the fact that one is most probably an independent lay and the other an episode which had to be fitted into the context of a great epic poem. It is precisely the few divergences (or some of them at any rate) which are of an undoubted value for us. The most important of them, which has often been pointed out, is a characteristic shift of emphasis in the episode. The *Beowulf* poet passes "over the matter of fighting . . . in the most cursory fashion,"[4] whereas he dwells on the pathetic situation of Queen Hildeburh and on the spiritual conflict of Hengest—both being the outstanding figures of the Episodes. The treatment is thus more heroic in the Fragment, more "sentimental" in the episode.

Now if the *Beowulf* poet thus stressed with obvious sympathy the human—one might even say psychological—element, it is not only because of its emotional appeal, which would naturally find an immediate response in an audience fond of such tragic situations; it is also because it considerably heightens the ultimate effect of the

3. Concerning the details, a greater harmony between the Episode and the Fragment could be attained if the name "Guðlafes" (l. 33 of the Fragment) were taken, as was suggested by Mr. Beaty in his study of echo-words, as a "common noun which means war-survivor and is an echo of the Guðlaf, proper noun, in l. 16" (J. O. Beaty, "The Echo-Word in 'Beowulf' with a Note on the 'Finnsburg Fragment,'" *PMLA*, XLIX [June, 1934], 373).

4. Klaeber, *op. cit.*, p. 236. "Whereas the *Fragment* is inspired by the lust and joy of battle, the theme of the *Episode*, as told in *Beowulf*, is rather the pity of it all; the legacy of mourning and vengeance which is left to the survivors: 'For never can true reconcilement grow / Where wounds of deadly hate have struck so deep.'" (R. W. Chambers, *Beowulf, An Introduction* [Cambridge: Cambridge University Press, 1932], p. 248.)

central theme. Could the elementary and irresistible force of the enmity between the two tribes be made more tangible and brought home to us in a more suggestive way than by the medium of such spiritual sufferings and conflicts? Hildeburh's distress vividly brings out the theme of the precarious peace, that even sacred human bonds are utterly unable to save.[5] And here we shall point out that the assumption that Hildeburh "had been given in marriage to the Frisian chief in the hope of securing permanent peace,"[6] or, to put it in the poet's words, had been used as *freoðuwebbe* seems to us extremely probable and satisfactory: in such a light the whole passage can only gain in dramatic force.

Hengest's dilemma and final resolve likewise brings out, and this time more directly, the theme of the precarious truce. However solemnly sworn and reasonable in its terms, the compact was doomed to be broken owing to the extraordinary power of the urge for vengeance. Two points are worth considering here. It is indeed on that point that the Episode again differs from the Fragment. Whereas the latter, in what has been called "epic exaggeration,"[7] reports that none of the defenders of the Hall were killed in the fight, the episode mentions, among others, the killing of Hnæf, the chief of the Danes himself. As Lawrence pointed out, the "*Episode* would have no point without the death of Hnæf and the obligation of vengeance, which motivate the entire tragic situation."[8] The death of Hnæf is indeed of the greatest importance both in the "Hildeburh part"—the unhappy queen thus losing her brother and her son who fought on opposite sides—and in the "Hengest part," as it is the main reason for the breaking of the oath to Finn, the duty of

5. The contrast between Hildeburh's innocence and the "dark background of treachery" (which is, after all, one element of the theme of the precarious peace) has been finely thrown into light by Professor Malone: the poet "is drawing for us a pathetic figure, a woman, innocent but helpless in the hands of an evil destiny. The poet protests for us. What had she done to bring upon herself such terrible suffering? And he answers, she was wholly without guilt. He thus contrasts, as strongly as he can, the background of treachery with the innocent figure who stands out in relief against it" (K. Malone, "The Finn Episode in 'Beowulf,'" *JEGP*, XXV [April, 1926], 161).

6. Klaeber, *op. cit.*, p. 231.

7. Lawrence, *Beowulf and Epic Tradition* (Cambridge: Harvard University Press, 1928), p. 119.

8. *Ibid.*

revenge for the fallen chieftain having been ultimately put before the "allegiance to an over-lord." On the other hand, to be really so effective, the dilemma had to be made particularly hard to solve and consequently the compact had to appear as a deliberate and responsible compromise. The poet insisted, therefore, on this trait: honor had been saved by the terrible fight in such a way that unless they intended to fight on to a complete and reciprocal extermination —like the famous lions of the fable, of whom only the tails were left —they had to make a truce. And the very terms of the truce which is *offered* by Finn (and not asked by the Danes)—especially the clause concerning a possible taunt about the awkward situation of the Danes—certainly preserve in the utmost measure the honor of the Danes.[9] But (there is so often a "but" after victories in *Beowulf*) the greater this victory, which had its motivation in the very circumstances in which the *Episode* was recited,[10] the sharper the

9. After having enumerated the six clauses of the truce, Professor Malone points out "that all these clauses represent concessions or promises on the part of Finn. Nothing is said about any obligations assumed by the Danes, and on the face of it, Hengest certainly drove a good bargain." That we have to deal here with a deliberate purpose on our poet's part, entailing some definite exaggeration, is likewise clear: "Finn is represented as entering into negotiations with Hengest out of dire military necessity—an explanation which one can hardly credit to the full, since the statement that he had lost all but a few of his thanes is obviously an exaggeration for the sake of increasing the prestige of Hengest and the little Danish band" (K. Malone, *op. cit.*, 163–164). This exaggeration is probably due to the circumstances as much as to the poet's sympathy for the Danes. See the following note.

10. As Professor Lawrence made clear, "the circumstances under which the minstrel sang his lay in Hrothgar's hall are important for an interpretation of the story. The subject was selected with a view to giving pleasure to the feasting Danish warriors, celebrating the triumph of a foreign hero, who had performed a feat that they had themselves striven in vain to accomplish. This might well be a little galling to them .... So the court poet adroitly selected a tale of Danish heroism and Danish vengeance, a tale of the complete and satisfying victory of the Danes over their ancient enemies, the Frisians" (Lawrence, *op. cit.*, pp. 109–110). This immediate motivation of the introduction of the Finn story and its character into the poem remains quite true even if we admit, with Professor Malone, that behind the "happy ending" the tragic note is still there. The assumption that Hengest himself "never took vengeance," in spite of his longings, and that this knowledge on the part of the audience constitutes a piece of dramatic irony casting "a pathetic shadow over the vengeance scene" (Malone, *op. cit.*, 169–170), is quite plausible, and would be in the manner of the *Beowulf* poet. It is, however, purely

contrast with the "clouds of future shadow" gathering behind the
subtle allusions of the following scene. Here we enter upon a more
speculative plane, without losing touch, however, with the reality of the text—and in the protecting shadow of an authoritative
critic.

As soon as the Finnsburg lay has been sung, convivial mirth
rises again and suddenly the whole attention is focused on Queen
Wealhtheow, who is about to address Beowulf. Before she has even
uttered a word, in the very brief picture of the scene in the hall—
and five lines only after the last words of the Finnsburg lay—the
poet puts in one of the clearest hints at Hrothulf's subsequent
treachery: *þā gȳt wæs hiera sib ætgædere.*[11] As to Wealhtheow's speech,
asking Beowulf "to act as protector of her sons,"[12] it ends with the
well-known hymn on the loyalty and harmony reigning among the
Danes which, in view of the poet's intimations of Hrothulf's treachery (and probable usurpation) may be considered as a fine piece of
dramatic irony. Be it as it may, the allusion to the future tragedy of
the Danish royal house is clear enough and its effect is obviously
heightened by its double contrast with the brilliant scene of splendor
and rejoicings in the Hall, and with the glorious Danish victory over
their enemies at Finnsburg.

The link with the *Episode*, moreover, transcends this element of
contrast, and Professor Lawrence wonders whether it may not be
"that the story of Queen Hildeburh was here designedly brought
into connection with the tragedy in store for Queen Wealhtheow,
which must have been well-known to the people for whom the poet
of *Beowulf* wrote?"[13] Asking the question is already solving it; the
parallel between Hildeburh and Wealhtheow is unmistakable. Yet a
further link of the greatest importance is to be stressed which makes
of that parallel the actual *trait d'union* between the Finnsburg and
the Heathobards episodes.

---

hypothetical, whereas the contrast between the Danish triumph—crushing enough
even in the case of Hengest's possible frustration—closing the Episode and the dark
implications of the following scene (to which we refer below) finds a real support
in the text.

11. *Beowulf*, l. 1164.
12. Klaeber, *op. cit.*, p. 179.
13. Lawrence, *op. cit.*, p. 126.

"The telling of the story of Hildeburh," writes Professor Law-rence, "in the presence of a queen who was herself of another people than that of her husband, whose efforts to keep the peace were destined to come to naught, and whose daughter Freawaru was to experience much the same melancholy destiny as the wife of King Finn, is surely not without significance." [14] The Wealhtheow scene is thus, in a way, the link connecting—in their striking analogy— the situation of Hildeburh in the Finnsburg Episode, and that of Wealhtheow's daughter Freawaru in the Heathobards Episode. Even if it is not quite certain (though extremely probable) that Hildeburh was likewise used as *freoðuwebbe* the similarity is obvious enough.

Now the point which is for us of the greatest interest is that the Heathobards Episode is thus not only definitely linked with the Finnsburg Episode but the central theme of both episodes is exactly the same: Beowulf's prophecy concerning Freawaru is in fact but another effective illustration of the theme of the precarious peace. [15] Ingeld's tragic dilemma is almost the exact counterpart of Hengest's, and in both cases the aspect of the sword (*billa sēlest* in the Finnsburg Episode, *dȳre īren* in the Heathobards Episode) [16] meant the decisive "call to action" resulting in the victory of the urge for revenge and the outbreak of fresh hostilities. We said "almost," because, if com-pared with the situation of Hengest, Ingeld's represents an even greater concentration of the dramatic element: not only does the claim of vengeance force him to break the compact with the former enemy, as in Hengest's case, but he is now connected by the bonds of marriage with Freawaru, the Danish princess, and such bonds render the dilemma even more tragic. It is, to a certain extent, as if Hengest had been married to a Frisian princess, say a daughter of

14. *Ibid.*, p. 127.

15. We here refer to Beowulf's "prophecy," but whether the passage is con-sidered as partly prophetic only (Malone) or as an instance of the use of the "historical present" (Olrik) is immaterial for us: the main effect of the tragedy is practically the same. We may safely adopt Malone's attitude, who "did not see that it made much difference, in interpreting the episode, whether the events were thought of as having occurred before or after Beowulf's visit to the Danish court" (K. Malone, "Time and Place in the Ingeld Episode of 'Beowulf,'" *JEGP*, XXXIX [Jan., 1940], 77; for Malone's interpretation of the episode, see *ibid.*, 87).

16. See respectively ll. 1144 and 2050.

Finn! And yet vengeance triumphs, again emphasizing how fateful indeed was a renewal of the enmity between the two tribes.[17] It should not be forgotten, moreover, that the dramatic effect is again heightened by the very similar contrast wrought between present harmony (the fine picture of Freawaru amid the rejoicing guests in the Hall) and future calamity.

Now only are we in a position to interpret the actual value of the *leitmotiv* of the precarious peace, common to both episodes, in connection with the organic structure of the poem. In a word we suggest that this element is to the background of the Danish part what the impending renewal of the Swedish-Geatish feud is to that of the Dragon part. Yet it is at the same time no less than a subtle preparation for that theme that looms so large in the background of the Dragon part, and gradually imposes itself in an admirable and oppressive crescendo.

If the episodes that deal with the former Swedish-Geatish feud are in fact inexorably leading to the great epic prophecy of the downfall of the Geatish people; if that downfall itself is a consequence of the inevitable renewal of the feud between the two nations, then the theme of the precarious peace, as illustrated in the background of Danish history, already strikes the first notes of the whole tragedy. After the vivid precedents of the Finnsburg and Heathobards stories, which are indeed its best warrant, the outbreak of the war between Swedes and Geats is felt to be all the more inescapable. The recurrent pictures of the former fights between the two hostile peoples—especially when involving the "fall of a prince"[18]—are so many milestones leading to the inevitable conclusion: the renewal of the feud is bound to come. And when it is actually prophesied, the

17. As a critic writes in reference to Beowulf's prophecy about Freawaru, "implicit in the whole story is the strain so dear to the poet of *Beowulf*, fatal inevitability (in the reader's knowledge) against which human bravery will struggle till the end which is fixed and even so contested" (B. F. Huppé, "A Reconsideration of the Ingeld Passage in 'Beowulf,'" *JEGP*, XXXVIII [April, 1939], 225). It should be added that the motive of the feud is not only emphasized by Ingeld's spiritual conflict but also by the "stern old warrior who will not let the feud die down" (Chambers, *op, cit.*, p. 22).

18. As in the case with Hrethric and Ongentheow. Compare with the fall of Hnæf in *Finnsburg* and Beowulf's allusion to swords seldom resting after "hæleða hryre" in connection with the Ingeld episode.

ground and atmosphere have been so admirably prepared that it acquires indeed a tremendous power—one shudders at the presence of such implacable doom.

In conclusion we may point out that if Beowulf's personality and actions represent the main thread which runs through the two parts of the poem, the theme that connects these episodes with the background of the Dragon part may be considered as a parallel and corresponding thread—both uniting the Grendel and the Dragon parts in a closer web. This is no mean artistic achievement on the part of the *Beowulf* poet.

Reprinted from Adrien Bonjour, *The Digressions in* Beowulf, Medium Aevum Monographs, V (Oxford: Basil Blackwell & Mott, Ltd., 1950), pp. 56–63. One reference has been moved from the text to the notes, and one footnote has been deleted.

# List of Contributors

RUDOLPH C. BAMBAS is Professor of English at the University of Oklahoma. His publications include "Verb Forms in -*s* and -*th* in Early Modern English Prose," *JEGP* (1947).

JESS B. BESSINGER, JR. is Professor of English at New York University. Among his publications are *A Short Dictionary of Anglo-Saxon Poetry* (1960) and *A Concordance to Beowulf* (1968). He is General Editor of the Harvard Old English Series. He was a Fulbright Scholar in 1950–1952, a Canada Council Fellow in 1960, and a Guggenheim Fellow in 1964.

N. F. BLAKE is Lecturer in the Department of English Language at the University of Liverpool. He has published editions of *The Saga of the Jomsvikings* (1962) and *The Phoenix* (1964). His edition of Caxton's *History of Reynard the Fox* for the Early English Text Society and his book *Caxton and his World* are now at the press.

MORTON W. BLOOMFIELD is Professor of English at Harvard University. Among his major publications are *The Seven Deadly Sins* (1952 and 1967), *Piers Plowman as a Fourteenth Century Apocalypse*, and *A Linguistic History of English* with Leonard Newmark. He is a member of the American Academy of Arts and Sciences, and a Fellow of the Mediaeval Academy, the Guggenheim Foundation, the American Council of Learned Societies, and the Center for Advanced Study in the Behavioral Sciences (1967–1968). His book on *Piers Plowman* won the Haskins Medal from the Mediaeval Academy.

ADRIEN BONJOUR is Professor of English at the University of Neuchâtel, Switzerland. His major publications include *Coleridge's Hymn Before Sunrise* (1942), an edition of the *Dialogue de St. Julien et son Disciple* for the Anglo-Norman Text Society (1949),

*The Digressions in Beowulf* (1950, reprinted 1965), *The Structure of Julius Caesar* (1958), and *Twelve Beowulf Papers, 1940–1960, with Additional Comments* (1962).

GEORGE LESLIE BROOK is Professor of English Language and Medieval Literature at the University of Manchester. He is editor of *The Harley Lyrics* (1948), co-editor of *Layamon's Brut*, Vol. I, with Roy F. Leslie for the Early English Text Society (1963), and author of *English Sound-Changes* (1935), *An Introduction to Old English* (1955), *History of the English Language* (1958), *English Dialects* (1963), and *The Modern University* (1965). In 1951, he was Visiting Professor of English at UCLA.

J. A. BURROW is Fellow of Jesus College, Oxford. His publications include *A Reading of Sir Gawain and the Green Knight* (1965) and various articles in learned journals.

ROBERT P. CREED is Professor of English at the State University of New York at Stony Brook. He edited *Old English Poetry: Fifteen Essays* (1967), co-edited *Franciplegius: Medieval and Linguistic Studies in Honor of Francis Peabody Magoun, Jr.* with Jess B. Bessinger, Jr. (1965), recorded "Lyrics from the Old English" with Burton Raffel for Folkways Records (1964), and wrote numerous articles for learned journals. In 1962–1963, he held a Guggenheim Fellowship.

ELEANOR DUCKETT is Professor Emeritus of Classics at Smith College. She is also an Honorary Fellow of Girton College, Cambridge. Her major publications include *The Gateway to the Middle Ages, Anglo-Saxon Saints and Scholars, The Wandering Saints of the Early Middle Ages, Carolingian Portraits,* and *Death and Life in the Tenth Century.*

STANLEY B. GREENFIELD is Professor of English at the University of Oregon. He is editor of *Studies in Old English Literature in Honor of Arthur G. Brodeur* and author of *A Critical History of Old English Literature.* Other publications include the bibliography for *A Guide To English Literature from Beowulf through Chaucer and Medieval Drama* and an essay on "The Old English Elegies" in *Continuations and Beginnings,* edited by E. G. Stanley. He was a Guggenheim Fellow in 1965–1966.

BERNARD F. HUPPÉ is Professor of English and Chairman of the English Department at Harpur College of the State University of New York at Binghampton. His major books include *Piers Plowman and Scriptural Tradition* with D. W. Robertson, Jr. (1951), *Doctrine and Poetry* (1959), *Fruyt and Chaff: A Study in Chaucer's Allegory* with D. W. Robertson, Jr. (1963), and *A Reading of the Canterbury Tales* (1964). He has held three Princeton Summer Research Fellowships and was a Fulbright Lecturer at the University of Vienna, Austria in 1955–1956.

W. P. LEHMANN is Ashbel Smith Professor of Linguistics and Germanic Languages and Chairman of the Department of Linguistics at the University of Texas. His publications include the following books: *Proto-Indo-European Phonology* (1952), *The Development of Germanic Verse Form* (1956), and *Historical Linguistics: an Introduction* (1962).

ROY F. LESLIE is Professor of English and Head of the Department of English at the University of Victoria, British Columbia. His publications include the following editions: *Three Old English Elegies* (1961 and 1966), Vol. I of *Layamon's Brut* with George Leslie Brook for the Early English Text Society (1963), and *The Wanderer* (1966).

JOHN C. POPE is Lampson Professor of English at Yale University. He is author of *The Rhythm of Beowulf* (1942, rev. ed. 1966), and editor of the *Homilies of Ælfric: A Supplementary Collection*, 2 vols., for the Early English Text Society (1967, 1968). He has also published a text edition of *Seven Old English Poems* (1968).

KENNETH SISAM, F.B.A., is an Honorary Fellow of Merton College, Oxford. His books include *Fourteenth Century Verse and Prose* (1921), *Studies in the History of Old English Literature* (1953), *The Structure of Beowulf* (1965), and an edition, with Celia Sisam, of *The Salisbury Psalter* for the Early English Text Society.

ROBERT D. STEVICK is Associate Professor of English at the University of Washington. His publications include the editions *One Hundred Middle English Lyrics* (1964) and *Five Middle English Narratives* (1967). His books *Suprasegmentals, Meter, and the Manuscript of Beowulf* and *English and Its History: The Evolution of a Language* are scheduled for publication in 1968. He has been awarded a Fulbright Research Grant for 1968–1969 at the University of Sidney, Australia.

GODFRID STORMS is Professor of English Language at the Catholic University of Nijmegen, the Netherlands. His published works include *Anglo-Saxon Magic* (1948) and *Compounded Names of Peoples in Beowulf* (1957).

TOM H. TOWERS is Assistant Professor of English at Wisconsin State College, Whitewater, Wisconsin. Among his publications are articles in the *Journal of English and Germanic Philology*, *College English*, and *American Literature*.

DOROTHY WHITELOCK, C.B.E., F.B.A., and Litt.D. (Cambridge), is Elrington and Bosworth Professor of Anglo-Saxon at the University of Cambridge. Among her numerous publications are an edition of *Anglo-Saxon Wills* (1930), an edition of the *Sermo Lupi ad Anglos* (1939), *The Audience of Beowulf* (1950), *The Beginnings of English Society* (1952), and *The Anglo-Saxon Chronicle: A Revised Translation* (1961). She is a Fellow of the Mediaeval Academy of America, a Fellow of Newnham College, Cambridge, and Honorary Fellow at St. Hilda's College, Oxford.

# Acknowledgments

WE WOULD like to thank The Research Council of Rutgers University for a grant-in-aid to defray incidental costs. We wish also to thank the authors, editors, publishers, and organizations listed below for their permission to reprint the specified material in whole or in part.

M.S.
J.M.

G. L. Brook and André Deutsch Limited for permission to reprint an extract from *English Dialects*.

W. P. Lehmann and the University of Texas Press for permission to reprint an extract from *The Development of Germanic Verse Form*.

Kenneth Sisam and The Clarendon Press, Oxford, for permission to reprint an extract from *Studies in the History of Old English Literature*.

Robert P. Creed and The Johns Hopkins Press, publisher of *ELH*, for permission to reprint "The Making of an Anglo-Saxon Poem."

Robert D. Stevick and The Mediaeval Academy of America, publisher of *Speculum*, for permission to reprint "The Oral-Formulaic Analyses of Old English Verse."

R. F. Leslie and Carl Winter Universitätsverlag for permission to reprint "Analysis of Stylistic Devices and Effects in Anglo-Saxon Literature" from *Stil- und Formprobleme in der Literatur*, edited by Paul Böckmann.

Stanley B. Greenfield and *Neuphilologische Mitteilungen* for permission to reprint "Syntactic Analysis and Old English Poetry."

Tom H. Towers and the University of Illinois Press, publisher of
*JEGP*, for permission to reprint "Thematic Unity in the Story of
Cynewulf and Cyneheard."

Eleanor Duckett and William Collins Sons & Co. Ltd. for per-
mission to reprint an extract from *Alfred the Great and His England*.
The text used in this book is reprinted from the American edition,
*Alfred the Great, The King and His England*, by Eleanor Duckett by
permission of The University of Chicago Press. © 1956 by The
University of Chicago.

Stanley B. Greenfield and New York University Press for permission
to reprint an extract from *A Critical History of Old English Literature*.
© 1965 by New York University.

Bernard F. Huppé and the State University of New York Press for
permission to reprint an extract from *Doctrine and Poetry*.

R. F. Leslie, Manchester University Press, and Barnes & Noble,
Inc., for permission to reprint an extract from *The Wanderer*,
edited by R. F. Leslie.

John C. Pope and New York University Press for permission to
reprint an extract from *Franciplegius: Medieval and Linguistic Studies in
Honor of Francis Peabody Magoun, Jr.*, edited by Jess B. Bessinger, Jr.
and Robert P. Creed. © 1965 by New York University.

Dorothy Whitelock and Cambridge University Press for permission
to reprint "The Interpretation of *The Seafarer*" from *The Early
Cultures of North-West Europe*, edited by Sir Cyril Fox and Bruce
Dickins.

Morton W. Bloomfield and The Modern Language Association of
America, publisher of *PMLA*, for permission to reprint "The Form
of *Deor*."

Rudolph C. Bambas and the University of Illinois Press, publisher
of *JEGP*, for permission to reprint "Another View of the Old
English *Wife's Lament*."

Jess B. Bessinger, Jr., and University of Oregon Books for permission
to reprint "*Maldon* and the *Óláfsdrápa*: An Historical Caveat" from
*Studies in Old English Literature in Honor of Arthur G. Brodeur*, edited by
Stanely B. Greenfield.

J. A. Burrow and J. B. Wolters' Uitgeversmaatschappij N.V., publisher of *Neophilologus*, for permission to reprint "An Approach to *The Dream of the Rood*."

N. F. Blake and Manchester University Press for permission to reprint an extract from *The Phoenix*, edited by N. F. Blake.

Dorothy Whitelock and The Clarendon Press, Oxford, for permission to reprint an extract from *The Audience of* Beowulf.

G. Storms and University of Oregon Books for permission to reprint "The Subjectivity of the Style of *Beowulf*" from *Studies in Old English Literature in Honor of Arthur G. Brodeur*, edited by Stanley B. Greenfield.

Adrien Bonjour and Basil Blackwell & Mott Limited for permission to reprint "The Finn and Heathobards Episodes" from *The Digressions in* Beowulf.

**DATE DUE**

| NOV 17 1982 | | | |
|---|---|---|---|
| DEC 2 82 | | | |
| | | | |
| | | | |
| | | | |
| | | | |
| | | | |
| | | | |
| | | | |
| | | | |
| | | | |
| | | | |
| | | | |
| | | | |
| 30 505 JOSTEN'S | | | |